85-1094

P9-DVG-413

LATIN AMERICA IN THE 1930s

Since 1975 Latin America has suffered an intensely severe crisis in response to events in the international economy. It therefore becomes fascinating, and indeed essential, to turn back to the last great crisis, that of the 1930s, and see what can be learnt by comparison and contrast. This book is the first attempt to write solid well-documented economic histories of the 1920s and 1930s for a wide range of Latin American countries, and study them comparatively. The book documents a surprising speed of recovery in most Latin American countries, often in advance of the international economy. But the reasons do not allow optimism about the outlook for the 1980s.

The book also illuminates the debate on the role of external shocks; it is found that the events of the 1930s do indeed accelerate forces leading to institutional development, though the emphasis is on showing that the degree of discontinuity is usually overstressed. Countries studied include Argentina, Brazil, Chile, Colombia, Mexico, Peru and those of Central America. The authors are all authorities on their respective case-studies, and Charles P. Kindleberger and Carlos F. Diaz Alejandro have contributed the comparative chapters.

Rosemary Thorp is a Fellow of St Antony's College and a Lecturer in Latin American Economics at Oxford University. She has worked extensively on current Peruvian economic problems and on the economic history of that country. She is the author with Geoffrey Bertram of *Peru 1890–1977: Growth and Policy in an Open Economy*, as well as articles on inflation and recent economic problems in Peru. Her interest is increasingly comparative; she has edited with Laurence Whitehead *Inflation and Stabilisation in Latin America*, is working on a further version of this, and on a long-run comparative study of Peru and Colombia. She has taught in Berkeley, California (1967–70), and in Peru (1977) as well as in Oxford, 1962–7 and since 1970.

LATIN AMERICA IN THE 1930s

The Role of the Periphery in World Crisis

Edited by Rosemary Thorp

WITHDRAWN

Shambaugh Library

St. Martin's Press   New York

HC
125
.L3448
1984

X

© St. Antony's College, Oxford, 1984

All rights reserved. For information, write:
St. Martin's Press, Inc., 175 Fifth Avenue, New York, NY 10010
Printed in Hong Kong
Published in the United Kingdom by The Macmillan Press Ltd
First published in the United States of America in 1984

ISBN 0–312–47329–X

Library of Congress Cataloging in Publication Data

Main entry under title:

Latin America in the 1930s.

    Includes index.
    1. Latin America — Economic conditions — 1918–1945 — Ad-
dresses, essays, lectures.   2. Depressions — 1929 — Addresses,
essays, lectures.   I. Thorp, Rosemary.
HC125. L3448   1984   330.98'0033   84–6901
ISBN 0–312–47329–X

WITHDRAWN

Contents

List of Tables

List of Figures and Maps

FIGURES

MAPS

Notes on the Contributors

Marcelo de Paiva Abreu is a member of the research staff of IPEA, Rio de Janeiro.

Victor Bulmer-Thomas is Lecturer at Queen Mary College, University of London.

Enrique Cárdenas is Professor of Economics at the Universidad de las Americas, Puebla, Mexico.

Carlos F. Diaz Alejandro is visiting Professor of Economics at the University of Columbia, New York and Professor of Economics (on leave) at Yale University.

E. V. K. FitzGerald is Director of the Institute of Social Sciences, The Hague.

Charles P. Kindleberger is Emeritus Professor at Massachusetts Institute of Technology.

Carlos Londoño is Assistant Research Officer at the Institute of Economics and Statistics, Oxford University.

José Antonio Ocampo is a member of the research staff of Fedesarrollo, Bogotá.

Arturo O'Connell is a member of the research staff of the Instituto Torcuato di Tella, Buenos Aires.

Gabriel Palma is Assistant Lecturer in the Faculty of Economics, University of Cambridge, and Fellow of Fitzwilliam College.

Flavio Rabelo Versiani is Professor of Economics at the Universidad de Brasilia.

Rosemary Thorp is a Fellow of St Antony's College and Lecturer in Latin American Economics at the University of Oxford.

Preface

It is hardly necessary to justify attention today to the 1930s. As Latin America contends with the most severe adjustment crisis since that date, it becomes both irresistible and of enormous importance to look again at that earlier occasion. What were the recovery mechanisms then, and are they available today? Did Latin America recover in advance of the international economy and did this assist the Centre in its turn? Something of the sort has certainly been suggested for the 1970s. As Japan competes for leadership with the USA, can we gain insight into the resulting disequilibria by reflecting on the last major shift in structure as the USA itself replaced Great Britain? As the consequences of a massive expansion of private international lending come home to roost, can we learn by examining the process last time it occurred – namely, in the 1920s? What difference does world inflation make, and how differently do monetary mechanisms operate given fifty years of institutional development and a total break with the gold standard?

Ambitious as these questions are, the goals behind the research project which produced this volume were in fact even more ambitious. The stimulus came in a letter from the Joint Committee on Latin American Studies of the US Social Science Research Council and the American Council of Learned Societies. The Committee was interested in bringing together scholars 'in areas where it was felt the time was ripe for a breakthrough in the development of the subject'. The hope behind our response to this invitation was, first, that solid economic research on the histories of the individual countries had now reached a point where we could move more easily than before into comparative work. Second, and from this base, it would be possible to explore freshly a period for which we have a 'Latin American stereotype' but little sense of how individual countries fit that picture. Third, we were conscious of course of the preoccupations outlined in the first paragraph: to examine carefully the mechanisms at work in that former crisis could not but be illuminating in relation to today's problems.

With welcome encouragement from the Joint Committee we were able to attempt these goals in a near-ideal format. We met as a workshop in September 1981, at St Antony's College, Oxford. We then rewrote our papers for the Congress of Americanists in Manchester in September 1982, where we had the benefit of a wider audience and were able again to revise and synthesise. We were able to invite a number of newcomers to our second meeting who patiently read and commented on all our papers. One substantial benefit of this is the chapter by Professor Kindleberger with which we conclude the volume – a chapter which invalidates by its content his claim in its opening sentence to be 'an impostor at a meeting of Latin American experts'. A further gain is seen in the overview paper by Diaz Alejandro which, while it was from the beginning a unique contribution, has along the way been able to synthesise and place in context our individual findings.

We would like to acknowledge the financial as well as intellectual support of the Joint Committee. Additional finance was received from the Nuffield Foundation and the University of Oxford (for the first workshop) as well as the IDRC of Canada and the Ford Foundation. In addition, the travel expenses of scholars were often paid by their own institutions. Caroline Wise typed and retyped much of the manuscript with patience and elegance, and with other staff of the Institute of Economics and Statistics worked hard on 'producing' both the conferences and the manuscript.

ROSEMARY THORP

1 Introduction

ROSEMARY THORP*

This Introduction attempts three tasks. First, it explains the context and main conclusions of the volume. Second, for readers like myself who come to 'world economy' issues from a 'peripheral' background, it attempts a survey of the international events leading up to the Great Depression and the prevailing views on recovery in the Centre. This section is not for, and is written with apologies to, those specialised in the Centre literature, and simply aims to give an introduction to that literature. Third, the chapter ends with some thoughts on issues for further research coming out of our papers and our debates.

THE CONTEXT AND CONCLUSIONS OF THE PROJECT

The dominant stereotypes concerning this period in Latin American economic history all stress the key importance of the 1929 Depression. Indeed, it is hardly an exaggeration to say that anything written since 1949 on Latin American development has given the 1929 Depression a special place, seeing it as a force both for good and bad. For some – in particular ECLA (Economic Commission for Latin America) – it is 'the' turning-point, the 'critical point at which the primary-export model broke down'.[1] In early ECLA formulations the trade cycle is the fundamental mechanism which implements the long-run worsening of the terms of trade, since prices move in favour of primary products during the upswing 'but, during the downswing, generally tend to fall more than they had risen'.[2] Rigid wages, hence rigid supply prices, and accumulation of stocks at the Centre mean

---

* While this chapter remains my responsibility, I would like to acknowledge the collaboration of all contributors to this volume, especially that of E. V. K. FitzGerald, Victor Bulmer-Thomas and Gabriel Palma.

1

curtailed demand for primary products: 'In the periphery, lower prices for primary goods naturally mean lower profits and adverse pressure on wages in communities in which labour organisations, where they exist, are far less powerful than in the cyclical centres.'[2] But the 1929 Depression was outstandingly severe, with a fall in real import capacity from peak (1928) to trough (1932) of 45%.[3] This had profound effects, both negative and positive, the latter particularly for industrialisation. However, the standard version of ECLA's views has perhaps tended to overplay the 'turning-point': particularly in the writing of the economic historians of the ECLA school – Sunkel, Paz, Pinto, Furtado are outstanding examples – we find emphasis on varying historical experiences, with prior development of industry, the state apparatus, and industrial groups prominent as explanatory variables of the degree of progress made following 1929. It is the more radical approach which perhaps has the simpler view: Frank, for example, draws a sharp and oversimplified distinction between pre-1930, when exposure to international trade and investment completely stifled all options and possibilities for 'genuine' local development, and post-1930, when enforced autarchy permitted a flourishing of local enterprise.[4] The same viewpoint is echoed in the orthodox Marxist interpretation[5] which sees a proletariat and bourgeoisie only arising in the 1930s as a result of the crisis of capitalism, and industrialisation thus dating from this period.

Rather to our surprise, our own vision comes quite close to the ECLA view, inasmuch as we stress historical continuity and the gradually developing role of the State. We find the Depression to be of enormous significance, but as building on and pushing further trends in industrialisation, state intervention and developing financial and other institutions which precede the 1930s. In other ways we complicate the ECLA generalisations. ECLA stresses the dichotomy between large and small countries in their capacity to react, while our case studies upset this: particularly those on Central America, Argentina, Brazil, Colombia and Peru. We give a new importance to financial mechanisms, and in contrast to Frank *et al.* we show the relevance of external trading and other relationships in influencing internal options even after the supposed 'rupture' of 1929 (see particularly Argentina/Brazil).

The story of rapid recovery from the Depression is probably the most dramatic conclusion of the papers here presented. Under 'issues for further research' below, we review the stimulating discussion which developed around alternative views of the recovery mechanisms; the papers themselves stress how often the upturn *preceded* export recovery, and the role in the domestic upswing of government spending as well as relative prices. It was the fact that, because of downward wage and price flexibility, devaluations, unlike today, could effectively be 'real' which facilitated the stimulus to internal activity as well as the improvement in the balance of payments.

An interesting debate also developed around the nature and role of the foreign-exchange constraint. The first issue concerned the relative importance of trade and capital flows: the traditional ECLA stress had been on the fall in export earnings, whereas several studies stressed that part of the problem which came from capital flight and the cessation of new inflows. FitzGerald's study of Mexico argues that the latter was the greater problem. The second issue concerned the point when, and the degree to which, foreign-exchange shortages *per se* generated policy measures. In general the view was that a 'classical' mechanism prevailed in 1929 and 1930, in which the fall in internal demand and 'naturally' changing relative prices led to a fall in imports; however, as early as 1931 in some cases the move away from the gold standard and into various degrees of expansionary behaviour also necessitated exchange controls and tariffs, which reinforced the stimulus to industry. This was most firmly argued for Colombia, Brazil and Chile where a foreign-exchange constraint clearly 'bit' and strongly influenced policy. The Mexican case was the most divergent, due to its special characteristics. FitzGerald argues that much of the effect of the Depression was felt via the direct transfer of price changes, rather than through the foreign-exchange constraint. Industry's recovery occurred with that of demand as exports and agriculture recovered, and the industrial recovery was not strongly import-substituting in nature. The Cárdenas chapter disagrees with this analysis and emphasises far more the direct impact and significance of the foreign-exchange shortage.

These points and others are taken further in the two overview chapters and in the appendix to FitzGerald's chapter; to say more here would be superfluous. Instead we now turn to a brief review of the international context of our case studies.

THE WORLD ECONOMY 1913–29

The key theme of the period is the replacement of Britain by the USA as the dominant trading and investing power – and particularly *vis-à-vis* Latin America.

The outbreak of the First World War was the turning-point in the decay of the classical capitalist world economy based on the dominating role of Britain and the operation of the gold standard. Although the supposed automatic adjustment mechanisms of the gold system were less perfect than was thought for many years, the system had worked reasonably smoothly by means of *ex ante* avoidance of substantial disparities in cost competitiveness.[6] But from significantly before 1913, forces making for change had been emerging. There were two major trends, both of which signalled a need for a radical restructuring of financial and trading institutions. First, the shift in trading and investment flows was already occurring – though its outcome was only to be apparent in retrospect. The role of the USA was increasing dramatically from the turn of the century: by 1913 many northwestern Latin American countries were importing almost as much from the USA as from the UK – already a major switch compared with the 1890s. US investment was making rapid headway in, for example, Peruvian and Chilean copper and Cuban sugar, as well as in the Central American economies. Second, changes were already coming which would lead to a growing oversupply of primary products, and to increasing market instability (though the buoyant conditions of the early century concealed underlying trends). These changes were on the side both of demand and of supply. On the demand side, population growth in the developed countries was slowing down, and rising income was leading to a proportionately slower growth in the demand for food. On the supply side, technical change and modernisation were leading to greater productivity.[7] These trends were only offset in the case of a few products by technical change which led to new products and new demands – a factor which would be of more importance by the 1920s.

The War, however, clearly represented a major discontinuity. In four years the shift in trading structures was tremendously accelerated, since on the one hand Britain's position in world trade declined sharply, never to recover fully, while on the other the opportunities for exporting by the USA and by Japan blossomed overnight. The War also stimulated a significant increase in production capacity in many primary products where there was already imminent danger of excess supply. Sugar was perhaps the most outstanding example, but the same was true of many other foodstuffs and raw materials where European domestic production was temporarily disrupted.

With the old system in disarray, and new forces for change emerging in forms such as an expanded role of the State and strengthened labour movements following the Russian Revolution, there was an opportunity for fresh thinking in 1919 and for an attempt to appraise and handle the underlying problems. But the problems were not perceived. The accepted wisdom of the post-war period, at least in the UK and USA, was the need to return to the old system – in particular to the gold standard and as far as possible to pre-war exchange-rate parities. From 1922 there was sustained economic expansion in the USA and many European countries – though Britain was struggling with deflation in the attempt to restore and maintain the pre-war parity. But the system was basically unsound, with capital movements only temporarily papering over the cracks. Pre-war, the system had operated with one centre – London – which meant low reserves, and no possibility of playing one reserve currency off against another. While far from perfect, the system was closer to an equilibrium than was now the case.

In the post-war period the reinstituted gold-exchange system never worked well: there were too many centres, the USA lacked experience, and neither France nor the USA was committed to making the new system work.[8] There was also a new instability arising from the increased volume of short-term and volatile funds, and parities for the major currencies were badly chosen. Further, the size of the American surplus was such that it urgently required policies for promoting imports and capital exports which would ease the payment problems of the recipients. But trade was not the important factor to the USA which it had been to the UK; policies in fact were exactly the reverse of the above. The USA continued its protectionist policies, dating back to the Civil War, and its capital export policies created major problems for the recipient countries. The 1920s saw a bonanza of private foreign lending on the part of the USA, unparalleled unless by the 1970s. Salesmen pressed loans on largely unsuspecting governments; borrowers were positively encouraged to overextend themselves.

Aided by such credits the volume of primary production continued to expand. Meanwhile the forces operating on supply and demand continued and strengthened. The 1920s was a period of particularly rapid technical progress in agriculture: for the first time in history the pace caught up with industry – with mechanisation of farming, and the introduction of new plant strains and fertilisers. There were also major structural changes in primary product markets, with substitutes damaging the markets for products such as rubber and nitrates. Price behaviour in the decade is complicated to review, since the sudden boom of 1920 was followed by as sudden a crash, to be followed in its turn by recovery for all commodities by 1925, then an uneven weakening of many markets. But underlying this was an unfavourable long-run trend; by 1925–9 the terms of trade for all primary products had fallen significantly below their 1913 level.[9]

Given the size of these forces making for disequilibrium, it can surely be no surprise that the system collapsed by 1929. But a number of specific points are typically made about the crisis itself. First, as the stock market boomed in the USA on a wave of speculation, rates of interest rose so high that even as early as 1928 USA capital exports began to fall sharply. This affected Latin America both directly and indirectly, as Europe's capacity to import was in turn affected.[10] As interest rates rose, so the cost of financing stocks of raw materials also rose, and enforced liquidation also affected prices. Second, the crash in the USA itself was the result of factors internal to the USA (though they interrelated in some measure with the international factors we have mentioned) and it was a combination of a list of structural problems within the USA with inappropriate policy responses which led to the Depression being as deep and as long as it was. The reasons often mentioned for the 'fundamentally unsound'[11] nature of the US economy by 1929 are: (a) the inequitable distribution of income in the 1920s when productivity had increased sharply but mass purchasing power had not; (b) an unhealthy corporate structure, described by Galbraith as a 'floodtide of corporate larceny';[12] (c) an unhealthy banking structure with an enormous number of small and ill-backed banks ripe for collapse. The question of inappropriate policy responses raises perhaps the most controversial issue in current debate over 1929–33: the clash comes between those who give the major causal role to monetary policy (Friedman and Schwartz, 1963) and those who stress an autonomous decline in expenditure (Temin, 1976) and see the supply of money adjusting passively to falling demand.[13] Fortunately we are not forced to choose, since what matters for our story is the fact of the strong recession in the USA, not the exact weighting of different possible causes.[14]

Turning now to recovery, since one of our main preoccupations here is the explanation of the recovery in the Periphery, we thought it might be helpful to review the mechanisms of recovery in the Centre countries, to see if by contrast and comparison they illuminate our findings for the Periphery.

What emerged, of course, is that it is no simple task: not only are the experiences exceedingly diverse, but the whole topic is extremely controversial. We deal briefly here with some of the European experiences and with that of the USA, but the reader should take what follows as no more than suggestive.

The European literature generally distinguishes some six recovery mechanisms:

(i) government policy
(ii) improving terms of trade
(iii) rising real wages
(iv) technological change and its influence on demand
(v) housing
(vi) the retaining at home of capital previously exported.

In perhaps the most remarkable recovery story – UK – all six interacted, though the analysis is complicated by the slow growth of the UK in the 1920s (due to misguided policies and the problems of the staple export industries) and the consequent existence of a backlog of opportunities for innovation and spread of mass consumption of new goods. While early writing stressed the role of policy, particularly cheap money, abandonment of the gold standard, protection and the limiting of exports of capital, a line of analysis started by Richardson and taken up by Landes stressed the role of new goods and rising incomes.[15] Wages fell less rapidly than prices, and improving terms of trade meant not only an income gain, but specifically lower food prices, so assisting the rise in the real wage. With significant unemployment there was a redistribution of income to those in employment and a sharp increase in the potential demand for non-essential goods. This coincided with an extraordinary and broad-based flood of cost-reduction and innovations in lines such as radios, small cars, electrical goods, synthetics, which in the critical years 1929–33 was enough to push many new industries over the hump and into mass production at low cost. New possibilities in consumer goods plus new transport possibilities[16] in turn fed the enormous increase in demand for new housing as industrial relocation at last occurred on a substantial scale – all this significantly helped by policy measures but hardly precipitated by them.

The correct balance between this line of analysis and factors such as the cheap money policy, the revival of house-building and the rise in real wages is still a matter of controversy, however.[17] In other cases the prominence of policy seems less disputed. In several European countries this is true in a negative sense: inappropriate policies aborted the growth factors that might have produced a UK-style recovery (though always less strong, given the 'backlog' factor in the

British case). This is particularly true for France, which clung to the gold standard until 1936 and only then embarked on expansionary policy. Sweden was the showcase of successful policy – first monetary and subsequently fiscal policy playing an important counter-cyclical role, with a strong influence of professional economists (Wicksell and others).[18]

In the case of the USA the main point to make is, of course, that there was remarkably little recovery. National income in real terms was by 1935 still 25% below its 1929 level,[19] there was a further recession in 1937/8, and agriculture in particular was in a poor state throughout the 1930s.[20] It is of some relevance to the weakness of recovery that a number of the mechanisms mentioned for Europe did not apply – e.g. since US exports and imports were rather evenly divided among primary and manufactured products, improving terms of trade for the former did not help[21] (and anyway trade was only 7% of Gross National Product (GNP), not 25% as in the case of the UK[22]). The 'new products' factor was relevant to the 1920s, not the 1930s. The lack of capital was not the problem – rather the lack of demand and confidence: in fact the *failure* of the USA to lend more abroad to balance its trade *surplus* continued to be the problem in this decade (what lending there was was tied to exports).[23]

Policy is, of course, the fascinating and controversial item in the list. Briefly, the main lines of early policy, such as it was, were protection (the Hawley–Smoot Tariff Act of 1930 precipitated world-wide and self-defeating protectionist policies[24]) and from 1932 attempts at cheap money.[25] With the New Deal in 1933, in addition to the dollar devaluation of that year, came policy innovations which were sometimes contradictory and paradoxical in their effects: the National Industrial Recovery Act, which tried to improve the position of *both* labour and capital by increasing wages, restricting cut-throat competition and instituting minimum prices, and the Agricultural Adjustment Act, which tried to restore profitability in agriculture by minimum prices, restriction of production and reduction of interest burdens. Gradually, public works spending and various forms of income generation became important, amounting to $3 billion in 1935 (over 5% of national income). Meanwhile, weak attempts to boost export trade failed to rescue agriculture – even with straightforward subsidisation of export sales.

Among the controversies involved in the discussion of these policies, the most suggestive for us would seem to be, first, the role of price rigidity, and the role in that of the NIRA and the AAA – did they actually slow down a recovery which without intervention would have come 'naturally'? – and, second, the contradictions involved in trying to favour, in a time of recession, *both* labour and capital, and/ or *both* agriculture and industry.

All of this discussion provides a suggestive context for our case studies. Clearly, in the case of the Periphery, we are dealing not simply with the *absence* of some of the European factors, but actually with their *reverse*. The terms of trade clearly continued to deteriorate; there was no chance of gain by retaining at home capital previously exported, but rather significant balance-of-payments and possibly other problems as capital fled and new flows dried up. But where the USA may have suffered from wage and price rigidity, on that score at least the Periphery could gain. And the room for import-substitution could be equated to the 'new products' factor in the UK case. The large subsistence sector perhaps made it more possible than in the USA to tolerate a shift in the internal terms of trade against agriculture, in those cases where industry was ready to lead the recovery.

ISSUES FOR FURTHER RESEARCH

It was implicit in the context of this attempt at comparative work that we would define questions we were not yet able to answer. In the debate a number of such questions emerged and it may be of interest to note briefly several areas where our debate suggested more research would be worth while.

The Role of the State and Policy-making

The case studies conclude rather confidently that in the sphere of institutions and the role of the state there are significant benefits to be observed from external shocks. (The political repercussions are another matter; but the important, widespread and often violent regime changes of 1929–30 were not much discussed in our debates.) Every study that touched on the State emphasised the importance of the change in its role, though Abreu and Versiani were inclined to argue that this had possibly been overemphasised in the recent literature on Brazil. In the case of Central America, Bulmer-Thomas found clear evidence of the role of the shock in inducing change, in this case in perceptions as to the need for state intervention and in the development of financial institutions. The case of Chile is consistent with this: Palma shows that there was a major quantitative and qualitative change in the role of the State, but in the *1920s*: however, this is precisely because Chile received a major shock with the nitrate collapse well before 1929. For Mexico the emphasis was admittedly far more on the endogenous development of capitalism: 1925 is seen as the start of a process of capital restructuring, shifting away from mining and foreign enterprise towards agrarian capitalism with strong state support (FitzGerald: Cárdenas places more emphasis on industry). But even here the Depression, by making clear the contradictions and limitations of an open enclave economy, helped considerably to strengthen state institutions, stimulate banking developments and protectionism (a view accepted in both papers). As FitzGerald puts it, the Depression *permitted*, rather than created, a new relationship between the Mexican State and both domestic and foreign capital.

The case of Colombia is somewhat similar, though the forces at work are weaker and less radical: the need for state intervention already in the 1920s had led to important developments, as seen by Thorp and Londoño, and the needs of coffee production and marketing had already resulted in a new and *sui generis* producers' organisation with the potential for links to the State. The authors in this case use the wording of Palacios[27] that the Depression 'weds' the coffee sector to the State. (Ocampo's chapter emphasised the *future* significance of these events more strongly.)

Equally we saw gains in terms of increased national control – best evidenced in Cuba, where the disastrous story of sugar at least forced a consolidation of national interests in the sugar sector, with labour and capital combining in the face of the catastrophe to wrest control from the foreigner and set up a model to be imitated subsequently in other sectors.[28] In Peru in a more passive fashion the lack of interest of foreign capital allowed domestic entrepreneurs to expand in the small mining sector.

Much more research, however, is needed to clarify the long-run relationship between producer and other interest groups and policymaking. The papers were limited in their exploration of the complexity of policy-making. The debate often opened up interesting avenues which need more work. On the one hand external shocks are the precipitating factor forcing elite groups to define and protect their interests; on the other, forces making for diversification strengthen other groups and increase the potential for policies opposed by traditional groups (for example, exchange control opposed by Colombian coffee exporters). The need to generate a basis for staying in power

and defence needs may well enter into an explanation of 'unorthodox' response. The whole issue of what was perceived at the time as
'orthodox' or 'unorthodox' would also be fascinating to explore more
fully. Also relevant to the understanding of policy would be the degree of foreign ownership: a wholly foreign-owned export sector facing collapse might be less likely to precipitate major institutional
changes internally than a domestically-owned sector.

Recovery Mechanisms

Turning to the more short-term aspects of the role of the State, we
also need to refine both theoretically and empirically our understanding of the recovery mechanism. The studies do not all consider this,
but it is clear in a number of cases, as we have stated, that recovery
occurred in *advance* of exports – Argentina, Peru, Cuba and Honduras being clear exceptions to this. Most authors stress the failure of
government spending to fall as fast as might have been expected, and
the early date of its beginning to rise again (often 1932 or even 1931).
In Colombia Thorp and Londoño point also to state incentives to
private sector spending, while Ocampo points to interest-rate policy.
All, as we have mentioned, stress relative prices and 'real' devaluations. FitzGerald took a 'Kaleckian' line, by contrast, stressing income distribution, internal terms of trade and the supply of wage
goods. His paper alone suggests an increase in the profit share as an
explanation of the rapid recovery in investment; other papers are
more tentative, but, while agreeing that profitability in industry increased strongly, are inclined to hint at an improvement in the share
of labour (this is most firmly stated for the Central American case,
where because of the dominance of the agricultural sector, Bulmer-
Thomas argues that there was a shift of income towards wages).[29]
In our discussion FitzGerald was led to develop his alternative framework quite fully, which we found sufficiently stimulating that we have
taken the unusual step of encouraging him to write it up and present it
as a rather substantial note appended to his chapter in this volume.
Clearly, this is an area where we need more precision and more data,
which links to the next preoccupation.

Who Bore the Burden?

This was an issue not addressed in most of the papers, principally for
lack of data. (For a tentative overview, see Diaz Alejandro's chapter,
section entitled 'Welfare performance'.) The research problem is

very great: this is an area where aggregate statistics are quite useless, since labour systems varied so much between regions, as did relative price behaviour. What is needed is (a) careful regional studies of real incomes of different groups, and (b) studies of foreign firms' pricing behaviour etc., to illustrate how the burden was shared between domestic and foreign factors. We have argued rather strongly that the Periphery as a whole recovered surprisingly quickly and often before the world market: it is essential to the interpretation of this finding to document the squeezing of the incomes of certain groups, and/or wage and price flexibility, which made it possible. A clearer empirical picture is also important to assess more fully than we could the ECLA cyclical model, which hypothesises surplus labour in the export sector and competition between exporters as the principal reasons for the 'ratchet' effect which provides the mechanism of terms of trade decline over the longer run. This is closely related to the next point.

The Role of the Periphery

One of the original ideas behind the workshop was that we might succeed in understanding how the Centre was able to recover the more quickly because of the way the burden of the crisis could be off-loaded on to the Periphery, and that this might suggest parallels for the crisis of the 1980s. Our studies, however, have thrown up some confusing findings. Admittedly the fall in primary product prices was huge, resulting in a 32% fall in Latin America's terms of trade between peak and trough, and the European literature on the Centre countries emphasises the significance of the corresponding improvement in terms of trade for the Centre. Also the cessation of capital outflows, which accounted for a further third of the fall in the capacity to import, gave some Centre countries room for manœuvre.[30] But we have found several studies suggesting that a disproportionate part of the fall in primary product prices would have been borne by the profits of Centre-based firms, while the Centre's creditors lost out by the inevitable defaults. (Kindleberger's paper makes the important point, however, that the losers then were mainly private individuals, not the banks – unlike today – hence there was 'only' a personal loss rather than damage to the financial infrastructure.) Also we have stressed the rapidity of the recovery in Latin America: in few cases does this appear to wait on the recovery of export markets, and in most the upturn comes as early as 1932.

It appears tempting, therefore, to explore the possibility that the

Periphery's recovery stimulated the Centre economies. Indeed, it is worth noting that although US imports from Latin America continued to fall in 1933 (and this was the only region where this happened), Latin America's purchases from the USA were already rising by that year, and although dwarfed in absolute terms by the rise in European demand, the 11% rise in Latin American imports represented more than one-third of the total rise in US exports in that year. In the following year the figure was 22% of a far larger increase. This must have helped consolidate the recovery in the international economy. But the point was well made in discussion that exports played only a small role in the US economy; perhaps further research will show that the more correct approach is to note that the Periphery was able to survive, without supply disruption, and so be there to respond once the Centre began to recover.

Parallels with the 1980s?

Few of our studies ventured explicitly into this topic, perhaps preferring to leave it to the reader to draw his or her own conclusions. Certainly much more research is needed here. We would stress, however, that our findings to date underline the *differences* between the 1930s and the 1980s and the dangers of superficial parallels. Bulmer–Thomas's chapter emphasised this most strongly for Central America: the social, political and economic complexity of the Central American republics have increased enormously, and the internal components of the widespread current crisis are correspondingly far more critical than they were in the 1930s (p. 305).

The *lack* of parallel again is emphasised in considering the sources of recovery in the 1930s. Important options were available then which are not available now: in particular rapid import substitution. Today not only are the 'easy' opportunities exhausted, but the conflict with the interests of 'old' Centre industries becomes ever more acute. Abreu points out how this has produced a new conflict between the Centre's financial interests, which badly need debtors such as Brazil to generate a trade surplus, and Centre industrial interests fighting for protection (p. 159).

The exhaustion of import substitution has produced a curious reversal, rather than a parallel: whereas in the 1930s the cry was for intervention and development based on the internal market, now the call is for a return to more reliance on exports, both non-traditional and traditional (Mexico and Peru are both emphasising mineral exports). With this goes a swing back to 'the market' and reduced intervention: the Southern cone cases are well known, and even for Mexico FitzGerald notes that 'the case for an active state is now argued by the opposition rather than the regime' (p. 261).

A second buffer that is much diminished is that provided by the subsistence sector. As agriculture has become more commercialised so the protection to the wages fund given by the subsistence sector has been reduced. This plus the rise in living standards mean that the wage bill now typically has an import component, thus further worsening the complexity of managing the external constraint. This is also worsened by the obviously reduced wage and price flexibility which, as we have seen, in the 1930s permitted 'real' devaluations, something hard to achieve today.

Given this and the new importance of exports of manufactures, wage policies have taken on a new significance. As Thorp and Londoño point out, in the protectionist environment of the 1930s wages could rise without detriment to the model in the short term: today wage control is a much more critical policy variable, with major politicial implications.

An element which was worse in the 1930s than today was the burden of debt as prices fell rather than rose. And today the far greater sophistication of financial institutions, national and international (a product partly of the stimulus of the 1930s), greatly increase the chances that today's burden can be handled sanely. We cannot escape the conclusion, however, that in general many of the safety-valves and recovery routes of the 1930s are simply not available today.

NOTES

1. ECLA (Economic Commission for Latin America) (1964) p. 2.
2. ECLA (1951) pp. 57–61.
3. ECLA (1951) p. 98 and the Statistical Appendix to the present volume, Table 1.
4. Frank (1969).
5. See, for example, Kadar (1980) pp. 36–7.
6. See Triffin's analysis as quoted in Aldcroft (1977). The topic is still very controversial; see Lindert (1969); McCloskey and Zecher (1981).
7. Hardach in Aldcroft (1977), Loveday (1931) p. 86.
8. The French returned to gold at an undervalued exchange rate and brought pressure to bear on the Bank of England through accumulating massive gold reserves. The restored gold standard was seen as a device conceived by Montague Norman to perpetuate Anglo-Saxon Hegemony.

9. Rowe (1965).
10. Fleissig (1972) p. 158.
11. The phrase is Erickson's, in Van den Wee (1972); the summary of reasons is taken from him also.
12. Galbraith (1955).
13. For summaries of the debate see Brunner (1981) and Van den Wee (1972).
14. Though given the numerous forces at work it appears very unproductive to argue for a monocausal explanation.
15. Richardson (1962); Landes (1970).
16. The number of registered motor vehicles on British roads grew from 1 524 000 in 1930 to 2 043 000 in 1935. The number of radio licence-holders rose from 1.7 m. in 1925 to 8 m. by 1936. Production of vacuum cleaners rose from 37 550 in 1930 to 409 345 in 1935, etc. Data from Richardson (1962).
17. See, for example, von Tunzelman's recent survey (1981).
18. See Jonung in Brunner (1981).
19. Kuznets (1941) p. 147.
20. Rasmussen and Porter (1972). They estimate that at the end of the decade nearly one-half of all farm families were at 'bare subsistence level' (p. 130).
21. Arndt (1963) p. 72.
22. Ibid. p. 80.
23. Ibid. p. 90.
24. Kindleberger (1973) p. 294, who describes it as 'irresponsible'.
25. Ibid. pp. 194ff. There were many complexities to this period which we cannot summarise here.
26. Weinstein (1981) argues for the negative role of the NRA.
27. Palacios (1979) p. 307.
28. This is based on an oral presentation at the Manchester Conference by Brian Pollitt. This paper provided a significant stimulus to the debate – unfortunately as a late addition it could not be included here for reasons of space.
29. Coffee prices fell in the 1930s to between 20% and 25% of their peak levels; labour costs must have been fairly close to subsistence in the 1920s, so they cannot have fallen as much. A rise in the profit share was thus logically impossible.
30. It also affected periphery import demand very directly, of course. The degree of room for manœuvre depended on which effect was the quantitatively more significant for a particular country.

REFERENCES

D. H. Aldcroft, *From Versailles to Wall Street, 1919–1929* (London, 1977)
H. W. Arndt, *The Economic Lessons of the Nineteen-Thirties* (London, 1963)
K. Brunner (ed.), *The Great Depression Revisited* (New York, 1981).
Economic Commission for Latin America (ECLA), *Economic Survey of Latin America, 1949* (New York, 1951).

—— 'The Growth and Decline of Import Substitution in Brazil', *Economic Bulletin for Latin America*, vol. x, no. 1 (New York, 1964).

E. A. Erickson, 'The Great Crash of October 1929', in Van den Wee (1972).

H. Fleissig, 'The USA and the Non-European Periphery', in Van den Wee (1972).

A. G. Frank, *Capitalism and Underdevelopment in Latin America*, 2nd edn (New York, 1969).

M. Friedman and A. Schwartz, *A Monetary History of the United States* (Princeton, 1963).

J. K. Galbraith, *The Great Crash 1929* (Boston, 1955).

G. Hardach, *The First World War 1914–1918* (London, 1977).

B. Kadar, *Problems of Economic Growth in Latin America* (London, 1980).

C. P. Kindleberger, *The World in Depression 1929–1939* (London, 1973).

S. Kuznets, *National Income and Its Composition, 1919–1938* (New York, 1941).

D. S. Landes, *The Unbound Prometheus: Technological Change and Industrial Development in Western Europe from 1750 to the Present* (Cambridge, 1970).

P. Lindert, *Key Currencies and Gold 1900–1913* (Princeton, 1969).

A. Loveday, *Britain and World Trade* (London and New York, 1913).

D. N. McCloskey and J. R. Zecher, 'How the gold standard worked, 1880–1913', in D. N. McCloskey, *Enterprise and Trade in Victorian Britain* (London, 1981).

M. Palacios, *El Café en Colombia 1850–1970: Una Historia Económica, Social y Política* (Bogotá, 1979).

B. Pollitt, 'The Great Depression in Latin America: Some Observations on the Experience of the Republic of Cuba' (unpublished MS., University of Glasgow, 1982).

W. D. Rasmussen and J. M. Porter, 'Agriculture in the Industrial Economies of the West during the Great Depression, with special reference to the United States', in Van den Wee (1972).

H. W. Richardson, 'The Basis of Economic Recovery in the Nineteen Thirties: A Review and a New Interpretation', *Economic History Review*, 2nd series, xv (1962).

J. F. Rowe, *Primary Commodities in International Trade* (Cambridge, 1965).

P. Temin, *Did Monetary Forces Cause the Great Depression?* (New York, 1976).

H. Van den Wee (ed.), *The Great Depression Revisited* (The Hague, 1972).

N. von Tunzelman, 'Britain 1900–45: A Survey', in R. Floud and D. McCloskey (eds), *The Economic History of Britain since 1700*, vol. 2 (Cambridge, 1981).

M. M. Weinstein, 'Some Macroeconomic Impacts of the National Industrial Recovery Act, 1933–1935', in Brunner, 1981.

2 Latin America in the 1930s

CARLOS F. DIAZ ALEJANDRO*

INTRODUCTION

Latin American development experienced a turning-point during the 1930s. The contrast between 'before and after 1929' may often be exaggerated, but there is little doubt that the decade witnessed a closing toward international trade and finance, and a relative upsurge of import-substituting activities, primarily but not exclusively in manufacturing. Other trends visible before 1929, such as urbanisation and a growing interest by the State in promoting economic development, continued into the 1930s and accelerated in some countries. Memories of the 1930s have profoundly influenced the region's attitude toward international trade and finance; per capita foreign trade indicators reached by the late 1920s were not surpassed in many nations until the 1960s.

At least some Latin American economies performed surprisingly

* This essay both expands and abstracts who earlier ones (Diaz Alejandro, 1980 and 1981). All tables have been omitted; interested or sceptical readers are referred to those papers, others in the references, and the Statistical Appendix to this volume for fuller, albeit still incomplete, documentation. Workshops organised by Rosemary Thorp at St Antony's College Oxford during September 1981 and in Manchester during September 1982 were very helpful for the preparation of this essay. I am grateful to her and to other participants in those workshops for many useful comments. Those of Victor Bulmer-Thomas, Enrique Cárdenas, José Antonio Ocampo, Arturo O'Connell and Gabriel Palma were especially influential in making me rethink a number of points. Virginia Casey edited and typed these pages in the cold from a sticky manuscript completed in the tropics. Sabbatical leave from Yale University and the joyful and stimulating hospitality of the Pontifical Catholic University of Rio de Janeiro are gratefully acknowledged. Two Rio colleagues, Edmar Bacha and Winston Fritsch, were particularly generous in sharing with me their reflections on the 1930s. The Ford Foundation kindly made possible both the trip to Oxford and the stay in Rio. The Social Science Research Council of the United States financed the Manchester trip. The usual caveats should apply.

well during the 1930s, relative to North America, and relative to what average opinion would have expected to happen in quite open, primary-product exporting nations. This essay will view the economic performance of each country as the result of the magnitude of the exogenous external shock received, of the policy measures undertaken by domestic authorities to speed adjustment to those shocks and to seek external and internal balance, and of the resilience of local private agents in responding to the new constellation of profit opportunities, including those opened up by new technologies and products. (This formulation owes much to the chapter by Bulmer-Thomas in this volume.) Shocks, policies and capacities to transform differed substantially from country to country.

Ability and willingness to manipulate policy instruments such as nominal exchange rates, tariffs and domestic credit were greatest in countries which were either relatively large, such as Brazil, or had relatively autonomous public sectors, such as Costa Rica and Uruguay. Smaller countries, e.g. Honduras, or those with highly dependent governments, e.g. Cuba, had less room for policy manœuvre. Large domestic markets encouraged resource reallocation in the circumstances of the 1930s and had already induced substantial industrial capacity before then. Other structural features, such as the production characteristics of traditional exports, and the extent of foreign control of local banking and land, also played a role in determining the elasticity of response to the new relative prices. The generalisation that largeness and policy autonomy were favourable to performance covers only republics with nominal sovereignty. Paradoxically, some clear-cut colonies in the Caribbean appear to have performed better than Cuba or the Dominican Republic.

An era of export-led growth culminated in Latin America during the 1920s. In some countries, such as Chile, Cuba and Brazil, the limitations of external demand for the traditional staple had become clear by the late 1920s, while in others those years witnessed unprecedented export booms. Foreign capital, both portfolio and direct, flowed massively into both types of countries up until 1929, so balance-of-payments surplus or at least equilibrium was the rule. As in the rest of the world, there had been a return to the gold-exchange standard in Latin America, and price stability was also the rule, for the last time in this century. It is a moot point whether the terms of trade and the capital inflow of the late 1920s could have been expected to persist. In fact such external and internal balances were rudely and repeatedly shocked from the outside, starting in 1929 and throughout the 1930s.

The external shocks were at once reflected in balance-of-payments deficits, which by themselves triggered mechanisms of adjustment, some very clumsy and painful.

The rest of the chapter will chronicle how various Latin American countries coped with the crisis and the extent to which they were able to mobilise mechanisms of adjustment beyond deflation. The nature and magnitudes of the external shocks will first be narrated. Second, the various policy reactions to those shocks will be discussed, covering measures seeking to regain external and internal balance, as well as policies targeted toward longer-term goals. Then the global, sectoral and welfare performances will be explored, and the sense in which economies did or did not do reasonably well will be analysed. In evaluating performance, emphasis will be placed on quantitative indicators. An overall interpretation of events during the 1930s will close the paper.

EXTERNAL SHOCKS AND TRENDS

The breakdown during 1929–33 of the international economic order was transmitted to Latin America first of all by sharp changes in relative prices: dollar export prices collapsed more steeply than dollar import prices. Within four years the terms of trade fell by 21 to 45% in countries for which comparable data are available (Naciones Unidas, 1976). Latin American terms of trade had, of course, experienced steep declines before, as during 1920–1, but the magnitude of the collapse combined, for many countries, with the continuation of unfavourable terms of trade throughout the rest of the decade, in spite of some post-1933 recovery, was unprecedented at least during the era of export-led growth. The terms of trade deterioration may be regarded as primarily exogenous to Latin America; countries which could influence the international prices of their exports, such as Brazil, had been doing so since earlier in the century. During the early 1930s other Latin American countries began regulating their traditional exports so as not to worsen further their dollar prices.

For a country with a ratio of exports to Gross National Product (GNP) of one-third a deterioration of the terms of trade by 30% would represent a loss in real income of about one-tenth, assuming no change in physical output. The blow to GNP appears to have been softened in some countries by a more than proportional fall in the profits of exporting foreign enterprises; data on the fall of real returned value are unavailable for most countries. On the other hand, there are hints that out of the lower foreign profits a larger share may have sought to be remitted abroad, especially during the early years of the crisis, which may have brought further pressure on the balance of payments.

Except for the spectacular Chilean and Cuban cases, the contraction in the export quantum during 1929–33 was substantially less than the terms of trade deterioration, and by the late 1930s the export quantum of several countries had surpassed the 1928–9 level. Latin American exports were predominantly rural and mining products, the former showing a smaller price elasticity of supply than the latter. Some rural products, such as coffee and livestock, followed *sui generis* output cycles rooted in their productive characteristics, contributing to short-run price inelasticity of supply.

The commodity lottery brought relief to some countries even in the midst of gloomy external conditions. Gold prices were raised by US monetary policy; US support programmes for silver and agricultural commodities also improved a few Latin American export prices (although sometimes at the expense of market shares, as with Cuban sugar). Droughts in North America favoured exporters of temperate foodstuffs. Post-1933 German expansion allowed export diversification for several countries, as to products and markets. Brazilian cotton, Argentine corn, Peruvian and Colombian gold, Mexican silver and Venezuelan oil are examples of generally 'lucky' staples. Tropical colonies with preferential access to metropolitan markets for sugar and bananas gained at the expense of sovereign producers.

As noted earlier, during the late 1920s Latin American payments balances were bolstered by large capital inflows, with New York replacing London as the leading source of long-term portfolio funds. Already during 1929, well before Latin American countries showed signs of skipping scheduled servicing of the external debt or blocking profit remittances, gross capital inflows fell sharply. After mid-1930 little fresh capital came in. With the dollar price level falling unexpectedly by no less than one-quarter between 1920–9 and 1932–3, debt servicing rose dramatically in real terms, compressing the capacity to import beyond what data on the purchasing power of exports suggest. During the early stages of the crisis the import quantum fell even more than the purchasing power of exports in most countries, as they struggled to meet debt obligations in spite of the cessation of capital inflows. Defaults started in 1931 and by 1934 only Argentina, Haiti and the Dominican Republic maintained normal servicing of their external national debt. From then to the end of the decade import volumes as a rule recovered faster than the purchasing power of exports.

Direct foreign investment, in magnitudes more significant for specific branches of production than for the balance of payments, did not disappear during the 1930s, but shifted its marginal orientation away from traditional exports, export-oriented services and social overhead capital, and toward import substituting activities, with the important Venezuelan exception. This trend had been visible already during the 1920s, particularly in the more developed countries of the region. Exchange controls and multiple exchange rates discouraging profit remittances may have induced in the short run some reinvestment of profits in new local activities, especially after the early 1930s. The late 1930s also witnessed the inflow of refugee capital from Europe, and there were even proposals to make Buenos Aires an international money centre, replacing those threatened by European tensions.

The emergence of a protectionist and nationalistic Centre was the greatest shock to Latin American economies during the 1930s, going beyond its direct negative impact on the region's terms of trade. As late as 1931 it was still unclear whether the decline in economic activity in industrialised countries was another passing recession or something more serious. But by that date it seemed very likely that one was witnessing the end of *laissez-faire* and of the commitment of leading countries to relatively free trade. Already during the 1920s imperial preferences were advocated in Britain by influential groups, and the 1928 presidential election in the USA was accompanied by a protectionist wave. That ferment was followed by passage of the Smoot–Hawley tariff in 1930 and the British Abnormal Importations Act of 1931. Even if prosperity returned to the Centre, the outlook for Latin American exports competitive with production in industrial countries or in their colonies or commonwealths, ranging from sugar and copper to meat, corn and wool, looked grim. As the Depression deepened, protectionism gained ground: British Commonwealth preferences were adopted in Ottawa in 1932, while France, Germany and Japan also reinforced their protectionism and discriminatory trade arrangements for areas under their political hegemony.

It is true that in 1934 Cordell Hull, US Secretary of State, started a policy of reducing US tariffs, but such policy made slow progress, and had to whittle down a tariff wall raised not only by the Smoot–Hawley Act, but also by the deflation-induced increase in the incidence of specific duties. The brightest and best-informed observers of the international economy as it stood by 1934 probably had difficulty in forecasting the shape of the new international economic order for the next ten years, but it is unlikely that they would have urged Latin American countries to wait for export-led expansion. As it turned out, by that date circumstances had pushed many Latin American policy-makers into considerable experimentation, without the need of sage foreign advice, which had sharply depreciated during the crisis.

POLICIES

Under gold-exchange standard rules, a deficit in the balance of payments set off automatic mechanisms of adjustment without the need for discretionary actions by policy-makers. As the slowdown in the Centre economies already visible in 1929 and rampant protectionism were quickly translated into a decline of export values in the Periphery, a balance of payments already weakened by a decline in capital inflows turned negative, and gold and foreign exchange flowed out of Latin America. Nominal money supplies declined during the early stages of the crisis, while interest rates were kept no lower than those in the major international financial centres, all in accord with the then orthodox rules of the game. Falling price levels helped maintain real liquidity, also as textbooks predicted, although setting off less textbookish expectations and fears of bankruptcies.

As early as 1930 some Latin American policy-makers began to reconsider the wisdom of remaining faithful to the orthodox rules of the game. The reconsideration was not due to new theoretical insights, but to the pressure of circumstances. Maintaining gold parities when foreign-exchange reserves were disappearing and foreign capital markets were practically shut to new Latin American bond issues became foolhardy. Balancing the budget when customs revenues were collapsing and civil servants were rebelling became nearly impossible. Timidly at first and loudly promising a quick return to late 1920s parities and practices, policy-makers in countries where instruments were at hand or where sufficient autonomy allowed their creation began to replace gold-exchange standard rules with 'emergency' discretionary tinkering. Peripheral shame and self-doubts gradually gave way to self-confidence, especially after Britain abandoned the gold standard in 1931 and Germany and the USA embarked on their own experiments.

The following description of measures undertaken throughout the

1930s risks attributing to 'Autonomous Policy' a series of improvisations more or less forced by circumstances, and whose logic may be clearer *ex post* than at the time of their adoption. One would search in vain among public statements by economic authorities of those days for reasoned explanations for the switch from the old rules to the new discretion; only by the late 1930s *ex post* rationalisations of some intellectual weight began to appear. Yet, whatever their political and ideological motivations, the thrust of policies adopted by the more autonomous and reactive republics may be viewed as attempts to avoid the costs of the deflation called for by the classical mechanism of adjustment, and to speed up the achievement of a new constellation of relative prices and resource allocation consistent with the post-1929 realities of the international economy.

Exchange-rate Policies

Reactive countries by 1933 had nominal exchange rates relative to the dollar significantly above the late 1920s parities. The use of multiple exchange rates buttressed by exchange controls became widespread following the September 1931 devaluation of the pound sterling. Rates applicable to imports suffered the sharpest depreciations. Fears that devaluation would further worsen foreign prices for traditional exports motivated lower depreciations for rates applicable to them, but non-traditional exports received more favourable rates. Fiscal self-interest led to advantageous rates for servicing the public debt; the spread between major buying and selling rates also became a convenient source of public revenue. Memories of late nineteenth-century inflations under the 'inconvertible paper standard', such as those of Argentina and Brazil, made policy-makers anxious about exchange-rate depreciations, and some domestic and foreign advisors urged either an eventual or an immediate return to the parities of the late 1920s. Lip service was paid to an eventual restoration of the gold standard, but policy-makers in reactive countries went no further than checking 'excessive' depreciations.

Small or very dependent countries, such as Honduras, Haiti, Dominican Republic, Panama and Cuba, maintained their peg to the US dollar throughout the 1930s. The last two countries did not even have a central bank or a corresponding monetary authority, such as those of Brazil or pre-1935 Argentina. Exchange-control measures in the small or passive countries were on the whole less forceful than in reactive countries.

Data on price levels and money wages are scarce for the 1930s, especially for the smaller countries. Nevertheless, available information indicates that nominal devaluations in the reactive countries had weak inflationary consequences, contrary to the experience in later years. By 1930–4, therefore, *real* import-exchange rates with respect to the dollar, which take into account price-level changes domestically and abroad, had risen (depreciated) between 30 and 90% in Argentina, Brazil, Chile, Colombia, Mexico, Peru and Uruguay, relative to 1925–9 levels. Such real prices of dollars in terms of local currency remained at those depreciated levels also during 1935–9. As money wages in those countries appear to have followed price-level movements, when the decade is regarded as a whole the ratio of exchange rates to nominal wages also rose significantly.

For the smaller or passive countries one may conjecture that there was no such rapid and large real depreciation of exchange rates. In the Caribbean and Central America the sharpest Depression-induced devaluation occurred in Costa Rica, with a smaller one occurring in El Salvador; other small countries maintained their pegs to the dollar or underwent monetary changes due to domestic turmoil. Some countries having a steady peg to the dollar attempted to raise the ratio of the exchange rate to nominal wages by extraordinarily repressive labour policies; such was the case of Guatemala under General Ubico, at least until 1934 (see Chapter 11 by Bulmer-Thomas).

Regardless of the exchange-rate policy followed, a country subjected to an exogenous and permanent worsening of its international terms of trade should witness over the long run a decline in the price of its non-traded goods and services (or money wages) relative to the domestic price of importable goods, encouraging a movement of resources, including fresh investments, toward the import-competing sector, additional to that generated by the decline in exportable-goods prices. A permanent decline in net long-term capital inflows would also induce a decline in the prices of non-traded goods relative to all traded goods. Under a gold-exchange standard with fixed rates and with collapsing international nominal prices for both imports and exports, non-traded goods prices and domestic liquidity had a long way to fall to adjust to the 1929–33 decline in terms of trade and the cessation of capital inflows. It is the working hypothesis of this chapter that countries willing and able to devalue their exchange rate moved toward the new constellation of domestic relative prices more speedily and less painfully than those with fixed rates, limiting both price and monetary deflation, containing their negative impact on real output, or reducing pressures to depress money wages by extraordinary measures. It is worth emphasising that the depreciating trend in the reactive countries appears smooth only in *ex-post* five-year averages focusing on exchange rates with respect to the dollar. Besides confusing signals emanating from promises to return to earlier parities the early 1930s also witnessed changes in the rates between major currencies, particularly the dollar–pound sterling rate, which added to fluctuations in *effective* exchange rates of several countries, especially in South America, and complicated the formation of expectations about the future price of 'foreign exchange'.

Other Import-repressing and Import-diverting Policies

The domestic price of importable goods relative to non-traded goods prices, or to money wages, also received an upward push in many Latin American countries as tariffs rose and quantitative restrictions, via import or exchange controls, were introduced. Contrary to what would happen in the late 1940s and 1950s, exchange-rate and *de facto* protectionist policies reinforced each other as import-repressing mechanisms, especially in Brazil and the Southern Cone. Indeed, by the mid-1930s in some of the reactive countries there may have been redundancy in this formidable battery of measures; this has been argued for the Chilean case, for example.

The small or passive countries appear to have been, with some exceptions, as impotent regarding protection as with nominal exchange-rate management. Cuba actually lowered tariffs in 1934, undoing much of the protectionist effect of her anomalous Tariff Act of 1927. Even larger countries were pressured into reversing some of their early-1930s tariff increases; wielding the threat of Commonwealth preferences and meat import quotas, the UK obtained tariff concessions from Argentina under the controversial Roca–Runciman treaty of 1933. Argentina and Cuba shared awkward memberships in 'informal empires', although the autonomy of the former country was, of course, much larger than the latter.

Tariff rates appear to have undergone few changes in levels or structure in Mexico and Peru. These countries also behaved in a manner more like the smaller countries in regard to import and exchange controls; in contrast with Brazil and the Southern Cone they employed those instruments only sparingly. Colombia, as usual, had an intermediate set of policies: most of the change between 1927 and 1936 in the prices of her imported non-traditional manufactures has been attributed to devaluation rather than tariff increases, although increments in effective protection stimulated some industries, including cement, soap and rayon textiles. Colombia also exercised import and exchange controls with greater vigour than did Mexico and Peru.

Import and exchange controls, together with multiple rates, had the additional task of managing key bilateral balances, especially in Brazil and the Southern Cone; in countries with less diversified trading and financial patterns such management was less of a problem. Argentine controls were practically forced upon her by the UK pressure for bilateral clearings; to achieve that goal Argentina had to discriminate against US exports. Such 'buying from those that bought from her' generated hostility in the US against Argentina, and some North Americans viewed her controls as a sign of Nazi rather than British influence. Brazilian controls, in fact, received impetus from her expanded trade with Germany during the 1930s.

Other Balance-of-payments Policies

Toward the end of the 1920s the stock of British and US investments of all kinds in Latin America amounted, in per capita terms, to about one-sixth those in Canada. The heaviest concentration occurred, in descending order and still in per capita terms, in Cuba, Argentina, Chile, Mexico, Uruguay and Costa Rica. Both in Canada and Latin America the two major foreign investors had accumulated claims of all kinds of around four times the annual value of merchandise exports. Assuming a 5% rate of return, profits and interests of foreign capital must have accounted for about 20% of annual export earnings, and were punctually transferred abroad. With the exception of Mexico the 'investment climate' appeared reasonably good; the nineteenth-century defaults on bonds issued in London had been settled, and while numerous frictions were generated by direct investments they seemed negotiable.

The unexpected post-1929 fall in dollar and sterling prices sharply increased the real cost of external obligations denominated in those currencies. Servicing the Argentine public debt, for example, which had absorbed about 6% of merchandise exports during the late 1920s, by 1933 reached nearly 16% of exports. Chile in 1932 faced interest and amortisation charges, including those on short-term maturities, far exceeding export earnings. The ratio of the stock of long-term external public debt to yearly merchandise exports for all Latin America rose from 1.5 in 1929 to 2.3 in 1935. The drying up of foreign capital markets made roll-over operations for both long- and short-term debt very difficult. The collapse of import-duty revenues cut a traditional budgetary source for payments on the external debt.

Starting in 1931, authorities delayed granting exchange to importers for settling their short-term debt and to foreign companies for profit remittances. Also in 1931, many Latin American countries began to skip scheduled servicing of the external long-term public debt. Defaulting countries did not dramatically repudiate their obligations, but asked foreign creditors for conversations aimed at rescheduling and restructuring the debt. Different countries carried out those conversations with various degrees of enthusiasm: Cuba, for example, while servicing her debt irregularly during the 1930s maintained better relations with her creditors than Brazil, whose dealings with creditors during the late 1930s, especially with British ones, were acrimonious. For many countries those negotiations were to stretch out well into the 1940s, and into the 1950s in some cases. The contrast between Argentine and Brazilian policies toward debt service in the 1930s casts light on the nature of international economic relations during those years; see Chapter 6 for a discussion of those policies. One may emphasise that the relative abundance of exchange reserves in Argentina, whose gold holdings remained one of the highest in the world, gaining an important windfall by the increase in the international gold price during the 1930s, plus the fact that a substantial amount of the Argentine sterling- and dollar-denominated debt was held by Argentines (just as a share of 'domestic', peso-denominated debt was held by foreigners) also contributed to punctual servicing of even dollar-denominated bonds, presumably mostly held in the USA, in spite of British hints about the convenience for Anglo-Argentine trade of defaulting on that part of the debt. Furthermore, tampering with the normal servicing of the Argentine debt would have involved not only a bruising commercial clash with the UK, but probably also a major restructuring of the Argentine domestic political scene at the expense of groups linked with Anglo-Argentine trade.

There is little reason to doubt the consensus among those who have examined the Latin American defaults of the 1930s: if the Depression had been mild, and if the steady expansion of world trade and capital flows had been continued, defaults would have been infrequent and could have been settled without much difficulty. Once the Depression came and productive resources were allowed to go to waste in idleness, while countries everywhere restricted imports to protect jobs, it made no economic sense to insist on the transfer of real resources as debt servicing. No doubt the capital markets of the 1920s contained significant imperfections: during the 1930s many underwriters were accused not just of negligence in seeking information about borrowers and their projects, but also of deliberately misleading bond-buyers, motivating New Deal regulatory legislation. Latin American countries were encouraged to borrow excessively, and a good share of the funds went into projects of doubtful social productivity. But one may question whether these microeconomic factors were decisive. One may also note that the industrialised countries themselves led in the undermining of belief in the sanctity of contracts; examples include the British default on the war debt, Germany's failure to make payments on the greater part of her international obligations, the derogation of the gold clause in the USA, and domestic moratoria legislated in several countries.

By the late 1930s foreign-exchange availability had improved and indeed some debt servicing was paid by defaulting Latin American countries throughout the 1930s. Some countries purchased their own partially or wholly unserviced bonds selling at a discount in foreign markets; those bonds by the late 1930s were probably held mostly by speculators. Such 'repatriations' of the debt avoided a rigid settlement schedule at a time when the international economic outlook was very uncertain, and were carried out by central banks, whose financial positions were generally better than those of the Treasuries, which still suffered from the fall and change in composition of imports and the induced decline in duties.

In spite of exchange controls regulating profit remittances abroad by foreign enterprises, direct foreign investments occurred throughout the 1930s, although in amounts more significant for the expansion of specific branches of production than for balance-of-payments equilibrium. It has been argued that the local reinvestment of foreign-enterprise profits may have been encouraged by limitations on remittances abroad, an argument more plausible in the short run than in the long. In some countries exchange controls were also employed to ward off unwanted short-term capital inflows, as in Argentina during the late 1930s; such 'hot money' movements were perceived as destabilising macroeconmic balance. Capital accompanying European refugees was considered a more permanent and welcomed addition to local resources and these combinations of entrepreneurship and finance were important in the expansion of several economic (and cultural) activities in many Latin American countries.

Monetary and Fiscal Policies

The decline in exports and capital inflows signalling the beginning of the crisis was accompanied at once by balance-of-payments deficits which drained reserves and money supplies, according to gold-standard, fixed-exchange rates rules. The export fall had important multiplier effects. This section will examine responses to those deflationary pressures on aggregate demand. In countries without well-developed financial markets it is difficult to isolate purely fiscal from monetary policies. During the 1930s only Argentina had financial markets of some sophistication, so this section will discuss aggregate macroeconomic policies without establishing fine distinctions between monetary and fiscal ones.

Money-supply data indicate that reactive Latin American countries show briefer or shallower post-1929 declines in nominal money supplies than the USA. By 1932 the Brazilian nominal money supply exceeded that of 1929; the corresponding Colombian date is 1933. The end of convertibility into gold was helpful in stemming the loss of liquidity among reactive countries. In contrast the Cuban inability to break out of the then orthodox rules led to a monetary deflation even greater than that of the USA.

Domestic price levels for 1930–4 were below those of 1925–9 excepting Chile, although the decline appears smaller for most reactive countries than that in the USA. By 1935–9 price levels in those countries had mostly returned to about 1925–9 levels, with only Chile and Mexico cleary surpassing them. *Real* money supplies in 1930–4 in most reactive countries were above those for 1925–9; by 1935–9 real money supplies in Argentina, Brazil, Chile, Colombia, Mexico and Uruguay were substantially above 1925–9 levels. The Cuban real money supply in 1935–9 was below that for 1925–9 and this probably was the case in many of the Central American and Caribbean republics. This contrast suggests that the increase in real money supplies of reactive countries was not just the result of automatic mechanisms of adjustment triggered by the fall in the international price level, but also the result of domestic policies.

Maintenance of liquidity was not simply a matter of ending convertibility into gold or foreign exchange at the old parities. Even after the abandonment of the gold standard some countries, such as Argentina, shipped gold to service the external debt and sold some foreign exchange to stem currency depreciation. Both measures cut the monetary base if orthodox practices were followed. But as early as 1931 South American monetary authorities adopted measures which would have been regarded as unsound during the 1920s. Thus, the Argentine Caja de Conversión whose only classical duty was to exchange gold and foreign exchange for domestic currency at a fixed price, and vice versa, starting in 1931 began to issue domestic currency in exchange for private commercial paper, relying on obscure and nearly forgotten laws, and later on even issued domestic currency against Treasury paper, which was also accepted as payment for gold sent abroad for public debt servicing. Young technocrats in charge of Argentine monetary policy successfully resisted pressures from the orthodox to 'redeem' the Treasury paper, recall the new currency issues, and return to the old parity. The Colombian Central Bank in 1930 for the first time engaged in direct operations with the public, discounting notes and lending on the security of warehouse receipts; during 1931 ingenious subterfuges were found by the Bank to grant credit directly to the central government, involving as 'collateral' future public revenues from a salt mine (Ocampo, Chapter 5, below). Government bonds were purchased from private banks in large quantities by the Colombian Central Bank since 1932. In Colombia, as in other reactive countries, since the introduction of exchange controls in 1931 international reserves ceased to govern monetary issue, which from then on was predominantly influenced by internal considerations of economic policy or budgetary expediency.

The South American and Mexican monetary policies, started around 1932, were in some ways a relapse into past inflationary propensities, a past which was supposed to have been exorcised by the adoption during the 1920s of gold-standard rules and up-to-date budgetary and monetary mechanisms. These mechanisms became popular in the region during the second half of the 1920s, often following visits of foreign 'money doctors'. Memories of wild inflation under inconvertible paper during the late nineteenth century, memories still fresh during 1929–31, as well as episodes of financial disorder as recent as the early 1920s, hampered and slowed down the adoption of more self-assured and expansionist monetary policies. It should also be remembered that as late as the first half of 1931 there were optimistic reports of an upturn in the major industrialised economies.

In contrast with the USA there are no reports of widespread bank failures in reactive countries during the early 1930s. Also in contrast with the USA, monetary aggregates fail to reveal in flight into currency and away from bank deposits; if anything, during the early stages of the Depression the opposite appears to have occurred in Argentina, Brazil, Colombia and Uruguay. In reactive countries monetary authorities simply did not let many banks fail, casting fears of moral hazard to the winds. In many of those countries a substantial share of deposits were held in state-owned banks, which may have been decisive in avoiding financial panics. While moratoria on urban and rural domestic bank debts were decreed in many countries (earlier than in the USA), thus freezing banks' assets, commercial banks were supported in a number of *ad hoc* ways, not all of them conducive to maintaining actual liquidity. For example, in Brazil as early as October 1930 withdrawals of bank deposits were restricted by decree. Domestic moratoria, of course, had an expansionary influence on debtors. Rediscounting of commercial banks' loans was also vigorously carried out by Central Banks and institutions such as the Banco do Brasil and the Banco de la Nacion Argentina. Unorthodoxy was sometimes cloaked by gestures to the old financial hocus-pocus; Argentina claimed to have used profits from increases in the peso price of gold to create an institution which supported commercial banks.

The financial impotency of passive countries may be illustrated by the contrasting experiences of Cuba and Mexico in their tinkering with silver for monetary and fiscal purposes. Although Cuba was not a major silver producer while Mexico was, both countries hit upon the expedient of issuing silver coins, which added to liquidity and yielded seignorage profits to the Treasury, justifying expenditures. Depending on the acceptance by the public, both countries planned to issue paper notes backed by silver stocks, increasing seignorage. In Cuba modest issues were made during 1932–3, and in 1934 a revolutionary government appeared to herald a bold new monetary system independent of the dollar by planning new issues and by making silver pesos full legal tender for the discharge of old as well as new obligations contracted in dollars or in old Cuban gold pesos. Shortly thereafter a mild form of exchange control was decreed. Foreign banks on the island apparently threatened to export all dollars from Cuba; capital flight followed. The government caved in, lifting rather than expanding controls. Only the legal tender status of silver for all contracts in such currency remained of the 1934 reform. Even a Central Bank was to wait until 1948.

Mexico, after some deflationary measures in 1930 and 1931, adopted early in 1932 expansionary policies, relying mainly on issues of silver pesos. Central Bank control over commercial banks was extended and strengthened. Foreign banks threatened to leave Mexico, and as the Mexican authorities held firm, most of them left. Mexican-owned banks took their place. Campaigns were launched to convince the public to use 'silver' paper notes rather than coins; remarkably, the share of paper notes in the money supply jumped dramatically in a few years, for reasons still somewhat obscure (see Chapter 9, by Cárdenas). Public banks were created or expanded to finance housing, public works, foreign trade, industry and agriculture, and these instruments were used with increasingly self-conscious expansionist purposes. By the late 1930s the Mexican monetary and financial system was quite different from that of the late 1920s. In contrast with the disastrous Chinese experience, Mexican reliance on a silver standard did not generate unmanageable problems when the USA raised silver prices; Mexico simply prohibited the export of silver money in April 1935 and ordered all coins to be exchanged for paper currency. A year and a half later, after the world price of silver had fallen, silver coinage was restored, partly due to pressure from the US silver lobby. As a major exporter of silver Mexico, of course, benefited from higher international silver prices.

Even during the confusion of the early 1930s, fiscal policy in reactive countries appears to have contributed to the maintenance of aggregate demand, at least in the sense of *not* balancing the budget in the midst of the crisis, in spite of the protestations of policy-makers that they intended to do so. Although data are particularly shaky in this field, real government expenditures were not significantly cut during the early 1930s, while real tax revenues fell as imports collapsed, inducing an increase in fiscal deficits in spite of new taxes and higher tariffs. The financing of budget deficits even in reactive countries during the early 1930s was not all particularly expansionary; payment delays to civil servants and government suppliers increased the 'floating debt', a debt whose holders usually could only turn into cash at huge discounts, thus coming close to forced loans (but see Chapter 4, by Thorp and Londoño, who argue that such debt came closer to quasi-money). A fiscal policy, expansionary in the sense of increasing the full-capacity real budget deficit during the early 1930s, has been amply documented only for Brazil; the Chilean experience has some similarities to the Brazilian case, according to Palma, in this volume. The cases of Argentina and Brazil will illustrate the variety of fiscal policies in reactive countries.

Real expenditures of the Argentine central government rose in 1929 and again in 1930; the provisional regime of General Uriburu, which took power in September 1930, pledging to eliminate populist budgetary excesses, reduced 1931 real expenditures slightly below those for 1930, but left them above 1929 levels. The lowest real expenditure figures for the 1930s, which were registered in 1933, were still higher than those for 1929; for the rest of the decade real government expenditures expanded so that by 1938–9 they were around 50% above 1929. A major road-building programme was undertaken by the government of General Justo (1932–8), adding 30 000 kilometres of all-weather and improved roads by 1938 to a system that had only 2 100 kilometres of such roads in 1932. This programme had important effects not just on aggregate demand, but also on productivity and aggregate supply, both complementing and competing with the vast Argentine railroad network. The late 1930s also witnessed an expansion of military expenditures. The ratio of all government expenditures to merchandise exports, a useful index suggested by Rosemary Thorp, which in 1928 was less than 0.4 had risen to more than 0.9 by 1938–9.

The technocrats in charge of the economic policies of the Uriburu and Justo Administrations, including Federico Pinedo and Raúl Prebisch, took a dim view of the large deficits registered in 1930 and 1931; the fall in revenues from import duties aggravated a fiscal situation which already in 1928 and 1929 yielded taxes covering only 76–80% of all government expenditures. Tariff rates were increased, an income tax was introduced (in 1932), a gasoline tax was coupled with the road-building programme and use was made of multiple exchange rates to generate government revenues. As in other Latin American countries, fiscal heterodoxy was discredited in Argentina by dubious expenditures and lax budgets during the late 1920s.

The budget deficits of 1930 and 1931 were financed primarily by delays in payments to suppliers and civil servants, or payments in public debt instruments of low liquidity, contributing to the unpopularity of government deficits. Starting in 1932, however, such floating debt was sharply reduced and by the second half of the 1930s the government placed in an active local market both short- and long-term public securities at rates of interest much below those of 1929–32. Refunding operations were also carried out to reduce the cost and improve the structures of domestic and foreign debts.

The countercyclical potency of Argentine fiscal policy during the early 1930s was reduced by the increased share in total expenditures of debt-service payments, largely made to foreigners. All payments on the public debt reached 29% of expenditures in 1932; this may be

Shambaugh Library

contrasted with the meagre 5% devoted to public works. By 1938 the figures were 15% for debt service and 20% for public works. Other Latin American countries were to find the budgetary weight of debt service, exacerbated by exchange-rate depreciations, a strong inducement to suspend normal payments.

In short there is no evidence that during the early 1930s the Argentine government sought to increase the full-capacity budget deficit to compensate for the fall in aggregate demand. On the contrary, attempts were made to shift upward the tax schedule and to lower that for government expenditures. But even during the early 1930s efforts to reduce the deficit induced by the decline in foreign trade and output were tempered by either common sense or the sheer inability to cut expenditures and raise taxes fast enough. The relative size of public expenditures in the income stream thus grew by default already in the early 1930s, helping to sustain economic activity. Since 1933 public expenditures expanded in a deliberate way, and this expansion had at least a balanced-budget–multiplier effect on the rest of the economy. In addition, since 1935 the new Central Bank encouraged the expansion of a market for the domestic public debt, facilitating modest deficit financing. Finally, the structure of expenditures during the late 1930s on balance favoured domestic expansion, in spite of some increase in the import content of military expenditures.

Brazil provides an example of a compensatory increase in government expenditure in the early 1930s. Since 1906 the State of São Paulo and the federal government sustained coffee prices via buffer stocks; during the sharp recession of 1920–21 the countercyclical potency of the coffee valorisation scheme had already been demonstrated. As coffee prices fell during the early 1930s the government again purchased large quantities of that product. A good share of those purchases were financed either by a foreign loan or new taxes, but about one-third were financed essentially by money creation. It has also been argued that the new taxes levied on exports, and the exchange-rate appreciation generated by foreign loans, improved Brazilian terms of trade, relative to the relevant counterfactual situation. Argentina also started regulating the production and export of major traditional exports during the 1930s, notably wheat, but without the massive fiscal impact of the Brazilian coffee purchases, partly due to the recovery of their international prices. The exchange differential profits were the Argentine counterpart to the Brazilian export taxes, both attempting to raise government revenues as well as to protect the terms of trade. Brazil also expanded public expenditures during the late 1930s, and probably reduced the import content of those expenditures even more than Argentina, as beginning in September 1931 it met debt-service obligations only partially. In 1937 Brazil announced the suspension of all debt servicing, and none occurred during 1938 and 1939. In both Argentina and Brazil the 1930s witnessed diversification of public revenues, with a remarkable expansion in non-customs taxes, which by 1932 (Argentina) and 1933 (Brazil) had exceeded the 1929 levels, at current prices. A similar trend toward tax diversification has been reported for Colombia, where direct taxes were increased during 1935–6, and Mexico. In the Brazilian case state revenues, especially those of São Paulo, appear to have expanded by more than those of the federal government.

Calamities, civil disturbances and border wars during the early 1930s led to increased real public expenditures in several countries, apparently financed directly by monetary expansion. Examples include political turmoil in Chile during late 1931 and 1932 (when that country had a short-lived socialist government); the war between Peru and Colombia over Leticia in 1932 (partly financed on the Colombian side by voluntary donations); the second Gran Chaco War between Bolivia and Paraguay, also in 1932; and the São Paulo rebellion of 1932, plus a severe drought in the north-east, which added to coffee deficits in Brazil (the former more than the latter). In some countries weak central control over regional governments also contributed to the maintenance of public expenditures.

Whatever the hesitations and improvisations of the early 1930s, by the second half of the decade the reactive Latin American countries had developed a respectable array of both monetary and fiscal tools, as well as the will to use them to avoid deflation. Thus, the 1937–8 recession in the USA was felt in the foreign trade statistics more than those for industrial output. South American countries damaged by the loss of European markets and shipping shortages in 1939–40 mobilised to adopt emergency stabilisation measures, such as the remarkable Plan Pinedo in Argentina, which included proposals for closer regional economic ties, particularly between Argentina and Brazil. That Plan was never adopted, due to Congressional opposition and an improvement in the economic outlook.

Much of the new state activism discussed in this section may have been motivated by a desire to help influential rural exporters. One may note, however, that it is difficult to imagine macroeconomic policies in Latin American countries at that time which did not involve heavy emphasis on traditional export activities. This is due not just to the large weight of those sectors in national income, but also to the need to regulate their sales abroad, to avoid further declines in their international prices. Thus, apparently sectorial policies had a major impact on both aggregate demand and the balance of payments.

In passive countries an activist fiscal policy continued to be checked by exiguous foreign and domestic demand for public debt, and by convertibility into dollars at fixed rates that limited monetary expansion not backed by international reserves.

Other Policies

While nominal exchange-rate behaviour during the 1930s is well documented, much less is known regarding wages and how they were influenced by public policy, except for a few cases. In Guatemala, for example, where the exchange rate fixed during the 1920s was maintained throughout the 1930s, the regime of General Ubico enforced until 1934 draconian labour practices, some originating in the Spanish conquest, generating a cheap supply of quasi-forced labour for both landowners and public works. (But see Chapter 11 by Bulmer-Thomas for changes after 1934.) Flexibility and moderation regarding money wages was induced by more subtle means in other countries, particularly where non-traditional labour markets already existed. In some of those countries, like Argentina, soft economic conditions during the early 1930s, rural–urban migration and cheap foodstuffs kept increases in nominal wages substantially behind exchange-rate depreciations. In others, such as Colombia, Brazil and Mexico, those market trends were accompanied by public policies encouraging trade unions which often controlled from above rather than promoted wage gains, especially *vis-à-vis* nationally-owned firms. Mass deportation of Mexican workers from the USA during the 1930s also added to the pool of mobile labour available in that country.

Public policies went beyond those seeking short-term adjustment to outside shocks, and Latin American governments, whose attachment to *laissez-faire* was never particularly deep, became increasingly committed during the 1930s to promoting long-term growth and structural transformations. The Lazaro Cárdenas Administration (1934–40) accelerated the land reform programme of the Mexican Revolution, and in 1938 nationalised the petroleum industry. Government regulation of the pricing and marketing of rural products, and of public utility rates expanded in most countries. As noted earlier for Mexico, the 1930s witnessed in several other Latin American countries the strengthening and creation of public institutions granting medium- and long-term credits, which the unregulated financial markets of the 1920s had not provided in amounts regarded as sufficient, or whose supply had been left in foreign hands. Housing, public works, agriculture and, increasingly, industry benefited from such credit, which during the 1930s, when inflation was moderate at worst, was still priced not far below plausible estimates for the shadow cost of capital.

The public works undertaken in many countries had a long-lasting impact on productive capacity and urbanisation patterns. Vast road programmes accelerated the transition from the railroad age to that of motor vehicles. That transition stimulated many manufacturing activities including cement, rubber, petroleum refining and the assembly and eventual production of cars, trucks, and buses; generated public revenues via gasoline taxes; diversified and completed transport networks, lowering their costs and encouraging new activities, such as US tourism in Mexico, while opening up new lands for rural production; and even helped to change international economic relations, as motor-vehicle activities were dominated by the USA, while railroads had been dominated by the UK. (See Fodor and O'Connell, 1973.) Irrigation works, like those undertaken in Mexico, together with new roads and credit facilities, encouraged the transition from traditional to modern capitalist agriculture.

During the 1930s governments and public opinion showed a keener interest in increasing the national share in value added by foreign-owned activities and the control over the processing and marketing of exports. Foreign-owned enterprises came under closer scrutiny and supervision by host countries; several traditional export activities witnessed a rise in the share owned by domestic capitalists, as in the case of Cuban sugar. Finally, as the European and Asian political scenes continued to deteriorate, the Armed Forces, especially in South America, showed increased interest in promoting the expansion of certain types of infrastructure and the local manufacture of steel and armaments.

PERFORMANCE

Even in countries performing reasonably well during the 1930s, structural changes were more impressive than overall growth; during that decade some economic activities stagnated or collapsed while others surged ahead. The former were generally associated directly or indirectly with external markets, while the latter typically involved domestic sales. Reactive countries on average performed better than passive ones, and in both types of nations some regions did much better than others. Pockets of profitability within agriculture and industry coexisted with liquidations; textile mills worked three shifts even in 1932 while meat-packing plants and sugar mills were idle. The larger the pre-1929 share of exports (or their returned value) in total output the smaller the absolute size of the domestic market, and the greater the institutional barriers to domestic resource mobility, the more difficult it was for the growing sectors to dominate the shrinking ones to yield a reasonably good overall performance. These factors, plus luck with external commodity prices, trade partners and local leadership, generated a continuum of quantifiable economic performances, rather than clear-cut typologies. In these still heavily agricultural economies, weather and pests remained important influences even on ten-year growth rates. In what follows, aggregate performance will first be examined as far as data allow, turning later to sectoral and welfare performances.

Macroeconomic Performance

National accounts for the four largest Latin American countries (Argentina, Brazil, Colombia and Mexico) register growth rates for Gross Domestic Product (GDP) steadier and higher than those of Canada and the USA for 1929–39. Neither the absolute GDP growth nor its level relative to the growth achieved during the 1940s and early 1950s, however, are impressive, ranging from around 2% per annum for Argentina and Mexico, to about 4% per annum for the two major coffee countries. Argentine and Colombian GDPs grew during the 1920s at clearly faster rates than those of the 1930s; Brazilian GDP during 1919–29 also seems to have outperformed the 1929–39 expansion.

Measurements of GDP ignore losses of real income from deteriorating terms of trade. Taking these losses into account would reduce Brazilian annual growth for 1929–39 by about 1 percentage point (while increasing those for the 1920s and 1940s). Population growth in Latin America during the 1930s was higher than that in industrialised countries. Thus, measuring performance by growth in per capita real domestic income during 1929–39 would reduce the differential favouring reactive Latin American countries compared with industrialised countries. Correcting for the reduction in factor payments abroad which occurred during the 1930s, to obtain real *national* income, is unlikely to offset corrections for terms of trade and population in evaluating overall performance. Even for reactive countries data for these calculations are shaky, however, and for others they are generally unavailable.

In reactive countries GDP recovery apparently started in 1932, earlier than in the USA. Neither the 1929–32 decline nor the 1932–7 recovery were as dramatic as those in the USA.

Consumption and investment also show disparate behaviour in their component parts, making the use of those aggregates of only limited value. Investment shares in GDP seem to have declined relative to the late 1920s, yet some sectors expanded their productive capacity while others experienced net disinvestment. Imports of machinery and equipment for railroads and electricity waned, while those for some manufacturing activities rose. It would strain available data to discuss the evolution of national savings during the 1930s relative to the 1920s, but it is clear that they rose relative to external savings and it seems that changes in the domestic financial system and in government budgets encouraged their mobilisation. Private consumption must have also undergone significant structural changes after 1929, some reflecting ongoing long-term trends such as urbanisation and the adoption of new products, others induced in the short- and medium-term by the income and substitution effects of higher prices for imported goods.

SECTORAL PERFORMANCE

Economic performance during the 1930s for the reactive Latin American countries looks more impressive when attention is focused on manufacturing. While growth in this sector during the 1940s and early 1950s was to exceed that for the 1930s in most countries, manufacturing growth rates for 1929–39, ranging from more than 3% per annum in Argentina to more than 8% per annum in Colombia, far outstripped those of the USA and Canada, which hovered around zero. The relatively modest Argentine manufacturing expansion was higher than that of Australia, even though both countries experienced roughly similar GDP growth rates between 1928 and 1938. In the important Brazilian case, manufacturing growth during the 1930s, of more than 6% per annum, was significantly higher than during the 1920s; the pace of Colombian industrialisation during the 1930s could not have been much behind that of the 1920s, if at all. Another interesting comparison involves Chile and Uruguay, on one side, and Cuba, on the other; the former reactive countries experienced manufacturing expansion of 3 to 5% per annum, while the latter country saw its total industrial production shrink even more than in the USA. Chilean industry also grew during the 1930s faster than during the previous decade (Palma, Chapter 3 below).

Pre-1929 Latin American manufacturing tended to grow only slightly ahead of the rest of the export-led economy. Beyond moderate protectionism, public policy departed little from neutrality toward industry. Important segments of manufacturing exported (slightly) processed primary products; examples include meat-packing plants and flour mills in the River Plate and sugar mills in several countries, which also sold their products domestically. Growth of manufacturing during the recovery phase of the 1930s relied heavily on import substitution, defined in the usual accounting sense (decrease in the share of imported goods in total supply), which focuses on output rather than on installed capacity. Manufacturing during the 1930s grew in reactive countries much faster than GDP, in contrast with pre-1929 experience.

The uneven performance in various GDP components is echoed by heterogeneous growth within manufacturing. Activities tied to pre-1929 export-oriented prosperity shrank, while others (sometimes a handful) made dramatic output advances. Leading sectors typically included textiles, petroleum refining, tyres, pharmaceuticals, toiletries, food-processing for the home market (e.g. vegetable oils), chemicals, cement and other building materials. Cotton and wool textiles were the most important leading sectors, often providing more than 20% of the net expansion of value added in manufacturing, and growing at annual rates above 10%. Between the late 1920s and late 1930s cement production multiplied by more than 14 times in Colombia, by more than 6 times in Brazil and by almost 4 times in Argentina. Even in passive countries one finds some import-substituting industries growing very fast, such as milk-processing and cotton cloth in Cuba, but in the midst of depressed export-related manufacturing. The remarkable industrialisation of major coffee countries (Brazil and Colombia) was partly due to having pre-1929 manufacturing sectors with few direct links to exports, in contrast with Argentina and Cuba. Pre-1929 growth, and the industrialization it had induced, were the more helpful to the import-substituting drive of the 1930s the greater the extent to which social overhead capital, trained labour force, and other productive capacity which had been created were not rigidly tied to specialised needs of exporting activities and could be reallocated quickly to serve other productive purposes.

Output growth in the booming industrial sectors far outstripped the expansion of total domestic absorption of those manufactured goods, which either followed more closely the somewhat sluggish growth of GDP, or declined in some cases even in reactive countries. Apparent domestic cement consumption, for example, increased by far less than the spectacular output increases noted earlier; it rose by 26% in Colombia, 12% in Brazil, and 50% in Argentina (in the USA it *declined* by 36%, in Canada and Haiti by 50% and in Cuba by 63%). Exports explain little of the gap between high output and low domestic absorption expansion; the share of local production in domestic absorption of cement rose between the late 1920s and the late 1930s from 6 to 72% in Colombia, from 14 to 89% in Brazil, and from 35 to 94% in Argentina) In contrast, in Cuba, Haiti, the Dominican Republic and Central America the share of domestic output in national cement absorption changed very little during that decade (although the Cuban share had reached levels higher than those of South American countries in the late 1920s). A similar import-substitution tale applies to textiles. For other commodities, such as automobiles, the decline in imports could not be matched by expansion of local production; for those goods, primarily consumer durables and machinery and equipment, domestic absorption fell, not to recover in per capita terms until the 1960s in many cases. Such 'postponement' of expenditures with high import content would become a standard feature of the mechanism of adjustment in the balance of payments of many Latin American countries in later years.

Capacity in manufacturing and ancillary social overhead capital expanded by less than output during the 1930s; statistics do not show either an upsurge in imports of machinery and equipment or a compensating expansion of local production of those goods. Indeed, in some countries imports of certain types of machinery (e.g. textile machinery in Brazil) were banned based on allegations of excess capacity. The late 1920s left substantial slack or malleable capacity in industry, electricity and some transport facilities. There are frequent reports of textile mills increasing their number of shifts during the early 1930s, and of large investments made during the late 1920s coming to fruition during the 1930s, as in the Brazilian cement industry.

Electricity capacity oriented toward export-related production during the 1920s could fairly easily be switched to supplying booming import substituting activities. Nevertheless, output expansions such as those registered for cement in Argentina, Brazil and Colombia *must* have relied on some increases in capacity, and imports of machinery and equipment. One may conjecture that there were substantial changes in the composition and allocation of capital goods imports between the 1920s and 1930s, so even if their total fell, plenty of room was left for the investment needs of dynamic branches of manufacturing.

The industrialisation of the 1930s, at least in South America, was quite labour-intensive, and involved many small- and medium-sized firms. Between 1930 and 1937 industrial employment in São Paulo grew at nearly 11% per year. The output elasticity of employment was about 1 in both Argentina and Brazil; increases in average labour productivity for specific activities seem to have been rare, in spite of the entry of new firms. In Argentina, for example, the increase in the number of textile firms accounted during the 1930s for approximately 65% of the increase in spindles held by the industry.

There are other indications that import-substitution relied heavily on new national and foreign-born entrepreneurs, including fresh immigrants from the troubled Europe of the 1930s. The rise of Hitler and Franco led to significant gains of human and financial capital for Latin America. There was also direct foreign investment in import-substitution by tariff-jumping enterprises, whose home markets showed weak prospects. For sectors like tyres and cement these investments and the technology they supplied provided significant impetus. There is little systematic evidence on the overall financing of manufacturing investment during the 1930s. It may be conjectured that traditional sources, e.g. reinvestment of gross profits and short-term and informal-market borrowing supplied the bulk of finance for national entrepreneurs as the contribution of public credit institutions to manufacturing capital formation was still modest.

New import-substituting activities clustered, not surprisingly, mainly around major consuming centres, such as Buenos Aires, Mexico City and São Paulo. While industrialisation thus contributed to support ongoing urbanisation trends, the latter appear to have had a dynamism of their own, making one sceptical of any close short-term links between the two phenomena.

Import-substitution was the engine of growth during the 1930s, but not just in manufacturing. The rural sector also witnessed gains in the production of goods sold in the domestic market relative to those primarily sold abroad. Food-importing countries, such as those in the Caribbean and Central America, engaged in either modest import-replacement, as in Cuba, or more ambitious efforts as in Guatemala. Countries which during the 1920s imported beverages and cooking oils, like Argentina, turned to domestic substitutes during the 1930s. Cotton textiles imported during the 1920s were replaced partly by value added in expanding local production of cotton, which later led to exports. In contrast with import-replacement in industry, much of agricultural import-substitution was at the expense of intra-Latin American trade, e.g. Argentine production of *yerba maté* was at the expense of imports from Paraguay.

Agricultural import-substitution naturally had a greater weight in overall growth in the smaller, less-developed countries. Land was an apparently malleable and not fully utilised 'installed capacity' which could be turned from export cash-crops to production for either the local market or subsistence, and could also be expanded using little foreign exchange. The ease of land reallocation and expansion depended partly on tenure arrangements and agronomic characteristics of export crops. Thus, it appears that the presence of foreign-owned banana and sugar plantations in Cuba and Central America reduced, *ceteris paribus*, flexibility in land use, while lands planted with coffee were more receptive to sharing at least their idle capacity with other crops. (An identification problem exists as bananas and sugar were often produced in foreign-owned plantations and coffee by local farmers; see Chapter 11, by Bulmer-Thomas.) As noted earlier, all types of rural production were encouraged by new irrigation works, feeder roads, credit facilities and price support programmes. Publicly-sponsored agricultural research programme also had important payoffs during the 1930s, as in the case of Brazilian cotton.

Import-substitution extended to services; those of foreign labour and capital were to a large extent replaced with local inputs or dispensed with, while it is likely that many Argentines substituted visits to Bariloche and Mar del Plata for vacations in Paris. Among expanding sectors one can also find, especially in reactive countries, some producing non-traded goods and services using relatively few imported inputs, such as construction, housing and government.

The level of imports and exports reflected primarily exogenous shocks and trends, but their structures responded to the differing sectoral performances described above. The shares in total imports of consumer goods and intermediate products like cement and textiles fell, while those for metallurgical and other intermediate products rose. Machinery and equipment imports going to export-related manufacturing and to social overhead facilities which had expanded during the 1920s fell, while those going to import-substituting manufacturing rose. Export bills also underwent changes, partly because of the collapse of traditional exports, but also due to exportable surpluses generated by expanding activities, such as Argentine fruits and Brazilian cotton. Tourism also became an important non-traditional Mexican export during the 1930s. Export diversification extended to regional origin within the country (Rio Grande do Sul in Brazil and Rio Negro in Argentina emerging as exporting areas), and to their geographical destination, with Germany becoming an expanding market for many Latin American exports. New markets and higher exports for one Latin American country often meant a loss in traditional exports for another; thus, Colombia and Central America gained shares in the international coffee market at the expense of Brazil; Venezuelan oil advanced, replacing Mexican crude; bananas from Honduras took the place of Colombian ones; and a large number of countries nibbled at Cuban sugar hegemony.

Welfare Performance

Since colonial times it has been noted that a boom in Latin American land-intensive exports may not improve the welfare of lower-income groups, as during booms prices of locally produced foodstuffs rose sharply, and access to land became more difficult. Where coercive labour systems were applied, booms meant longer and more intense working hours. Busts frequently led to cheaper home-grown foodstuffs, a greater availability of land for subsistence crops, and slacker working regimes. One may conjecture that part of these ancient effects were still visible in the 1930s; for those employed in reasonably competitive labour markets it is likely that real wages in terms of foodstuffs rose, even as they fell in terms of importable goods. Access to rural land in many countries appears to have become easier and cheaper for lower- and middle-income groups, as the opportunity cost for land held by exporters declined and plantations were parcelled. These market trends were carried further in Mexico by a major land reform, while in Colombia and Cuba milder public measures also pointed in the same direction, increasing the tenure security of lower-income farmers.

Primarily coercive labour systems survived into the twentieth century in several Latin American localities where descendants of American Indians were concentrated, such as Bolivia, Peru and Central America, coexisting with freer labour arrangements. During the 1930s in Guatemala roads and public works were built using taxed Indian (and convict) labour, as had been the case during the 1920s under the Leguía dictatorship in Peru. Even in Guatemala, however, labour legislation was liberalised after 1934.

In the more urbanised countries where free labour systems predominated, at least in the cities, open unemployment seems to have been rare after the initial years of the crisis. A lack of strong institutional barriers to downward money wage flexibility and a rapid end to immigration contributed to the elimination of open unemployment; during the early 1930s many European immigrants returned to their old countries, and some recent arrivals to urban centres returned to their rural birthplaces. In Cuba the seasonal importation of Jamaican and other West Indian labour for the sugar harvest was eliminated. Nevertheless, the welfare consequences of the crisis appear worse in Cuba than in some Central American countries which had larger and more flexible subsistence sectors.

On the whole income and wealth distribution during the 1930s were buffeted by contradictory influences. Groups linked to traditional exports must have seen their relative and even absolute position decline, in spite of government actions aimed at ameliorating the external blows. Entrepreneurs in import-substituting agriculture and industry must have accumulated handsome profits, with their output fetching high domestic prices while labour and raw-material costs were unusually low. Entrepreneurs who had inherited excess capacity from the 1920s were especially fortunate, receiving unexpected capital gains. High- and middle-class families, with budgets having low shares for foodstuffs and high shares for imported consumer goods, faced unfavourable relative price trends. Beloved durable goods, such as automobiles, or European vacations, became very expensive, and their consumption often was to be postponed for many years. For lower-income groups, whether urban or rural, it is unlikely that real income gains in terms of foodstuffs could have been very substantial; the best guess is that even in reactive countries performing reasonably well by the late 1930s real wages for unskilled and semi-skilled labour, taking into account all components of their consumption basket, were no higher than a decade earlier. Gains in employment security arising from new labour legislation were limited to pockets in the labour force and of moot significance even for them. The tax reforms carried out in several countries were more important for public revenue raising and diversification than for significant changes in income distribution. Perhaps with the exception of Mexico, the 1930s did not witness a discontinuity in the inherited trends for public services in education and health. Secular improvements in literacy and health indicators appear to have continued without obvious leaps or retardations, seemingly following more the sluggish urbanisation trends than the vagaries of import substitution.

A CONCLUDING INTERPRETATION

Much of the evolution of Latin American economies during the 1930s, particularly the coexistence in reactive countries of vigorously growing branches of agriculture and manufacturing with declining or stagnant foreign trade, can be explained as a response to incentives created by policies aimed primarily at coping with balance-of-payments disequilibria generated by the unexpected worsening of the terms of trade and the abrupt cessation of capital inflows. As it became clear that the new constellation of external and domestic relative prices were not fleeting phenomena, and that the international economy was not to return to the pre-1929 rules of the game, both private and public agents reoriented their production and investment plans.

Admittedly incomplete evidence appears to support the view that countries willing and able to devalue their exchange rate forcefully early in the decade moved toward the new pattern of accumulation more speedily than those nations which kept their exchange rate fixed or devalued slightly. For the latter type of country the required deflationary process involved the marking down of a myriad of non-traded goods prices (and wages) without clear guidance from either markets or governments as to what the correct new level should be. The confusing circumstances of the 1930s, whose macroeconomics are debated even today in industrialised countries, made guessing about the new equilibrium non-traded goods prices singularly difficult. In contrast, devaluing the exchange rate involved a clear signal and a species of 'price guideline', reducing uncertainty for economic agents in reactive countries.

As devaluations typically occurred while exports of goods and services exceeded imports of goods and non-factor services (i.e. excluding immigrant remittances and those of profits and interest abroad) their expansionary effects were strengthened. Note also that purchasing-power parity should not be expected to hold in an economy subjected to real shocks, so it is not surprising that the nominal devaluations of the 1930s, in contrast with those occurring in Latin America since the Second World War, were offset only to a slight degree by movements in domestic price levels. Plentiful idle resources, of course, contributed to this outcome. One may also conjecture that in several reactive countries during the late 1920s an unusually large inflow of foreign capital financing domestic public works had resulted in what during the 1970s became known as *atraso cambiario*, i.e. a low price for dollars and sterling and a high price for non-traded goods and services, which made the real depreciations of the early 1930s the more dramatic. The late 1920s may have also left a legacy of plentiful liquidity in some countries, cushioning the impact of the crisis.

The abandonment of the old parities and of unlimited convertibility into foreign exchange allowed in several countries the maintenance and expansion of domestic liquidity, which combined with other policies led to the reasonably good economic performance in reactive countries. The balance-of-payments crisis and the threat of financial collapse were of greater significance in the adoption of those policies than whether the new governments which came to power during the 1930s represented a shift to the right, as in Argentina, or toward more reformist positions as in Colombia and Mexico. Purely domestic political factors may have accounted for whether or not a country engaged in land reform during the 1930s, but those factors had much less to do in reactive countries with the adoption of policies which induced import substitution. The latter depended on the magnitude of the foreign-exchange and financial crisis, and on country-specific characteristics of the external sector. Thus, revolutionary Mexico was more timid regarding exchange control than conservative Argentina, largely because of its open border with the USA. Policy-makers who abandoned gold convertibility, allowed the exchange rate to depreciate, supported banks at the edge of bankruptcy, permitted budget deficits induced by economic and foreign trade decline, and financed them by monetary expansion, on the whole did so moved by survival instincts rather than inspired by the writings of economists, either defunct or live. But in reactive countries, including Chile and Uruguay, the institutional structure was compatible with actions involving a degree of policy autonomy, while in smaller or passive countries, such as Cuba, it was less so.

While the economic performance of reactive countries was reasonably good, per capita real incomes grew less during the 1930s than during the 1920s or 1940s. Had the industrialised countries maintained full employment, open markets for foreign goods and bonds, and a peaceful international environment, it is likely that the aggregate output performance in reactive countries (and of course in passive ones) would have been better. Sectoral patterns of growth would have been different, and it is likely that under such counterfactual circumstances some activities, like cement and textiles, would have grown less than they actually did during the 1930s. The diversification which took place in agriculture, manufacturing, exports and government revenues, as well as in the geographical sources and destination of exports, could very well have been less under the hypothesised counterfactual conditions. It is also conceivable that institutional reforms in banking, taxation and even land tenure would have been weaker. Under the counterfactual circumstances there might have been less structural change but more growth not just in aggregate output, but also in physical and technical capacity. Output growth during the 1930s wore out much of the capital stock accumulated during the 1920s and earlier and was accompanied by relatively little fresh investment and technical change. At the outbreak of the Second World War, a good share of the Latin American social overhead capital and industrial capacity was already stretched thin and at the verge of obsolescence; war shortages were to aggravate these conditions.

The crisis at the Centre did induce policy experimentation in the Periphery; as in the Centre, not all innovations were attractive. Bold foreign examples were plentiful: the New Deal in the USA; Fascism in Italy, and later in Germany and Spain; and radical Socialism in the Soviet Union. Examples of a successful maintenance of old-fashioned orthodoxy were fewer. The collapse of international financial markets encouraged attempts to mobilise domestic savings and the creation of new domestic financial institutions. The lamentable state of banks in the USA and other industrialised countries during the early 1930s made Latin Americans think twice about the wisdom of capital flight, increasing the potency of domestic monetary and tax policy. Rivalries among industrialised countries, exacerbated by the crisis, plus the Good Neighbour policy of Franklin Delano Roosevelt also encouraged, directly or indirectly, policy initiatives favouring the geographical diversification of foreign trade, greater national control over natural resources, and the rescheduling of external debt obligations. A poor profits outlook at the Centre encouraged some direct foreign investment into Latin America, and helped to concentrate the animal spirits of local entrepreneurs within the domestic market. Schemes for closer Latin American economic integration were proposed from the Southern Cone to Central America, although very little was done to carry them out. In short the disastrous news from the rest of the world reaching Latin America during the 1930s made policy-makers and informed opinion feel not only that local conditions were not so bad, after all, but also that no one knew, in Centre or Periphery, exactly what were the roots of the crisis nor how it could be overcome. After a terrible fright, this stimulated an almost exhilarated creativity. The old authorities and rules on economic policy were shattered. It was a time calling for reliance on one's discretion.

REFERENCES

C. F. Diaz Alejandro, 'A America Latina em Depressao 1929/39', *Pesquisa e Planejamento Económico 10* (1980) 351–82.

──── 'Stories of the 1930s for the 1980s', *NBER Conference Paper* no. 130 (November 1981).

J. Fodor and A. O'Connell, 'La Argentina y la economía atlántica en la primera mitad del siglo *XX*', *Desarrollo Económico*, vol. 13, no. 49 (April–June 1973) 3–66.

Naciones Unidas, *América Latína: Relación de Precios del Intercambio* (Santiago, 1976).

3 From an Export-led to an Import-substituting Economy: Chile 1914–39

GABRIEL PALMA[*]

It is commonly argued that the process of industrialisation began in Chile only in the 1930s. Attention is drawn to a 'frustrated' attempt at industrialisation between 1830 and 1960 due to its 'incompatibility' with export-led growth, and hence it is held that local manufacturing industry could only flourish after the collapse of the export sector.[1] Chile thus fits neatly into the conventional model which at its simplest divides post-colonial economic development in Latin America into two major phases, 'outward-oriented' growth up to 1930 and 'inward-oriented' growth thereafter.[2] This assumes that in the first phase the export sector acts as the engine of growth, but generates little *diversification* throughout the rest of the economy, and in particular into manufacturing, while in the second phase a process of import-substitution is launched, and the State takes an active role in promoting local economic development.

Given this conventional view that export-led growth acts as a brake upon local manufacturing activities, the crisis of the 1930s plays an important part in the explanations of the origins of industrialisation.

* Earlier versions of this chapter were written for two conferences organised by Rosemary Thorp on the effect of the 1929 Depression on the Latin American economies (Oxford 1981 and Manchester 1982). I would like to thank the participants of both conferences for their comments and contributions to the chapter, in particular Marcelo Abreu, Paul Cammack, Carlos Diaz Alejandro, Charles Kindleberger, Brooke Larson, Oscar Muñoz, José Antonio Ocampo and Rosemary Thorp. I am also grateful to Luis Ortega, John Sender, Ignes Sodre and Elizabeth Spillius for their contributions to the finished chapter. A grant from the Social Science Research Council (New York) made this research possible. Responsibility for the judgements expressed is mine alone.

The collapse of the export sector is seen as leading to a restructuring of the articulation of Latin American economies with those of the Centre achieved through an inward-oriented pattern of development that gave priority to local manufacturing activities.

I have argued elsewhere that the first part of this model misinterprets the nature of local manufacturing development before 1930, and does scant justice to its extent. Even those studies which describe the development of manufacturing before 1930 trace its origins back only to the closing years of the nineteenth century; I suggest, however, that because of the nature of export activities, the economic policies pursued and the structural characteristics of the international economy in the period, export-led growth in fact *stimulated* the diversification of the local economy. The origins of the resulting process of industrialisation[3] can be clearly located in the late 1860s and the early 1870s.[4]

I shall argue in this chapter that, for the Chilean case at least, the impact of the Depression of the 1930s upon the local economy has been exaggerated not only because a process of industrialisation had already been under way for fifty years, but also because the import-substituting phase of Chilean industrialisation had commenced with the First World War. The early transition was mainly a consequence of the acute instability of the nitrate market after the First World War. Thus, I shall conclude that the crisis of the 1930s does not represent so much a break with the immediate past, as far as the Chilean economy is concerned, *as an acceleration of a process of transition from export-led growth to import-substituting industrialisation which was already under way*.

The chapter is divided into three sections. The first gives an account of the Chilean economy on the eve of the First World War. The second discusses the period from 1914 to 1929, and the third, dealing with the first half of the 1930s, discusses the changes taking place in the economy as a result of the Depression and reveals the continuities with the previous period.

THE CHILEAN ECONOMY IN 1914

On the eve of the First World War Chile was among the most highly developed nations of Latin America. In terms of US dollars of 1980 (hereafter US*) income per capita was approaching US* 1 000, and exports per capita stood at US* 330 (a figure not repeated again until

1981, with the exception of 1929), with returned value at approximately US* 250. Some 40% of public expenditure was devoted to education and investment in physical capital, 40% of the population was resident in towns of over 2000 inhabitants, and 16% of the economically active population was engaged in some kind of manufacturing activity. Those employed in establishments with five or more workers provided practically half of the total supply of manufactures, with a volume of production 1.7 times that corresponding to a 'Chenery-normal' level. Many new manufacturing firms had been founded in the years preceding the outbreak of the War. Among those were the Compañía Industrial (1901), the Compañía Cervecerías Unidas (1902), the Sociedad Industrial de los Andes (1903), the Sociedad Nacional Fábrica de Vidrios (1904), Cemento Melón (1905, the successor to the Fábrica Nacional de Cemento de la Cruz founded two years earlier, destined to become the largest producer of Portland cement in Latin America and the fifth largest cement works in the world), a subsidiary of Établissements Américaines Grety (1906), the Compañía de Molinos y Fideos Carozzi (1906), a Santiago-based subsidiary of Siemens-Schuckeet Ltd (1907), with branches opened subsequently in Valparaiso, Concepción and Antofagasta, and the Compañía Industrial El Volcán (1908).[5]

This process of economic development was, of course, very different from that of advanced capitalist countries, and manifested itself in diverse ways in the different branches of the Chilean economy; it generated inequalities at regional levels and in the distribution of income, it was accompanied by such phenomena as underemployment and unemployment, it took on a cyclical nature, and benefited the elite almost exclusively. In other words, the development of capitalism in Chile in this period, as everywhere else and at all times, was also characterised by its contradictory and exploitative nature. Nevertheless, for the authors mentioned above,[6] it seems that capitalism in Chile in this period was characterised by these negative sides (to the analysis of which they have made significant contributions) for they have failed to see both the process of capitalist accumulation under way and the modifications in the different structures of Chilean society that this process of accumulation induced as it evolved (such as modifications in the composition of productive forces, in resource allocation, in class relations and in the character and nature of the State). Thus, they have been unable to detect the specificity of the historical progressiveness of capitalism in Chile in this period.

One of the many examples of these transformations in Chilean society in this period is the early development of the trade union movement in the country. Under socialist, anarchist and christian influence the Gran Federación Obrera Chilena (FOCH) led by Luis Emilio Recabarren 'transformed itself from a mutual aid society into a revolutionary sindical organisation' (Angell, 1972, p. 23). It provided one of the bases for the Partido Obrero Socialista, founded in 1912 and affiliated to the Third International in 1920.

From 1830 onwards Chile had developed as an export economy, with the 'engine' of growth provided by the exports of copper, silver, wheat and flour before the War of the Pacific (1879), and nitrates thereafter. By the First World War nitrate exports represented 80% of total exports (and hence US* 263 per capita), and provided half of ordinary public revenues through taxation.[7] By this time though the absolute supremacy of nitrates within the export sector was coming under challenge with the initiation of large-scale copper mining. Chile had been the leading world producer of copper in the 1850s and 1860s despite its distance from major markets and its low degree of technological development, but these factors had led to its gradual marginalisation in the world market; nevertheless the opening of El Teniente in 1912 and Chuquicamata in 1915 (respectively the largest underground and open-cast mines in the world) signalled the reversal of this trend. On the eve of the European hostilities, then, Chilean foreign trade had reached very respectable levels, and the recent process of diversification augured well for the future.

CHILE 1914–29: AN ECONOMY IN TRANSITION?

During the First World War (with the exception of the first few months) Chilean export trade continued relatively unaffected, while imports were substantially reduced. The result was hitherto unknown surpluses in the balance of trade. Demand for nitrates, of which Chile was the only producer, was increased due to its role in the production of explosives. This more than made up for decreased demand from the fertiliser industry, and led to record exports in 1916 of three million tons.[8] Imports meanwhile fell by more than half in both value and quantum terms, with inputs into manufacturing, particularly capital goods, most seriously affected; imports of metal products, machinery and transport equipment fell to less than a quarter of pre-war levels.[9] While export activity permitted aggregate internal demand to remain relatively stable, the sharp reduction in imports channelled this demand toward the internal market. Local manufacturing activity showed an impressive ability to respond: the data provided by Muñoz suggest that during the four years manufacturing production rose by 53%. Even allowing for an underestimation of the value of production in the base year of 1914, this represents a substantial achievement.[10]

The Compañía de Azucar de Viña del Mar, for example, increased production substantially and began exports to Argentina; the Compañía Industrial increased production of industrial oils by 70% between 1915 and 1917; the Compañía de Tejidos and the Fábrica Nacional de Envases experienced substantial increases in sales, and the latter carried out a significant programme of expansion; and the Fundación Las Rosas produced a selection of machinery, particularly converters, for copper mining. These had previously been imported. Other foundries produced cement mixers and machinery for tanneries, again replacing former imports.[11] Employment statistics confirm the expansion in manufacturing output.[12].

Much of the capacity shown to respond to increased demand is explained by the presence of firms founded in the years preceding the outbreak of the War.[13] Other establishments were created during the War, such as the paper factory Ebbinghaus, Haemsel & Co. (1914), subsequently converted into the largest manufacturing establishment in the country, the Compañía Manufacturera de Papeles y Cartones, and the Compañía Electro-Metalúrgica ELECMETAL (1917), a producer of steel and various types of metal products, machinery and transport equipment. Statistics on corporate investment in the first decade of the century reinforce the argument.[14]

Nevertheless, the bonanza enjoyed by exporting and manufacturing interests during the War came to an abrupt end. In the wake of the Armistice demand for nitrates in the explosives industry fell sharply, while depressed demand for fertilisers showed no sign of immediate recovery. Indeed, increased supplies of ammonium sulphate and the rapid development of the synthetic nitrates industry spelt the irreversible decline of the Chilean nitrate sector. The immediate impact was disastrous. Nitrate exports in 1919 fell to a quarter of 1918 levels in volume, and a fifth in real value. For their part, terms of trade fell by 38% between 1917 and 1919. As exports represented some 30% of GNP, this deterioration meant a loss of real income of around 11% (assuming no changes in physical product).

TABLE 3.1   *Instability of export value, quantum and prices: alternative methodologies, 1883–1929*

	Value			Quantum			Prices		
	P.V.[a] nominal	P.V. real	Net P.V. real	Gross P.V.	Net P.V.	S.D.[b] $\bar{Q}$	P.V. nominal	P.V. real	S.D. $\bar{P}$
1883–1913	8.0	8.2	6.9	9.4	8.6	11.4	5.9	7.5	17.7
1914–1918	27.3	14.0	14.2	14.0	12.8	12.9	14.2	12.1	19.3
1919–1929	37.5	28.5	26.5	29.8	27.7	20.3	12.3	11.0	19.3
(1919–1924)							(19.8)	(12.2)	

[a] *P.V.* = average absolute percentage annual variation.
[b] *S.D./$\bar{X}$* = standard deviation of the residuals from an exponential trend, corrected by the average of the variable.

SOURCE: For statistics see Palma (1979, appendices 20, 21, 31, and 32). For the methodology see note 16.

Despite some recovery in the nitrate industry and the terms of trade in the 1920s, both were marked by severe instability. While the index of export prices fell rapidly and continuously throughout the 1920s, declining by 43% overall, the terms of trade index behaved erratically, reflecting violent fluctuations in import prices.[15] The increasing degree of instability of exports can be seen from different points of view in Table 3.1.[16]

As the table reveals, in whatever way one measures instability the decade between 1919 and 1929 shows a much higher degree of revenue, price and quantum instability than the three decades between the end of the War of the Pacific and the outbreak of the First World War (1883–1913). In the case of export revenues, for example, the average percentage annual variation during the 1920s is 4.6 times higher than that of 1883–1913. Even more remarkable, *instability in the 1920s was greater than that of the First World War years*. The only exception seems to be in export prices; but if one compares the four years of the War with the following five (1919–24) there is also an increase in the average percentage annual variation of export prices (from 14.2% to 19.8%).

Thus the foreign trade sector, for so long the principal motor of local economic development, became a major source of general economic instability, with its principal product losing its position to natural and synthetic substitutes, the export price index falling and the import and export trade subject to rapid fluctuations.

The response to these difficulties in the foreign trade sector was a relatively systematic attempt to pursue a different growth model, with the accent on production for the internal market. A more detailed analysis of the demand and supply factors behind this transition allows us a better understanding of the dynamic of change.

On the demand side the essential characteristic of the period was the implementation of a number of economic policies *intended to increase the proportion of aggregate demand oriented to the internal market*. First, between 1914 and 1929 there were several revisions of import tariffs. The first general revision took place in 1916, and provoked from the *Report on Trade* issued by the US Federal Trade Commission the complaint that the tariff on imported manufactures had risen by between 50% and 86%, and that 'in various cases the increase was even greater' (1916, pp. 52–3). The *Report* calculated that taking into account the tariff and other customs dues American preserved foods were paying a tariff of 250%.[17] The Sociedad Nacional de Agricultura achieved even more 'effective' protection for its products by blocking the completion of the Chilean section of the Salta to Antofagasta railway, and thus denying access to the nitrate zone for Argentine production. The tariff structure was revised again several times in the 1920s. The 1928 revision introduced significant increases on a number of manufactured goods and gave the President the right to increase the tariff on any product to a maximum of 35%. Within two years Ibañez had used this provision to raise the tariff on the products contained in 440 customs classifications.[18] With protectionism increasing in the countries of the Centre, the few remaining local critics of the policy were losing the argument.

The second relevant economic policy was that of currency devaluation: between 1913 and 1929 the peso fell by 60% in real terms.[19]

Finally, for the first time in over half a century there were years in which the internal rate of inflation fell below the international rate, and this also helped to direct aggregate internal demand towards the local market. In conjunction with currency devaluation, falling terms of trade and the import tariff, this contributed to relative increases in the prices of importables in relation to non-traded goods, and provided further stimulus to transfers of resources into import substitution.

These developments helped to alter the structure of relative prices and orient aggregate demand towards the internal market, thus stimulating local production. But in addition to the more radical use of this range of policy instruments this period was also characterised by an expansion in state intervention in economic activity. The internal structure of the State was modified, with the creation of a number of public bodies charged with promoting a range of productive activities, and the attribution to the State itself of a direct role in production.

Among the agencies which gave the State a greater degree of control over economic activity in general were the Banco Central (1925), the Servicio de Minas del Estado (1925), the Caja de Crédito Agrícola (1926), the Caja de Crédito Minero (1927), the Caja de Crédito Carbonífero (1928) and the Instituto de Crédito Industrial (1928). To these should be added the Instituto de Fomento Minero e Industrial de Tarapaca, and of Antofagasta, and the Caja de Colonización Agrícola. These institutions provided finance and in some cases became responsible for commercialisation. For example, the Caja de Crédito Minero marketed the production of small and medium copper producers, and engaged in prospecting, infrastructural work, technical assistance and the provision of machinery.

In the area of direct production the State already possessed two manufacturing establishments, the Imprenta Nacional and the Fábrica y Maestranzas del Ejercito (FAMAE), both producing exclusively to fulfil the needs of the State itself.[20] In this period, though, it began to produce inputs for private industry, steel being the most important. Despite the presence of private steel producers, established in Chile for over a decade at this time, the State took a majority share in the Compañía Electro-Siderúrgica e Industrial of Corral (1926) in order to accelerate production in this area.

From the point of view of the supply factors behind this transitional

TABLE 3.2 *Index of manufacturing and export
production, 1914–35*
(real values, 1914 = 100)

	Manufacturing production	Exports
1914	100.0	100.0
1918	153.0	111.0
1919	153.4	39.6
1922	158.6	68.3
1925	189.1	126.1
1928/9	181.0	167.1
1932	145.5	30.6
1935	208.3	48.7

SOURCE: Palma (1979) appendices 31 and 47.

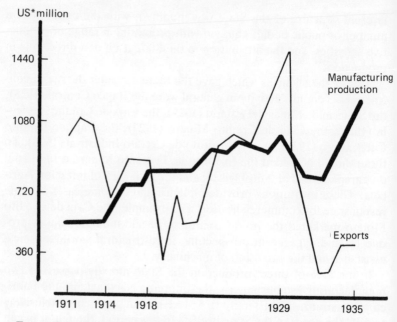

FIGURE 3.1   *Real value of manufacturing and export production, 1911–35*

SOURCE: Palma (1979) appendices 31 and 47.

process, one of the most significant characteristics of the period was the markedly different performances of the export and manufacturing sectors.

As Table 3.2 reveals, manufacturing production grew 4.2 times more rapidly than exports during the war years, and the subsequent disparity between the two sectors was even greater. The contrast, then, dates from the war period and the years immediately following it, rather than from the 1930s, as has commonly been supposed. In fact the performance of the two activities could scarcely have been more in contrast. This can be seen clearly when comparing the real value of production of both activities, as in Figure 3.1.

It is difficult to reconcile this picture with the notion of an 'export economy', in which the export sector acts as the engine of growth, and other activities move in relative harmony with it. Further evidence regarding this increasing degree of independence of manufacturing industry from the export cycle can be found by testing the log-linear relationship between real manufacturing production (MP)

and real export revenues (X) between 1914 and 1929. The numbers in brackets under the estimated coefficient are their t-ratios:

$$Ln\ (MP) = 9.463 + 0.035\ Ln\ (X) \quad R^2 = 0.0254 \quad \bar{R}^2 = -0.044$$
$$\qquad\qquad (14.9) \qquad (0.604) \qquad RHO = 0.959 \quad DW = \quad 1.28$$

The value of R^2 indicates how badly the regression line fits the observations. In fact only 2.5% of the variation of manufacturing production during these years can be attributed to the variations of the fitted values of exports. Furthermore, if the value of R^2 is adjusted for the degrees of freedom (the corrected coefficient of determination) it ends up negative! At the same time the coefficient on *ln* (X), as shown by its t-ratio, is not significantly different from zero (even at the 25% level). Therefore it is clear that, from the First World War onwards, manufacturing activities do not follow the export cycle any longer. Evidence such as this, that in the Chilean case *it was the First World War which marked the beginning of the break with the 'export economy', and the start of the process of import-substitution*, corrects the view advanced previously by the most important accounts of the period, those of Muñoz and Kirsch, that manufacturing activities still followed the export cycle during these years.[21]

Further information regarding the transition taking place can be derived from a detailed analysis of the structure of manufacturing production between 1914 and 1929. The most significant trend is the decline in the high share accounted for by current consumption goods (food manufactures, beverages, tobacco, footwear and clothing), and the rise in the low share represented by durable consumer goods, and intermediate and capital goods (textile manufacture, paper and printing, chemical products, metal products, machinery and transport equipment).

As Table 3.3 shows, during the First World War rates of growth in each group of activities were similar, but thereafter the second group experiences much more rapid growth. Between 1918 and 1929 production of current consumption goods grew at an average of only 0.6% per annum, while that of the second group grew at 6% per annum. Its relative share rose in consequence from 18.3% to 28.5% and the process continued after 1929.

The rapid growth in production of consumer durables and intermediate and capital inputs relative to current consumption goods can be seen in Figure 3.2, which compares the production indices of both activities.

TABLE 3.3 Production indices and relative shares in manufacturing production for current consumption goods, and durable consumer goods, intermediate and capital goods: 1914–35
(real values, 1918 = 100)

	Current consumption goods		Durable consumer, intermediate and capital goods		Total manufacturing production
	Index	Relative share %	Index	Relative share %	
1914	67.1	(82.6)	63.0	(17.4)	65.4
1918	100.0	(81.7)	100.0	(18.3)	100.0
1925	115.5	(76.3)	165.9	(23.7)	123.6
1929	107.0	(71.5)	190.5	(28.5)	122.2
1933	89.7	(68.8)	181.1	(31.2)	106.9
1935	104.4	(62.6)	278.0	(37.4)	136.1

SOURCE: Palma (1979, appendices 47, 59 and 60).

The changing pattern described above was also reflected in the relative shares of domestic production by sector in total internal supply. On the eve of the War, manufacturing establishments employing five or more workers were providing practically half of total supply, but the picture in each of the two sectors examined was radically different: the local production of current consumption goods accounted for 80% of internal supply, while that of the second type of goods did not account for even 20%.[22]

The picture changed as a result of the War. As we have seen, the level of imports fell, while aggregate internal demand was kept up by export activities. Given the very different share accounted for by imports in the supply of the two groups examined, the falling level of imports affected them differently. In the case of current consumption goods it was possible for domestic production to make up the difference and in fact even increase total supply, while in the second group total supply declined by 15% over four years, despite a 59% increase in domestic production over the same period. At the end of the War, therefore, there were shortages of manufactures in the areas of durable consumer goods and manufactured inputs only, and it was in these sectors where import tariffs rose most substantially. Thus the strong stimulus to local production continued after the war for these products, while it did not where current consumption goods were

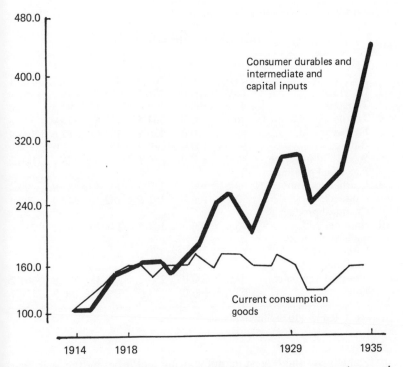

FIGURE 3.2 *Indices of real production values for current consumption goods and consumer durables, intermediate and capital inputs, 1914–35*

SOURCE: Palma (1979) appendices 59 and 60.

concerned. This is reflected in the comparative production indices, as we have seen.

As a result of these changes the share of local manufacturing production in total supply rose from 51% to 66% between 1914 and 1925; the increase for current consumption goods was from 80% to 85%, and that for the second group of goods from 17% to 35%.[23]

Changes in the structure of production and the local market for manufactured goods can best be appreciated from the data in Table 3.4, which gives production indices for the different activities into which I have divided current consumption goods and durable consumer, intermediate and capital goods.

The two activities which best illustrate the transition to which I have referred are those of food-processing on the one hand, and metal products, machinery and transport equipment on the other. The

TABLE 3.4   *Production indices for the different manufacturing activities,*
1914–35
(real values, 1918 = 100)

	1914	1918	1925	1929	1933	1935
1. Food manufactures	71.1	100.0	103.9	110.4	91.7	106.1
2. Beverages	68.5	100.0	135.0	94.8	78.7	91.0
3. Tobacco	46.0	100.0	159.3	125.1	92.3	106.8
4. Textile manufactures	76.2	100.0	164.5	157.5	223.9	363.8
5. Footwear and	49.1	100.0	116.9	104.9	87.6	104.4
clothing	90.3	100.0	140.0	107.8	98.5	124.0
6. Wood and furniture	62.2	100.0	96.1	171.6	148.7	246.2
7. Paper and printing						
8. Leather and rubber	63.5	100.0	122.3	103.4	85.9	99.4
products	73.1	100.0	151.6	192.7	144.9	200.4
9. Chemical products						
10. Non-metallic	46.4	100.0	104.5	148.2	131.1	217.0
mineral products						
11. Metal products						
machinery and						
transport equipment	57.8	100.0	250.2	289.5	217.8	301.2
Total	65.4	100.0	123.6	122.8	106.9	136.1

SOURCE: Palma (1979) appendix 46.

first, which was the largest manufacturing sector before the War, was relatively stagnant after it; the second grew rapidly both during and after the War, increasing by 73% overall in the war years, and at a rate of 11.2% per annum thereafter. Its share in total Chilean manufacturing doubled, and its share in total internal supply of these products tripled.[24]

The rapid growth in production of consumer durables and intermediate and capital inputs, and in particular of metal products, machinery and transport equipment, reflected a clear trend toward a structure of production with a higher degree of diversification and autonomy; as a consequence, some of the potential advantages of a greater degree of specialisation were lost, but in any case the international economy did not display in the period the minimum level of stability required if such potential advantages were to be realised.

Very preliminary estimates of the share of manufactures from establishments with five or more workers in GDP place it at 9.6% in 1914, 10.8% in 1918 and 13% in 1925.

Along with the changes taking place in the model of growth in these years went a number of social and political developments. While economic policies were designed seeking to accelerate the

growth and diversification of manufacturing production and to increase the degree of local economic autonomy, a very progressive
social legislation was introduced, the Constitution was modified, and
the socio-political composition of Congress changed radically. This
reflected the emergence of new groups and social forces and the de-
stabilisation of the oligarchic political regime which had dominated
national politics in the first hundred years of independence. Given
these changes on the economic, social and political fronts, the country which had to face up to the crisis of the 1930s was in some ways
strikingly different from that which had existed before the First
World War.[25]

Before the War the 'export economy' was relatively successful, as
was its capacity to promote diversification of the local economy.
Thereafter, with the crisis of the export sector, a process of transformation began. With the loss of compression in the 'engine' of
growth, as a result of export instability, there was a turn to manufacturing industry as a new source of stimuli for local development. The
transition was marked by difficulties, ambivalence, political conflict,
indecision and improvisation, but its central characteristic was the
shift from the *export economy to a process of import-substitution*.

The process of import-substitution has been examined in the literature from two perspectives. The first, related to the supply of manufactured products, concerns the increase in the proportion of total
supply of manufactures met by net local production (Chenery, 1960).
A variant of this approach, mainly focused on short-term changes,
restricts attention to the local production of previously imported
goods (Sutcliffe). A second approach observes the process from the
point of view of demand and distinguishes between a 'natural' process
of industrialisation and one that is 'forced' or based upon import-
substitution (Clark, 1975). The first relates to the increase in manufacturing production which would normally accompany an increase in
per capita income in a country. The second, in contrast, stems from
an attempt to raise the rate of growth of manufacturing activities
above this 'natural' level by introducing economic policies designed
specifically for that purpose. In other words, from this point of view,
the difference is between a process of industrialisation resulting from
normal economic growth and a deliberate policy designed to accelerate industrial growth by the forced transformation of the productive
capacity of a country.

On any analysis Chile was in transition between 1914 and 1929
from an export economy to one based on import-substitution. The
net contribution of local production to the internal supply of manu-

factures was increasing; industrial growth was based upon the local production of previously imported goods, intermediate and capital inputs in particular; and economic policies were devised and applied in order to orient aggregate demand toward the internal market, and hence to accelerate the growth of manufacturing production in the country and the degree of internal economic autonomy. The efficiency of the set of policies applied may be questioned, but not its direction.

In the light of this discussion I must record my dissent from the views of the authors like Sergio de Castro and Sergio de la Cuadra, who choose this period, of all periods of Chilean economic history, to support their pro-free-trade hypotheses. According to these economic historians, during the years immediately prior to 1929 the economy experienced one of the highest rate of growth on record 'in an environment of free-trade which made it possible to take advantage of the opportunities created by the international market while demanding at the same time, efficiency in the domestic allocation of resources' (1971: 1). First, these authors, although referring to the Ballesteros and Davis estimates, choose to ignore their warning that the 1928 and 1929 figures probably are misleading because of high copper prices and the large transitory inflow of foreign capital. Therefore, they emphasise the 2.7% growth rate for 1908–29 instead of the 1.5% growth rate for 1908–27. Second, whatever the benefits of trade liberalisation are and whatever the correct growth rate is for the Chilean economy, the years between the First World War and 1929 are certainly the worst possible ones to use as an example of free-trade and 'positive' opportunities created by the international market.

CHILE 1929–35: A BREAK WITH THE PAST?

A major difference between the First World War and the crisis of the 1930s, as far as the Chilean economy is concerned, was that the former had a negative impact mainly on the import trade, whereas the latter saw the collapse of both exports and imports. In real terms exports in 1932 stood at *one-sixth* of their level in 1929; in quantum terms they stood at less than one-quarter, while the export price index was down by one-half, and continued to fall in 1933, reaching one-third of what it had been in 1929, and one-fifth of its level in 1920.

This fall in the level of exports, added to the unavailability of foreign credits and the limited stocks of gold reserves, forced imports to follow the same downward path. By 1932 these too stood in real terms at only one-sixth of their 1929 levels, and fell even further in 1933. In quantum terms they also fell to one-sixth of their 1929 level in 1932. The import price index however fell far more slowly, standing at three-quarters of its 1929 level in 1932, and continuing a gradual decline thereafter, but far less severe than that experienced by export prices. The terms of trade therefore moved against Chile, declining by 36% between 1929 and 1932. By the same token, of course, they were moving in favour of the countries of the Centre: for Britain, for example, the terms of trade reached their highest point in the whole 95-year cycle covered by Feinstein.[26]

According to calculations made by the League of Nations, *Chile's economy was worse hit than any other in the world by the crisis.* A study covering countries accounting for 90% of world trade showed Chile suffering the largest percentage decline in value of imports and exports alike; while in quantum world trade showed a decline from 100 in 1929 to 74.5 in 1932, Chile registered an export decline from 100 in 1929 to 24 in 1932, with a low of 13 in November of that year, and an import decline from 100 to 18, with a low of 10 in May 1932.[27]

As if the balance of trade was not bad enough, the unavailability of international loans made the balance of payments worse. Chile had gone heavily into debt in the late 1920s, in particular under the Ibañez government, in order to balance its international account and service its early borrowing, but also to finance a large programme of public investment. In the USA alone Chile sold bonds to the value of US* 1.76 billion during the 1920s. Foreign loans received amounted to US* 338 million in 1929 and US* 563 million in 1930, falling to US* 53 million 1931, and US* 23 million in 1932 before disappearing altogether in 1933.[28]

Nevertheless, the fact that Chile was at least able to borrow until 1930 made her an exception in Latin America. The rest of the subcontinent was hit hard – as Professor Kindleberger explains (see Chapter 12) – by the abrupt halt in US foreign lending in June 1928, when the New York stock market started its meteoric rise and interest rates tightened on the call money market. For this reason a number of Latin American countries date the start of the Depression from the second half of 1928, while in Chile it could be delayed until 1930.

In the circumstances the shrinking export revenues went increasingly to service the foreign debt. This commitment absorbed US* 326 million in 1929 and US* 394 million in 1930, while the decline of the peso made the burden even heavier in terms of domestic currency. With Chile on the gold standard, the growing balance-of-payments deficit had to be covered by drawing on the gold reserves of the central bank. As gold reserves declined the balance-of-payments situation became unbearable. On 17 March 1931 import tariffs on a broad range of goods were raised by 20 to 35 per cent, but despite this it proved necessary, on 15 June 1931, to declare a moratorium on the foreign debt and to impose exchange controls. This was a bid to halt the flow of gold from the central bank, slow the rapid decline of the peso, and ensure that essential imports would still be obtained. By this time, though, the crisis had begun to affect the political system, forcing Ibáñez to resign on 26 July 1931 and thus inaugurating an eighteen-month period of greater instability than the Republic had known before, marked as it was at its peak by the rise and fall of the short-lived 'Socialist Republic' of 100 days.

With the default on the foreign debt and the introduction of exchange controls in June 1931, the deflationary process produced by adherence to the gold standard in conditions of crisis in the foreign trade came to a halt. Nominal money supply (M_1) had fallen by 38% between September 1929 and June 1931, while over a similar period (July 1929 to November 1931) the cost-of-living index had fallen by 11% and the wholesale price index by 30%.[29]

In the meantime the dramatic decline in revenues from export taxes had produced a substantial budget deficit. Taxes on exports produced 48% of 'ordinary' public revenues before the First World War, and 28% in 1925; by 1930 they contributed only 13%, and by 1935 a mere 0.1%.[30] Despite the drastic economies, it was impossible to balance the budget in these circumstances. The deficit in 1931 stood at 31% of total expenditure, rising to 37% in 1932. The collapse of exports also affected production for the internal market.

If we first consider the most difficult years, 1929–32, it is clear that agriculture was least affected by the crisis, undoubtedly because of its reduced need for imported inputs and machinery. It is also agriculture, however, which shows the lowest growth rate throughout the rest of the decade. The experience of the mining sector was radically different. Average annual production fell to one-quarter of 1929 levels in 1932, reaching its lowest point in December of that year.[31] Of the 91 000 workers employed in the sector in 1929 less than one-third remained in work two years later. Mining thus accounts for fully half of the unemployment created in the period.[32] Construction too suffered heavily. Activity by 1932 was only one-third of what it had been in 1929, and in August 1932 the number of contracts signed touched a low point of 6% of the monthly average for 1929.[33] In contrast manufacturing industry was less directly affected, *reflecting the greater independence from the export cycle which resulted from the structural transformations of the 1920s, and the degree of diversification that had been achieved.*

TABLE 3.5 *GDP and production by activity, 1929–40*
(real value, 1929 = 100)

	Agriculture	Mining	Manufacturing	Construction	GDP
1929	100.0	100.0	100.0	100.0	100.0
1930	103.1	71.1	94.8	77.6	85.4
1931	83.0	48.3	76.8	34.6	64.3
1932	84.5	26.3	77.5	43.9	63.6
1933	104.8	32.8	87.1	58.0	75.3
1934	111.5	53.4	98.5	103.4	85.7
1935	97.5	61.1	111.0	110.7	87.3
1936	102.4	62.4	117.3	95.6	90.6
1937	94.0	85.8	123.5	114.6	97.5
1938	100.6	76.7	128.0	104.9	101.7
1939	109.3	75.0	130.4	133.7	98.8
1940	104.6	81.1	150.9	152.2	103.1

SOURCES: ECLA (1950) and Palma (1979).

The decline in annual levels of manufacturing production was relatively slight, and by 1934 the fall had practically been made up. Furthermore, monthly production figures suggest that production continued to rise until August 1930 (to a level 11% above the average for 1929), then fell for only twelve months. The lowest point (August 1931) was 25% below the average for 1929, and the ground lost was recovered in only seven months.[34]

GDP fell by over one-third between 1929 and 1932, largely due to the importance of mining, whose contribution to GDP in 1929 fell only 8% short of those of agriculture, manufacturing industry and construction combined.

Turning now to the years of recovery from 1932 onward, we note that from the point of view of demand factors connected to it, the monetary policies pursued after the fall of Ibañez were scarcely orthodox, particularly between June and September 1932, when the 'Socialist Republic' was in power. In fact M_1 doubled in less than two years, between August 1931 and April 1933.[35] This was not simply the result of government borrowing from the central bank in order to fund budget deficits. It was in part a consequence of a decree law issued by the 'Socialist Republic' instructing the central bank to print money in order to make loans to a number of Development Boards (Instituciones de Fomento) *with the explicit purpose of stimulating production*. The presence of positive actions of this kind, in addition to inevitable deficit spending aimed at partially compensating for falling public revenues, seems to suggest a 'pre-Keynesian' orientation to public spending in the period.

This is not to imply that those charged with shaping economic policy had a clear and coherent global alternative to the orthodox economic model. It implies that being faced with a crisis of great magnitude and having lost faith in conventional economic theory they sought alternative ways of alleviating the chaos into which the economy had fallen. A deliberately expansionist monetary and fiscal policy was, in any case, no more heretical than the new import tariffs, the default on the foreign debt, the abandonment of the gold standard or the introduction of exchange controls, all of which had gone before. All these policies pointed away from conventional remedies. In any case, flexibility over such matters was a time-honoured custom. As a famous treasury Minister had remarked in the middle of the nineteenth century, 'time and other circumstances modify principle' (*Memoria*, Ministerio de Hacienda, 1849, p. 321).

Law 4321 of 1928 had raised tariffs, and given the President of the Republic the power to introduce further increases. The result of the use made of this provision by Ibañez was that between 1928 and 1930 the tariff rose on average by 71%, affecting 73% of imports. Ibañez introuduced further increases early in 1931, and in 1932 the short-lived government of Juan Esteban Montero imposed a further 10% tariff on 'luxury goods'. In March 1933, virtually on taking power, Alessandri increased tariffs across the board by 50%, and a year later that increase was replaced by a surcharge on the tariff, based upon its value in gold, of 100%. In January 1935 this was increased to 300%.[36]

This increase in the tariff, in conjunction with exchange controls and import licences and quotas, greatly stimulated domestic production and accelerated the tendency toward diversification noted in the previous decade and a half.

The effect on the structure of relative prices was reinforced by the behaviour of the exchange rate. Between 1930 and 1935 the peso lost two-thirds of its real purchasing power; without the measures taken to save foreign exchange and reduce imports it would undoubtedly have lost more. Between 1914 and 1935, then, the peso had seen an 80% decline in its purchasing power. In addition, rises in the internal price index had not kept pace with the rate of devaluation. The net effect was a devaluation of 44% in real terms in the period. This clearly favoured domestic production of importables and exportables.

Thus, after 1931 the combined effect of monetary and fiscal policy, import tariffs, exchange controls and devaluation of the peso was to orient a very high proportion of existing and newly created demand to the internal market. The stimulus to domestic production that this represented was effective, as we shall see.[37]

Economic recovery was also encouraged by a number of acts of legislation. Law 5314 of 1933 exempted all private construction started after August 1933 and finished by the end of 1935 from all taxes except that relating to paving and sewage. It was subsequently modified to include all buildings on which the basic structural work had been completed by the end of 1935, thus extending its effective life. Within a year it had led to an increase of 77% in finished construction (measured in square metres).[38]

Finally, economic recovery owed much to the reactivation of the international market and the increased demand in volume terms for Chile's exports. Exports rose in value terms by 59% and in quantum terms by 156% between 1932 and 1935. The monthly index (1927–9 = 100) rose from 13 in November 1932 to 68 by the end of 1933; nitrate production went from 694 000 metric tons in 1932 to 1 200 000 in 1935, while production of refined and blister copper rose by 270% over the same period. Increases in volume exported thus offset to some extent the continued decline in international prices.[39]

From the point of view of the supply side of the recovery, with the exception of agriculture, local production showed an impressive ability to respond to stimuli on the demand side. As Table 3.5 shows, agricultural production returned to 1929 levels by 1933 (in real value) after a shallow decline, but stagnated thereafter. Mining, however, including gold, silver, copper, nitrates, iron, coal, iodine and sulphur, reached a low point in December 1932, with production standing at one-fifth of 1929 levels, and recovered slowly to two-thirds of those levels by 1935. At this stage it remained the most adversely affected sector, with its share in GDP reduced to 18%, in comparison with 23% in 1929. Given its weight in total GDP, it bore most of the responsibility for the decline in the wider measure of 12.7% over the same period. The aggregation of all mining activity concealed wide variation, however. Nitrate exports in 1935 were at 42% in volume terms of those in 1929, while those of copper had recovered to 86%. The same trend was to continue thereafter.

The construction sector proved the most sensitive to short-term fluctuations in the period. It fell sharply, then recovered rapidly to reach in 1935 a level 11% higher than that of 1929; in residential and industrial/commercial construction respectively completed square metres rose 3.5 and 4.1 times between 1931 and 1935.[40]

As we have seen, manufacturing industry experienced a rapid and permanent recovery after a relatively limited decline, to reach in 1935 the highest relative level of production of all economic activities. Important structural changes also took place during the period. A comparison of the first and second National Censuses of Industry and Commerce, made in 1927 and 1937, reveals an increase in the number of establishments with five or more workers from 8 539 to 18 328, an increase of 170%.[41] The total number employed in such enterprises increased by 83%, from 82 494 to 151 157. Whereas in 1920 only one-quarter of total employment in manufacturing industry was provided by such establishments, they accounted for 41% in 1930 and practically 50% in 1937.[42] There were also a growing number of establishments with over 100 workers. They accounted for substantial proportions of those workers in establishments with five or more workers: 31% in processed foods, 71% in beverages, 89% in tobacco, 70% in textiles, 36% in clothing and footwear, 56% in paper, 43% in printing, 48% in chemical products, 67% in non-metallic minerals and 60% in metal products, machinery and transport equipment.

Figures on industrial investment reveal continued real growth despite adverse circumstances in 1930 and 1931, a decline in 1932 and 1933, and a rapid recovery in 1934 to levels above those of 1929.[43]

Estimates of manufacturing production, as we have seen, show improvements from mid-1931. Once again, though, disaggregation reveals a number of contrasts.

By 1935 production of current consumption goods had not yet returned to 1929 levels, while in the second group it had surpassed them by 44%, Over the longer term the first group showed a 70% improvement (in real terms) over 1914, while the second group showed a 340% increase. As a result, current consumption goods fell from an 83% share of total manufacturing production to a 63% share, with the second group gaining ground proportionately. The implicit average annual rates of growth for each group between 1929 and 1940 were 1.6% and 6.8% respectively; for the period 1931–40 they were 5.1% and 11.5% respectively.

As regards the structure of local supply of manufactures the rapid decline in manufactured imports (from US* 206 per capita in 1929 to US* 26 per capita in 1934) and the rapid recovery of local production

TABLE 3.6   *Indices of manufacturing production and relative shares for current consumption goods, and durable consumer goods, intermediate and capital inputs, 1929–40*
(real values, 1918 = 100)

	Current consumption goods		Durable consumer intermediate and capital goods		Total manufacturing production
	Index	Relative share %	Index	Relative share %	
1929	100.0	(71.5)	100.0	(28.5)	100.0
1930	92.7	(68.9)	100.6	(30.2)	94.8
1931	76.6	(71.3)	77.1	(28.7)	76.8
1932	75.3	(69.4)	83.3	(30.6)	77.5
1933	83.8	(68.8)	95.1	(31.2)	87.1
1934	90.3	(65.4)	119.9	(34.6)	98.5
1935	97.5	(62.6)	143.9	(37.4)	111.0
1936	106.5	(64.8)	144.8	(35.2)	117.3
1937	106.2	(61.9)	163.8	(38.1)	123.3
1938	106.0	(61.1)	168.8	(38.9)	128.0
1939	108.2	(60.9)	174.1	(39.1)	130.4
1940	119.5	(59.7)	205.3	(40.3)	150.9

SOURCE: Muñoz (1968) and Palma (1979) appendices 47, 59 and 60.

meant that by that time domestic production represented 90% of total internal supply, against 60% in 1928–9.[44] Per capita consumption of manufactures fell by more than half between 1929 and 1931 (from US* 452 to US* 216 respectively), but reached US* 256 in 1934, and US* 400 toward the end of the decade.[45]

Domestic production was already supplying more than 80% of current consumption goods in the 1920s. By 1935 97.3% of such goods were locally produced, but this owed more to reductions in imports than to increases in domestic production. The decline in the value of imported current consumption goods from US* 148 million in 1929 to US* 18 million in 1933 had relatively little effect upon consumption in view of the limited weight of imports in total consumption. Per capita consumption fell only from US* 194 in 1929 to US* 127 in 1932, recovering to US* 150 by 1935.[46]

For durable consumer, intermediate and capital goods, on the other hand, local production had been responsible for some 30% of total supply in the late 1920s. With the crisis it rose to a peak of 74% in 1933, and remained at 71.1% in 1935. Here the rapid response of local production was as significant as the decline in imports, which slumped from US* 712 million to US* 93 million in 1933. They recovered quickly thereafter, but domestic production rose sufficiently fast for relative shares to remain virtually constant.[47]

If we return to Table 3.4 we gain a clearer view of manufacturing activity by sector in the period. In the first half of the 1930s the most outstanding performance came from textiles, which experienced a small decline in 1930, but grew thereafter at 30% per annum. By 1935 real annual production grew to more than double the level of 1929. Despite the sharp fall in imports, per capita internal supply in 1935 reached 80% of 1929 levels.[48]

The rapid increase in textile production pushed the share of domestic production in total domestic supply from 30% in 1929 to 77% in 1935, and the share of textiles in total manufacturing production rose from 6% to 13.7% over the same period.[49] Rapid increases in textile production were common in Latin America in the period.[50]

Other dynamic sectors in manufacturing in the period were non-metallic minerals, chemical products, timber and furniture, paper and printing, and metal products, machinery and transport equipment. The production of non-metallic minerals followed the fortunes of the construction sector closely, expanding at 29% per annum between 1933 and 1935. Between 1929 and 1935 the share of domestic production in total supply rose from 39.5% to 86.8%[51] In real terms by 1935 production was over 4.6 times what it had been in 1914. Production of chemicals recovered from 1933 onward, rising by 38% over two years; the share of domestic production in total supply rose from 25% in 1929 to 54% in 1935.[52] In real terms by 1935 production was almost 3 times what it had been in 1914.

Where metal products, machinery and transport equipment was concerned, domestic production was by 1935 supplying 60% of the domestic market, as against 30% in the mid-1920s, and 7% in 1914.[53] In real terms by 1935 production was 5.2 times what it had been in 1914.

Conclusions

By Latin American standards manufacturing in Chile was relatively well advanced on the eve of the First World War. It was thus increasingly able to take on the role of the 'engine' of local economic growth as the export sector entered into difficulties which were to culminate in the crisis of the 1930s. The instability of the export sector would provide the *stimulus* and the level of manufacturing development before the First World War *the material base* for this transition from export-led development to development based upon import-substitution.[54] The essential characteristic of the transition was the growing degree of *autonomy* of the local economy with respect to an increasingly unstable international economy. This was achieved through rapid increases in the diversification of the structure of production. Nevertheless, given the limited size of the internal market, the process of diversification unavoidably had significant costs in terms of the inefficiency attendant upon the lack of specialisation.

However, those who would criticise the process of 'inward-oriented' development on these grounds should recall that it was precisely the instability of the international economy between the wars which led to its adoption. In the circumstances it is hardly surprising that the form of development adopted involved some degree of disengagement from the world economy.

The economic policies adopted and the changes in the structure of production during the 1920s foreshadowed the lines along which economic development would continue not only during the 1930s, but for the following three decades as well. In other words the principal characteristics of development after 1930 were already present beforehand. Even so, the recognition that the transition toward import substituting industrialisation began early does not take away from the significance of the crisis of the 1930s for the Chilean economy. No other economy in the world suffered more acutely, and the effects were not easily borne. The point is that the two decades following the outbreak of the First World War must be seen *as a single unit*, whose principal characteristic was the instability of the external sector and, in response to it, an attempt to carry through a radical transformation of the economy, in order to create a greater degree of local productive automony. The crisis which began in 1929 contributed new elements which affected the *degree* but not so much the *nature* of the change to a strategy of 'inward-oriented' development'.

Finally, this analysis stands in sharp contrast to the views of those like Frank, Ramirez Necochea, Veliz, Nolff, Cademartori, and Hinkelamert, who unequivocally argue for the 'positive' nature of the crisis of the 1930s. In my opinion, from the point of view of the 'benefits', the 1930s represent an acceleration and strengthening of a process of transition already under way for over a decade; from the point of view of the 'costs' no other economy in the world suffered as much as Chile, and the recovery was difficult. In fact the levels of exports per capita prevailing before the crisis were not regained until the 1980s. Equally, Chile had to wait until the second half of the 1940s to re-establish the levels of per capita GDP and consumption of manufactures achieved in the 1920s; and there is no evidence that distribution had really improved. As we have seen, there were equally high costs of a social and political nature too. Labour organisation, for example, suffered a tremendous setback, especially in the northern half of the country. Thus, I would argue that even those who regard as decidedly positive the fact that the crisis accelerated and strengthened the transition to import-substituting industrialisation and the strategy of 'inward-oriented' development can scarcely be right to argue that the impact of the crisis as a whole was unambiguously positive.

NOTES

1. See Segall (1953), Jobet (1955), Ramirez Necochea (1958 and 1960), Veliz (1961 and 1963), Nolff (1965), Frank (1967), Cademartori (1968), Hinkelamert (1970a, 1970b and 1975), Garcia-Huidobro (1971), Godoy (1971) and de Vylder (1973 and 1974).
2. For a description of the model see Bianchi (1973).
3. I understand by 'the origins of a process of industrialization' not merely a process of increasing simple production of manufactures, but one in which an increase in the net volume of production (value added) of manufacturing activities is accompanied by a process of fundamental and relatively generalised transformation of the organisation of production and the complexity of the technology employed: wage labour gradually becomes the basic relation of production, and the capital equipment used grows not only in volume, but also, and crucially, in range and variety.
4. For my own account see Palma (1979). For descriptions of manufacturing development before 1930 see Lagos (1966), Hurtado (1966), Muñoz (1968), Carmagnani (1971 and 1973), Kirsch (1973) and Cariola and Sunkel (1976). For a parallel study which reaches conclusions similar to my own see Ortega (1979).
5. For sources of calculations and different statistics see Palma (1979).
6. See n. 1.
7. Palma (1979) appendices 30, 31 and 40.
8. In 1915 and 1916 the value of exports was 2.3 times that of imports. See ibid., appendix 32. For exports of nitrate and copper, appendices 30 and 31.
9. Ibid., appendix 38.
10. Muñoz (1968) p. 160; Palma (1979) p. 329. For an analysis of the problem of the 1914 statistics see Palma (1979) pp. 333–6.
11. Palma (1979) p. 333–4; Kirsch (1973) pp. 85–6.

12. Ibid., appendix 45. These statistics are subject to the underestimation of levels of production in 1914 mentioned above.
13. See p. 52.
14. See Zegers (1968) p. 7 and Espinoza (1909) p. 310.
15. Palma (1979) appendix 32.
16. The method for Table 3.1 is as follows: The average absolute percentage annual variation is calculated with the formula

$$\frac{100}{n} \sum_{2}^{N} \left| \frac{X_t - X_{t-1}}{X_{t-1}} \right|$$

With respect to 'net' values (revenues or quantum) the variables were 'deflated' by their respective average annual rate of growth to take into account the positive trend in export capacity and revenues. The new index was calculated using the formula

$$\frac{100}{n} \sum_{2}^{m} \left| \frac{(X_t - X_{t-1})(1 + r)}{(X_{t-1})(1 + r)} \right|$$

Real export prices correspond to the terms of trade. The S.D./$\bar{X}$ is calculated with the standard deviation of the residuals from an exponential trend corrected by the average of the variable. The exponential trend is obtained from the linear relationship between the log of the dependent variable (price, quantum or value) and time. See Ffrench-Davis (1981), Leith (1970), Masell (1970), Kenen and Voivodos (1972) and Yotopoulos and Nugent (1976) for discussion of the methodologies. The first indicator measures instability on a year-to-year basis, regardless of its position with respect to 'normal' or trend values. The second is a measure of deviation from a trend.
17. Wright (1975) p. 7.
18. Palma (1979) p. 284; Ellsworth (1945) p. 11. Taxes on exports meanwhile fell from 46% of ordinary public revenues in 1910 to 39% in 1915, 29% in 1920, 28% in 1925 and 13% in 1930. Taxes on imports meanwhile rose from 12% in 1915 and 1920 to 20% in 1925 and 28% in 1930. Revisions of the tariff may have been as much designed to restore public finances as to stimulate manufacturing industry.
19. Palma (1979) appendix 27.
20. The first, founded in the 1850s, produced official publications; the second, founded in the 1890s, provided the Armed Forces with armaments and other materials. A National Foundry existed between 1866 and 1874, but was closed when the diversification of its products range away from war materials threatened private competition.
21. See Muñoz (1968) pp. 44–7, and Kirsch (1973) p. 46–7.
22. Palma (1979) appendices 47, 59 and 60.
23. Ibid.
24. Ibid., appendices 48 and 58.
25. For the first time, for example, 'the great latifundistas' no longer were a majority in the Senate; see Bauer (1975) p. 215. The social legislation

concerned the regulation of labour contracts, unions and social security. It also created the Dirección General del Trabajo.

26. For Chilean terms of trade see Palma (1979) appendices 18 and 32; for those of Great Britain see Feinstein (1972) table 139.
27. See Ellsworth (1945) pp. 23–69; Palma (1979) appendix 31.
28. See Ellsworth (1945) pp. 4 and 9.
29. See *Estadística Chilena* for the years in question.
30. By this stage import taxes were producing 38% of 'ordinary' public revenues. Internal taxes, responsible for 0.2% of 'ordinary' public revenues in 1905, generated 9% in 1920, 18% in 1925, 30% in 1930, and 39% in 1935. See Palma (1979) appendix 40. 'Ordinary' public revenues were those which came from regular sources of revenue.
31. *Estadística Chilena*, relevant years.
32. Ellsworth (1945) p. 14. Many Bolivians worked in the nitrate areas, and they were repatriated during the crisis. This helped to reduce the official figures of unemployment.
33. *Estadística Chilena*, relevant years.
34. Ibid. and Palma (1979) appendix 47.
35. *Estadística Chilena*, relevant years.
36. Ellsworth (1945) pp. 45–73. By the end of the decade import tariffs on tyres (150 KB) were equivalent to 1 693.5 pesos, while its c.i.f. value was only 605 pesos. See ibid., p. 50.
37. As in any 'small' economy faced with an exogenous deterioration in its terms of trade the price of tradeables rose in comparison to that of non-tradeables. Thus the 39% deterioration in the terms of trade between 1930 and 1933 was an important stimulus on the demand side to domestic production of importables. Price indices in *Estadística Chilena*, relevant years; rates of exchange in Palma (1979) appendix 27.
38. *Estadística Chilena*, relevant years.
39. Palma (1979) appendices 30 and 34.
40. *Estadística Chilena*, relevant years.
41. Palma (1979) appendix 44.
42. Ibid., appendix 45.
43. Ellsworth (1945) p. 21.
44. Palma (1979) appendix 47.
45. Ibid., appendices 1 and 47; Muñoz (1968) pp. 160–1.
46. Palma (1979) appendix 59.
47. Ibid., appendix 60.
48. In real terms by 1935 production was over 4.7 times what it had been in 1914.
49. Palma (1979) appendices 46 and 51.
50. See Diaz Alejandro (1980) p. 26.
51. Palma (1979) appendix 57.
52. Ibid., appendix 56.
53. Ibid., appendix 58.
54. As 80% of imports were manufactured goods, and these represented half the total internal supply, this appears to be the only area providing the opportunity in the short term for local economic growth once the export sector enters into crisis.

REFERENCES

A. Angell, *Politics and the Labour Movement in Chile* (London, 1972).

P. Aquirre Cerda, *El Problema Industrial* (Santiago de Chile, 1933).

O. Alvarez Andrews, *Historia del Desarrollo Industrial de Chile* (Santiago de Chile, 1936).

M. A. Ballesteros and T. E. Davis, 'The Growth of Output and Employment in Basic Sectors of the Chilean Economy, 1908–1957', *Economic Development and Cultural Change*, vol. II (January, 1963) 152–76.

A. J. Bauer, *Chilean Rural Society from the Spanish Conquest to 1930* (Cambridge, 1975).

J. R. Behrman, *Foreign Trade Regimes and Economic Development, Chile* (New York, 1976).

A. Bianchi, 'The Theory of Latin American Development', *Social and Economic Studies* (March, 1973).

J. Cademartori, *La Economía Chilena: un enfoque marxista* (Santiago, 1968).

C. Cariola and O. Sunkel, 'Expansión Salitrera y Transformaciones Socioeconómicas en Chile, 1860–1930', manuscript, University of Sussex (1976).

M. Carmagnani, *Sviluppo Industriale e Sottosviluppo Económico: Il Caso Chileno (1860–1930)* (Torino, 1971).

———*Les Mecanismes de la Vie Economique dans une Societé Colóniale: Le Chili 1680–1830* (Paris, 1973).

H. B. Chenery, 'Patterns of Industrial Growth', *American Economic Review* (September, 1960).

Chile, *Anuario Estadístico* (Santiago de Chile, relevant years).

——— *Congreso Nacional* (Santiago de Chile, relevant years).

——— *Memorias*, Ministerios del Interior, Hacienda, de Guerra, Justicia y Relaciones Exteriores (Santiago de Chile, relevant years).

——— *Estadística Commercial* (Valparaiso, 1862–1910).

——— *Censo Industrial y Comercial* (Santiago, 1927).

——— *Anuarios de Minería e Industria* (Santiago, 1910–26).

——— *Segundo Censo Industrial y Comercial* (Santiago, 1937).

——— *Sinopsis Estadística* (Santiago, 1916–39).

P. Clark, *Planning Import Substitution* (Amsterdam, 1975).

M. Concha, *La Lucha Económica* (Santiago, 1909).

F. Cotapos, *El Aporte del Capital Extranjero en la Industria Minera de Chile* (Santiago, 1947).

S. de Castro and S. de la Cuadra, 'Towards a New Trade Policy for Chile', mimeo, AID (Santiago, 1971).

Diario Oficial, newspaper (Santiago, 1877–).

C. Diaz Alejandro, *Essays on the Economic History of the Argentine Republic* (New Haven, 1970).

ECLA, *Economic Survey of Latin America, 1949* (New York, 1950).

P. T. Ellsworth, *Chile: an Economy in Transition* (New York, 1945).

F. A. Encina, *Nuestra Inferioridad Económica* (Santiago, 1955).

R. Espinoza, *Cuestiones Financieras de Chile* (Santiago, 1909).

C. H. Feinstein, *Statistical Tables of National Income, Expenditure and Output of the UK, 1855–1965* (Cambridge, 1972).

F. W. Fetter, *Monetary Inflation in Chile* (Princeton, 1931).

R. Ffrench-Davis, 'Old and new Forms of External Instability in Latin America: Sources, Mechanisms of Transmission and Policies', CIEPLAN, *Notas Tecnicas*, 30 (1981).

V. Figueroa, *Diccionario Histórico y Biográfico de Chile* (Santiago, 1931).

A. G. Frank, *Capitalism and Underdevelopment in Latin America: Historical Studies of Chile and Brazil* (New York, 1967).

L. Galdames, 'La Industria', in *Geografía Económica de Chile* (Santiago, 1911).

G. Ganderillas, *Recopilación de Leyes y Reglamentos sobre Fomento de las Industrias Mineras, Agrícolas y Fabril* (Santiago, 1930).

G. Garcia Huidobro, 'El Desarrollo Económico Chileno durante el Siglo XIX: una historia critica', B.A. dissertation, Universidad de Chile (Santiago, 1972).

K. Glaucer, 'Orígenes del Régimen de Producción Vigente en Chile', *Cuadernos de la Realidad Nacional*, 6 (1971) 78–152.

H. Godoy (ed.), *Estructura Social: de Chile* (Santiago, 1971).

P. L. Gonzalez, *La Sociedad de Fomento Fabril, su labor durante veinticino años* (Santiago, 1913).

P. L. González, *Chile Industrial* (Santiago, 1919).

——— *Chile: Breves Noticias de sus Industrias* (Santiago, 1920).

——— *Las Fábricas de Tejidos de Algodón en Chile y los Derechos de Aduanas* (Santiago, 1924).

——— and M. Soto, *Album Gráfico e Histórico de la Sociedad de Fomento Fabril y de la Industria Nacional* (Santiago, 1926).

——— *50 años de labor de la Sociedad de Fomento Fabril, 1883–1933* (Santiago, 1933).

C. Silva Cortez and E. Gajardo Cruzat, *El Esfuerzo Nacional; estudio de la política industrial; reseña de las industrias nacionales; rol de industrias* (Santiago, 1916).

Great Britain, *Report on the Industrial and Economic Situation in Chile* (London, relevant years).

R. Hernández, *El Salitre: Resumen Historico desde su Descumbrimiento y Explotación* (Valparaíso, 1930).

F. Hinkelamert (1970a), *El Subdesarrollo Latinoamericano: un Caso de Desarrollo Capitalista* (Santiago, 1970).

——— (1970b), 'Teoría de la Dialéctica del Desarrollo Desigual', *Cuadernos de la Realidad Nacional*, 6 (December 1970).

——— 'La Teoría Clásica del Imperialismo, el Subdesarrollo y la Acumulación Socialista', in M. A. Garreton, *Economía Política en la Unidad Popular* (Barcelona, 1975).

J. Hormann, *Chile Industrial y Económico, 1897–1917: efecto de las leyes de impuestos N. 980 del 23 de diciembre de 1897 y N. 3066 del 1°de marzo de 1916* (Santiago, 1918).

C. Hurtado, *Concentración de la Población y Desarrollo Económico: El Caso Chileno* (Santiago, 1966).

T. Jeanneret, 'El Sistema de Protección a la Industria Chilena', in O. Muñoz (1972).

J. C. Jobet, *Ensayo Crítico del Desarrollo Económico Social de Chile* (Santiago, 1955).

P. Kenen and C. Voivodos, 'Export Instability and Economic Growth', *Kyklos*, 4 (1972).

H. W. Kirsch, 'The Industrialization of Chile, 1880–1930', Ph.D. dissertation, University of Florida (1973).

—— *Industrial Development in a Traditional Society: The Conflict between Entrepreneurship and Modernization in Chile* (Florida, 1977).

R. Lagos, *La Industria en Chile: Antecedentes Estructurales* (Santiago, 1966).

C. Leith, 'The Decline in World Export Instability: A Comment', *Bulletin of the Oxford University Institute of Economics and Statistics* (1970) 267–72.

S. Machiavello-Varas, *Política Económica Nacional: Antecedentes y Directivas*, two vols (Santiago, 1931).

D. Martner, *Historia de Chile: Historia Económica* (Santiago, 1929).

B. Masell, 'Export Instability and Economic Structure', *American Economic Review* (September 1970).

O. Muñoz, *Crecimiento Industrial de Chile, 1914–1965* (Santiago, 1968).

—— *Proceso a la Industrialización Chilena* (Santiago, 1972).

M. Nolff, 'Industria Manufacturera', in CORFO (ed.), *Geografía Económica de Chile* (Santiago, 1965).

L. Ortega, 'Change and Crisis in Chile's Economy and Society, 1865–1879', Ph.D. dissertation, University of London (1979).

J. G. Palma, 'Dependency: A Formal Theory of Underdevelopment or a Methodology for the Analysis of Concrete Situations of Underdevelopment?', *World Development*, vol. 6, no. 718 (1978) 881–924.

—— 'Growth and Structure of Chilean Manufacturing Industry from 1830 to 1935: Origins and Development of a Process of Industrialization in an Export Economy', D.Phil. dissertation, University of Oxford (1979), forthcoming Oxford University Press.

J. Perez Canto, *Chile: An Account of its Wealth and Progress* (London, 1912).

J. Pfeiffer, 'The Development of Manufacturing Industry in Chile, 1820–1940', Ph.D. dissertation, University of Chicago (1947).

F. Pike, *Chile and the United States: 1880–1962* (Indiana, 1963).

A. Pinto, *Chile, un Caso de Desarrollo Frustrado* (Santiago, 1959).

C. D. Quintano, 'La Crisis de 1929 y sus Efectos', *Memoria de Prueba para optar al grado de licenciado en la Facultad de Ciencias Juridicas y Sociales de la Universidad de Chile* (1945).

H. Ramirez Neocochea, *Balmaceda y la Contrarevolución de 1891* (Santiago, 1958).

——*Historia del Imperialismo en Chile* (Santiago, 1960).

L. E. Recabarren, *Obras Escogidas* (Santiago, 1965).

C. W. Reynolds, 'Domestic Consequences of Export Instability: An Empirical Look at Chile and its Copper Industry, 1925–1959', *American Economic Review* (May 1963).

—— 'Development Problems of an Export Economy: the Case of Chilean Copper', in M. Mamalakis and C. W. Reynolds, *Essays on the Chilean Economy* (Illinois, 1965).

J. F. Rippy, *Latin America and the Industrial Age* (New York, 1944).

—— and J. Pfeiffer, 'Notes on the Dawn of Manufacturing in Chile', *The*

*Hispanic American Historical Review,*xxviii, no. 2 (May, 1948) 293–303.

F. Rivas Vicuña, *Nuevas Bases para el Establecimiento de la Industria Suder-urgica en Chile* (Santiago, 1917).

L. S. Rowe, 'Early Effects of the European War upon the Finance, Commerce and Industry of Chile', in D. Kinley (ed.) *Preliminary Economic Studies of the War* (New York, 1918).

A. Ruffat, 'La Politica Monetaria y el Sector Externo en Chile entre las Dos Guerras Mundiales: Una Evaluación, mimeo (Santiago, 1969).

G. Salazar, 'Formas Económicas de Transición: Chile 1844–1914, Ph.D. dissertation in progress, Hull University.

M. Segall, *Desarrollo del Capitalismo en Chile: cinco ensayos dialecticos* (Santiago, 1953).

R. Simon, 'Determinación de la Entrada Nacional de Chile', in CORFO, *Cuentas Nacionales de Chile, 1940–54* (Santiago, 1957).

Sociedad Nacional de Agricultura, *Boletín de la Sociedad Nacional de Agricultura* (relevant years).

Sociedad de Fomento Fabril, 'Censo Industrial', in *Industria*, Boletin de la Sociedad de Fomento Fabril, no. 1 (1896) 5–7.

——*Industria, Boletín de la Sociedad de Fomento Fabril, (relevant years).*

——*Resúmenes Generales de la Estadística Industrial* (Santiago, 1908).

——*Estadística Industrial de la Republica de Chile* (Santiago, 1910).

—— *Chile: Breves Noticias de sus Industrias* (Santiago, 1920).

C. Solberg, 'Immigration and Urban Social Problems in Argentina and Chile, 1890–1914', *Hispanic American Historical Review*, vol. 49 (1969) 215–32.

G. Subercaseaux, *Monetary and Banking Policy of Chile* (Oxford, 1922).

—— *Historia de las Doctrinas Económicas en América Latina y en especial en Chile* (Santiago, 1924).

R. B. Sutcliffe, *Industry and Underdevelopment* (London OUP Reading, Mass., 1971).

UNESCO, *'Immigration in Chile'* (Santiago, n.d.).

G. Urzua Valenzuela, *Evolución de la Administración Pública Chilena: 1918–1968* (Santiago, 1970).

USA, *Statistical Abstract* (Washington, relevant years).

J. Valdivieso, *El Instituto de Crédito Industrial y su Labor de Desarrollo en Beneficio de la Economía Nacional* (Santiago, 1947).

C. Véliz, *Historia de la Marina Mercante de Chile* (Santiago, 1961).

——'La Mesa de Tres Patas', *Desarrollo Económico* (April-September 1963).

S. de Vylder, 'The Roots of Chile's Underdevelopment and the Factors Perpetuating it: an historical interpretation', mimeo (Stockholm, 1973).

—— *From Colonialism to Dependence: an Introduction to Chile's Economic History*, SIDA (Stockholm, 1974).

C. T. Wright, 'Agriculture and Protectionism in Chile, 1880–1930', *Journal of Latin American Studies*, vol. 7 (May 1975).

P. Yotopoulos and J. Nugent, *Economics of Development* (New York, 1976).

J. Zegers, *Estudios Económicos 1907–8* (Santiago, 1908).

4 The Effect of the Great Depression on the Economies of Peru and Colombia

ROSEMARY THORP AND CARLOS LONDOÑO*

This chapter would like to[1] answer the following questions. What can we learn, from comparing two economies, of the factors which determine the severity of the impact of the Depression? How does the nature of the response vary, and why? What is the relative importance of the factors much discussed elsewhere: countercyclical government spending and the role of wars?[2] (It adds perhaps to the interest of our choice of countries that their 'War' was actually fought with each other.) Or do longer-term factors have more to do with the recovery? Is there some kind of 'institutional breakthrough' occurring anyway by that point? Who bears the burden of adjustment? Is there a distinct change in growth strategy, and/or a greater degree of autonomy? Is recovery itself independent of international market factors? Is the Depression rightly seen as a discontinuity in any sense? Finally, how does the response compare with the response to the crisis of the 1970s?

* We would like to acknowledge the substantial contribution made to this chapter by Juan José Echavarría in sharing with us his research materials and working papers. We thank the Social Science Research Council of the UK for financial support, and the following for extensive helpful comments on the paper: José Antonio Ocampo, Marco Palacios, Miguel Urrutia, Carlos Diaz Alejandro, Malcolm Deas.

The plan of the chapter is as follows. In the first section we review some trends of the 1920s we consider of importance for what follows, and in so doing sketch in briefly the main features of our two economies. The second part considers the severity of the Depression in the two cases, and looks briefly at the relative degree of recovery in the medium term. The third section explores the character of the adjustment process, and tries to explain the very different responses in the two cases. The fourth section looks at who bore the burden, and the chapter concludes in a speculative vein.

THE 1920S: DANCING WITH FOREIGN BANKERS

'The Dance of the Millions' is at the centre of our stereotype of the 1920s: a decade when North American salesmen pressed loans and American products upon unsuspecting governments, who, overwhelmed by this sudden access to credit and to goods, borrowed with a recklessness only to be equalled in the 1970s. Both our countries were at the forefront of this process, experiencing an inrush of private and public capital and a boom in public works as a consequence. By 1924 Colombia had borrowed $18 million, Peru $25 million. In two years, 1926 and 1927, Colombia received a gross inflow of $135 million,[3] or $67 million a year, while her annual exports only brought her something over $100 million. Peru had one such incredible year – 1927 – when $60 million arrived in external finance, $117 million in export revenue.[4]

Both countries looked desirable to the outside – and both were interested in doing what was required to make themselves more attractive. Both requested Kemmerer Missions: Kemmerer was a US financial adviser whose 'acceptance of an invitation to provide financial counsel would be sufficient to improve prospects for a country's future and would seem tantamount to financial and economic reform itself'.[5] Under his guidance, and that of a number of other foreign experts, both countries carried out serious banking and administrative reforms. More importantly, outstanding issues involving foreign interests were settled rather rapidly. In Colombia the dispute was the matter of the indemnisation owed by the USA in compensation for the Panama Canal; by the early 1920s US investors were seriously interested in oil, railroads and coal and were pressing for a settlement. When it came, in 1922, it amounted to $25 million, payable in annual instalments of $5 million, and representing an obvious guarantee of the credit-worthiness of the Colombian government.[6]

In the case of Peru the 1920s is the decade of the dictatorship of Augusto Leguía, who was financed in his bid for power in 1919 by various foreign interests. He paid his debts in many forms, and pursued an extremely friendly policy towards foreign firms. In 1922 also the long-standing issue of La Brea-Parinas[7] was settled with the International Petroleum Company (IPC), on terms extraordinarily favourable to the company. The deal shows the interplay between one form of financing and another, since as part of the arrangement IPC assisted in the placing of $2.5 million worth of bonds in the USA.

Each country experienced substantial export growth as well, and in each case the effect of the flood of foreign exchange was appreciation of the exchange rate and an enormous increase in imports. In neither case was there strong protectionist pressure;[8] the growth of industrial production was slow in each,[9] though in the case of Colombia there was substantial demand-induced expansion of capacity.

Both countries were considered to suffer from waste and corruption in the utilising of foreign money. In Colombia Olaya Herrera would claim in his 1930 election campaign that the bankers' estimate to him was that only 30% of the money filtered through to public works.[10] 'The bankers' commenting on Peru gave a similar estimate.[11]

There is, in other words, a basic similarity in the manner of interaction with the outside world and in the pattern of saturation with foreign money beyond the absorption capacity of the economy. But if we look a little more closely we shall begin to find differences which may

TABLE 4.1   *Colombia: composition of exports by value[a] 1905–30*
(percentage shares)

	Coffee	*Bananas*	*Oil*	*Gold[b]*	*Tobacco*	*Hides*
1905	39	3[c]	0	14	3	6
1910	31	9	0	19	2	10
1915	52	6	0	17	1	12
1919[d]	69	3	0	1	3	11
1925	80	7	0	2	0	4
1930	61	8	23	8	0	3

[a] Components do not sum to 100, as only principal exports are included.
[b] Non-monetary exports only.
[c] 1906 figure.
[d] 1920 figures are not given.

SOURCE: Urrutia and Arrubla (1970), insert between pp. 108 and 109.

TABLE 4.2   *Peru: composition of exports by value,ᵃ 1890–1930*
(percentage shares)

	Sugar	Cotton	Wool	Silver	Rubber	Copper	Petroleum
1890	28	9	15	33	13	1	–
1895	35	7	15	26	14	1	–
1900	32	7	7	22	13	18	–
1905	32	7	8	6	16	10	–
1910	20	14	7	10	18	18	2
1915	26	11	5	5	5	17	10
1920	42	30	2	5	1	7	5
1925	11	32	4	10	1	8	24
1930	11	18	3	4	–	10	30

ᵃ The percentage shares are only very approximate, since some exports were valued fob, some cif – it often being unclear what the practice was. The rows sum to less than 100% owing to the exclusion of minor export items.

SOURCE: Thorp and Bertram (1978) p. 40.

be of far more interest to our analysis. Certain obvious differences at the start of our period lie in the resource endowment and political and economic structure of the two countries. Tables 4.1 and 4.2 show the variation in export composition: in Colombia coffee dominated – locally owned and produced by a mix of large and small farms, the mix varying regionally, but in most areas with a heavy preponderance of small producers. The foreign-owned enclaves of oil and bananas were of less significance than Peru's foreign-owned sectors, oil and copper. Peru had far more diversity, with significant agricultural exports in sugar and cotton, and even wool from the Sierra.

As of 1920 the degree of industrialisation was greater in Peru. While Peru had experienced a not-inconsiderable period of industrial development in the 1890s and early 1900s, Colombia was at that time enmeshed in civil war. While individual factories can of course be traced back to earlier years, 'industry' only really began to take shape in the years following 1910.[12]

A third and most important point of difference lies in the political structure of the two countries. In Colombia the departmental and even municipal governments have considerable (if varying) importance. They have powers to collect taxes[13] and their joint expenditure actually *exceeds* that of the national government.[14] By contrast, local government in Peru is minuscule in importance, with expenditure levels less than 10% of the national government. This difference had implications for foreign borrowing: in Colombia the external debt accumulated in the 1920s by departments and municipalities exceeded that of the national government.

Related with these basic differences of structure we find some important differences when we look more closely at the developments of the 1920s, in particular when we focus on the infrastructural needs and likely demands of the main productive sectors of the economy and relate this to the role of the State and to foreign finance. In the case of Peru the leading export products of the 1920s become immediately evident from Table 4.2. What we observe there is an important shift with two main implications. The move away from cotton, sugar, wool and rubber to a leading role for oil and copper represented, first, a shift from Peruvian to foreign control, and, second, an accentuation of the regional concentration already begun in the 1910s with the decline in rubber and wool. (Oil production was on the Coast; the booming mineral centres were in the Central Sierra, already well connected in by rail to the Coast, thanks to important investments at the turn of the century.)

This pattern, and the character of the resource base underlying it, had some quite definite implications for the infrastructure required and the consequent development of the role of the State. The multinationals who were anxious to develop copper and oil were prepared and able to provide their own infrastructure; indeed, the major investments underlying the expansion of the 1920s – in port works, refineries and railways – had already been completed. Transport was not a problem, and marketing was carried out within the companies' multinational network. There was a need for order and regulation, particularly of oil claims, which would become serious by the 1940s,[15] but did not affect this period. What the companies did need from the State was negative: an absence of interference and in particular of taxation. It is in this way principally that they fit into our story: the 'price' for absurdly low taxation, and a favourable settlement of the La Brea–Parinas dispute, was paid in part in direct financing of the government, and in part, as we have mentioned, in IPC's services in the negotiation of international loans.

By contrast the sectors which had greater need in principle of government support were either not in political favour or were facing serious economic decline. The industries of the Selva and the more remote Sierra – rubber and wool – gave no motivation whatsoever for an opening up of the country; sugar also faced adverse conditions and a number of the most prominent producers spent the 1920s in political exile. Cotton clearly needed the State, for irrigation, but was composed for the most part of fairly small producers, who did not carry much weight at the national level. (We have already noted that the spending of local governments was tiny.) In fact it would seem that irrigation needs did meet with some response, and that the investments were in part genuinely productive (largely owing to the efforts of Charles Sutton, consultant engineer in the Direccion de Aguas e Irrigación).[16] However, a closer examination is revealing. Irrigation expenditure was made up as follows:

	Thousand libras
Imperial	922
Olmos	3453
Esperanza	612
Chira	60
Total	5047

Source: Labarthe (1933).

The imperial scheme was in Cañete, Leguía's home ground: the list of beneficiaries makes revealing reading.[17] Esperanza and Chira represented state takeovers of private enterprise ventures by the Graña and Checa families respectively.[18] Olmos was perhaps the greatest scandal of the Leguía projects, with Lp 170 000 being spent on fraudulent 'expropriations' of land owned by political favourites, with the son of the President and his friends deeply involved.[19] So also was the Lima merchant house of Ayulo & Co., which sold the machinery to the government.[20] The project was apparently *opposed* by local landowners, who feared it would create a labour shortage and interfere with their comfortable monopoly of water rights.[21] In all cases disbursement lagged badly. What is really noticeable is how *little* was done that bore any relation to the real needs of the sector.[22]

The real beneficiaries of the schemes, therefore, tended to be based in Lima, and this was even more true of the extensive urban improvements carried out.[23] Heavily involved were a number of foreign construction companies – notably the Foundation Co. and Frederick Ley & Co., and construction and real-estate interests. A clear symptom is the rise in property values in Lima: between 1921 and 1925 alone property values in general rose over 100%, and 'property values of territory adjacent to the city have increased more than 500%'.[24] Political favouritism, corruption, speculation, luxury importing and capital flight were all commonly observable.[25] It is hard to disagree with the summing up in 1932 by a critic of the Leguía regime: the foreign loans of the 1920s 'fictitiously and considerably increased the purchasing power of Peruvians. . . . Every individual who, honestly, or not, but with relative facility, obtained some share of this money, became a larger consumer of what are called the "good things of life" such as jewels, autos, wines, dresses, materials for the construction of their chalets, etc.'[26]

Colombia also by the late 1920s had a rapidly growing and foreign-owned export sector in the shape of oil. But as Table 4.1 shows, the main basis for her expansion remained coffee, and coffee was a domestically owned sector badly in need of infrastructure. At the beginning of the 1920s Colombia's transport system turned on rivers, with the Rio Magdalena as the main artery connecting the coffee-growing regions to the port of Barranquilla and bringing imports to the main internal centres of population (see Map 4.1). But the Magdalena was vulnerable to drought, which paralysed the transport system every few years.[27] And with time erosion was making the rivers even less dependable.[28] A patchy but useful railway network did exist, as Map 4.1 shows. However, there were a number of obvious and crucial needs as of the early 1920s. First, the Magdalena route itself needed improvement, in the form of canals and the major port works of Bocas de Ceniza to clear the river entrance. Second, with the opening of the Panama Canal in the 1910s the Pacific had begun to assume a new importance; the new coffee areas in Caldas and Antioquia needed an efficient and reliable route linking them by rail to the Pacific coast, and a new port needed building at Buenaventura.

Maps 4.1 and 4.2 show how in the course of the 1920s both national and departmental governments responded to this challenge, and with the aid of foreign finance integrated and transformed the production and trading patterns of the country. In addition to the main shift there were many smaller ones, and many improvements in existing routes.[29] The key national project was the extension of the Pacific railway,[30] from Cali to Popayan and from Cali to Ibagué. For Antioquia it was the finishing of the Amaga railway up to the Cauca river, opening the Amaga coalfields and linking coffee-growers to the Pacific railway. Caldas, which by the 1930s was to displace Antioquia as the leading coffee department, was busy building its own links to the Pacific railway, as well as completing a cable link up to the Magdalena. Cundinamarca improved the links between Bogotá and the Magdalena. The coffee and commerce sectors in Norte de Santander pushed to shift exports from a route through Venezuela to the Magdalena.[31] Roads played a role too, but were of less importance.

This is the background to the figures on transport investment: we

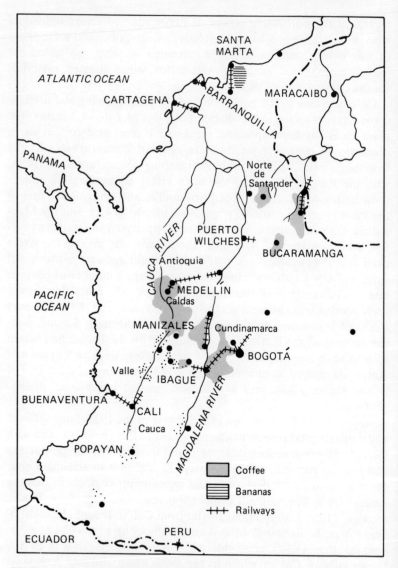

MAP 4.1　Coffee Distribution in Colombia

Sources:　Garcia (1937), McGreevy (1971), Beyer (1947), *Colombian Review*, *Commerce Reports*, *Diario Oficial*.

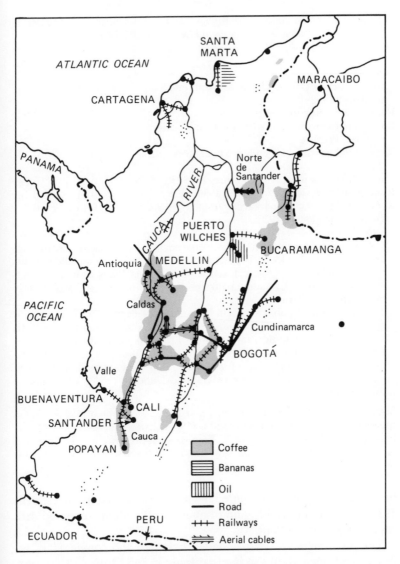

MAP 4.2   Coffee Distribution in Colombia, 1934

SOURCES: as Map 4.1, plus *Memoria de Obras Públicas* (1926), *Revista de Ministerio de Obras Públicas* (enero – abril 1925), *Anuario General de Estadística*, Federación Nacional de Cafeteros (1933).

TABLE 4.3   *The significance of foreign finance, government spending and public works: Peru and Colombia, 1925–30*

	Colombia	Peru
Ratio of stock of US and UK investments and loans to exports, 1929	2.4	2.2
Ratio of debt only to exports, 1929	2.6[a]	0.9
Ratio of public expenditure (national and local) to exports, 1925–30	1.1	0.71
Ratio of public works expenditure to exports, 1925–30	0.49	0.12
Ratio of public works to expenditure, 1925–30	0.43	0.18[b]
Ratio of debt servicing to exports, 1930	0.21	0.16
Ratio of debt servicing to total government revenue (national and local), 1930	0.19	0.25

[a] Colombian debt includes national, departmental and municipal borrowing, and that of the banks. It is possible that more has been included in this figure than in the estimate for investments plus loans from the *South American Journal*. Excluding banks gives a ratio of 1.6 – still significantly higher than the Peruvian figure.

[b] The total value of public works in Peru in the 1920s probably amounted to about Lp 25 million. The estimates vary according to the pro- or anti-Leguía bias of the author, ranging from Lp 19 million (Labarthe, 1933) to Lp 32 million (Capuñay, 1951) for 1919–30, the latter being inflated by the inclusion of an imputed value for forced labour used in road-building. The estimates used here are those of Garland Duponte (n.d.), which take a middle value.

SOURCES: US and UK investments and loans – Normano (1931). Public spending: CEPAL, *Anexo* for Colombia (1957), *Extracto Estadístico* for Peru. Peruvian public works: see note[b]. Exports in local currency: Urrutia and Arrubla (1970), *Extracto Estadístico*. Exports in dollars: Wilkie (1974). Colombian debt: Echavarría (1981).

find that transport represented nearly 80% of public investment 1925–30[32] – an incredible sum of about $280 million compared with some $30 million in Peru.[33]

The investment clearly responded to coffee and commercial[34] interests and opened up the internal trade in foodstuffs.[35] There was also an obvious political element: that of national unity. The lack of a national transport system diminished the power of the central government while increasing the 'caciquismo' of distant regions and towns.[36]

Given this analysis it is hardly surprising that when we compare the countries, as in Table 4.3, we find marked contrasts. Peru gave a larger place to private foreign investment – this fits with the picture we have painted. Colombia relied more heavily on borrowing than did Peru; the consequence was an expansion of the State, seen in the higher ratio of public expenditure to exports, and a *far* higher use of that expenditure in public works, producing the remarkable difference in the ratio of public works expenditure to exports. Whatever the sense in Colombia that there too there was waste and disorganisation in the 1920s, in *relative* terms we see surely a highly proportion of a larger sum going through to answer real development needs. In Peru the relative lack of such needs in relation to the points of expansion in the 1920s, meant that the pattern of corruption and extravagance which developed was not in fundamental contradiction with the economic model.

The contrast is illuminated by occasional fascinating documents appearing in the *Boletin de la Controlaría General* in Colombia, showing a degree of sensitivity to the need for control over expenditure which we have not been able to find in the case of Peru. In one case the accounts of Ulen & Co., working on the Bocas de Ceniza project, were examined with a fine-tooth comb.[37] In another the corruption and inefficiency in the Ferrocarril del Carare project was exposed.[38] Such items, of course, bear eloquent witness to corrupt practices – but the care taken to prevent them contrasts with Peru of the 1920s rather strongly.

The different patterns we have identified had other implications too. First, the Peruvian pattern generated a less rapid rate of growth overall. The increasing share of foreign-owned export sectors, with correspondingly lower proportions of export revenue returned to the local economy, meant that 'returned value'[39] from exports actually stagnated during the 1920s, while the high component of luxury consumption generated by the public spending programme meant a high leakage into imports. We would hypothesise that Colombia gained relative to Peru on both these counts; although in the late 1920s returned value grew less rapidly than total export revenue, as oil exports expanded, still total export growth was faster than for Peru.[40]

A second effect comes from the increasingly small scale[41] and locally controlled[42] nature of the coffee expansion, though it has much to do also with the nature of the international coffee market. This was the emergence of a coffee producers' organisation with a very special relationship to the State. It was clear by the 1920s that some such organisation was needed. First, Brazil had been working hard since the 1900s to introudce some measure of control into the supply side; numerous schemes had been tried and the need to articulate and defend Colombian interests itself required an organisation. But also, as those interests become defined, it became clear that Colombia's future lay in differentiating her product and promoting her higher-quality carefully selected beans. This in turn required organisation: classification schemes and, above all, control to prevent Colombian producers of inferior coffee trying to hide behind her growing reputation.[43] The small-scale nature of the sector, however, led the organisers to feel that the usual voluntary contribution scheme would never work;[44] by 1927 a most unusual organisation had been set up, the Federación Nacional de Cafeteros Colombianos, a private organisation but empowered to collect and spend an export tax on coffee.[45]

Third, it will be clear that the effect of public spending and the expansion of exports was felt throughout many regions of Colombia and in rural areas, while in Peru the effect was much more concentrated and felt much more in urban centres, particularly in Lima. Thus is Colombia it is clear in the qualitative literature, and suggested by the scanty quantitative wage data, that the effect of the public works programme was felt in rural labour markets:[46] the coffee sector complained endlessly of the growing labour shortage and rising wages.[47] There was an increase in wage labour and a distinct move away from traditional systems, especially in coffee regions.[48] Land conflicts became sharper, as the demand for land increased both for productive and speculative reasons.[49] Several authors link these changes, plus the distaste for corruption and 'old-style' politics, to the political change which with the Depression ended more than twenty-five years Conservative rule and produced a Liberal government.[50]

In Peru, corresponding to the pattern we have identified, there were no repercussions observable in rural labour markets: it was, of course, public sector wages which increased.[51] Certainly strong discontent focused around the repression, corruption and favouritism of the Dictatorship, and around reaction against the role of foreign capital; in due course these resentments would lead to more violent and incoherent political change than in Colombia.

But this is to anticipate our story: we must turn now to explore fully what happened as midnight struck and the dance came to an end.

THE EFFECT OF THE DEPRESSION

The first indicator we might look at to measure the effect of the Depression makes it appear that the event was more serious for Peru than for Colombia. The dollar value of exports in the case of Colombia fell 58% from its peak in 1928 to its low point in 1933. For Peru the fall was 72% between 1929 and the most adverse point, which for Peru was 1932. This difference was not a matter of prices; as Figure 4.1 shows, the prices of all their main export commodities moved in a rather similar fashion in the first three years. The difference is principally copper, where there was a heavy fall in volume as well as price, owing to the defensive action of the USA and preferential treatment of the UK and France for their colonial territories.[52]

However, if we explore further we find a number of factors which tend to diminish the difference between the two cases. The first of these is the matter of foreign ownership. While in the boom of the 1920s increasing foreign ownership was a negative factor for Peru, reducing the domestic impact of the export expansion by its effect in lowering returned value, now at least Peru could gain, since much of the impact of the fall in prices fell on the repatriated profits of foreign firms. This was true too for oil and bananas in Colombia, but the share of exports coming from foreign firms was only about one-quarter, while for Peru it was well over one-half.

The second concerns the size of the capital inflow during the 1920s. As we have seen, the loan component of this inflow, compared to exports, was significantly higher in the case of Colombia. Again Peru could benefit from what we have generally found to be a negative factor: the large role of foreign firms.[53] At least with the Depression the reduction in the outflows on account of profits was automatic, and the imports financed by such inflows likewise came to an automatic end. With public sector loans the adjustment lacked these characteristics. Debt had still to be repaid and the higher general demand for imports produced by the model would not adjust downwards quite so naturally.

If we attempt a crude back-of-the-envelope calculation to see the significance of some of these factors we might suggest tentatively that, as shown in Table 4.4, while total exports in dollars fell 58% and 72% for Colombia and Peru respectively, allowing for the different behaviour of returned value might reduce the difference to 56% and 63%.[54] If both countries had paid their full bill on account of amortisation and interest on the external debt in the second year (on which) more anon) – and at the pre-Depression exchange rate – the fall in dollar import capacity might then be of the order of 78% for Colombia, compared with 79% for Peru. It begins to seem more reasonable that the fall in the dollar value of imports was actually rather similar in the two cases.[55]

The more important factor, however, in measuring the medium-

TABLE 4.4   *Peru and Colombia: visible trade and debt service, peak and trough* (US $ m.n.)

| | Colombia | | Peru | |
	1928	1933	1929	1932
Exports	131	54	134	38
Returned value only	(106)[a]	(46)[a]	(63)[a]	(23)[a]
Imports	145	40	76	16
Balance	14	14	+58	+22
Debt service	−16	(−23)[b]	−13	(−14)[b]

[a] See text.

[b] See the text for the nature of this figure. It represents what *would* have been due, in the absence of default and devaluation. The Combination figure includes national, departmental and municipal debt, and that of the Banco Agricola.

SOURCES: Trade: Wilkie (1974); Bertram (1974) appendix G. Debt service: our own estimates from *Extracto Estadístico del Peru*, *Anuario General de Estadística* (Colombia) and *South American Journal*.

term effect and real severity of the Depression can readily be observed from Figure 4.1. We can see at once that for all the severity of the Depression for Peru, it was short-lived, while Colombia had to struggle on with unpromising coffee prices through the decade. The key to Peru's recovery was cotton, this being the principal income-generator in the economy, produced by numerous small farmers, with widespread multiplier effects. There was at least one benefit from world recession for countries lucky enough to own gold deposits, as country after country was forced off the gold standard and the price shot up: both countries were in a position to benefit from this, but Peru also had the advantage of lead and zinc, which both faced favourable prices. Overall these movements were enough actually to allow Peruvian terms of trade to reach again their 1929 level by 1937, while Colombia's were still 25% below their 1928 peak.

THE RESPONSE TO CRISIS

In this section we consider first the immediate reaction, in the first years of the Depression, and then the medium-term recovery process.

The short-term response comprises basically balance-of-payments crisis measures and compression of government spending. The range

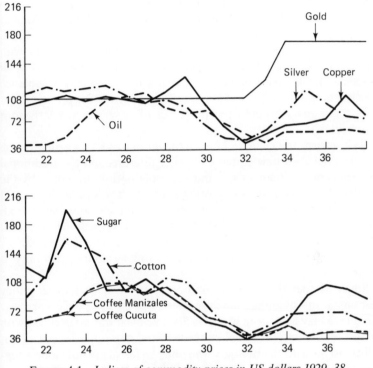

FIGURE 4.1   *Indices of commodity prices in US dollars 1929–38*
(1926–28 = 100)

SOURCES: *Statistical Abstract of the United States, 1944–5*; *Metal Statistics 1938*, pp. 46–53; *Lamborn's Sugar Data*; Beyer (1947).

of choices in regard to the balance of payments included default, abandonment of the gold standard and devaluation, exchange controls and tariffs. It is important to bear in mind that devaluation and default are closely interconnected: once devaluation occurred the incidence of external debt service on internal revenues in domestic currency became so high there was a strong incentive to at least partial default (or multiple exchange rates). (Equally an international context which condoned default encouraged devaluation.)

Before we consider the different policy choices made by our two case studies it is important to recall the context of policy-making. As we mentioned above, in the case of Peru the dictatorship of Leguía produced a ferment of reaction; the association with foreign capital led to a growth of nationalism, not just as embodied in APRA, but on a wider front too. This plus the corruption and elitism and repression of popular movements gave rise not simply to the military uprising of August 1930 which overthrew Leguía and put Sanchez Cerro into office, but to a growth of middle-class and popular discontent with oligarchic rule which underlay three years of almost civil war. 'For all practical effects this struggle was a civil war . . . the acts of violence which it occasioned spread from one end of Peru to the other and for over three years brought the processes of government nearly to a standstill.'[56]

By contrast, the changes being wrought in Colombia with growing conflicts between new coffee and other interests and the traditional politicans and bureaucrats,[57] and the mobilisation promoted by the degree of rural change and development which was occurring, could be accommodated into a relatively peaceful electoral shift from Conservative to Liberal in 1930. The three years which saw such lack of government in Peru were in Colombia years of *relative* peace,[58] with the Liberal Party anxious to use its long-awaited opportunity to make policy.

Small wonder then that we find contrast when we look at policy responses. In Colombia, however 'non-autonomous' public works expenditure may have been in the 1920s, by now it was intertwined with important domestic regional interests whose new importance had not a little to do with the new government. As far as possible a development programme had to be maintained, and for this the government was aware of the importance of foreign capital. It was also acutely aware of people's fear of currency depreciation, given memories of the '1000 days' War'.[59] It therefore fought against default and to maintain the exchange rate, even when almost every other Latin American country had defaulted.[60] In this it was able to benefit from its 'federal structure'; departmental and municipal government went into default at an early stage,[61] but the *national* government was able to point to *national* virtue, conveniently ignoring the fact that the non-national debt was actually the larger of the two. As default became more of a necessity, the government resorted to the issuing of 'scrip' bonds, in lieu of the greater proportion of interest due. The maintenance of the exchange rate was done for two years at considerable cost to the reserves. But the 'reward' was that the USA and other creditors were apparently prepared to take a tolerant view of the alternative measures – exchange controls, multiple exchange rates and tariffs[62] – seeing these as preferable to default and abandonment of the gold standard.

The strength of the regional interests behind public works programmes meant that while of course many had to be abruptly suspended, there were strong efforts made to maintain others. Departmental and municipal governments fought particularly hard, and were able to succeed partly because of the weakness of central control. The legal position was apparently that departments could embark on public works and *tell* the national government what subsidy it now owed them; by 1931 of course such subsidies were simply not being paid – but in the meantime local governments had raised loans on the basis of such anticipated subsidies.[63] By 1931 the national government owed the departments 11 million pesos on account of such subsidies[64] – more than the total of actual departmental expenditure on public works in that year. The municipalities were even less willing to cut and were assisted by private money: in October 1930, for example, the municipality of Cartagena raised a loan from Canadian sources to begin work on an aqueduct.[65] Local initiatives were also important, as the following rather remarkable description suggests:

> Bajo la iniciativa de las respectivas gobernaciones, se agruparon las principales capitalistas de las grandes cuidades, las cuales a través de préstamos permitían al departamento o a los municipios emprender obras que a su vez necesitaban de brazos para llevarse a cabo; así fue como en Cali se adelantaron toda una serie de mejoras . . . en Antioquía esos fondos iba a ayudar a impulsar la construcción de la Carretera al Mar y a la colonisación de Urabá i en Barranquilla igualmente hubo iniciativa similar.[66]

At national level too, while there was stricter adherence to orthodox economics, there were some surprising initiatives. The *Memoria* of the Ministry of Industry records in 1931 its endeavours to reduce unemployment. A system of free railway passes for the unemployed in Bogotá willing to return to agriculture, had been made use of by 1699 persons in its first year of operation.[67] But the more specialised workers were the problem; here the Ministry had made contacts with firms in the private sector, offering them public sector contracts preferentially, 'even when their products could not compete in price with the imported good',[68] if they would take on extra workers.

How far reflationary pressures actually led to state spending itself leading the recovery is hard to analyse precisely given the data problems. CEPAL's claim that the Colombian government played a strong reflationary role from 1929 on is clearly based on incorrect statistics:[69] in fact expenditure did fall more rapidly than prices at both national and departmental levels in 1929 and 1930, leading to a fall in real terms of some 20% compared to 1926–8.[70] Very early however, pressures from the coffee sector and other quarters pushed the government into unorthodoxy: as Ocampo and Montenegro have shown,[71] the monetary data indicate that by 1971 (and well in advance of the Leticia 'War') the government was indeed using deficit financing to expand activity quite strongly. We can conclude that Colombia even in 1929 and 1939 probably avoided a total collapse partly by borrowing from and promoting the private sector, possibly partly by lack of control over regional spending,[72] while from 1931 on policies were decidedly Keynesian – a characteristic accentuated by the Leticia 'War' and fear of invasion by Peru.

Peru, needless to say, was hardly in a position to implement such a set of measures. What we see instead is initially wholesale cuts in public sector programmes, resulting in 1929 in the beginning of the total political chaos we have already described. Once defaulting is legitimised the opportunity is grabbed: Peru is the second country in the continent to default,[73] followed at once by abandonment of the gold standard and abrupt devaluation. Meanwhile, though the public spending pattern of the 1920s implied the need for political change, it also implied its efficacy: at least with the abrupt downfall of all political favourites public spending could be cut overnight, as it were, by wholesale abandoning of projects and above all by the cessation of payoffs and bribes which had comprised so large a part. (Not that the new political system would prove free of such things: but at least in the first instance major economies were possible.) In the first years, 1929 and 1930, real expenditure fell 27% from its 1926–8 level, compared with 20% in Colombia; more importantly, it continued to fall heavily in the following two years.

However, these measures were certainly effective in gaining room for manœuvre: the default alone in 1931 increased import capacity by some 20%. There was thus less need for other measures: exchange controls were not used and although there were some increases in tariffs they did not compare with Colombia.

In the medium term we find a similar pattern. Peru simply waited upon the turnaround in export prices which we saw in Figure 4.1 (p. 95). The following figures giving an index of cotton sector export incomes in constant domestic purchasing power tell their own story:

1928	100
1929	90
1930	76
1931	61
1932	70
1933	128
1934	168
1935	164
1936	178
1937	161

SOURCE: *Extracto Estadístico.*

There was some supply response, particularly in small and medium mining where favourable prices for zinc and lead brought increased production, and in gold, exports of which rose by 162% in value by 1938, compared with 1925–9. But the overall recovery to 80% of the 1929 peak was achieved with an increase in the aggregate quantum index of exports of only 12%.[74]

Government spending recovered with exports in 1933 and continued to rise, though less rapidly than export revenue. The Leticia War may have somewhat increased spending, but not by much.[75]

As to relative prices, Figure 4.2 below shows that the exchange-rate movement gave some additional protection to the industrial sector, but it was slight compared with Colombia. There was rather little pressure for protection; an invasion of Japanese cotton textiles did result in import quotas in 1934,[76] but the new tariff schedule introduced in 1936 had a minimal effect on the overall level of protection.[77]

Colombia, however, could not afford to wait on international prices, as Figure 4.1 revealed above. Only in the case of gold did price developments bring much joy. Colombia's export quantum index had risen by 32% by 1937.[78] Specifically, coffee exports were 2.9 million bags in 1929, and 4.0 million by 1938.[79] Gold exports were 3% of the total 1925–9 and 17% in 1937, providing 28% of the export recovery 1933 to 1937.[80] The increase in gold production was from 143 000 fine oz. in 1928 to 442 000 fine oz. in 1937.[81]

The success in coffee-exporting in the 1930s emphasised and built on the points we have made concerning the 1920s. With the Depression, co-ordination and skilful promotion became even more essential, and the FNCC became ever more solidly established, with an office in Paris by 1931, and international missions to fight tariffs and

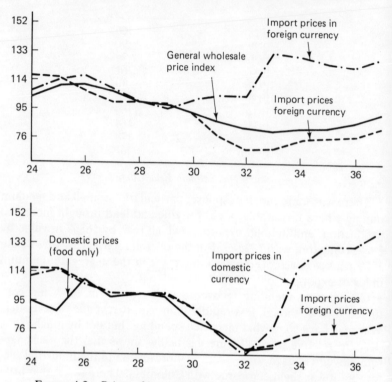

FIGURE 4.2   *Prices of imported and domestically produced goods*

SOURCES: Hunt (1974); *Extracto Estadístico.*

promote Colombian interests. The story of Brazil's attempts to control supply, and Colombia's gains from not co-operating, is well known.[82] At the same time much development occurred on the domestic front: in 1932 the FNCC brought in a classification scheme, credit schemes were developed, warehouses built, etc. The need to oppose foreign interests anxious to infiltrate the FNCC was important in the definition and articulation of group interest.[83] A succession of powerful presidents symbolised the claim made by Palacios, that the Depression wedded the coffee bourgeoisie to the State – with the solidity of a traditional Catholic marriage.[84]

Another story of developing producer co-operation and pressure resulting in an increased role of the State, occurred at this period in the sugar sector, where the Depression is described by Lopez as 'obliging' the producers to associate and count on state help.[85]

The supply response in gold seems to be in part yet another tale of Antioqueño enterprise, but unlike coffee, with growing foreign participation, which reached 44% of production by 1932 and 47% by 1937.[86] With the rise in the gold price countless mines opened up or expanded, chiefly in the department of Antioquia, producing the rather extraordinary rise in output we have cited above.

We have seen that the government sector played a countercyclical role in the early years of the Depression. What is particularly remarkable is the rise in real terms in the *absence* of any recovery in exports at this stage. Then came Leticia: while the Peruvians were relatively unaffected, the incident provoked a strong nationalistic response and patriotic effort in Colombia, with defence loans being oversubscribed and jewellery and ornaments being donated to the effort.[87] Real revenue does not appear to have risen:[88] internal loans financed the gap, in part drawing on private wealth. Once Leticia was over, however, the role of the state was not expansionary. Its importance lay more in the development of its role relative to coffee, than in the macro significance of its spending plans.

But the greater significance of the 'War' was probably that it at last provided an honourable excuse for default and devaluation. Much care was taken in the public relations associated with the default to make the connection clear.[89]

Once the exchange rate could move, then we see in Figure 4.5 how far industry received protection. The gap which opened up between import prices and domestic prices can be seen to be considerably larger than in the case of Peru. More importantly, tariff reforms significantly increased protection on a number of items which led in the acceleration of industrial growth which now occurred. The level of nominal protection for non-traditional manufactures rose from 25% in 1927 to 76% in 1936 (weighting by pre-Depression market size[90]) while in Peru, in textiles for example, nominal tariffs rose from 19 to 20%, and tariffs fell on many other consumer goods.[91] Certain important sectors received a significantly larger increase in effective protection in Colombia than in Peru, notably all kinds of yarn, wool and rayon cloth, and cement.[92]

We can now turn to the indicators of recovery shown in Table 4.5. What Colombia experienced was at least in relative terms an autonomous recovery, in advance of the upturn in export prices, and owing much to the countercyclical effect of government spending. What followed thereafter represented a distinct shift in structure, with the industrial sector leading the recovery and much progress being made

TABLE 4.5   *Measures of medium-term recovery by 1937*
(1926–8 = 100)

	Colombia	Peru
Volume of industrial production	205	n.a.
Volume of cotton textile production	449	126
Export quantum	150	132
Terms of trade	78	106

SOURCES: Industrial production – CEPAL (1957). Textiles – Colombia: Chu (1972); Peru: estimate made by Thorp and Bertram (1978). Trade data – Colombia: CEPAL (1957); Peru: Hunt (1973) and import price index estimated by Thorp and Bertram (1978).

in import-substitution. The policies which aided this formed a logical continuum with the trends of the 1920s, and reinforced those trends – though it must be stressed that some of the contrast with Peru is explained by Colombia's prior underdevelopment of industry rather than by policy. However, if there is a 'learning-by-doing' process in policy-making and economic management, then surely Colombia's path was more rewarding in its elements of unorthodoxy than Peru's instant-default, gaining of room for manœuvre, and move back into a pattern of following exports. This route we see reflected in the relatively slow growth of industry and the few signs of progress in import-substitution. The state sector might actually have grown more than Colombia's if measured by money spent, but in terms of more qualitative and meaningful measures it certainly did not.

WHO BORE THE BURDEN?

The contemporary views of this question are of some interest. For Kemmerer the problem was that those in employment did not bear enough of the burden. An article entitled 'Kemmerer Speaks on Latin America' in July 1931 summarises his view of the adjustment problem: in the 1920s Latin American nations obtained money too easily from US sources, and spent it on high-employment public works schemes which artificially pushed up the price of labour. There was then a ratchet effect: the high wages failed to fall when loans ceased, and unemployment followed. The sudden unemployment and the contraction of government sectors was now making all Latin America politically very unstable.[93]

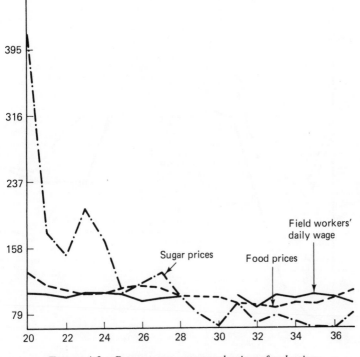

FIGURE 4.3   *Peru: sugar wages and prices, food prices*

SOURCES: Hunt (1974); *Extracto Estadístico*.

A different point was constantly being made, however, in contemporary Colombian sources: there the return migration of labour released from public works and the effect of this on wages were being continually mentioned as the life-saving factors for the coffee sector and the catalyst leading to the opening up of numerous new gold mines.[94] In other words, there was *no* ratchet, and its absence was crucial in smoothing the adjustment process.

Needless to say the data are still too scanty and unreliable to enable a very coherent discussion, but given the importance of the topic it is perhaps worth presenting what figures we have, in the hope of provoking more research.

Data for the cotton, sugar and coffee sectors in Peru and Colombia respectively are shown in Figures 4.3–4.5. It will be seen that both in coffee and cotton there is a remarkably close parallel between com-

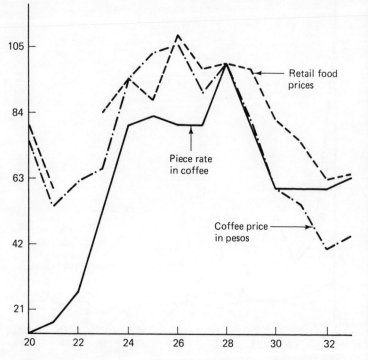

FIGURE 4.4   *Colombia: coffee price, coffee piece rate, food prices*

SOURCES: Coffee price from Beyer (1947), wage rate from Palacios (1979), food prices from Urrutia and Arrubla (1970).

modity prices and money wages in the first few years of the recession, with wages falling ahead of the cost of living.[95] (Sugar is difficult to evaluate because of the gap in the series, but does not appear to fit quite so well.) There is at least a suggestion here then that a substantial part of the burden of adjustment was borne at the lowest level, though this needs far more research, and that downward wage flexibility did smooth the adjustment.

In urban areas in Colombia, and possibly in non-export agriculture, there was les rapid adjustment, with a resulting *rise* in real wages initially as food prices fell, as shown in Table 4.6. Some series suggest no fall, and where there is a decline, it is notable that the decline is not great – considerably less than that in Peru in the recent stabilisation crisis 1976–8. Unfortunately for Peru the urban data are very incomplete. We saw above that in Peru the events of the 1920s

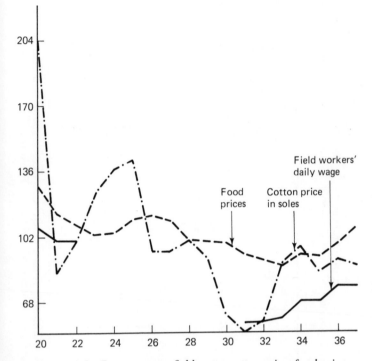

FIGURE 4.5   *Peru: cotton – field wage, cotton price, food prices*
SOURCES: Hunt (1974); *Extracto Estadístico*.

led to a substantial rise in public sector wages; however, there is a ten-year gap in the series 1930–40 so it is hard to judge the effect of expenditure cuts: this is yet another point on which research is needed. Perhaps the most accurate point to make would be that the difficulty of reversing such a rate of increase underlined the necessity of political change, which could permit economies in numbers as well as the other routes we have suggested.

In general then, in urban areas, the burden was borne in part by the *un*employed – quite a considerable number in Peru, smaller in Colombia. It was also borne by those whose wages or accounts in the public sector were simply not paid.

Looking at the other end of the scale it is clear from the fall in imports of consumer goods in both countries that the rich suffered a considerable loss, at least in satisfaction, and clearly too there were

TABLE 4.6 Wage levels in Colombia, nominal and real

	(i) Peon, livestock, Sinú	(ii) Coffee piece-rate	(iii) Peon, coffee mill Medellin	(iv) Textiles av. for Colombia[a]	(v) Cigarette manufacture Medellin	(vi) Peon, public sector, Bogotá	(vii) Teacher, monthly salary
				Wage in pesos			
1928	0.40	1.35	0.79½	1.72	2.17	1.06	61.9
1929	0.45	1.08	0.76	1.87	2.22	1.05	62.0
1930	0.39	0.81	0.67	1.49	2.24	0.99	56.2
1931	0.28	0.81	0.53	1.20	1.92	1.04	44.7
1932	0.25	0.81	0.45	1.01	1.88	1.06	35.7
1933	0.26	0.86	0.51	—	1.84	0.60	35.4
1934	0.34	—	—	—	2.44	0.70	46.7
1935	0.39	—	—	—	2.69	0.80	46.4
				Index of 'real' wages[b]			
1928	100	100	100	100	100	100	100
1929	114	82	97	111	104	101	102
1930	120	73	103	106	126	114	111
1931	94	80	89	94	118	132	97
1932	99	96	90	94	139	160	92
1933	101	99	99		132	88	88
1934	95				125	74	84
1935	105				134	81	81

[a] A series taken from the archives of one leading firm (Fabricato) gives a different picture. It shows a substantial rise, continuing through 1932/3 in real terms. Employment *also* rises. (Data provided by J. J. Echavarria.)

[b] See Thorp (1983) for a full discussion of the various prices series and the problems with them.

SOURCES: (i) comes from the archive of the Sociedad Agricola de Sinú: Hacienda Marta Magdalena 1926–35. This is held in the Archivo Ospina, FAES, Medellín. Our warm thanks go to Juan Manuel Ospina and his staff for their collaboration.

(ii) Palacios (1979).
(iii) *Boletín Estadístico de Antioquia*, various issues.
(iv) Ministerio de Industria, *Revista de Industria*, several issues.
(v) Archives of Coltabaco, Medellín. Data provided by J. J. Echavarría.
(vi) Urrutia and Arrubla (1970).
(vii) *Boletín Estadístico de Antioquia*, various issues.

bankruptcies, particularly among farmers. But – perhaps partly be-cause of lack of availability of imports – interview and personal ar-chive data for Colombia indicate a surprising number of people with money to spend. Given the lack of opportunity for spending it abroad the speed of the urban recovery in Colombia, shown in every index we have looked at so far, and the ability of local government in Col-ombia to continue tapping private savings, begin to make sense.

SOME SPECULATIVE CONCLUSIONS

Our first conclusion underlines the fundamental continuity between the 1920s and the 1930s. This sounds obvious, but it must condition any view of 1929 as a 'turning-point' or of the decade of the 1930s as a 'breakthrough'. We have told two perhaps surprisingly different stories of adjustment: Colombia moved with some degree of coher-ency to a more inward-looking growth-path, aided by reflation: a path with clear implications for the developing role of the State. Peru reacted, rather than moved, and essentially let recovery come of its own accord via international prices. Our analysis has tended to play down the argument that this reflects the lesser severity of the crisis in the case of Colombia, since we have shown that the difference was less great than might be thought at first sight. Rather, we have shown how these two stories flow naturally from the developments of the 1920s. Turning back to explanations emphasised in the literature, we can see that what normally appear as alternative explanations are actually, in the case of Colombia, one and the same. It is precisely the institutional breakthroughs and developments of the 1920s, and the interests which lie behind them, which make it difficult to abandon projects totally in 1929 and lead to countercyclical policy – well be-fore the War provides an excuse for more.

What conclusions can we draw on the comparison between the crises of the 1930s and the 1970s? The difference in the options faced stands out. Default was both more necessary then, since world prices were falling and the burden of debt becoming heavier, in contrast to today – and accepted without sanctions by the international system. This certainly provided a means of off-loading some of the burden of adjustment on to creditors outside the country, and considerably in-creased the chances of autonomous recovery. The story of Colombia is a clear illustration of how the option of more protection and fairly ready response of an incipient industry system was there in the 1930s in a way it could not possibly be forty years later after intensive use of that very route. Instead today apparently the only accepted route is promotion of exports, both traditional and non-traditional. This has strong implications for the role of wages: in the 1930s market forces let wages in primary sectors absorb some of the burden of adjustment, while sticky urban wages were 'only' a fiscal problem, since protection was increasing sharply. Today the significance of real wages in the adjustment process is different and crucial: if the adjustment is to centre around a move into non-traditional exports, with manufactures playing a large role, then the unfortunate logic of the process appears to be that it is precisely urban industrial wages which must be controlled.

NOTES

1. We must stress from the start that we choose the phrase 'would like to' advisedly. The analysis is still at a tentative stage, perhaps particularly with regard to Colombia, where a number of severe data problems are still unresolved. Problems with price series and their implications are discussed elsewhere (Thorp, 1983); other problems arose, for example, over data on the external debt; after several days of effort, we were only moderately consoled to encounter the opinion of Sr Quijano Mantilla, who having struggled with the same problem wrote in *El Tiempo* in 1930 that it was 'even more difficult than that of the famous labyrinth of Crete' (Villegas, 1930, p. 15).
2. Of the limited literature existing on the recovery from the Depression in Colombia, Urrutia emphasises the role of the Leticia War (Urrutia, 1980, p. 181).
3. Calculated from *Anuario Estadístico* and *South American Journal*. For details see Echavarría (1981).
4. Calculated from *Extracto Estadístico*.
5. Seidel (1972) p. 524. Seidel points out that US investment increased more rapidly in those countries Kemmerer visited than in any other Latin American country except Cuba and Venezuela (p. 543).
6. See Rippy (1931) for an account of the history of the negotiations.
7. Thorp and Bertram (1978) pp. 108–10. The issue was one of a disputed property claim in regard to an oilfield, and the taxes due under alternative views of the property rights. It was, of course, to return to Peruvian politics with a vengeance in 1968.
8. For discussion of protection see Thorp and Bertram (1978) chap. 6, and Boloña (1981) for Peru. For Colombia Ospina Vásquez (1955), especially p. 495. He argues that after a period of rapid growth up to 1923, industry lost impetus. Also Palacios (1979) p. 292 on the effect of the exchange rate, and on Ospina Vásquez's *over*-estimate of the importance of protectionism.

9. For Colombia CEPAL's estimates begin in 1925. They show total industrial growth of nearly 5% a year 1925–9, but concentrated in export and construction-oriented activities. Import-substituting sectors grew very slowly. For Peru we have few indications, but they suggest even slower industrial growth (see Thorp and Bertram, chap. 6).
10. Villegas (1930–5), p. 8. Of course such a claim cannot be taken too seriously.
11. Despatch no. 325, 30 July 1929, Mayer to Secretary of State, D.F. 923. 51/433, quoted in Bertram (1974) p. 51.
12. See the sources quoted in n. 8, p. 3 above.
13. Only the 'impuesto de industria y comercio' is legally totally their own. But the revenue from certain other taxes goes to them, and they may be able to vary the rate. And see, for example, *Mensaje del Presidente* (1933) for complaints about governments' illegal levying of taxes.
14. This applies also to public works. In 1926–7 CEPAL estimates departmental and municipal investment expenditure at some 70% of the total. (CEPAL (1957) tables 35 and 36.)
15. Thorp and Bertram (1978) chap. II.
16. Sutton (1929a), (1929b).
17. We owe thanks to Felipe Portocarrero for this list and other helpful material found in his research in the Ministerio de Agricultura archive in Lima.
18. Low (1979) p. 131.
19. Bertram (1974) p. 52.
20. Bertram (1974) p. 52; Labarthe (1933).
21. WCL 15.9.31.
22. Low (1979) p. 131.
23. Carey (1964); Bertram (1974) p. 279.
24. WCL 1.9.25, quoted in Bertram (1974) p. 277.
25. McQueen (1926), Bertram (1974).
26. Carlos Ledgard, quoted in WCL 26.1.32. Of course some productive expenditure did result. The chief example was probably the investment in the Port of Callao – undoubtedly necessary and of real benefit to the country.
27. There was a particularly severe drought in 1926–7, which is described as 'paralyzing the country'. See PRO 1927.
28. Beyer (1974) p. 193.
29. The fact that many projects were not actually completed in the 1920s does not affect our argument: the point is that there were substantial economic interests pushing for and benefiting from these projects.
30. The section Cali-Buenaventura was built before 1915. Law 129 of 1913 decreed the joining of Ferrocarril del Tolima with the Buenaventura line and renamed it Ferrocarril del Pacífico. See *Diario Oficial*, 1913 onwards.
31. *Colombian Trade Review* (March 1926).
32. CEPAL, *Anexo* (1957).
33. A very rough estimate based on the three sources described in the notes to Table 4.3.
34. The question of the direction of causality is fascinating. Palacios de-

scribes the public works as 'non autonomous', i.e. *precipitated* by external financial interests (1979, p. 303). McGreevey has been roundly criticised for too simplistic a suggestion that railways caused coffee expansion (McGreevey, 1971). For our purposes it is enough that the public works were closely tied in to productive interests and needs – but reading, for example, the *Revista Nacional de Agricultura*, the mouthpiece of the Sociedad Nacional de Agricultura, one finds endless examples of pressure and interest in transport expansion – of course not only in the context of coffee, but many products.

35. For example, the Pacific railway connected the sugar-producing area of Valle with the home market, the Canal de Dique opened up the interior to purchasing meat, rice and sugar. The North and North-east railway opened the wheat and fruit regions of Boyaca and Santander. (See *Boletin de Comercio e Industria* and *Boletin de Agricultura*.)
36. Ospina Vásquez (1955) chaps. 5–8.
37. A gentleman travelling from New York to Puerto Colombia made two unauthorised stopovers and had his hotels and taxis disallowed; many wages were challenged as above the maximum, expenses were disallowed because the travel costs were too high, etc. See *Boletin* (June – July 1927).
38. *Boletin de la Controlaria* (February – March 1930).
39. The sum of local expenditures: wages and salaries, taxation, local purchases of materials, local investment in construction, etc.
40. 102% for 1921–9 in dollar value as compared with 65% in the same period for Peru (Wilkie (1974) pp. 263, 276).
41. Beyer (1947) p. 289ff.
42. After the crash of 1920, large US coffee importers moved in to play a big role in coffee *marketing*. But production was always in local hands.
43. Beyer (1947) p. 262.
44. Koffman (1969) p. 1.
45. Beyer (1947) p. 236. The tax was at this stage rather small; the importance lay in its potential significance. Later the resources of this organisation would become very considerable.
46. Beyer (1947) p. 163.
47. The FNCC even petitioned the government at this period to have public works employees made available to them for the coffee harvest (Kalmanovitz, 1978, p. 20).
48. Molina (1974) p. 117.
49. Kalmanovitz (1978) p. 20. Conflicts with foreign companies also became important in certain regions.
50. See Ospina Vásquez (1955) for example.
51. Hunt (1974).
52. Copper was hit especially hard for several reasons. The world's leading copper producers had several times formed cartels to hold prices above market levels, and the latest of these had been successful until late 1929 in holding the world price at record levels (hence Peru's peak in 1929, not 1928 as in Colombia). This had generated a rapid increase in world supply, much of which came from new low-cost producing areas. These new entrants could afford to accept low prices for their copper, and the

slump following the collapse of the cartel was correspondingly a severe one. In May 1932 the USA imposed a prohibitive duty on foreign copper, while shortly afterwards Britain announced preferential tariffs for Empire producers and France for Katanga (see Thorp and Bertram (1978) p. 156).

53. The case for their negative role in this period in Peru is argued in Thorp and Bertram (1978).

54. The calculation for Peru is a serious one – see Bertram (1974) appendix G for the methodology and assumptions. The calculation for Colombia is as yet no more than a guess based on Peruvian experience. The phenomenon of low returned value was accepted by contemporary opinion. See, for example, the view of Esteban Jaramillo in the *Memoria del Ministro de Hacienda 1934*, that returned value from oil was zero (an exaggeration), while in parliament in 1928 an estimate of 50% returned value was given for bananas (*El Tiempo*, 23.8.28).

55. In fact from maximum to minimum, it fell by 80% in both cases. In Colombia imports reached their minimum in 1932, so Table 4.4 shows a fall of 72% 1928–33.

56. Pike (1967) p. 249.

57. See Palacios (1979) pp. 304ff.

58. PRO – *Annual Report, 1930–3*; Molina (1974) vol. II.

59. Drake (1979) stresses the importance of the need for foreign capital. Ocampo and Montenegro (1982) consider the second factor the more important.

60. And when *regional* elites were pressing for national default too. See Echavarría (1981).

61. Lewis (1938).

62. See, for example, the 1931 Report of the Committee of Foreign Bondholders. Exchange control was introduced in November 1931, aimed specifically at the control of gold. See, however, PRO Annual Report 1933 for fascinating insight into the complexity of implementing exchange control when a foreign company controls an export sector – and when in particular the government is in debt to the firm and needs to borrow more.

63. See the 1931 *Presidential Message*, p. 31. In that year legislation was introduced to eliminate such subsidies, following the firm counsel of the Kemmerer Mission.

64. *Presidential Message* (1931) p. 31.

65. *Boletin de Comercio e Industria* (November 1930).

66. *Boletin Nacional de Estadística* (1976) p. 126.

67. *Memoria del Ministerio de Industria* (1930) p. 370.

68. *Memoria del Ministerio de Industria* (1931) p. 244.

69. On this see Thorp (1983). Part of the problem is that the CEPAL GDP deflator exaggerates the fall in prices 1928–32, so producing a spurious 'real' increase. A larger part is that CEPAL uses municipal income and expenditure figures which are budget data, not actual income and expenditure; they show, for example, virtually no fall in nominal terms in either category despite a 20% price fall 1928–30, which cannot be correct.

70. External debt servicing has been excluded throughout in this analysis, on the grounds that to cut it did not have a domestic deflationary impact.
71. Ocampo and Montenegro (1981).
72. A further possibility is the use of 'vales' to pay both bills and wages and salaries, though this is not mentioned in the literature. Alternatively, non-payment of wages would have led to private informal credit markets developing.
73. Lewis (1938) p. 399.
74. Hunt (1973) p. 28.
75. In September 1932 Peruvian forces in the department of Loreto, in the Amazon bason, took over a Colombian customs post at Leticia. Peru's initial line was that it could not do anything in the face of the department of Loreto's decision to keep the post to put right the injustice perpetrated by the original treaty. Colombia eventually mobilised a considerable war effort to resist what it saw as a threat of further invasion; Peru appears to have done rather little; defence spending in 1933 and 1934 barely rose above trend.
76. Thorp and Bertram (1978) p. 190.
77. See Boloña's careful study of protection (1981).
78. CEPAL (1957) table 2.
79. Beyer (1947) p. 356.
80. Urrutia and Arrubla (1970), insert between pp. 108 and 109.
81. *South American Journal*, various numbers.
82. And well told in Beyer (1947).
83. PRO (1932).
84. Palacios (1979) p. 307.
85. A. López, *El Mes Financiero y Económico* (November 1937).
86. H. López Castaño, y M. Arango Restrepo (1977); *Mineria* (February – March 1933; article by J. Ramírez).
87. See *Revista* del Banco de la República (July 1934); *Memoria* of Minister – io de Hacienda, 1934; PRO/F.O. 371/15833/p. 13.
88. For the data see Thorp (1983).
89. See, for example, the *Memorias* of the Ministerio de Hacienda.
90. Chu (1972) p. 21.
91. Boloña (1981) chap. 6.
92. We plan to explore further the question of protection. The only existing study (Chu (1972)) does reveal increases in effective protection in certain products which were important in the expansion of the 1930s, but it calculates the median level of effective protection for non-traditional manufactures in 1927 and 1936 and concludes there is no change over-all. We are doubtful about this in view of the shift in nominal protection, and want to examine his methodology further (e.g. he uses 1945 input – output data, which in certain industries could introduce big distortions).
93. *West Coast Leader* (7 July 1931, p. 14). Kemmerer had fairly recently left Peru, where in three months he had witnessed three armed revolts, various street riots and four presidents (*West Coast Leader*, 21 April 1931, p. 1).
94. See numerous comments in the weekly *Commerce Reports*, in the *Revista del Banco de la República*, in *El Tiempo* etc.

95. But note what a doubtful measure this is here, being an *urban* index and telling us little or nothing about the costs faced by peasant families paid partly in kind, and sometimes producing and even marketing food themselves. A picture of the real burden borne by peasants producing under the complex conditions typical of these countries would seem impossible to get.

REFERENCES

Books and Journal Articles

J. A. Bejarano, 'El fin de la economia exportadora y los origenes del problema agrario', *Cuadernos Colombianos*, nos. 6, 7, 8 (Medellín, 1975).

P. L. Bell, *Colombia: A Commercial and Industrial Handbook* (Washington, 1923).

I. G. Bertram, 'Development Problems in an Export Economy: A Study of Domestic Capitalists, Foreign Firms and Government in Peru, 1919–30', D.Phil. thesis (Oxford, 1974).

B. C. Beyer, 'The Colombian Coffee Industry: Origins and Major Trends', Ph.D. thesis (University of Minnesoto, 1947).

C. Boloña, 'Protection and Liberalism in Peru 1880–1980', D.Phil. thesis (Oxford, 1981).

M. Capuñay, *Leguía: Vida y Obra del Constructor del Gran Perú* (Lima, 1951).

J. C. Carey, *Peru and the United States* (Notre Dame, South Bend, Illinois, 1964.)

Comisión Económica para America Latina (UN, CEPAL) *Anexo: Analísis y Proyecciones del Desarrollo Económico: El Desarrollo Económico de Colombia: Anexo Estadístico* (Mexico, 1957). (Reproduced in part in DANE, *Boletin Mensual de Estadística*, no. 226, May 1970.)

D. S. C. Chu, 'The Great Depression and Industrialisation in Latin America: Response to Relative Price Incentives in Argentina and Colombia 1930–45', Ph.D. thesis (Yale University (unpublished), 1972).

P. Drake, 'The Origins of United States Economic Supremacy in South America: Colombia's Dance of the Millions 1923–33', Wilson Center Working Paper no. 40 (1979).

J. J. Echavarría, 'The History of Colombia's Foreign Debt', unpublished MS (Oxford, 1981).

Federación Nacional de Cafeteros Colombianos, *Mapa Cafetera de Colombia* (Bogotá, 1933).

A. Garcia, *Geografía Económica de Colombia* (Caldas, 1937) (2nd ed, Bogotá, 1978).

A. Garland Duponte, *Lo Que el Oncenio Hizo por el Perú bajo el Mando del Presidente Leguía* (Lima, n.d.).

S. J. Hunt, *Price and Quantum Estimates of Peruvian Exports 1830–1962* (Princeton, N.J., Discussion Paper no. 34, 1973).

—— 'Real Wages and Economic Growth in Peru', Princeton MS (1974).

S. Kalmanovitz, *Desarrollo de la Agricultura en Colombia* (Medellín, 1978).

B. E. Koffman, 'The National Federation of Coffee Growers of Colombia', Ph.D. thesis (University of Virginia, 1969).

P. A. Labarthe, *La Política de Obras Públicas del Gobierno de Leguía* (Lima, 1933).

C. Lewis, *America's Stake in International Investments* (Washington, D.C., 1938).

A. López, *Problemas Colombianos* (Paris, 1927).

Hugo López, 'La inflacion en Colombia en la década de los veinte', *Cuadernos Colombianos*, no. 5 (Medellín, 1975).

H. López Castaño and M. Arango Restrepo, *La Pequeña y Mediana Minería Aurifera en el Bajo Cauca y Nechi*, C.I.E. (Medellín, 1977).

A. M. Low, 'Agro-exporters as Entrepreneurs: Peruvian Sugar and Cotton Producers 1890–1945', D.Phil. dissertation (Oxford, unpublished, 1979).

W. McGreevy, *An Economic History of Colombia 1845–1930* (Cambridge, 1971).

C. A. McQueen, *Peruvian Public Finance*, US Department of Commerce Trade Promotion Series, no. 30 (Washington, 1926).

G. Molina, *Las Ideas Liberales en Colombia 1915–34* (Bogotá, 1974).

J. F. Normano, *The Struggle for South America* (Boston, 1931).

J. A. Ocampo and S. Montenegro, 'La Crisis Mundial de los Años Trienta en Colombia', *Desarrollo y Sociedad*, no. 7 (January 1982).

L. Ospina Vásquez, *Industria y Protección en Colombia 1810–1930* (Medellín, 1955).

M. Palacios, *El Café en Colombia 1850–1970: Una Historia Económica, Social y Política* (Bogotá, 1979).

F. Pike, *The Modern History of Peru* (Praeger, 1967).

PRO, *Annual Reports* (different years), London.

J. F. Rippy, *The Capitalists and Colombia* (New York, 1931).

R. Seidel, 'American Reformers Abroad. The Kemmerer Missions in South America, 1923–1931', *Journal of Economic History*, vol. xxxii, no. 2 (1972).

C. W. Sutton (1929a) 'El Projecto de Irrigación de Olmas o Lambayeque', mimeo (Lima, August 1929).

——— (1929b) Letter of September 1929, archive of Ministerío de Fomento (Lima, 1929).

R. Thorp, 'Price and Fiscal Data in Colombia in the 1920s and 1930s', unpublished working paper (Oxford, 1983).

R. Thorp and G. Bertram, *Peru 1890–1977: Growth and Policy in an Open Economy* (London, 1978).

M. Urrutia (ed.), *Ensayos sobre Historia Económica* (Bogotá, 1980).

M. Urrutia and M. Arrubla, *Compendio de Estadísticas Históricas de Colombia* (Bogotá, 1970).

J. Villegas, 'Recopilacion de articulos de prensa Colombiana', mimeo (DANE, *without date*). (Note dates in references refer to the years the collection refers to.)

J. White, 'The United Fruit Company in the Santa Marta Banana Zone, Colombia: Conflicts of the 1920s' (B.Phil. thesis Oxford, 1971).

J. W. Wilkie, *Statistics and National Policy*, Supplement 3 to UCLA Statistical Abstract of Latin America (Los Angeles, 1974).

Periodicals, Journals, Statistical Series, Official Papers

Anuario Estadístico, 1915–27; *Anuario General de Estadística*, 1928, Bogotá.
Boletin de Agricultura, Min. de Industria, monthly, Bogotá, 1927–35.
Boletin de la Controloría General, Bogotá.
Boletin de Comercio e Industrias, Bogotá, monthly.
Boletin Estadística de Antioquia.
Boletin Nacional de Estadística, Bogotá.
Colombian Trade Review 1921–9, London, weekly.
Commerce Reports, USA, Department of Commerce, Washington (weekly).
Desarrollo y Sociedad, CEDE, Bogotá.
Diario Oficial (1920–), Bogotá, weekly.
El Mes Financiero e Económico, Bogotá.
El Tiempo, daily newspaper, Bogotá.
Extracto Estadístico del Perú, Lima: Direccion Nacional de Estadística 1918–43; subsequently *Anuario Estadístico del Perú*.
Lamborn's Sugar Data, New York, annual.
Memoria del Ministerio de Industria, Bogotá.
Memoria del Ministro de Hacienda, Bogotá.
Memoria del Ministro de Obras Publicas (1925), Bogotá.
Mensaje Presidencial, Bogotá.
Metal Statistics, 44th annual issue 1947–56, Frankfurt.
Minería, Asociación Colombiana de Mineros, 1932–, Medellín.
South American Journal, Buenos Aires.
Revista del Banco de la República, Bogotá (monthly).
Revista de Industrias, Min. de Industria, Bogotá.
Revista de Ministerio de Obras Publicas, Bogotá.
Revista Nacional de Agricultura, SNA, Bogotá.
Statistical Abstract of the United States, Washington, DC, US Department of Commerce, 1944–5.

5 The Colombian Economy in the 1930s

JOSE ANTONIO OCAMPO

THE EXTERNAL SHOCK

By Latin American standards Colombia was a late-comer to the age of export-led growth. After a period of stagnation in the first half of the nineteenth century the country went through a stage of slack and unstable export growth in the second half, which induced a slow internal transformation of the economy. However, by the early twentieth century, real per capita exports were only 36% higher than at the end of the colonial period and the country had, together with Haiti, the lowest indices of per capita foreign trade, foreign investment and railroads in Latin America (Ocampo, 1982).

After the Thousand Days War (1899–1902), the last and bloodiest of the nineteenth-century civil wars, political stability was guaranteed by a moderate elite in control of the two major political parties. Export-led growth accelerated on the basis of peasant coffee production and the enclave sectors. Both forms of export development represented a break with the unstable forms of production for the foreign market which had prevailed in the nineteenth century. The coffee culture was rapidly assimilated in the peasant regions of *Antioqueño* migration on the western side of the country. On the other hand, the gold, platinum and banana enclaves that had developed in the last years of the nineteenth century grew and were consolidated in the first decade of the twentieth century, followed in the 1920s by the petroleum enclave. As shown in Figure 5.1, export growth was fast in the two and a half decades before the 1929 crisis, the export quantum increasing at an average rate of 7% between 1905/9 and 1925/9.

The explosion of modern capitalist development was felt particu-

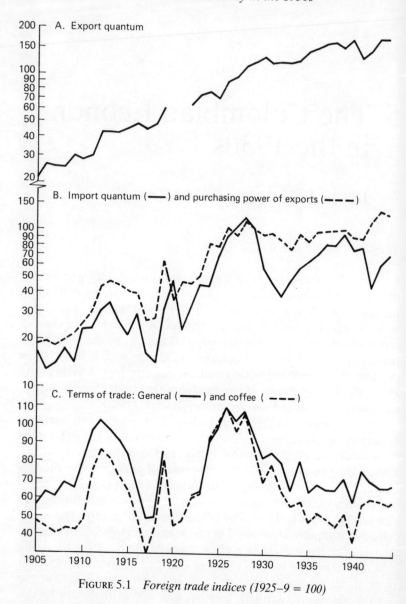

FIGURE 5.1 *Foreign trade indices (1925–9 = 100)*

larly strongly in the hectic 1920s, when export expansion and an improvement of the terms of trade were accompanied by the indemnity paid by the USA for the independence of Panama and a significant inflow of foreign capital (Figure 5.2), mainly in the form of public

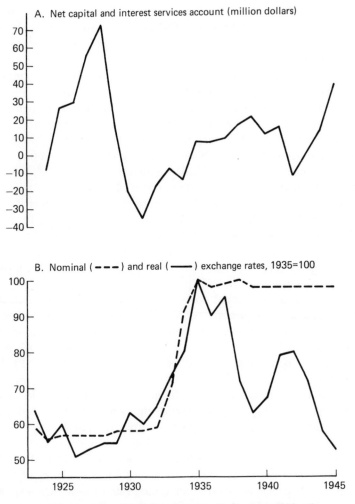

FIGURE 5.2 *Other foreign sector indicators, 1923–45*

debt. At the same time crucial institutional reforms in the financial and fiscal systems were introduced by the Kemmerer mission during the Pedro Nel Ospina Administration (1922–6). The joint effect of institutional transformation, export growth and fiscal expansion was a period of substantial prosperity, inflation and corruption. From 1925 to 1928, when the first national accounts are available, Gross Domestic Product (GDP) increased at a rate of 8.6%. Although some industrial sectors did not do particularly well during this period (textiles in particular) there are clear indications that economic prosperity was reflected in an investment boom in the modern manufacturing sector in the second half of the 1920s (CEPAL, 1957, p. 250; Montenegro, 1982, table A–2).

The Great Depression thus reached Colombia at a time when modern capitalism was rapidly consolidating itself in the country, a process which some other Latin American nations had lived through decades before. The first signs of the crisis were felt rather soon, in the second half of 1928, when long-term financial flows were suddenly interrupted. These flows had been increasing at an exponential rate since 1924, reaching a peak of US $69.8 million during the first half of 1928. In the second half the country received only US $5.6 million and in 1929 US $9.9 million. Aside from the effects of restrictive monetary policies in the USA from mid-1928 on, the reasons for this sudden interruption of capital flows were the disputes between the USA and Colombia on oil concessions and the rationalisation of public works policy (Patiño, 1981, pp. 125–44; Echavarría, 1982; Rippy, 1970, pp. 202–9).

The interruption of capital flows was followed in the latter part of 1928 by a fall in coffee prices. The fall continued throughout 1929 and was very sharp after October, when the world banking crisis, coupled with the deflationary policy of the federal government of Brazil, put an end to the 'permanent defence' of coffee prices by the São Paulo government.

As shown in Figures 5.1 and 5.2 the major effect of the world crisis on Colombia was the sharp reversal of the capital account. Indeed, from the point of view of the export quantum and purchasing power the crisis was not severe at all. Real coffee exports continued to increase in the 1930s at a rate which was only slightly below that which had been typical up to the 1920s (5% v. 7.2%), while from 1929 to 1941 gold production boomed at an annual rate of 14%. The expansion of coffee and gold exports was more than sufficient to counteract the poor evolution of oil, bananas and minor exports. On the other hand, the expansion of the aggregate export quantum counterbalanced the deterioration of the terms of trade: export purchasing power declined only slightly during the first years and soon recovered the exceptional levels of the late 1920s.

Despite the positive evolution of exports, the contraction of capital imports was strongly felt internally. The sharp internal contraction of demand was particularly reflected in imports, which declined 68% between 1928 and 1932. The contraction of imports was mainly the result of the decline of investment and textile consumption. It was helped by the reduction of excess inventories of imported goods, the paralysation of commercial credit and the protective effect of specific import taxes. However, even the sharp induced contraction of imports was insufficient to correct the balance-of-payments deficit. The tariff reforms of 1931 contributed to the decline in import demand, but only direct foreign-exchange rationing put an end to the decline of international reserves in late 1931. Even then, imports did not recover immediately, since the government maintained foreign debt payments during the first months of exchange controls. When this policy was abandoned imports recovered, reaching by the late 1930s levels which, in historical perspective, were quite acceptable for Colombia (Figure 5.1B). By then they were also helped by inflows of direct foreign capital investment into the oil sector. The rapid recovery of real imports after the sharp contraction of the first years, together with important changes in the composition of imports, were quite favourable to rapid growth in the modern manufacturing sector, as we will see below.

COLOMBIA AND THE INTERNATIONAL COFFEE MARKET

The evolution of the international coffee market in the 1920s and 1930s was largely determined by Brazilian intervention (Delfim Netto, 1979, chaps 2–3; Peláez, 1973; Rowe, 1932; Wickizer, 1942, chap. 10). Production capacity increased in the late 1910s, induced by high prices associated with the second valorisation scheme of the São Paulo government, the frost of 1918 and the post-First World War boom. The effects of these plantings were felt only in the mid-1920s, as is typical in the traditional forms of coffee culture. The third valorisation scheme of the federal government of Brazil in 1921, together with the policy of 'permanent defence', adopted by the São Paulo government in 1924, contributed to the exceptional price levels of the 1920s. World production capacity increased from 3 209 million trees in 1926 to 5 014 million in 1933 (Wickizer, 1942, p. 117); plantings were particularly extensive in Brazil during the 1927/8 harvest, due to the excessive liquidity of planters. Although the following harvest was not exceptional the São Paulo government was unable to sell the stocks accumulated in the previous year. Faced with excess inventories, an exceptional harvest under way and the financial difficulties created by the world banking crisis and the deflationary policies of the federal government, the policy of 'permanent defence' collapsed in October 1929. Brazilian coffee prices tumbled, bringing down Colombian prices at a slower rate; the premium of Colombian over Brazilian prices, which was decreasing before the crisis, thus increased rapidly in the months following October, but was soon back at more normal levels.

The evolution of the international coffee market was determined in the 1930s by two major factors: changes in world demand and enormous Brazilian overproduction. There was a continuation of the autonomous displacement of world demand towards soft and particularly Colombian coffees which had been typical of world and especially US demand since the early part of the century. Colombia had thus no difficulty in disposing of all her production in the world market at prices above those of Brazilian coffees. In fact, the differential in favour of Colombian coffees was normal during most of the 1930s, while the elasticity of substitution between Colombian and Brazilian coffees was low (-0.5 in the US market) and can hardly explain any important changes in relative demands (Delfim Netto, 1962, pp. 715–22). Besides, bilateral trade agreements, especially with Germany, were quite favourable to Colombia during the Depression. Exports to Germany, some of which were re-exported to other European countries, increased from an annual average of 45 000 bags in 1925/9 to 592 000 in 1935/9, accounting for 36% of the expansion of Colombian exports during the period.

Under these conditions, overproduction was mainly a Brazilian affair and a serious one indeed, given the magnitude of excess capacity created in the late 1920s. Three exceptional harvests in 1929/30, 1931/2 and 1933/4, pushed the Brazilian government into very active intervention in the market. Brazilian production between 1929/30 and 1933/4 was 119.2 million bags, of which only 76.7 were disposed of; to the excess of 42.5 million bags thus resulting, we have to add 10.3 million accumulated in the interior of Brazil in mid-1929 due to previous defence policies (Kingston, 1973, table 1; IIA, 1934, table VIII). It was politically unviable, and possibly economically so, given the characteristics of coffee investment and demand, to manage such an overproduction through the market. The Brazilian government thus decided to intervene and destroy coffee from mid-1931 on.

In this way the federal government corrected the errors of the 'permanent defence' policy of the São Paulo government in the 1920s. Colombia was favoured by such a development, both in the 1920s, when the São Paulo policy pushed up international prices, and in the 1930s, when the federal government of Brazil defended them in the downswing. Brazil could not accept such externalities and thus attempted to reach an international agreement early in the crisis. However, neither the trends in the world coffee market nor internal conditions in Colombia were favourable to an international pact (Ocampo and Montenegro, 1982, part II; Lleras, 1978; FAO, 1947, pp. 481–504; Beyer, 1947, chap 19; Palacios, 1979, pp. 319–23).

The first attempt was made at the São Paulo International Coffee Congress of May 1933, without success. Two years later, in the London Economic and Monetary Conference, the Colombian delegate, Alfonso López Pumarejo, was more inclined to an agreement. He thought that there were sufficient economic reasons for an international pact (the complementarity of Colombian and Brazilian coffees), although at the time his reasons were political: the support of Brazil for the Colombian claims in the dispute with Peru (Tirado, 1981, pp. 83–4). The head of the National Federation of Coffee Growers, Mariano Ospina Pérez, wrote a strong rebuttal of López in November 1933, arguing that changes in world demand were favouring Colombia and that a peasant culture meant that the country was very strong in case of a price war, since monetary costs were minimal and peasant farming was almost self-sufficient in basic necessities; besides, he argued, peasant coffee culture was democratic and should thus be encouraged; under these conditions there were no reasons for controlling production or exports (Ospina Pérez, 1934, pp. 49–69).

When López was elected president in 1934 the internal balance of forces was temporarily favourable to an agreement. In the Seventh National Coffee Congress in 1935 the government insisted on an equal representation of the government and the coffee-growers in the National Coffee Committee, and gave the president the power to elect the head of the Federation of Coffee Growers. The new head of the Federation, Alejandro López, gave the lead in a more significant intervention in the internal market, where since 1929 intervention had been limited to the regulation of local markets. He also called a Pan-American Coffee Congress in Bogotá in October 1936, in which an agreement between Colombia and Brazil was reached. On 3 December a secret pact was signed in New York, establishing minimum prices for Santos 4 and Manizales coffees (10.5 and 12 cents per pound) and a minimum differential (1.5 cents).

The Federation intervened in the market on a large scale in the six months following the Bogotá conference, purchasing 8% of the harvest at a cost of 6 million pesos. However, the policy soon faced very difficult financial conditions. The total income of the Federation, coming mainly from coffee taxes, was at the time less than one million pesos, while the central bank, which at first collaborated in the intervention policy, began to argue that the credits granted to accumulate stocks were inflationary. The financial burden was increased early in 1937 due to the paralysation of exports to Germany, while a new bilateral trade agreement was negotiated. Faced with an increase in Santos 4 prices above the minimum level in February, the Federation argued that it could not defend the differential; moreover, when prices fell soon afterwards, it was out of funds, and had to stop purchasing coffee. A very heated debate against the international agreement then took place in the midst of an overall political crisis. Mariano Ospina Pérez, then conservative candidate for the presidency, was the leader of the opposition against the interventionist policy. In the following months the policy was continued at a slower pace, coffee taxes increased and new credits from the central bank extended to the Federation. However, the differential between Manizales and Santos 4 remained less than half a cent. In Colombia the political climate was not favourable to more intervention, while in Brazil the reduced price differential was seen as a sure sign of further displacements of Brazilian coffees from the market. Besides, after seven years of almost unilateral defence of coffee prices, some sectors in Brazil were in favour of stronger competition in the international market. The negotiations for the extension of the international agreement started badly in the Havana Conference in August and broke off finally two months later in New York. In early November Brazil eliminated the restrictions of coffee exports and reduced export taxes, while maintaining the policy of destruction of excess stocks.

The 'coffee war', as this policy was called, did not affect Colombia significantly. After an initial fall Colombian coffee prices recovered, while her share in US imports (which represented 77% of Colombian exports in 1935–9) remained at about 22%. Brazil gained a small share of the US market from the Central American producers at the expense of a significant fall in relative prices. None the less, the coffee war clearly manifested that overproduction continued to be the major feature of the world coffee economy in the late 1930s. It is thus not surprising that coffee prices did not participate in the world price recovery of the second half of the 1930s. The real price of coffee thus tended to deteriorate as the decade progressed (Figure 5.1c).

Soon afterwards the coffee crisis became acute, as the world political situation grew worse and the Second World War broke out. The

Colombian terms of trade fell in 1940 to levels significantly lower than those of the 1930s. Given world political conditions, pressure by the USA, the major consuming market even at peacetime and the magnitude of the crisis, the first Inter-American Coffee Agreement was signed in November 1940. The recovery of world coffee prices soon ensued.

ECONOMIC POLICY

Regardless of the important institutional reforms of the 1920s, modern state interventionism was not firmly established before the crisis. State support was mainly limited to the development of infrastructure and moderate protectionism. The State had intervened in the development of infrastructure since the colonial period. Intervention was made more necessary by the high costs of railroad developments in the nineteenth century, and was much in evidence in the early twentieth century. On the other hand, after a period of domination of liberal ideas on the international division of labour, a mixture of protectionism for some domestic industries and export-orientedness gained the ideological upper hand in the final decades of the nineteenth century. Protectionism was further encouraged by the Reyes government in the first decade of the twentieth century, at a time of deep economic crisis. Modern manufacturing production had started in the late nineteenth century, and on a more important scale in the first decade of the twentieth century and the First World War. Developments in manufacturing industry gave new force to protectionist ideas, which continued to coexist with export-orientedness. The dominant ideology was thus the exploitation of all market opportunities, both in the international and internal markets, as well as in primary and secondary production. The free-trade Kemmerer proposals were not accepted in the 1920s, the only tariff reductions adopted in the decade being the Emergency Law of 1927 by which tariffs were reduced on agricultural products to control inflation (Ospina Vasquez, 1955; Bejarano, 1979).

On the monetary front the country had experienced a fiduciary system at the end of the nineteenth century which evolved into hyperinflation during the Thousand Days War. This traumatic experience had a determining influence on monetary developments in the first four decades of the twentieth century. Reyes's attempt to reconstruct a central bank in the first decade was defeated and a constitutional amendment in 1910 forbade fiat money as a 'civil right'. The creation of the Banco de la Republica in 1923 was possible only on the condition that it clung to the gold standard and the government had minority representation on the Board. Monetary policy was thus very orthodox, both in the 1920s and the early part of the crisis. Moreover, in the early 1930s all proposals for monetary expansion had to be justified on the basis that they did not represent a return to fiat money (Patiño, 1981, pp. 365–70, 517–45, 558–9). The inflation which resulted from expansionary policies resurrected the fears of paper money and led to stabilisation policies soon afterwards, and a return to the ideals of 'healthy money' during the López and Santos Administrations (1934–42).

Regardless of the constraints imposed by the fear of a fiduciary system the government was for a time forced by the strength of the crisis and political pressure to implement expansionary fiscal and monetary policies. They were part of a larger package of interventionist policies, which strengthened protectionism through tariffs and import restrictions, led to the first modern devaluation, increased intervention in the banking sector and direct regulation of some productive activities. After 1934, although monetary, fiscal and foreign-exchange policies were principally aimed at stability, import restrictions and intervention in the banking and productive sectors were increased. In addition, a whole new series of interventionist policies were implemented: direct taxation as a major fiscal source, redistribution of income through government expenditure, social reform (both in the rural and urban sectors) and direct promotion of new industries, among others. Indeed, a whole new conception of the State was developed, based both on the economic and social reality and the change in the dominant ideology of the Liberal Party in power. According to the concept of a 'national economy', developed at the time by major representatives of the Liberal Party, a country such as Colombia could not rely on primary production for the world market, characterised by deteriorating terms of trade and control by international monopolies, and had to promote growth through import-substituting manufacturing and other forms of production for the internal market; these ideas were part of a larger conception of the need for a type of 'national capitalism' conscious of its 'social responsibilities' (Vargas, 1938, pp. 151–7; Lleras, 1946, pp. 52–3).

In our discussion of the development of economic policies during the crisis and the 1930s we will differentiate four periods: the orthodox management of the crisis (1929–31), the implementation of anti-cyclical policies (1931–4), the stabilisation policies of the reformist López Administration (1934–7) and the defensive policies in the face of a deepening coffee crisis (1937–41). Our analysis stops in 1941, when the industrial boom of the 1930s ended, the economy started to face supply problems associated with war import restrictions and economic policy became increasingly concerned with monetary expansion associated with the accumulation of international reserves.

Orthodox Management of the Crisis (1929–31)

International reserves peaked in July and the money supply in December 1928. Starting in 1929 the balance-of-payments deficit generated a strong monetary contraction (Table 5.1). From December 1928 to December 1931 international reserves fell 78.7%, central bank bills in circulation 63.4% and the money supply 48.6%. Price deflation came with a lag and was equally dramatic. Central bank policy was extremely cautious. Although its own reserve ratio fell it remained always significantly above legal requirements. The discount rate was maintained at 8–9%, above the pre-Depression level (7%). Discounts to member banks peaked very early in the crisis: they increased from $4.3 million in July 1928 to $17 million in March 1929, a level which was surpassed only during the September 1931 crisis. During most of the downswing the discount policy was thus contractionary. On the other hand, credits to the national government increased by less than $2 million, as the 1930 Kemmerer reforms increased slightly the legal availability of such loans. The expansion generated by these credits was minimal.

Within orthodox principles the contraction was well-managed. The public never lost confidence in the central bank or the financial system and there were no bank failures. Private banks adopted a very cautious policy, which further encouraged monetary contraction but allowed them to survive the crisis.

Following orthodox principles, fiscal contraction was equally dramatic. With the interruption of capital inflows and the fall in import duties collected, government expenditure contracted dramatically (Table 5.2). The new Olaya government (inaugurated August 1930) insisted on the punctual payment of the foreign debt, in the hope of getting new loans and direct capital investments. The foreign debt policy was extremely contractionary, as the government was unable to get significant amounts of new financing. The resulting contraction was especially acute in the case of national government in-

TABLE 5.1 Monetary indicators, 1928–41

	Central Bank bills in circulation (million pesos)	Money supply (million pesos)	Growth in money supply and contributing factors[a]				Inflation rate (foodstuffs)	
			Total	International reserves	Government deficit[b]	Private credit policy[c]	Unweighted	Weighted
1928	56.2	110.6						
1929	39.1	80.9	−26.8%	−31.8%	3.4%	8.2	− 0.4%	− 8.6%
1930	27.4	64.2	−20.7	−15.7	2.4	− 7.0	−20.7	−24.2
1931	20.6	56.9	−11.5	−25.8	6.1	8.9	−13.5	−18.6
1932	22.5	68.2	19.9	6.8	17.7	− 9.6	−23.3	−15.3
1933	31.8	84.6	24.1	− 0.7	7.3	19.0	5.0	1.4
1934	40.1	100.7	19.0	− 0.9	4.7	10.4	38.8	41.5
1935	43.2	103.2	2.5	− 1.8	− 3.5	1.0	4.3	− 0.5
1936	57.2	124.2	20.3	11.4	− 0.6	4.8	6.0	
1937	53.0	128.0	3.1	6.6	0.6	9.3	3.3	
1938	58.3	141.7	10.7	10.5	2.9[d]	0.2	12.5	
1939	60.4	146.3	3.3	− 4.5	2.8	3.9	7.1	
1940	62.3	158.3	8.2[e]	1.0	11.1	4.4	− 5.6	
1941	74.4	176.0	11.2	− 4.5	3.4	9.5	− 0.9	

[a] Contribution to the growth in the money supply = multiplier × change in the monetary base due to the factor indicated as % of money supply.

[b] Loans to the national government net of deposits of the government in the central bank.

[c] Loans and discounts to member banks; 1932–5: also purchase of government bonds and investments of central bank in Banco Central Hipotecario.

[d] Excludes deposits for $13 million due to distribution of profits from devaluation.

[e] Contraction via non-monetary liabilities equivalent to 10.6% of money supply.

SOURCES: *Revista del Banco de la República*; Ocampo and Montenegro (1982) table 8.

TABLE 5.2   National fiscal indicators, 1926–41
(million current pesos)

| | Current income | Expenditure, net of debt payments | | Fiscal surplus (+) or deficit (−) | |
| | | Accruals | Payments in the year corresponding to current and previous year's budgets | (1−2a) | (1−2b) |
	1	2a	2b	3a	3b
1926	60.6	61.1		− 0.5	
1927	63.4	78.4		−15.0	
1928	75.5	107.4		−31.9	
1929	75.2	73.3		1.9	
1930	49.4	51.3		− 1.9	
1931	43.7	42.5		1.2	
1932[a]	41.5	34.4		7.1	
1933	49.7	56.6		− 6.3	
1934	63.6	61.6		2.0	
1935	72.3	58.0		14.2	
1936	85.1	69.3		15.8	
1937	98.2	80.6	78.9[b]	17.6	19.2
1938	98.9		97.2		1.7
1939	110.1		99.7		10.4
1940	97.9		111.2		−13.2
1941	108.8		126.5		−17.8

[a] Since 1932 it includes current income (net of transfers to the nation) and expenditure of Consejo Administrativo de los Ferrocarriles Nacionales.
[b] Including a $3.6 million difference between accruals in 1936 according to Anuarios of 1936 and 1938.

Sources: Anuario General de Estadística (AGE), 1932–41.
Series (2a): 1926–31, AGE 1932; 1932–34: AGE 1936; 1934-37: AGE 1938.

vestment, which was practically non-existent by the beginning of 1931. Indeed, the contraction was stronger than shown in the figures of Table 5.2, since Treasury payments were delayed, such delayed payments reaching more than $20 million in 1930.

Fiscal contraction was equally strong at the departmental level, especially in those departments which had relied heavily on foreign loans in the late 1920s. For the most important of them (Antioquia, Cundinamarca and Valle) expenditures excluding debt payments decreased 66% between the fiscal years 1928/9 and 1931/2.

During this phase anti-cyclical policies were adopted only on the tariff front. There was from the beginning of the crisis strong pressure to protect agriculture by repealing the Emergency Law of 1927. The Congress finally did so on 8 January 1931. In May a new tariff code was adopted, benefiting both manufacturing and agriculture. Protectionism was not seen as a break with orthodoxy since, as we saw, it was already embedded in the dominant ideologies before the Depression.

Pressure was mounting before September 1931 for a more active anti-cyclical policy. From 1930 on, some former ministers of finance were pushing for more expansionary credit management, including loans from the central bank to the national government. Early in 1931 a Congress Commission asked the government to implement such a policy (Patiño, 1981, pp. 303–6, 363–72, 389–90). Coffee-growers were particularly interested at this stage in credit policy. They asked for the creation of an agrarian bank, and preferential treatment for the bonds issued by the Federation warehouses in the discount policy of the central bank. Such a treatment was in fact granted, by establishing a lower discount rate for them in November 1929 and direct discount for the public holding those bonds in October 1930.

Anti-cyclical Policy (1931–4)

The single event which impelled a change of policy was the sterling devaluation of 4 September 1931. There was a run on the scarce reserves of the central bank, which forced upon the government a change in policy. Authorised by the Congress to act on an emergency basis, it established exchange controls on 24 September. Having direct control over international reserves there was now no reason to follow orthodox rules regarding monetary and fiscal policy. In the following months the central bank rapidly increased its loans to the national government. They grew from 2.6 million pesos in August

1931 to 14.4 million in mid-1932, turning for a time into the major source of growth in the money supply (Table 5.1). Most of these credits were probably used to reduce the backlog of payments of the Treasury and are thus not reflected in the fiscal accruals of 1932 (Table 5.2 above). Monetary expansion to finance the national government was not as rapid in the following years. However, the War with Peru accelerated the recovery of fiscal expenditures in 1933 and 1934, which were partly financed by the central bank.

Private credit policy also became expansionary behind exchange controls. Three new government institutions were created: the Agrarian Bank (Caja Agraria), the Central Mortgage Bank and the Colombian Credit Corporation. Due to the extremely conservative policy of private banks the former two were the major source of credit expansion even in the mid-1930s. Both the Central Mortgage Bank and the Colombian Credit Corporation were created to purchase the risky portfolios of private institutions. The government also established maximum interest rates for private loans, extended the terms of all credits and allowed debtors to pay half of their obligations in mortgage and government bonds at face value. These bonds could be purchased early in 1932 at 50%; although they immediately rose in price, the policy was in fact equivalent to a 20% reduction in the capital value of all debts. The central bank was forced to rediscount half of the bonds received by the banks as debt payments. Discount rates were also reduced, starting September 1931, reaching a minimum by mid-1933: 4% for ordinary and 3% for preferential discounts (warehouse bonds). Finally, in mid-1933 the capital value of all mortgage loans was reduced 40% by agreement with all banks. This policy, which was strongly pushed by the coffee-growers, meant in fact the liquidation of private mortgage banks and the purchase of their portfolios by the Agrarian Mortgage Bank.

The monetary effect of the credit policy was counteracted at first by the very conservative management of private banks. As shown in Table 5.1, in 1932 the decline in discounts to member banks, reflecting their own demands, prevailed over the expansionary elements of the private sector credit policy. However, in 1933 and 1934 this policy became the major source of monetary expansion.

Despite growing pressures foreign debt and exchange-rate policies were still very conservative for a time after September 1931. Due to the loss in foreign reserves in the month following the establishment of exchange controls, the government decided in October that it would pay the foreign debt of departments and municipalities with a scrip issue; departmental and municipal governments were obliged to deposit in the central bank the amounts due in Colombian currency. The departments and municipalities decided in April 1932 to suspend such deposits, since they were suffering the disadvantage of paying the debt with none of the benefits, and they were in desperate fiscal condition. The national government suspended these scrip issues, but decided that it would continue to pay the interest on its own debt as usual and issue scrip to pay the amortisations due. By these means payments on the long-term foreign public debt were reduced from 16 to 5 million pesos in 1932. The making of these payments was strongly opposed, but the government defended it on the basis that the country had to maintain its good reputation in the international financial market. None the less, forced by the fiscal conditions created by the war with Peru, it suspended all payments early in 1933. The interest and amortisations due in 1933 and 1934 were still paid with scrip issues. A total moratorium was only declared in 1935, and even then the nation continued to pay the interest and amortisation on the scrips issued and the short-term loans.

On the exchange-rate front, the tenacity of the government was equally difficult to overcome. Regardless of exchange controls the government still viewed the fixed parity with gold as a sign of 'monetary stability'. However, the strong pressure of the coffee-growers forced it to take the first steps away from a fixed exchange rate. Coffee-growers skilfully used the black market created by exchange controls as an argument for devaluation. They argued that they were in fact being discriminated against, since if they could have sold their foreign exchange in a free market their incomes would have been higher. On 15 March 1932 they were given a 10% bonus, which was in fact paid by the central bank. A year later exchange rates were temporarily set at 1.13 pesos per dollar for exporters and 1.16 for importers, leaving the maximum gold parity of 1.05 for government transactions. The foreign-exchange policies of the USA in March and April 1933 led the government to maintain a fixed rate with the dollar, thus abandoning gold parities. Finally, in September 1933, the pressure of coffee-growers and a seven-week delay in the exchange control office led the government first to a 10 cent devaluation, and later to the establishment of a system of foreign-exchange certificates, which were sold in a free market to importers. By the end of the year the exchange rate had reached 1.57, and continued to climb in 1934; in early 1935 it stabilised around 1.75.

As part of the emergency policies of late 1931 the government also increased tariffs, thus strengthening the protective policies adopted earlier in the year. Finally, the crisis of the sugar industry in 1932 led it in 1933 to its first direct intervention in a productive sector. A semi-public institution was created which granted credit to the sugar mills, regulated the internal market, controlled sugar imports and led the campaign against the sugar leaf disease (Eder, 1959, pp. 585–8). This type of direct intervention was soon to become more general.

Stabilisation Policy and Social Reform (1934–7)

The rapid devaluation of late 1933 and early 1934 led to inflation in 1934 (Table 5.1). As it coincided for a time with a recovery of international prices internal coffee prices increased 68%, stimulating the inflationary impact of devaluation (Table 5.3). Fears of monetary inflation and fiat money reappeared and led the reformist López government, inaugurated in August 1934, to undertake a harsh stabilisation policy. Fiscal expenditures were reduced and a fiscal surplus developed in 1935 (Table 5.2). The objectives of social reform and stabilisation policy were reconciled in the 1935–6 tax reform, which considerably raised income-taxes and introduced wealth and excess profits taxes as a means to tax incomes from profit more heavily (Restrepo, 1936, pp. 26–30). The increase in government taxes from 1936 on led to the growth of expenditure, but a fiscal surplus was maintained up to 1937. The surplus was used to reduce the outstanding internal debt, a contractionary policy, since government bonds were by then owned mainly by the central and private banks, as a result of the private sector credit policies of the Olaya Administration. Economic policy and a coffee recession curbed inflation in 1935. The government also stabilised the exchange rate around 1.75; this rate was in fact fixed in May 1936, suspending temporarily the issue of the foreign-exchange certificates.

Social reformism was manifested in several aspects of the López Administration, aside from direct taxation. Expenditure was redirected to social ends, agrarian land reform and credit encouraged, the trade unions supported and several reformist labour policies adopted. State interventionism became the official ideology, leading to strong political opposition. Interventionism was particularly active on the agrarian front, where conflicts had been mounting since the late 1920s.

On the protectionist front devaluation and the recovery of world prices decreased the protective effect of the 1931 tariff reforms, which

TABLE 5.3 *Coffee and macro-economic indicators, 1928–41*

	(1) Internal coffee price (pesos, per bag of 60 kg. pilado)	(2) Coffee exports (million current pesos)	(3) Gross production (million 1953 pesos)				(4) Volume of manufacturing production (1945 = 100)	
			Gross Domestic Product	Primary sector	Secondary sector		Total	Dynamic sectors
1928	30.48	88.2	2 806	1 667	433		28.8	15.0
1929	24.85	76.9	2 907	1 688	397		30.2	14.5
1930	17.65	61.7	2 882	1 767	338		29.3	14.9
1931	16.43	55.2	2 836	1 675	319		28.7	17.2
1932	12.83	42.9	3 024	1 761	356		32.9	18.6
1933	13.17	49.3	3 194	1 839	422		38.6	25.1
1934	22.15	82.5	3 395	1 905	431		41.0	33.6
1935	17.66	79.2	3 478	1 933	491		45.4	36.5
1936	19.40	92.0	3 662	2 042	533		49.5	39.8
1937	20.84	99.2	3 719	2 045	627		58.2	52.2
1938	18.24	88.8	3 961	2 165	642		59.5	55.8
1939	19.69	87.1	4 204	2 212	789		73.0	67.7
1940	14.88	74.0	4 295	2 279	765		68.3	62.0
1941	20.66	83.3	4 367	2 300	873		81.7	91.7

SOURCES:
(1) *Revista del Banco de la República*, Girardot price.
(2) *Anuario de Comercio Exterior*.
(3) CEPAL (1957) appendix, table 1.
(4) (a) Ibid.
(b) Cotton and rayon textiles, beer, sugar and cement. Ocampo and Montenegro (1982) table A-7, series (lb) and (4); table A-9, series (1) and (4); table A-10, series (2); weighted by value added in 1944–5 (table 9).

had maintained a system of specific taxes. The rapid recovery of import demand also threatened the balance-of-payments equilibrium. Finally, protectionist policies in some advanced countries had affected Colombian exports in some cases. The government managed all these problems mainly by a system of bilateral trade agreements with countries with which Colombia had a commercial deficit. The policy was implemented with Germany, Italy, Japan, Czechoslovakia and Great Britain. It meant in fact that import controls were established, discriminating according to the country of origin. Prior registration of imports was also established in 1935 and import licences in 1936. On the other hand, the country signed a very generous trade agreement with the USA, which was Colombia's major export market and a net source of foreign exchange. The only important concession for Colombia was the guarantee that the USA would not establish import tariffs on coffee, something feared by Colombian growers since 1931.

Deepening Coffee Crisis (1937–41)

As we saw above, conditions in the world coffee market deteriorated in the latter part of the 1930s and early 1940s. The average coffee terms of trade in 1937–41 were 51% lower than in 1925–9 and 28% lower than in 1930–4. Conditions were particularly difficult in 1937–8 and in 1940; in the latter year the real price of coffee decreased to the lowest level of any year since 1905, with the exception of 1917.

Due to the increasing demand created by the expanding manufacturing sectors, and in the early part of the Second World War by precautionary import demand, deteriorating conditions in the coffee market were reflected in a new balance-of-payments crisis. In order to maintain exchange rate stability the government decided to use direct rationing of foreign exchange as the equilibrating mechanism. The exchange rate was only allowed to devalue by 5% in late 1937, bringing it back to the $1.75 level in the second half of 1938. In November 1937 imports were divided in two groups according to how 'essential' they were, new permits allocated according to the foreign-exchange purchases of the central bank during the previous week and a 5% prior import deposit established. In February 1938 these norms were reaffirmed, and in April most textile imports temporarily prohibited. By this time accumulated import licences had reached US $11 million, which had their counterpart in unpaid commercial loans; the Minister of Finance argued that it was essential to restrict imports as a way to restore the commercial credit of the country. In the following months textile imports were reopened, establishing a quota equivalent to 50% of 1937 imports.

Restrictions subsequently eased, to be re-established in December 1939 when imports were divided again into two groups and an exchange rate allocated according to the previous week's purchases. In April 1940 four groups of imports were established with differential exchange rates ranging from 1.75 to 1.95 pesos per dollar. The lowest exchange rate was kept for essentials, which according to the government's definition encompassed 65% of the previous year's imports. Textiles were, of course, classified in the fourth category. Further, since the War had closed the German and other European markets, the government established a system by which non-essential imports were in fact paid for with coffee, a system which did not work very well under war conditions.

In order to defend coffee incomes, in addition to the attempt to tie coffee exports to non-essential imports, the government established an export bonus for an eight-month period starting in May 1940, which was equivalent to 11.5% of the average Girardot price in 1940 and was paid by the government. Interest rates were reduced and the amortisation terms eased for credits granted to coffee-growers. Finally, the government supported the Inter-American Coffee Agreement. In order to handle the obligations thus contracted a National Coffee Fund was created in November 1940 and generous financial resources were allocated to it.

Monetary and fiscal stability were retained as objectives of economic policy, both during the last year of the López Administration and during the Eduardo Santos Administration, inaugurated in August 1938, but they were more difficult to maintain than exchange-rate stability. The fiscal surplus disappeared in 1938 as customs collections declined (largely as a result of rationing of textile imports), and although it reappeared with the increased custom duties of 1939 it turned into a substantial deficit from 1940 on (Table 5.2 above). In 1940 the government renegotiated the foreign debt and contracted a US $10 million loan with the Export–Import Bank, both to supply foreign exchange and to cover the fiscal deficit. As shown in Table 5.1 above, in that year the deficit became again an important source of monetary expansion.

Although income redistribution was maintained as a policy objective, social reformism in fact slackened under the Santos Administration. The government gave a special impetus to the development of new credit institutions, which encompassed several aspects of economic life. Long-term rural credit was encouraged through the Caja Agraria, including the creation of a National Fund for Cattle Development, and rural housing credits granted through the newly created Instituto de Crédito Territorial. The Industrial Development Institute was designed as a way to encourage new industrial activities through direct government investment. The Institute was also granted the task of searching for new industrial opportunities in the country. Long-term industrial credit was also increased through the Central Mortgage and Agrarian Banks. Finally, as part of a larger set of reforms on the municipal front, the Municipal Development Fund was created, to support the development of modern public services. In this way, although state interventionism continued to be the dominant ideology of the government, its emphasis changed under the Santos Administration.

ECONOMIC DEVELOPMENT IN THE 1930s

The crisis had a strong effect on aggregate demand, which according to ECLA statistics declined 53.4% in nominal terms in 1928–31 and 14.6% in real terms. In the same period real gross investment fell 54%, while the apparent consumption of some goods decreased dramatically (29% in the case of cotton textiles, 24% in beer, 59% in cement, etc.). However, adjustment processes guaranteed that the decline in demand was only minimally reflected in aggregate production, which, as shown in Table 5.3, declined only 2.4% between 1929 and 1931, remaining always above 1928 levels.

Non-tradable non-agricultural activities were badly hurt. This was true of construction, internal transportation and some manufacturing activities (beer, soft drinks, glass and brick production, for example). Some export activities, notably bananas and oil, were also affected. However, as we saw, their contraction was amply compensated by the growth of coffee and gold exports during the crisis years and the 1930s. On the other hand, the rapid decline in import demand reserved the internal market for import-competing production, which in many cases displaced imports from the market. This was partly an autonomous development and partly an induced effect of specific import taxes and of tariff reforms and exchange controls in 1931. The most important effect was observed in the case of foodstuffs imports, which declined from 134 792 tons in 1930 to 30 704 tons in 1932; in fact they had been decreasing since 1928, when they peaked at 154 045 tons. Import-competing agricultural production (sugar, rice, cocoa and wheat) increased during the crisis years, as well as pork production, which was partly displacing lard imports. On the average, foodstuffs production increased 44% between 1925–9 and 1930–4 according to ECLA estimates, and pork production 24%.

Agricultural production in general did very well during the crisis years, even apart from the positive evolution of coffee and import-competing foodstuffs production. There were several reasons for this. First, the sector reacted to the crisis with downward price flexibility, thus minimising real contraction. Second, it was favoured by inelastic demand; the strongest effects of demand contraction were thus felt on non-agricultural commodities. Third, fragmentary evidence indicates that urban and possibly also rural wages declined less than foodstuff prices, thus acting as an automatic stabiliser of the demand for necessities (Urrutia and Arrubla, 1970, chap. II; Palacios, 1979, p. 400). Fourth, the intensive development of an internal transportation network in the 1920s had a lagged effect on agricultural production. On the whole, since the rural sector represented more than half of GDP, the evolution of agricultural production by itself had a very important stabilising effect on aggregate production.

The recovery of demand was fast between 1931 and 1934, aggregate real expenditure increasing at an annual rate of growth of 8.2% and GDP at 6.2%. Although growth was obviously faster in those sectors which had done worse during the crisis (especially construction and non-tradable manufacturing activities), growth was balanced during these years. Industrial-led growth was thus a feature of the Colombian economy only after 1934, when nominal coffee exports stagnated (Table 5.3) and fiscal and monetary policy ceased to be expansionary. Indeed, after 1934 aggregate growth was not very fast, real expenditure increasing at a rate of 4.1% in 1934–41 and GDP at 3.6%. Secondary production was then the only dynamic sector. Although it was sensitive to nominal coffee exports and stabilisation policies (especially in 1935, 1938 and 1940) the rate of growth of secondary production was 10.6% in 1934–41, representing 45% of GDP expansion in the period. Growth was even faster in the five dynamic sectors included in Tables 5.3 and 5.4. After 1941 growth rates declined rapidly, especially in the dynamic sectors.

Four different factors account for the rapid growth of manufacturing production in Colombia in the 1930s. The crisis reached Colombia at a time when the prerequisites for modern industrialisation were

TABLE 5.4 Dynamic industrial sectors

	Value added 1944–5 (thousand pesos)	Value of machinery and equipment, 1944–5 (thousand pesos)	Growth rate[a] 1929–41	Growth rate[a] 1933–41	Production in 1945 compared to highest level in the 1920s	Per capita consumption in 1945 compared to 1927–9
Cotton textiles	19 748	18 961	15.8	20.3 (14.5)[b]	8.9	0.8
Rayon textiles	5 430	12 669		27.6 (24.9)[b]	(7.3)[c]	5.2
Beer	11 897	14 949	15.3	13.8	6.1	4.7
Sugar	5 254	11 707	6.3	7.7	4.0	1.9
Cement	4 640	5 839	27.3	17.6	30.3	1.7
Total manufacturing industry	144 804	118 549	9.0	9.1	3.3	

[a] Slope of the regression $\ln P = a + bt$, P = production, t = time
[b] Apparent consumption of raw materials
[c] Compared to production in 1934

SOURCE: Ocampo and Montenegro (1982) table 9.

rapidly accumulating. Export-led growth in the two decades prior to the crisis had considerably expanded the market, while the construction policy of the 1920s had finally created the first modern internal transportation network in a traditionally fragmented market. The first experiences for more than four decades with modern manufacturing had taken place and in the late 1920s an investment boom had occurred in the manufacturing sector, reflecting favourable market conditions. Industrial development in the 1930s was thus to a large extent the result of a momentum coming from the previous decade. Due to the late character of export-led growth the share of manufacturing in aggregate production was in fact very low before the crisis (6.8%, compared to 11.7% for Brazil, 14.2% for Mexico and 22.8% for Argentina) and became normal only after the industrial boom of the 1930s (12.3% in 1941) (CEPAL, 1957; Furtado, 1971, p. 111).

A second favourable condition for manufacturing growth was the change in the demand patterns that accompanied the modernisation of the economy, particularly the relative growth of the urban sector. While income per capita increased only 21% between 1929 and 1945, the demand for many industrial goods grew much more. This is reflected in Table 5.4 in the case of the more dynamic manufacturing sectors. Indeed, aside from cotton textiles, where we can talk of a pure case of import-substitution, the growth of demand was crucial for the expansion of production.

Government policy was also very effective in reorienting demand towards internal production. Protectionist policy went through three different phases. In 1931, as we saw, tariffs were considerably increased. In 1932–5 a significant real devaluation took place (Figure 5.2B); prior to 1932 a small real devaluation had also taken place within the fixed-exchange-rate system, but as a product of strong internal deflation. Finally, as the real effect of devaluation declined the government used direct import controls as a protective device.

Evidence on internal manufacturing prices suggests that neither tariffs, devaluation nor import controls were transferred to consumers, as traditional tariff theory suggests. Rather, according to imperfect competition rules, domestic production prices followed internal costs of production, and the effect of protection was to raise the relative price of imported goods, thus displacing demand towards internal producers (Ocampo and Montenegro, 1982, pp. 80–3; *El Tiempo*, 29 March 1939, pp. 1–2). Import quotas directly redistributed demand towards internal production. In this way profit margins did not increase as the result of protectionism, while the relative price of industrial goods declined in the 1930s, reflecting faster productivity growth. It is impossible with existing evidence to assert whether the gains from increasing productivity were partly retained by the producers in the form of higher margins. It is clear, however, that part of the profit margins in the manufacturing sector were transferred to the State through direct taxation. Indeed, one of the most important arguments used by liberal governments to support direct taxes was that it returned to the State part of the benefits granted to manufacturing industries by protection from imports (López, 1937, pp. 270–1; Lleras, 1946, pp. 58, 65).

It must finally be remarked that the capacity to import was not a significant constraint on manufacturing growth in the 1930s. Export purchasing power did not decline significantly, as we saw in the second section, while imports recovered in the late 1930s the exceptional levels of 1925–9. After 1933 economic policy reserved scarce foreign exchange for the importation of goods rather than capital services and was successful in changing the composition of imports. In particular the share of foodstuffs and textiles declined from 41.7% in 1925–9 to 25.8% in 1935–9 and 16.9% in 1940–4. In this way the growing manufacturing capital-intensive sectors (Table 5.4) had sufficient foreign exchange to finance the expansion of production capacity and the imports of intermediate goods. In these sectors there is evidence that most of the capacity expansion in textiles took place in the 1930s and not in the 1920s, as is commonly assumed. At the same time, while in beer, sugar and cement production there was excess capacity in the early 1930s, productive capacity more than doubled in the decade.

OVERVIEW

Colombian development in the 1930s was a highly successful story, not only in terms of the rate of growth achieved – one of the highest in Latin America – but most importantly from the point of view of the institutional and structural transformations of the State and the economy. The crisis came after a period of late but fast export-led growth, in which some primary (foodstuffs) and secondary sectors had lagged behind. Conditions were especially favourable for the expansion of the secondary sector in the 1930s, based on the market created by export growth in the previous decades.

The crisis was transmitted through a sharp reversal of the capital account, falling coffee prices and pro-cyclical government policies. In the context of an underdeveloped secondary sector, adjustment in the downswing came mainly through price deflation rather than output contraction. The pressure of interest groups, especially the coffee-growers, under severe balance-of-payments, monetary and fiscal crises, forced the government to adopt expansionary policies in 1931–4. The economy responded with expansion of import-substituting and non-tradable activities in the primary and secondary sectors, while world market conditions were favourable for the expansion of coffee and gold exports.

In 1934 the inflationary effect of devaluation, in the context of recovering world coffee prices, resurrected the fears of fiat money, which had led to hyper-inflation at the turn of the century. Thus, although social reformism gained momentum, the economy was managed in line with stabilising macroeconomic principles after 1934. Economic policies, coupled with deteriorating world coffee conditions, led to a slower rate of growth. Development then concentrated in the secondary sector, encouraged by market conditions created in the previous decades, growing urbanisation, protectionist policies and the successful rationing of foreign exchange.

REFERENCES

J. A. Bejarano, *El Régimen Agrario: de la Economía Exportadora a la Economía Industrial* (Bogotá, 1979).

R. C. Beyer, 'The Colombian Coffee Industry: Origins and Major Trends', Ph. D. thesis (University of Minnesota, 1947).

CEPAL, *Análisis y Proyecciones del Desarrollo Económico*, vol. III: *El Desarrollo Económico de Colombia* (Mexico, 1957).

A. Delfim Netto, 'O Café Brasileiro no Mercado dos Estados Unidos no Período de 1922–39', in Instituto Brasileiro do Café, *Curso de Economía Cafeteira*, vol. II (Rio de Janeiro, 1962).

―――― *O Problema de Café no Brazil* (Rio de Janeiro, 1979).

J. J. Echavarría, 'La Deuda Externa Colombiana durante los 20s y los 30s', *Coyuntura Económica*, 12. 2 (1982).

P. J. Eder, *El Fundador, Santiago M. Eder* (Bogotá, 1959).

FAO, *The World's Coffee* (Rome, 1947).

C. Furtado, *La Economía Latinoamericana desde la Conquista Ibérica hasta la Revolución Cubana*, 2nd edn (Mexico, 1971).

IIA, *Coffee in 1931 and 1932* (Rome, 1934).

J. Kingston, 'A lei Estadística da Demanda de Café', in Instituto Brasileiro do Café, *Ençaios sobre Café e Desenvolvimiento Económico* (Rio de Janeiro, 1973).

C. Lleras, 'La Obra Económica y Fiscal del Liberalismo', en *El Liberalismo en el Gobierno, 1930–40*, vol. II (Bogotá, 1946).
―――― 'Crónicas de mi Propia Vida', *Nueva Frontera* (1978) nos 198–205.
A. López, 'La Gestión Económica y Fiscal del Estado', *Revista del Banco de la República* (1937) 270–1.
S. Montenegro, 'La Industria Textil en Colombia: 1900–1945', *Desarrollo y Sociedad*, no. 8 (1982).
J. A. Ocampo, 'Desarrollo Exportador y Desarrollo Capitalista Colombiano en el Siglo XIX; *Desarrollo y Sociedad*, no. 8 (1982).
J. A. Ocampo and S. Montenegro, 'La Crisis Mundial de los Años Treinta en Colombia', *Desarrollo y Sociedad*, no. 7 (1982).
M. Ospina Pérez, *Informe del Gerente de la Federación al Sexto Congreso Nacional de Cafeteros* (Bogotá, 1934).
L. Ospina Vasquez, *Industria y Protección en Colombia, 1810–1930* (Medellín, 1955).
M. Palacios, *El Café en Colombia (1850–1970): Una Historia Económica, Social y Política* (Bogotá, 1979).
A. Patiño, *La Prosperidad a Debe y la Gran Crisis, 1925–1935* (Bogotá, 1981).
C. M. Peláez, 'Analise Económica do Programa Brasileiro de Sustentaçao do Café, 1906–1945: Teoría, Política e Mediaçao', in Instituto Brasileiro do Café, *Ençaios sobre Café e Desenvolvimiento Económico* (Río de Janeiro, 1973).
C. E. Posada, *La Crisis del Capitalísmo Mundial y la Deflación en Colombia, 1929–1933* (Medellín, 1976).
G. Restrepo, *Memoria de Hacienda* (Bogotá, 1936).
F. J. Rippy, *El Capitalísmo Norteamericano y la Penetración Imperialista en Colombia* (Medellín, 1970).
J. W. F. Rowe, 'Studies in the Artificial Control of Raw Materials', no. 3, *Brazilian Coffee* (London and Cambridge Economic Series, 1932).
A. Tirado, *Aspectos Políticos del Primer Gobierno de Alfonso López Pumarejo, 1934–1938* (Bogotá, 1981).
M. Urrutia and M. Arrubla, *Compendio de Estadísticas Históricas de Colombia* (Bogotá, 1970).
H. J. Vargas, *Memoria de Hacienda* (Bogotá, 1938).
V. D. Wickizer, *The World Coffee Economy, with Special References to Control Schemes* (Stanford, 1942).

6 Argentina and Brazil during the 1930s: The Impact of British and American International Economic Policies*

MARCELO DE PAIVA ABREU

The accumulation of recent work on the impact of the 1929–33 Depression on specific Latin American economies provides an adequate basis for serious comparative studies trying to detect cross-country reactions in terms of shifts in economic policy and their results as well as to define homogeneous groups of countries in terms of economic performance.[1]

There are, however, important pitfalls which should be made clear when such generalisations are produced as apparently homogeneous behaviour of certain variables frequently conceals important differences concerning other variables. This seems to be the case when links of particular countries with the world economy are concerned. Indeed, following the trend established by ECLA's early writings, it

* Paper presented to the 44th International Congress of Americanists held in Manchester, 5 to 10 September 1982, in a symposium organised by Rosemary Thorp on 'The Effects of the 1929 Depression on Latin America'. A preliminary version was presented in a workshop held in St Antony's College, Oxford, 21 to 23 September 1981. Participants are thanked for their comments. The author also thanks: Rosemary Thorp for her invitation to attend both events, Gelson Fonseca Jr and Winston Fritsch for their comments in Brazil, Ricardo Markwald for help in obtaining Argentinian publications, CAPES – Coordenação do Aperfeiçoamento do Pessoal de Nível Superior and IDRC – the International Development Research Centre – for financial support. The views expressed in this paper are those of the author alone.

144

is possible to detect a definite stream in the literature tending to stress the shift from exogenous to endogenous inducements to economic growth, particularly in the case of large economies such as those of Argentina, Brazil and Mexico. This is generally related to the very simple fact that the relative importance of foreign trade and payments in the 1930s was much diminished in comparison with the pre-1929 period in the wake of a sharp fall in export prices, the imposition of controls of a diversified nature and the reduction of financial flows associated with the closure of capital markets and defaults. However, even superficial acquaintance with the economic policy formulation process in many Latin American countries in the 1930s will confirm that, in spite of the reduced importance of foreign trade and capital flows, the generation of foreign exchange and its distribution was the central problem which had to be faced by policy-makers throughout the 1930s, leaving few degrees of freedom for the definition of other aspects of economic policy.

Over-enthusiastic extensions of the useful transition model from *desarrollo hacia afuera* to *desarrollo hacia adentro* are at the root of at least two important misconceptions or exaggerations concerning Latin American economies in the 1930s: on the one hand the allegedly increased elbow-room for Latin American countries which resulted from increased 'interimperialist rivalries' and, on the other, the autonomous nature of development given the diversified characteristics of the industrial sector as a result of import-substitution in the capital goods and intermediate goods sectors. In this chapter concern will centre on questions related to the 'increased-elbow-room' interpretation rather than on the *endogenista* issue.[2]

This chapter consequently is very much against the current as it stresses the importance of taking into account developments in the world economy, in particular different international economic policies adopted by the USA and the leading European countries and their unequal impact on different Latin American countries. Had the foreign economic policies of Britain and the USA been similar in the 1930s there would be no room for what follows.

Argentina and Brazil have been selected for this comparative exercise because they illustrate quite clearly two radically distinct situations in terms of the relative bargaining power of Britain and the USA and the resulting constraints on domestic and foreign economic policies in these two countries. It must be stressed, however, that the chapter is written very much from a Brazilian point of view, a result both of the author's limitations and of the lack of Argentinian materials in Brazil.

This chapter is divided into four sections. The first section deals with the structural characteristics of the commercial and financial links of both Argentina and Brazil with Britain and the USA before the Depression, emphasising their different nature. The second section is mainly concerned with the impact of American foreign economic policy during the 1930s on Brazilian economic policy – especially concerning trade and payments – and on Brazilian economic growth. The third section is similar in scope to the second, dealing with the impact of British foreign economic policy on Argentinian economic policy and growth. Finally, the fourth section presents the main comparative conclusions and attempts to draw lessons which could possibly be useful in the 1980s.

ARGENTINIAN AND BRAZILIAN TRADE AND PAYMENTS BEFORE THE DEPRESSION

The triangular nature of Argentina's commercial and financial links with Britain and the USA before the 1930s is now well known.[3] While the British market typically absorbed about 30% of Argentina's total exports, not more than 20% of total imports were of British origin. In contrast with pre-war years the clear trend was towards a structural trade imbalance favouring Argentina as the British share of total exports remained stable and British goods were displaced from the Argentinian market by sterling's overvaluation as well as by changes in the composition of imports in favour of 'modern' goods such as consumer durables and machinery in whose production Britain was unable to face competition, especially from the USA. The importance of the British market for Argentinian products, however, was not evenly distributed. In the case of meat, which corresponded to about 15% of Argentinian exports, Britain absorbed more than three-fourths of Argentinian exports. The importance of the British market was even more pronounced for chilled beef exports, which were rapidly gaining ground over other types of meat as a proportion of meat exports.[4]

This trade imbalance during the late 1920s was at least mitigated by compensatory financial flows resulting from interest, profit and dividend remittances and the net inflow of foreign capital. As the USA superseded Britain as the main capital exporters and the amount of British capital invested in Argentina was very considerable, in the case of the Britain–Argentina and the Argentina–US sides of the triangle, financial flows tended to compensate trade imbalances.[5]

The triangular nature of Argentina's commercial and financial links with the USA and Europe and particularly the importance of the British market for Argentinian meat were to have crucial significance for Argentina's foreign economic policy in the 1930s, especially in relation to the criteria governing the distribution of foreign-exchange earnings between competitive uses.

The nature of Brazil's links with the world economy in the late 1920s was also quite peculiar. The US market absorbed about 45% of total Brazilian exports, while less than 30% of Brazilian imports came from the USA. This imbalance had been more important in the past as typically the US import share had remained below 15% before 1914. Britain, on the other hand, which had lost her position as Brazil's main market around 1870, absorbed only about 5% of Brazil's total exports. The British share of the Brazilian market declined for roughly the same reasons as in Argentina: by the late 1920s Britain held 20% of the Brazilian market constrasted with around 30 % before the First World War. Besides being by very far Brazil's main export market, the USA in the case of coffee – which corresponded to 70% of total Brazilian exports – absorbed around 50% of Brazil's exports.[6] Brazil not only depended even more on her main export market than Argentina, but depended much more on coffee exports than Argentina on meat exports. That consumption of Brazilian coffee was more evenly distributed than that of Argentinian meat – especially chilled beef – was in consequence a rather limited consolation.

The pattern of Brazilian trade was such as to comprise an 'inverted' triangle if compared with Argentina: the balance of trade with the USA was structurally favourable to Brazil, while the balance of Anglo-Brazilian trade was favourable to Britain.

In the case of Brazil, in contrast with Argentina, financial flows – related to both interest, profit and dividend remittances and to the net inflow of foreign capital – underlined rather than mitigated the trade imbalances. Indeed, financial flows, bilaterally defined, tended to be favourable in the case of the new lender and unfavourable in the case of the old one.

This pattern of Brazilian trade and payments was to have important consequences in the 1930s – more for what did not happen than for what in fact happened – since, in spite of American leverage in

Brazil being at least as powerful as Britain's in Argentina, Brazil was never under real pressure to adapt her foreign economic policy to the advantage of the USA. In fact, the US record concerning the extraction of special privileges when its bargaining power was sufficiently strong was not beyond repair until the early 1920s, when the Fordney – McCumber tariff made the most-favoured-nation clause a basis for American commercial policy. During the 1930s, however, the USA, in contrast with Britain, consistently adopted policies based on such clauses.[7]

ECONOMIC RELATIONS BETWEEN BRAZIL AND THE USA IN THE 1930S AND THEIR IMPACT ON BRAZILIAN ECONOMIC GROWTH

The impact of the Great Depression on the Brazilian economy has been extensively discussed in the literature.[8] From the end of 1928 the Wall Street boom had as a main consequence the draining of funds from the Periphery either directly or by diverting 'normal' capital flows: the inflow of foreign capital which had been above £25 million a year in 1926–8 was reduced to practically nil in 1929. This strain on the balance of payments was considerably aggravated by the almost complete breakdown of traditional capital markets after 1929 and the contemporary very heavy fall in coffee prices. While the quantum exported fell below the 1928 level only in 1932 (by about 16%) and had expanded 70% above this level by the end of the decade, export prices fell quite rapidly (by almost 40%) until 1930 and only recovered their 1928 level in 1941, remaining about 25% below this level for most of the decade. The terms of trade deteriorated quite sharply by almost 45% by 1931 and then further after the 1937 recession until they reached less than 40% of their 1928 level. The capacity to import remained as a rule about 30% below pre-Depression levels. Brazil then faced a massive balance-of-payments crisis originating both from the fall in export earnings and the interruption in the flow of both portfolio and direct foreign capital. Equilibrium was restored during the 1930s by successive appeals first to gold and foreign-exchange exports and then to a combination of exchange-rate devaluation, exchange controls, foreign debt default and the accumulation of commercial arrears.[9]

Brazilian GDP, however, remained practically stable even during the worst Depression years[10] while industrial output contracted by not more than about 10% in relation to 1928 (in the worst year which was 1930) and was 5% above 1928 output in 1933. It is now accepted that recovery was at least partly related to economic policy concerning both public expenditure *and* the generation of sizeable trade balances through import controls. Between 1932 and 1939 both industrial output and GDP increased rapidly – at yearly rates of 7.9% and 5.7% respectively – in spite of difficulties in 1938–9 in the wake of the American recession.

Political and economic relations between Brazil and the USA in the early years of the Vargas regime were rather strained due both to the Americans having backed the wrong side in 1930 and to New York's lack of 'co-operation' with the Brazilian banks, by withdrawing their short-term lines of credit, a behaviour which contrasted with London's more accomodating mood. However, as the structural characteristics of trade between Brazil and the USA, which have been mentioned in the first section, persisted after the recession, it was inevitable that these difficulties would not continue for long, especially as the British after 1932 concentrated their efforts in Brazil mainly on financial (i.e. public foreign debt) questions and seemed resigned to a fast further decline of their export trade.[11]

The US share of the Brazilian market during the 1930s remained roughly stable around 25% (after due allowance is made for the overvaluation of imports from Germany) while exports of Brazilian goods to the US market slowly fell from 45% to 35% of total exports as the importance of coffee exports was much reduced, coffee prices fell more than the prices of non-coffee exports and Germany increased very considerably her purchases in Brazil in 1934–8. Consequently, there was still room for the exertion of US bargaining power if the USA had chosen to do so. The US business community in the early 1930s was strongly in favour of full exploitation of US leverage to obtain preferred treatment in the transfer of foreign exchange: the proposed stick was often the threat to impose a duty on coffee imports. US official circles, however strongly opposed such a course of action as it would make US exports to other markets, where the bargaining power of the USA was weaker, vulnerable to similar treatment. The issue was not decided in fact until 1934 when George Peek's proposed trade policy based on bilateralism was turned down in favour of Cordell Hull's unshakeable faith in multilateralism. In sharp contrast with Argentina, as will be seen in the next section,

Brazilian foreign-exchange regimes throughout the 1930s did not discriminate between countries with which Brazil had a favourable balance of trade and those in the reverse position.

While in some specific episodes the Americans eventually made use of their stick – the main occasion being the negotiation of a new Brazil–US Trade Agreement extracting some minor advantages from Brazil in 1935 – important Brazilian decisions concerning foreign economic policy, in some instances patently unfavourable to the USA, were not influenced by American pressure. At the same time that US commercial and financial arrears accumulated due to the lack of foreign exchange, between 1932 and 1937 Brazil paid £6–8 million yearly (around 20% of the import bill) of public debt service mainly to British holders.[12] Debt settlements in the early 1930s in fact not only stressed the priority of debt service over commercial needs, but were consistently unfavourable to dollar loans, which were on the whole less well secured than sterling loans.

In no other instance is US sacrifice to long-term objectives and to multilateralism more evident than in relation to the expansion of Brazilian bilateral trade, particularly with Germany from 1934. Following the adoption of Schacht's new foreign trade policy Germany expanded her share in Brazil's total imports and exports quite substantially, by means of compensation arrangements which involved both direct export subsidies to German industries and flexible foreign-exchange rates considerably undervalued in relation to the Reichsmark theoretical parity. The relative stability of bilateral trade was assured by the increase of Brazilian exports to Germany, especially of cotton whose exports before the Depression were negligible and – ironically – whose production had increased in Brazil under the umbrella of the US cotton price support program.

Given the lack of complementarity between the US and Brazilian economies in respect to cotton and the American incapacity to absorb further quantities of goods which accounted for much of the expansion of Brazilian exports in the second half of the 1930s, it is difficult to think how the output of such goods could have expanded at the rate it did in the decade in the absence of German bilateral trade based on compensation, since there were no alternative markets where they could be sold.[13] Furthermore, from a balance-of-payments point of view, exports to Germany corresponded in those foreign-exchange-starved years to about 20% of total exports, generating inconvertible foreign exchange to pay for much valued imports. Data on Brazilian imports in the 1930s indicate that it was the

British rather than the US exports which were displaced by the expansion of German compensation trade: both the Americans and the aggregate German–British shares of the Brazilian market remained fairly stable during the 1930s. Damage caused by German competition to US exports was eventually recouped by American inroads in the market shares of other Brazilian trade partners (including Britain). The contraction of British trade exports to Brazil resulted both from the well-known competitive difficulties which were faced by British goods and from structural changes in the Brazilian import bill resulting from balance-of-payments problems which had a relatively stronger effect on British staple exports, especially textiles, as they were displaced by domestic production.

In spite of the fact that Brazilian – American bilateral trade in the 1930s generated between £10 million and (more typically) £15 million yearly of convertible foreign exchange in excess of the requirement of US imports[14] the US government – both because of its attachment to multilateralism and for considerations related to its strategic aim to enhance Brazil's influence in Latin America in order to counter Argentina's more independent leadership – turned a blind eye to the Brazilian adoption of policies which ran clearly against US interests. US bondholders – or, more precisely, holders of Brazilian dollar bonds – 'lost' between £7 and £5 million yearly in the 1930s due to Brazilian partial or total defaults[15] and compensation trade 'diverted' £8 million of Brazilian imports to Germany.

The net effect of a hypothetical US policy in Brazil which mirrored British policy in a country such as Argentina, i.e. based on the full exertion of available bargaining power, would probably have been to reduce quite drastically Brazilian imports and, to a lesser extent, Brazilian exports.

Relative scarcity of foreign exchange was, of course, of paramount importance to explain the fast expansion of Brazilian output, especially in industry after 1932. Domestic industry was protected from foreign competition by the imposition of import controls and the substantial changes in relative prices of domestically produced and imported goods as from 1930–1. But a fast-expanding economy depends on the availability of foreign exchange to pay for intermediate goods, raw materials, capital goods and non-competitive consumer goods. While in the early 1930s increased output did not depend on increased capacity as idle capacity was very substantial, by the end of the decade Brazil was importing only 15% less industrial capital goods – in quantum – than in the late 1920s.[16]

Data on the import structure during the 1930s are notoriously fragile. There is no doubt, however, that even modest import cuts would have not only resulted in the interruption of the flow of some residual consumer goods which were being imported partly because of political arguments – such as motor-cars, radio sets and refrigerators – but also would have badly affected imports of inputs and raw materials which were essential for current industrial production. One of the reasons related to the reversal in the late 1930s of Brazilian policy in relation to the priority accorded to public debt payments was the need to accommodate the increasing demand for capital goods by Brazilian industry as fast expansion based on the use of idle capacity was losing momentum.

Brazil's adoption of a constrained foreign economic policy similar to Argentina's, would thus very probably have resulted in a slowing down of the rate of expansion of GDP owing to a scarcity of imported inputs and – later in the decade – capital goods imports for industrial use, the deterioration of services such as transportation which depended on imports and a reduction in the output of agricultural goods which could only find markets under bilateralist arrangements.

ANGLO-ARGENTINIAN ECONOMIC RELATIONS IN THE 1930S AND THEIR IMPACT ON ARGENTINIAN ECONOMIC GROWTH

The impact of the Depression on Argentinian terms of trade was substantial but rather more limited than in the case of Brazil: not only was the minimum level – reached in 1931–3 – around 35% below its 1928 peak[17] (as opposed to almost 45% in Brazil), but in 1936–8 it practically regained this peak level in the wake of a fast recovery of export prices related to the US drought. Capacity to import in the 1930s somewhat puzzlingly was not notably below its level in the 1920s: perhaps not more than 10% if contrasted with a typical 30% in Brazil.

GDP in Argentina fell during the worst years of the Depression rather more than in Brazil. By 1932 it had fallen about 15% in relation to its 1929 peak level. Recovery as a result of moderately expansionary policies was also rather slower than in Brazil: the pre-Depression peak level was not reached until 1935. In fact, while between 1928 and 1939 Brazilian GDP increased at 3.7% a year,

Argentinian GDP increased at 1.8% a year in spite of its less stringent foreign-exchange constraints, both in the early 1930s and later in the decade. Argentinian industrial output increased between 1928 and 1939 at the yearly rate of 3.2% while the more 'mature' Brazilian industry increased its output during the same years at the rate of 5%.[18]

Argentinian foreign economic policy during the 1930s, as is well known, was very much a corollary of British foreign economic policy. It is, in fact, difficult to speak of a coherent British foreign economic policy in the 1930s as it was basically defined in the light of the evaluation of British bargaining power in each particular country. A comparison between British policy in Brazil and in Argentina is, in this context, particularly instructive. While in Brazil, British policy was strictly defined on a multilateral basis – due to the lack of leverage – in Argentina there was room for the extraction of advantages given the structural deficit of Anglo-Argentinian trade, the political preeminence of cattle interests and the importance of the British meat market.[19] Britain's preferred slogan in Argentina – 'comprar a quien nos compra' – had to be drastically changed in Brazil to 'buy from whom sells you the best', to the increased embarrassment of British officials who had to answer queries about the ambiguity of British policy on trade and payments.[20]

British bilateral devices, of course, did make sense from the point of view of maximising *British exports*. In this context it is relevant to mention Keynes's sharp criticism of the American religious belief in the advantages of free trade for all countries:

we desire meat and will pay £110 for it; the Argentine desires a motor car price £110 in U.K. and £110 in U.S.A.; U.S.A. does not desire the meat, has a tariff against it and will not pay more than £50 for it, if that; the Argentine has the meat and will gladly accept £100 for it rather than not sell it but cannot take less than £100; we, having no dollars, can only afford to buy meat if we sell the car. Under *laissez faire* the trade cannot take place; for if we pay for the meat in money, whether at £100 or £110, the Argentine will spend the money in buying the car in U.S.A., and we became insolvent. Some system by which our buying the meat is made contingent on the Argentine buying our car is the only way by which trade can take place. Otherwise the Argentine's meat producers and our motor-car producers are both thrown out of work.

He went on:

this possibility is excluded in [some American economists'] philosophy because of latent assumptions, assumed in [their] classical theory and not realised in practice, that, if you buy the Argentine meat for cash and the Argentines buy the American car for cash, it necessarily follows that America will buy from us some export worth £100. In other words, [their] fundamental philosophy has assumed the non-existence of the very problem we are out to solve.[21]

The 'traditional' interpretation concerning Argentinian foreign economic policy in the 1930s would claim that this policy was defined not in the light of national interest but in the light of sectional (meat) interests, that the relative importance of the meat trade if compared with total exports was not such as to warrant the adoption of such a policy and that Britain had a concrete interest in the availability of Argentinian meat in the British market as diversion of meat purchases would prove to be rather costly for the British consumer. Underlying this interpretation is the view that Argentina had in fact more degrees of freedom than implied by its rather passive position in relation to Mr Runciman's exertions.[22]

Argentina's foreign-exchange policy immediately after the recession was very much like Brazilian foreign-exchange policy, i.e. a foreign-exchange control was established which allocated exchange on the basis of the nature of foreign-exchange operations without discrimination based on the nationality of recipients.

However, the well-known Roca–Runciman Convention and its Supplementary Convention, both signed in 1933 – extracted by Runciman on the basis of what Argentina had to offer to have the *status quo ante* with regard to the entry of Argentinian meat in the British market maintained in terms of tariffs (but not of quantities) – assured discriminatory favourable treatment of Argentinian remittances to the UK as well as the reduction of import duties on manufactured goods mainly supplied by Britain and sympathetic treatment of British capital invested in Argentina. Moreover, the second stage of foreign-exchange control adopted in late 1933 favoured British goods which almost invariably could be imported at the more favourable official exchange rate.[23]

This is not the place to examine in detail the rather controversial literature on the inevitability of Roca – Runciman and its damaging consequences for Argentina and on whether its main objective was to defend national or class interests. However, some recent attempts to revise the traditional interpretation that it was indeed an arrangement through which cattle interests, in exchange for rather limited advantages, were prepared to offer quite substantial concessions to Britain, seem so peculiarly objectionable that they must be commented upon.[24]

These interpretations suggest that the terms obtained in 1933 were the best Argentinian negotiators could have achieved, that the pact was designed to defend the national interest and not cattle interests and that it protected Argentina from the 'vicissitudes of the world economy'.[25] They are based on a rather one-sided evaluation of what could have been Britain's reaction concerning the entry of Argentinian meat in the British market had not Roca–Runciman's terms been obtained: there was unquestionable British interest in the continuation of the meat trade based both on general grounds (availability of cheap good-quality meat)[26] and on particular grounds related to the protection of British capital invested in meat-related activities. On the other hand, the Roca–Runciman Convention cannot be evaluated exclusively in terms of its impact on Anglo-Argentinian trade as so many concessions concerning British capital were obtained in its wake and that of the 1936 renewal. Moreover, the fact that the 'actual pattern of trade between the two countries was not unfavourable to Argentina after 1933'[27] is rather irrelevant to show the 'advantages' of Roca–Runciman as had not British goods enjoyed preferential treatment the British unfavourable trade balance with Argentina would have undoubtedly widened quite considerably. It is consequently strange to read that the British were 'willing to sacrifice the investment that Argentina held hostage behind the wall of exchange control, and even came to support Argentine efforts to nationalize the railroads'.[28] It is rather questionable if there was ever any question of a 'sacrifice': the future would in fact show that even General Perón made this eventual 'sacrifice' rather sweet – pricewise – for the British. The wall of exchange control, on the other hand, worked clearly in favour of British goods whose access to the Argentine market was guaranteed by thinly disguised bilateral devices. The conventional view of Roca–Runciman still seems to hold water in the light of the available evidence.

Renewal of the Roca–Runciman Pact in 1936 by Malbrán and Eden further reduced British 'concessions' to Argentina and aggravated previous pledges.[29] While the British trade deficit with Argentina did not appreciably decrease during the 1930s in comparison with pre-Depression years, Britain was able to obtain throughout the decade preferential treatment of British capital invested in Argentina and of British trade. There is little doubt that had not British goods enjoyed preferential treatment from the point of view of foreign-exchange allocation, government purchasing policy and import duties, the British share of the Argentinian market would have shrunk very considerably.[30]

While in the case of Brazil it is relatively clear that economic performance in the 1930s would have suffered if the USA had pressed for the payment of dollar bonds and for the interruption of bilateral trade, specially with Germany, the impact on the Argentinian economy of the adoption of a less sanguine bilateral policy by Britain is perhaps less clear-cut as the foreign-exchange constraint seems to have been less stringent than in Brazil.

To the extent that Argentina's policies discriminated in favour of imports of British origin they fostered the purchase of less competitive goods, at the expense of the Argentinian consumers or of the efficiency of domestic industry, or even the purchase of consumer goods at the expense of capital goods as Britain was an important supplier of capital goods. Indeed, it is a striking feature of Argentina's import bill that capital goods imports remained even in the good years around 1937 at least 30% below (in quantum terms) their pre-Depression level.[31] This is at least partly related to the continued importance of consumer goods imports: textile imports (including inputs), for instance, remained in the second half of the decade roughly at the same quantum level as in pre-Depression years.

It is likely that had Argentinian foreign economic policy been less pliable in relation to British pressures it would have been possible, in spite of foreign-exchange scarcity, to achieve a faster rate of capital accumulation in import-substituting industries and, consequently, a faster rate of growth. Moreover, a less well-behaved policy concerning financial matters – involving, for instance, rescheduling the foreign debt – would have freed resources for the adoption of expansionary domestic policies by the federal government and for further consolidation of Argentine industry through the expansion of capital goods imports.

CONCLUSIONS

During the 1930s Britain's leverage in Argentina was decisive in view of the importance of the British market for Argentina's exports and American bargaining power in Brazil was strong because of the important share of Brazilian exports – particularly of coffee – absorbed by the American market.

However, from the early 1930s Britain adopted a foreign economic policy which placed emphasis on the extraction of privileged treatment in those countries where she had a strong bargaining power, as was the case in Argentina. The USA, in contrast, especially after 1934, adopted a policy which had as its main tenet the substitution of multilateralist trade and payments practices for the bilateralist formal or informal arrangements which were becoming common practice among European countries.

These developments in the international scene accounted for the very considerable differences in the international economic policies of Argentina and Brazil during the 1930s. While Argentina, because of British pressure and of the political importance of cattle-raisers for the stability of *Concordancia*, adopted policies which favoured British trade and capital, Brazil was able to follow a foreign economic policy defined on an *ad hoc* basis practically without American interference.

These differences between the foreign economic policies adopted by Argentina and Brazil had, of course, quite different implications for their balance of payments as relatively more foreign exchange cover was available in Brazil – given the US reluctance to adopt either bilateral trade and payments or restrictions to the entry of Brazilian goods in the American market. Had the Americans adopted stronghand methods to balance their payments in relation to Brazil in a manner similar to the British in Argentina a very substantial reduction in the availability of foreign exchange could have been expected.

Scarcity of foreign exchange was vital for the fast expansion of the output of import-substituting industries in Brazil during the 1930s. If, however, the reduction in the value of imports had been such as to interfere with the level of intermediate and – to a lesser degree – capital goods imports, this was bound to constrain the growth of industrial output. It is in fact claimed in this chapter that the fast rate of industrial growth in Brazil during the 1930s was possible, among other things, because of American 'strategic leniency' towards Brazil.

The output of other sectors of the economy also depended on the availability of foreign exchange as in the case of transport services which relied on imported capital goods, components and fuel. Agricultural diversification, on the other hand, which was a striking feature of the economy during the decade, depended on the stability of new export markets supplied under the umbrella provided by the unwavering American adoption of a global foreign economic policy based on multilateralism.

Argentina's foreign economic policy in the 1930s was defined under the heavy constraints placed by British bilateralism. Given the political basis of *Concordancia*, Argentinian concessions tended to assume a shape which distinctly favoured cattle interests to the detriment of the national interest. This policy had costs in the long run in terms of a slower rate of growth of the economy – and particularly of industry – than would have been the case had it made less concessions towards British interests.

It would seem, in the light of the cases of Argentina and Brazil, that comparative studies of Latin American economies in the 1930s must indeed take into account the diversified characteristics of the links of different countries with the international economy, which by their very nature may have imposed quite different constraints on economic policy and, consequently, on the economic performance of specific countries.

The experience of these two countries also makes clear the continued importance of links with the world economy to explain economic policy formulation and growth in the 1930s in spite of reduced integration of the international economy (measured, for instance, by the value of trade and capital flows in relation to income).

It is not very easy to draw lessons for the 1980s for such countries as Brazil and Argentina based on their experience during the 1930s. A marked feature of the international economy today is the absence of a hegemonic country – such as was the case of the USA in the 1930s. It is unlikely, consequently, in a context of stiff international competition, that any country will be able to exploit for extended periods any structural advantages it may have, as Brazil did in the 1930s. Multilateralism today, in spite of assertions to the contrary, is much qualified by strictly bilateral arguments and the expansion of LDC exports frequently faces the competition of the more senile segments of industry in advanced countries. In this sense the lesson to be drawn from the Brazilian experience in the 1930s seems to be rather limited.[32]

In spite of its well-known economic and political difficulties Argentina in the 1980s by virtue of its more diversified basis of natural resources – especially her self-reliance concerning energy – is likely to depend less crucially on the world economy than Brazil.

The generation of a sizeable and permanent surplus in the Brazilian trade account is today of paramount importance in order to reassure lenders about the country's capacity to pay its foreign debt service and to make possible further indebtedness. As the capacity of oil-exporting countries to absorb Brazilian exports is limited, trade surpluses have to be generated in other markets frequently facing the competition either of well-established suppliers as in the markets of Africa and Latin America or of heavily protected lameducks in Western Europe and the USA.

It is in fact in the balances of payments of countries such as Brazil that the incoherent claims of the financial and the less-competitive industrial interests in advanced economies are portrayed. At the present stage of its economic growth Brazil needs to keep its indebtedness under control. To do this in a non-damaging way it needs to increase its trade surplus, carving off markets from traditional suppliers. Outcry would be easy to understand if Brazil were not a rather marginal supplier of the world market: indeed Brazil's share of the world market in the early 1980s (less than 1%), in spite of increasing integration with the world economy since 1967, is still considerably below its 1928 level.

As it is, the Brazilian task in the 1980s of trying to align its commercial share of the world market with its importance as an outlet for international financial flows is going to be a particular hard one – especially so, when a comfortable umbrella similar to that provided by the USA in the 1930s is wanting.

NOTES

1. A good example of such work is Diaz Alejandro (1980).
2. It may be said, however, that while there was substantial diversification of the industrial structure in the 1930s, the reduced importance of non-traditional industrial sectors, at least in Brazil, seems to indicate that excessive stress has been placed on the endogenous model.
3. See Fodor and O'Connell (1973). See also Chapter 8 by O'Connell in this volume.

4. See Diaz Alejandro (1970) pp. 19–21 and Salera (1941), pp. 26 and 42.
5. Fodor and O'Connell (1973) pp. 5–7. Unbalanced trade resulted in unbalanced trade volumes since a large proportion of Argentina's exports were rather bulky in comparison with typical imports, a fact reflected in the disparity between import and export average values per ton. This resulted in highly differentiated rates for inward and outward freights and was only partly compensated by Brazilian freights. Brazilian exports in fact had a higher value per ton than Brazilian imports. Aggregate Argentinian and Brazilian imports were roughly equivalent in weight to aggregate Argentinian and Brazilian exports. See Fodor and O'Connell (1973) p. 6.
6. See Instituto Brasileiro de Geografia e Estatistica (n.d.) pp. 1366–74.
7. For twenty years before 1923 certain imports of American origin enjoyed discriminatory rebates of 20–30% in Brazil.
8. The classical interpretation is by Furtado (1963). This has been challenged by revisionists, but Fishlow (1972) provides a well-balanced evaluation of such revisions, confirming, in spite of several important qualifications, the main lines of the classical interpretation.
9. For foreign trade indices and a comprehensive treatment of Brazil's foreign economic policies in the 1930s see Abreu (1977) p. 34, and chaps 1 to 6. It would seem that the first balanced general treatment of the standard reaction of primary goods exporters to foreign exchange problems in the 1930s was provided by J. H. Williams's 1934 report on 'Foreign Exchange Problems in Brazil, Argentina and Chile', Department of State (1954) pp. 393–422. Williams also stressed the limited usefulness of devaluation in Latin America, since it could involve reduction in export proceeds as agricultural products faced inelastic demand and many countries controlled a sizeable share of the world market for their main exports.
10. It is of course true that real income was more substantially affected as terms of trade turned against Brazil.
11. That this line, which was clear in the case of Brazil as shown by Abreu (1977), passim, corresponded to a general priority of British foreign economic policy is confirmed by Tasca (1939) p. 85.
12. These payments were equivalent to about one-third of normal payments.
13. Cotton output in Brazil increased from around 100 000 metric tons in the late 1920s to more than 400 000 tons in 1937–9. Much of this expanded output was absorbed by foreign markets: total exports increased from less than 12 000 tons in 1926–8 to more than 270 000 tons in 1937–9. The British share of Brazilian cotton exports fell from 80% in the late 1920s to about 20% in the late 1930s in spite of quite a substantial increase in the absolute value of British imports. Germany in 1937–8 absorbed about 30% (60% in 1935) and Japan about 20% of Brazilian cotton exports.
14. Information concerning profit remittances by US firms in the period is rather scant but data on capital stock suggest that total remittances were very reduced in comparison with the typical trade imbalance.
15. Part of it not permanently. See Abreu (1978).
16. 1927–9 compared to 1936–8.

17. It must be mentioned that in 1928 terms of trade improved very considerably if compared with earlier years in the 1920s: average terms for 1921–7 were not more than 76% of the 1928 level. See UN (1951) p. 98.
18. For data on GDP and industrial production in Argentina see Diaz Alejandro (1970) statistical appendix. For Brazil see Fishlow (1972) appendix . Population increased at the rate of 2% a year during the same period in both countries.
19. See, for instance, Tasca (1939) p. 156: 'the rigidities in the British economic structure have inspired the British government to seek to retrieve and maintain its competitive position in export markets through the full utilization of Britain's bargaining weapons'.
20. See Mason's memo, 1.9.39, Foreign Office 371: A6297/1082/6, PRO, London, complaining that 'this country remains with one foot on the path of quotas and tariffs and the other still in the realm of most-favoured-nation agreements'.
21. Keynes (1980) pp. 239–40, Keynes's notes (5.1.42) on Pasvolsky's memo, 'Possibilities of Conflict of British and American Official Views on the Post-War Economic Policy'.
22. See, for instance, Fodor and O'Connell(1973).
23. See Salera (1941) chaps 2, 3 and 4, as well as section 2 of Fodor and O'Connell (1973).
24. See, for instance, Tulchin (1975). Attempts to reassess Roca – Runciman on the basis of its indirect effects seem in the light of events in other Latin American countries similarly fragile.
25. Tulchin (1975) pp. 86–7.
26. O'Connell(1982) shows that in the late 1920s the significance of Argentine meat for British consumption had led the British government to take a very different line if compared with the USA, based on the same scientific evidence concerning foot and mouth disease, as meat imports from Argentine into Britain were allowed to continue unhindered while they were embargoed in the USA.
27. Tulchin (1975) p. 97.
28. Tulchin (1975) p. 100.
29. See Di Tella and Zymelman (1973) for comments on the hard terms of the Malbrán – Eden agreement in the context of a fast recovery of Argentinian exports. See also Salera (1941) chap. 5.
30. The USA, obviously hurt by British-sponsored Argentinian discriminatory policies, was of course in a weak position to avoid damage to its interests especially in the first half of the decade. Secretary Hull's words of condemnation of British policy were thinly disguised: 'the establishment of an effective regime of equality of treatment, however, requires not only that nations refuse to grant preferences in their own markets, but also that they refrain from seeking a preferred position in markets of other countries', US Department of State, *Press Releases,* no. 347, 23.5.36, pp. 535–6, quoted in Kreider (1943) pp. 72–3.
31. See UN (1951) pp. 115 and 144.
32. There is no need to deal with Argentinian experience in the 1930s, as this hardly provides an example to be followed.

REFERENCES

M. de P. Abreu, 'Brazil and the World Economy, 1930–1945: Aspects of Foreign Economic Policies and International Economic Relations under Vargas', unpublished Ph. D. dissertation (Cambridge, 1977).

—— 'Brazilian Public Foreign Debt Policy, 1931–1943', *Brazilian Economic Studies*, 4 (1978) 37–88.

Brazil. Instituto Brasileiro de Geografia e Estatistica, *Anuário Estatístico do Brasil, 1939/40* (Rio de Janeiro, n.d.).

C. Diaz Alejandro, *Essays on the Economic History of the Argentine Republic* (New Haven and London, 1970.)

——'A América Latina em Depressão: 1929–39', *Pesquisa e Planejamento Econômico*, 10 (1980) 351–82.

G. Di Tella and M. Zymelman, *Los Ciclos Económicos Argentinos* (Buenos Aires, 1973).

A. Fishlow, 'Origins and Consequences of Import Substitution in Brazil', in L. Di Marco, *International Economics and Development: Essays in Honor of Raúl Prebisch* (New York, 1972).

J. Fodor and A. O'Connell, 'La Argentina y la Economia Atlántica en la Primera Mitad del Siglo xx', *Desarrollo Económico*, 13 (1973) 13–65.

C. Furtado. *The Economic Growth of Brazil* (Berkeley, Calif. 1963).

J. M. Keynes, *The Collected Writings of John Maynard Keynes, Activities 1944–1946: Shaping the Post-War World: Bretton Woods and Reparations*, vol. xxvi (London and New York, 1980).

C. Kreider, *The Anglo-American Trade Agreement: A Study of British and American Commercial Policies, 1934–1939* (Princeton, N. J., 1943).

A. O'Connell, 'The American Sanitary Embargo against Meat and the U-turn to Bilateralism in Argentine Commercial Policy' (unpublished paper, 1982).

V. Salera, *Exchange Control and the Argentine Market* (New York, 1941).

H. J. Tasca, *World Trading Systems: A Study of American and British Commercial Policies* (Paris, 1939).

J. S. Tulchin, 'Foreign Policy', in M. Falcoff and R. Dolkart (eds), *Prologue to Perón: Argentine in Depression and War, 1930–1943* (Berkeley, Calif. 1975).

7 Before the Depression: Brazilian Industry in the 1920s

FLAVIO RABELO VERSIANI

INTRODUCTION

The literature on the economics of the Depression in Brazil may be said to have passed through three stages. Initially, the classical ECLA–Furtado theory on the positive effects of the slump on the diversification of Brazilian productive structure reigned supreme (Furtado, 1959, chaps. xxx–xxxiii). The theory was influential not only in the field of economics, but was also widely used as a basis for sociological and political analyses of the period. A radical generalisation of that vision has been presented as part of the '*dependencia*' theory of Latin American underdevelopment (Frank, 1969).

In the second stage the reasoning of Furtado was attacked on various fronts. The fire was chiefly concentrated on his main line of argument, according to which the relatively rapid recovery of the Brazilian economy in the 1930s had been a by-product of the coffee policy (which caused an increase in demand for domestically produced import-substitutes, especially manufactures, early in the decade). Furtado's emphasis on the 1930s as the starting-point of significant industrial growth was also criticised, on the grounds that it underestimated previous developments (Peláez, 1972; Villela and Suzigan, 1973).

The third phase has been characterised by a closer scrutiny of the debate on the relation between coffee and the recovery (Silber, 1977; Fishlow, 1972; E. Cardoso, 1979). It has been found that Furtado's original argument, in its general lines, withstands quite well the

163

charges of its critics – even though it has been subject to factual corrections of some importance.

On the other hand, research on the supply side of the picture – on
how the production system was able to respond to the increase in
demand for manufactures during the Depression – is in a much less
satisfactory state. It is generally agreed now that unused productive
capacity inherited from the 1920s played a crucial role in the expansion of the 1930s; however, not much is said in the literature on the
reasons for the existence of such excess capacity. Industry, it is said,
grew slowly or not at all after the mid-1920s; in spite of that, indices
for capital formation would indicate an acceleration of investment
activity in the last half of the decade (Villela and Suzigan, 1973; Fishlow, 1972; Baer and Villela, 1973; Haddad, 1974).

The purpose of this paper is to contribute to a better understanding
of the period of the Depression, by studying some characteristics of
industrial growth in the preceding decade. The main contention is
that the overall performance of industry in the 1920s was rather better than is commonly realised. That performance laid the foundations
for an appreciable number of new initiatives in industrial investment,
so that a good basis was established for the diversification of industrial output in the following decade.

The chapter is organised as follows. In the next section data on
industrial output growth and investment for the interwar period are
examined. The third section presents an overview of the economic
policies of the period; the fourth section deals with the effects of
those policies on the development of industry. The fifth section discusses some features of industrial investment in the period. A final
section presents the main conclusions.

INDUSTRIAL PERFORMANCE IN THE 1920S

The available indices of Brazilian industrial output in the 1920s are
shown in Table 7.1 (a). The three series apparently tell somewhat
different stories. In the Villela – Suzigan index, the 1923 output level
is not reached again in the remaining years of the decade; these
figures have been taken as evidence of the stagnation that is supposed
to have dominated Brazilian industrial activities in the period (cf.
Villela and Suzigan, 1973; Baer and Villela, 1973; Silber, 1977). On
the other hand, both Haddad's and Eishlow's indices suggest a respectable increase in out put between 1923–4 and 1927–8; Haddad's,

TABLE 7.1   *Brazil: industrial output 1917–30*
(a) Indices (1920 = 100)

Year	*Villela–Suzigan*	*Haddad*	*Fishlow*	*Cotton textiles*
		Overall industrial output		
1917	–	84	–	103
1918	–	83	–	93
1919	–	95	–	97
1920	100	100	100	100
1921	99	98	98	96
1922	114	117	117	118
1923	136	132	117	117
1924	114	131	117	109
1925	115	132	120	101
1926	114	135	122	101
1927	123	150	134	112
1928	133	161	142	109
1929	128	157	137	90
1930	122	147	127	89

(b) Yearly growth rates (%)

Year	*Villela–Suzigan*	*Haddad*	*Fishlow*
1925	0.8	1.1	2.1
1926	−1.0	2.4	2.0
1927	8.1	10.7	10.0
1928	8.0	7.0	5.5
1929	−3.5	−2.2	−3.5
1930	−4.7	−6.7	−7.1

SOURCES: Basic data from: Villela and Suzigan (1973) p. 431; Haddad (1974) p. 147; Fishlow (1972) p. 357; for cotton textiles, Brazil, Departamento Nacional de Estatística (1933) p. xiv. Growth rates computed from original data.

however, indicates a much higher average growth rate during the 1920s.

These differences, however, spring from a problem common to all these series: the numbers for the years 1919 to 1923 are not consistent with those for the rest of the period, in the official statistics on which the indices are based.[1] If those years are excepted the three indices point basically in the same direction; this is better seen by comparing the growth rates derived from them (Table 7.1 (b)).

Having in mind the statistical problem for 1919–23, the numbers in Table 7.1 suggest a division of the period between the First World War and the Depression into four well-defined phases, in respect of overall industrial growth:

(a) 1917/18–1923/4. As a whole a period of vigorous, if irregular, expansion in manufacturing output; the Haddad index shows an average yearly growth of 6.8% between 1917–18 and 1924–5. However, 1921 was a slack year.
(b) 1924–6. A period of sluggish growth.
(c) 1927–8. Rapid output increase again, the 1928 output level exceeding that of 1924 by 17% and 22%, depending on the index considered.
(d) 1929–30. Negative growth rates.

Table 7.1 (a) also contains information on the performance of the cotton textile industry, the first manufacturing activity to assume substantial proportions, and still the main sector at the time.[2] The cotton textile output index (in which the statistical problem for 1919–23, referred to above, has been eliminated) shows that that sector did experience a marked setback after 1922–3; the output level of those two years was never reached again in the 1920s. Therefore, even though the idea of widespread stagnation in industry after 1923 is open to challenge a weaker proposition remains true: stagnation prevailed in the most important industrial sector. This fact has been used in support of the idea that the import-substitution process suffered a reversal in the 1920s (cf. Fishlow, 1972).

To what extent were the difficulties of the textile industry shared by other sectors as well? The data in Table 7.2 suggest that the evolution of cotton textile production in the second half of the 1920s was not typical of manufacturing activity as a whole.[3] 'Traditional' industries such as food, hats and footwear did suffer output declines after 1924; however, a recovery took place after 1926 so that the 1924 production level was surpassed by a large margin by 1927–8 in those industries. (The same was true in textiles as a whole, due to rapid advances in wool and jute production.) On the other hand, newer sectors such as chemicals and metallurgy, along with tobacco products, showed remarkable growth in those years.

Table 7.3 compares the aggregate performance of manufacturing activities with and without textiles.[4] It is seen that non-textile manufactures, on the whole, moved in a direction quite opposite to that of the cotton sector (cf. Table 7.1) after 1922: a steady growth, at rates that increase up to 1928, and, quite remarkably, a positive growth rate of almost 5% in 1929 (as compared to a drop of −3% in the overall manufacturing index for that year).

Also in the pattern of industrial investment a difference between

TABLE 7.2 *Brazil: manufacturing output, 1924–30*
(indices 1924 = 100)

Year	Textiles	Food	Beverages	Footwear	Hats	Chemicals	Tobacco	Printing	Furniture	Metallurgy	Total manuf.
1924	100	100	100	100	100	100	100	100	100	100	100
1925	92	99	101	99	94	100	131	122	119	121	100
1926	92	106	108	93	76	163	104	92	119	109	102
1927	111	108	115	109	108	185	132	77	131	103	113
1928	116	114	121	116	135	198	150	90	135	151	121
1929	92	119	125	135	118	222	156	103	115	193	118
1930	89	129	104	99	63	157	141	95	85	158	110

SOURCES: For metallurgy: Villela and Suzigan (1973) p. 433; other series from Haddad (1974). Base year changed to 1924.

TABLE 7.3   *Brazil: manufacturing output, 1920–30*
(indices 1920 = 100)

Year	Total output		Total output excluding textiles	
	Index	Growth rates (%)	Index	Growth rates (%)
1920	100		100	
1921	98	−2.0	96	−4.0
1922	118	20.4	118	22.9
1923	133	12.7	120	1.7
1924	129	−3.0	122	1.7
1925	129	0	126	3.3
1926	132	2.3	130	3.2
1927	145	9.9	137	5.4
1928	154	6.2	148	8.0
1929	150	−2.6	155	4.7
1930	142	−5.3	147	−5.2

SOURCE AND METHOD: The overall index is a weighted average of indices for the manufacturing sectors in Table 7.2, the weights being the respective shares in those sectors' total value added in 1919. The second index is of similar construction, textiles being excluded. Basic data from Haddad (1974).

the textile sector and the remaining industries can be seen. Given that internal production of industrial equipment at the time was negligible, the evolution of investment is usually estimated from machinery import data. Table 7.4 compares import values for textile machinery and for other machinery. It is seen that while in the case of the former series there is a marked decline after 1925, imports of 'other' machinery actually increased in the second half of the decade, the peak value being reached in 1929. As before, general indices, being strongly influenced by what happened in the textile industry, may be a misleading indicator of the behaviour of other sectors.[5]

ECONOMIC POLICIES AND INDUSTRIAL DEVELOPMENT IN THE 1920S

Three factors are undoubtedly important to explain the performance of industry in the period: the behaviour of the coffee sector, the evolution of the exchange rate, and the monetary and fiscal policies followed by the government. This section briefly reviews these points.[6]

TABLE 7.4   *Brazil: imports of industrial machinery, 1918–30*
(£1 000)

Year	Textile machinery[a]	Other machinery[b]
1918	314	760
1919	416	1 189
1920	752	3 587
1921	954	3 137
1922	839	1 443
1923	934	1 537
1924	1 128	2 744
1925	1 778	3 433
1926	1 050	3 306
1927	740	2 985
1928	755	3 415
1929	562	4 095
1930	283	2 220

[a] Items 265 to 268 of the import statistics.
[b] Items 269 ('Industrial machinery, unenumerated') and 283 ('Machinery, unenumerated') of the import statistics.

SOURCES: *Comercio Exterior do Brasil* (various issues).

As to coffee, the main characteristic of the period is the successful operation of the price-support policy, in so far as prices were pushed upwards and kept at high levels (after a sharp drop in 1919–21). Export proceeds reached in 1924–9 values never attained before.

The *mil-réis* underwent a sharp devaluation at the beginning of the decade; the rate of exchange of sterling almost trebled from 1919 to 1923. This can be partly attributed to the fall in coffee prices: the interactions between coffee market fluctuations and the behaviour of the exchange rate in Brazil are well known.[7] But the exchange market was also affected by the expansion of money supply in 1921–4. This expansion was largely associated with the operatons of the Carteira de Redescontos of the Banco do Brasil, created in 1921. Established to rediscount commercial paper, the new department was soon made to discount Treasury bills as well, and became a basic source of finance to cover the deficit of the federal government. The Carteira was also instrumental in financing the purchase of coffee by the government, through the 'valorisation' scheme.

A marked change in economic policies took place beginning in 1923, under the new Bernardes Administration.[8] A very restrictive monetary policy was followed; the monetary base suffered a marked contraction from 1924 to 1926, and the rediscounting activities of the

Banco do Brasil were drastically curtailed (particularly as far as commercial paper was concerned). The external value of the *mil-réis* increased; from the last quarter of 1923 to the third quarter of 1926 the
average quotation of the pound sterling dropped from 53.4 *mil-réis* to
31.6.[9]

At the end of 1926 the favourable balance-of-payments position
(caused by high coffee prices and an increased inflow of foreign capital) induced the new Administration, under President Washington
Luis, to embark on a policy of making the *mil-réis* into a convertible
currency. Newly issued *mil-réis* notes were to be exchangeable for
gold, or convertible currencies, at a new parity rate (40.69 *mil-réis*/
£1). That rate meant a substantial devaluation of the *mil-réis*, in relation to the 1926 exchange rates (an average of 33.6/£1). As a result of
that, and of the ample supply of foreign exchange in the market, the
flow of convertible currencies into the 'stabilisation fund', in exchange for the new *mil-réis* notes, was rather high in 1927–8. The
corresponding increase in money supply was instrumental in easing
the credit situation.[10] In the words of a contemporary observer, the
convertibility policy was 'an attempt to take into consideration the
desire for cheap money, the aversion of coffee producers to a high
exchange rate and the striving of the new industrial classes towards
stable money' (Normano (1968) p. 189.). If that was the case, the
policy was a successful one up to 1928: the exchange rate was stabilised at a lower level and money was more easily available.

In 1929–30, on the other hand, the outflow of capital caused a
decrease in the circulation of convertible notes, until the reserves of
the stabilisation fund were exhausted. The monetary base diminished
by about 10% from late 1928 to the end of 1929 (Peláez and Suzigan,
1976, table A. 3). In 1930 the price of coffee began its plunge, which
was to last up to the mid-1930s.

The tariff legislation was subject to few changes in the 1920s, apart
from some *ad hoc* alterations in response to demands from specific
groups.[11] The only general change of importance was an increase in
the proportion of tariff dues to be paid in gold, which went up from
55% to 60%, starting in 1923.[12] In fact, the 1900 tariff schedule was
not changed until 1934; this stands in marked contrast to the frequent
revisions in the last decades of the nineteenth century. The previous
alternation of 'liberalising' and 'protectionist' tariff reforms was now
replaced by a deadlock: neither proposals to lower the general level
of tariffs nor motions for an across-the-board increase in protection
were able to muster sufficient support in both houses of parliament.[13]

However, the absence of large revisions in the tariff legislation was in effect a change of policy by default, since, in spite of unchanged tax-rate schedules, the relative level of taxation on imports was greatly reduced in the period. This was a result of the increase in import prices (see below, p. 172) and of the fact that the tariff was fixed in nominal terms. The proportion of import duty proceeds to the total value of imports, which had averaged 45% in 1901–10, now dropped to half that figure (an average of 23%, in 1920–9).[14]

The general effects of the above developments on the growth of industry in the 1920s can be *a priori* described as follows. The success of the coffee valorisation scheme, given the weight of coffee export revenues in aggregate income, must have had a positive effect on the overall level of activity during the decade. On the other hand, monetary policy was highly contractionary in 1924–6 and 1929–30. As to the exchange rate, the substantial devaluations in the early 1920s, and again in 1926–9, must have increased the competitiveness of local producers; on the other hand, the appreciation of the *mil-réis* in 1923–6 had the opposite result. Finally, the tariff policy was in principle detrimental to the interests of local industry, allowing as it did a deterioration in the relative level of taxation on imports.

The literature on the period shows different views as to the reasons for the supposed decline in industrial activity after 1924. Fishlow (1972), for instance, stresses as the main factor the increase in imports of manufactured goods in the period. This in turn he attributes to the strengthened competitive position of imports due to the appreciation of the *mil-réis*, and to the reduced protection afforded by the tariff system. According to him, 'there was no lack of demand in general'; the problem was basically one of relative prices (Fishlow, 1972, p. 327). Others put more emphasis on the effect of the deflationary policies in force after 1923 (Villela and Suzigan, 1973; Baer and Villela, 1973), implying that the phenomenon was more general, not necessarily restricted to import-substituting industries. It is interesting to examine more closely these two lines of argument, with a view to seeing what light they may throw on the question of the differential behaviour of the texile industry.

IMPORT PRICES AND CREDIT SHORTAGE: TEXTILES V. NON-TEXTILES

Taking first the question of the relative price of imports it is important to realise that their movements were related not only to the ups and downs of the exchange rate and the erosion of tariff protection

TABLE 7.5   *Brazil: cotton texile import prices, 1912–30*
(Indices 1912 = 100)

Year	Sterling prices A	Exchange rate (mil-réis/£) B	Mil-réis prices (A × B) C	Internal price level D	Real import prices (C/D) E
1912	100	100	100	100	100
1918	236	125	296	147	201
1919	312	114	356	152	234
1920	405	112	452	167	270
1921	348	186	645	172	375
1922	235	231	543	188	289
1923	239	298	714	207	345
1924	239	273	650	242	269
1925	224	267	597	259	230
1926	198	224	443	266	167
1927	185	274	507	273	186
1928	208	272	568	269	210
1929	186	272	507	267	190
1930	178	293	521	243	215

SOURCES AND METHOD: Column *A*: Index of average prices of 'piece goods, dyed' (the main item of textile imports, in the period); basic data from *Comercio Exterior do Brasil* (various issues). Column *B*: Index of the rate of exchange implicit in the import statistics of cotton manufactures, in *Comercio Exterior do Brasil* (various issues). Column *D*: Cost-of-living index for Rio de Janeiro from Brazil, Instituto Brasileiro de Geografia e Estatística (p. 1384).

(as implied in Fishlow's reasoning). The sterling price of imported manufactures was itself subject to large variations in the period, reflecting the post-war shifts in prices in the industrialised economics. We may recall that the British wholesale price index, after reaching in 1920 a level more than three times that of 1913, fell sharply in the 1921 Depression, and followed a general downward trend in the rest of the decade. Prices in the USA showed a similar pattern.

The figures in Table 7.5 show the extent of variation in sterling import prices, in the case of cotton textiles, and its effect on the domestic price of imports. In the years right after the war, for instance, in spite of a rise in exchange, the *mil-réis* price of imported textiles *increased* markedly, even if deflated by an index of the general level of prices in Brazil.[15] From 1920 to 1923 sterling prices went down and the *mil-réis* depreciated; those opposing movements caused wide oscillations in the internal price of imports. In the next three years, on the other hand, both forces tended to pull downwards

TABLE 7.6   *Brazil: estimated domestic consumption of cotton textiles,*
1919–30
(million metres)

Year	Domestic Productuon A	Imports B	Exports C	Domestic consumption (A + B − C) D	Imports/ consumption (B/D, %) E
1919	516	56	1	571	9.8
1920	533	73	1	605	12.0
1921	512	30	6	536	5.6
1922	627	47	8	666	7.1
1923	624	59	8	675	8.7
1924	580	88	1	667	13.2
1925	536	110	0	646	17.0
1926	539	110	0	649	17.0
1927	594	109	0	703	15.5
1928	582	125	0	707	17.7
1929	478	74	0	552	13.4
1930	476	20	0	496	4.0

SOURCES: Column *A*: See Table 7.1. Column *B*: Data in kilograms from *Comercio Exterior do Brasil*, converted into metres by means of the ratio 15m/kg, derived from comparison of British and Brazilian trade statistics. Column *C*: As in *B*, using the conversion factor 10m/kg.

the internal price of imports, which was cut by half in real terms from 1923 to 1926. Notwithstanding a reaction in 1927–8, the *mil-réis* price never again reached the 1925 level in the remaining years of the decade.

Given such an evolution of relative prices it is not surprising that competition from import cottons should have been strong after 1924. It can be estimated that the share of imports in domestic consumption went up from around 7% in 1921–3 to 17% in 1925–8 (see Table 7.6).

The figures in Table 7.6 lend some support to Fishlow's contention (1972) that the bad performance of the industry in the second half of the 1920s was more related to unfavourable trends in relative prices than to slack demand.[16] It is important to notice, however, that the shifts in the import price of textiles were rather more extreme than those of import prices in general. The price increase in cotton textile import in 1918–21 was much steeper than the average, and the drop after 1924 was also steeper. This is apparent from the numbers presented in Table 7.7. There is therefore good reason to suppose that the relative-price argument is particularly applicable to the textile industry.

TABLE 7.7   *Brazil: import price indices, 1912–30*
(1912 = 100)

Year	All goods	Cotton textiles
1912	100	100
1918	290	296
1919	269	356
1920	322	452
1921	377	645
1922	299	543
1923	320	714
1924	281	650
1925	288	597
1926	237	443
1927	288	507
1928	273	566
1929	257	507
1930	276	521

SOURCES AND METHOD: The overall index is taken from Villela and Suzigan (1973) p. 441 (base year changed). For the cotton textile index see Table 7.5. The indices are for *mil-réis* prices.

On the other hand, it was to be expected that the stringent monetary policy followed in 1924–6 should have affected the manufacturing sector. The industries were hit especially hard as the credit difficulties came on top of a rising trend in the exchange rate, which had forced local producers to extend more liberal credit terms to their customers, so as to face competition from imports.[17] Industrial firms generally depended on the banking system for working capital, and apparently the previous years of ample credit supply had made that dependence even more marked. This made them especially vulnerable at that time.[18]

Contemporary accounts of the evolution of the economy stress that the 1925–6 crisis was felt with particular force in the cotton textile industry. The sudden rise of the exchange in the first half of 1926, for instance, was said to have 'created a panic in local industries, especially in the cotton mills'.[19] But the appreciation of the *mil-réis* was not considered to be the main problem of textile producers: 'The improvement in exchange facilitated importation, but the difficulties of the textile industry are to be attributed less to any increased importation than to the general tightness of money, and to overproduction.'[20]

The same point was emphasised by another observer: the problems of the textile industry were 'much less the result of foreign competition than of over-production'.[21]

References to over-production are abundant in the period in relation to the texile industry (see Stein, 1959). Recalling that the 1924–6 period witnessed a spurt of investment in textile production (cf. Table 7.4 above), it is easy to see what was meant by that. It is important, for our purposes, to ask why, in spite of the crisis, many entrepreneurs thought that it was an appropriate time to expand the productive capacity of their mills or to enter the market as new producers.

To some extent the 1924–6 investment spurt may be seen as a predictable reaction of textile producers to their good results in previous years. This pattern was a very general one in the early development of industry in Brazil: periods of depreciating exchange and increased demand were often followed by periods of greater investment activity in industry, coinciding with a revaluation of the *mil-réis* which made machinery imports easier (F. R. Versiani, 1980). Increased investment in 1924 might thus be considered a response to high 1923 profits, and a better exchange rate for the *mil-réis*. But it would be difficult to reconcile the idea of a three-year period of generalised crisis in the industry with a simultaneous drive for expansion of productive capacity.

The solution to the riddle seems to be that the impact of the crisis did not fall evenly on all producers in the industry. There is evidence that the textile machinery installed in the 1920s had cost advantages over existing productive installations, so that the owners of the former fared better in the period than old-established producers. Those mills that had not been re-equipped were thus confronted not only with an increase in imports, but also with the rise of competition at home.[22]

The expansion of productive capacity in the period was especially noticeable in certain states such as Pernambuco, where the founding of various new mills was reported in 1925–6.[23] But the process was not geographically restricted; the late 1920s witnessed a veritable mushrooming of small mills in various States, a development viewed with alarm by owners of existing mills.[24]

It is therefore understandable that 'over-production' was indeed a serious problem from the viewpoint of the older mills. It reflected basically the entry of new, more efficient producers, in a market

TABLE 7.8   *Brazil: unit prices of the main products subject to consumption tax, 1925–9*
(indices, 1925 = 100)

Product	1925	1926	1927	1928	1929
Cotton textile	100	76	74	77	75
Shoes	100	103	109	111	105
Beer	100	107	97	97	101
Sugar-cane brandy	100	82	71	88	86
Ground coffee	100	100	100	100	100
Cigarettes	100	103	101	101	n.a.
Glass	100	97	97	101	98
Furniture	100	100	102	101	100
Screws and bolts	100	99	99	92	92

SOURCE: Derived from data in Brazil, Departamento Nacional de Estatística.

already burdened by rising imports and credit shortage. The reaction of the owners of large pre-war mills to such a state of affairs was strong enough to force an intervention by the government, with the purpose of checking the expansion of productive capacity: in 1931 importation of machinery to be used in industries 'in a state of over-production' was prohibited (see Stein, 1959).

The combined effect of the fall in the relative price of imports and the increase of productive capacity in textiles was apparent in the second half of the 1920s. The average price of domestically produced cotton textiles fell by about 25%, from 1925 to 1927 (Table 7.8). It is relevant to point out that such a fall contrasts with the evolution of prices in most other manufacturing activities, as shown by the data in Table 7.8; this is still more evidence that the performance of the textile industry was not typical of industry in general. In 1928 cotton textile producing was described as 'the biggest cloud on a clearing horizon' in domestic manufacturing industry.[25] But the clouds were not everywhere: in the State of Pernambuco, for instance, production of cottons increased by more than 60% in the last half of the decade, and the share of the State in total output grew from 9% in 1925 to 15% in 1926.[26]

To sum up, there are reasons to suppose not only that import price movements in the 1920s were more unfavourable in the case of cotton textiles, but also that the credit restrictions of the Bernardes Administration had an especially strong effect on the textile industry. The case of textiles was indeed a special one.[27]

SOME FEATURES OF INTERWAR INDUSTRIAL DEVELOPMENT

The data presented above indicate that, if the textile industry is excepted, the 1920s may be seen as a period of appreciable output growth rates and investment activity in manufacturing. An important aspect of that was the diversification of industrial production. Writing about São Paulo, Dean lists the following manufactures whose domestic production started in the inter-War period: pig iron, cement, electrial hardware, electric motors, textile machinery, sugar-processing equipment, automobile parts, accessories and tools, agricultural implements, gas appliances, timekeeping and weighing devices, and rayon textiles (Dean, 1969, p. 110). In fact, in all these cases domestic production had already begun in the 1920s (cf. sources quoted in n. 29 below).

Except in the case of a few industries the initial development of these activities has not been much studied; the sources of the capital invested, and the social origins of entrepreneurship, in particular, are still to be investigated.[28] However, some general observations are worth making, in connection with industrial investment initiatives in the period. They concern: the importance of repair shops as the initial nucleus of some industries; the role of capital reinvestment and of foreign capital; and the question of governmental support.

(a) Many of the initiatives in the field of machinery and equipment production had their origin in small repair shops. Dates of foundation of industrial firms in these sectors seem to be concentrated in the early 1920s, and to a lesser extent in the last years of the decade. That is, following periods of increased production – and profits – in the industry.[29] The experience and profits accumulated during the War were an important source of stimulus. A common story was that a repair shop, given the importation difficulties imposed by wartime, had found it profitable to produce replacement parts for sale; after the War, it was decided that production on a regular basis was a worth-while proposition.

Many examples can be cited: in fact, a good number of leading present-day firms in those sectors were founded in the 1920s. Villares, for instance, the largest private Brazilian producer of machinery and equipment, was established in 1920; the firm evolved from an elevator repair shop founded at the beginning of the War. Dedini, the leading maker of equipment for sugar and alcohol production, was also founded in 1929, and started as a machine repair shop; Mr Dedini had worked as a mechanic in a sugar-grinding mill during the War. Very similar stories can be told of Romi, the machine-tool giant (founded in 1929), Ribeiro and Andrighetti, the makers of equipment for textile production (1920 and 1922, respectively); other important firms dating from the 1920s include Lorenzetti (water-heating equipment, 1923) and Nardini (machine tools, 1924).[30] In the words of Dean (1969, p. 116): 'The origins of this new group of entrepreneurs are in most cases obscure; however, if a generalization can be extended from a few cases, it appears that they were generally town-bred members of the lower fringes of the middle class, most often first or second generation immigrants, who had obtained a technical education of sorts.'

(b) As in previous periods, profit reinvestment seems to have played a crucial role (cf. F. R. Versiani, 1980). The capacity to manage adequately the profits obtained in periods of favourable market position may have been the distinguishing mark of those firms that started as very small concerns.

A contemporary report on 'Brazilian Industrial Progress' sustained that the reinvestment capacity of São Paulo industrialists was high in 1923 (a year when industries were 'humming'): a random sample of forty balance-sheets revealed that 'most concerns . . . were strengthening their position by placing large sums to reserve'. While the average proportion of net profits to paid-up capital was 33%, dividends paid averaged less than 15%.[31] Profits were being invested also in different fields of production: see Dean (1969, pp. 113ff.).

(c) The participation of foreign capital in the establishment of the cement and steel industries in Brazil in the period has been pointed out in the literature (Villela and Suzigan, 1973; Baer, 1969). But the 1920s marked also the beginning of a new and important trend in foreign investment: the establishment of local productive units by foreign firms (especially U.S. concerns). The bulletin of the American Chamber of Commerce for Brazil in the 1920s repeatedly urged US firms to set up factories in Brazil, in order to circumvent the tariff barrier. 'Several firms from the U.S. have already done this, and others will in the near future', wrote a business analyst in 1923.[32]

The prediction was quite correct (and also applicable to firms from other countries). A list of foreign corporations that established production units in Brazil between the Wars includes: General Electric (1919), RCA (1919), IBM (1924), Ericsson (1924), Philips (1925), Standard Electric (1926), Burroughs (1929) and Pirelli (1929).

Assembly plants were also set up in the period by Ford and General Motors.[33]

As a whole, the available data indicate that the capital inflows resulting from such moves were not very significant. The importance of the process lies, however, in the fact that it helped to establish the foundations for an expansion and diversification of industrial output in the following decade.

(d) It is known that the Brazilian government sometimes offered some sort of assistance to the founding of new industries in the period we are concerned with. Such assistance could assume various forms: tax exemptions for importation of equipment, guarantee of interest, loans, cash prizes (Villela and Suzigan, 1973, pp. 345ff.).

The granting of such benefits did not follow any particular plan or pattern, however, generally resulting from isolated initiatives; often the legal instrument introducing a given benefit was revoked after a short time. This has led some analysts to consider the governmental incentives as ineffective. In line with this idea the economic policies of the period before 1930 are seen as entirely dominated by agricultural or commercial interests (Villela and Suzigan, 1973; Suzigan, 1975). This is, however, a questionable argument. In the first place it is necessary to recognise that, even though the class of large landowners associated with the export business was undoubtedly preponderant in the social system, it does not follow that the State would in all circumstances act in strict accordance with the interests of that class (nor that all lines of governmental policy could be explained only by reference to the social structure). Political scientists warn us against a simplistic association between class relations and the political system in Brazil; and it has been shown that in some important instances policies quite contrary to the interests of the coffee elite were consistently pursued in the pre-1930 era.[34]

As to the question of the effectiveness of incentives to industry in our period, it is difficult to make any general statement. The very fact that benefits took so many forms and were so subject to change makes it difficult to analyse their effects; indeed, our factual knowledge about this matter is still quite limited. But it is doubtful that we can pronounce the incentive system ineffectual; for one thing, contemporary observers seemed to think that it was quite effective. It is significant, for instance, that economic reports prepared by the British and American embassies usually gave emphasis to the introduction of industrial promotion measures by the government. In 1923 'the willingness of the Government to assist in establishing new industries' was mentioned as 'a great factor' of industrial growth in the preceding years (along with the War, high tariffs and depreciation of the *mil-réis*).[35]

There are some specific instances, in the inter-war period, when the establishment of new industries was certainly related to governmental incentives. The cases of cement and steel come to mind at once (Villela and Suzigan, 1973, pp. 176–7, 349–51). Another example is the various incentives given to silk spinning, in a period when the domestic production of silk textiles increased rapidly (Department of Overseas Trade, 1926, pp. 26–7; 1927, p. 18).

Another case in point is that of caustic-soda production, actively promoted by the government in 1918–19, through the offer of loans corresponding to 75% of the cost of the factories. Various firms bid for that incentive, four finally being chosen; the total credits opened by the government amounted to about US $1.2 million.[36]

Other examples could be added; what is needed, however, is a systematic study of the question. But is is clear that we cannot rule out *a priori* as unimportant the role of governmental incentives in the process of industrial diversification of the inter-War period. Governmental policies in the coffee era were not always anti-industrialist.

CONCLUDING REMARKS

The broad effects of the 1929 crisis on the Brazilian economy are well known. Contraction of export revenues and decrease of capital inflows opened the way for a sharp devaluation of the *mil-réis*, and for exchange and import controls; on the other hand, government policies – in particular the coffee support programme – had an anti-cyclical effect. The combined result of these price and income movements was an increased demand for locally produced importable goods, especially manufactures. From this resulted an early recovery in the internal production of those goods, with unusually high rates of growth 1932–6 and a remarkable diversification of internal supply, with a rapid growth of non-traditional sectors (see Table 7.9).

The argument of the previous sections shows that on both accounts – high growth and diversification of manufacturing production – developments previous to 1929 are rather important in explaining the effects of the Depression. The performance of the textile sector, for instance, stands in marked contrast to that of other traditonal sectors such as food, beverages and footwear during the 1930s: the average

TABLE 7.9   *Brazil: manufacturing output, 1928–39*
(indices 1928 = 100)

Year	Textiles	Food	Beverages	Foot-wear	Hats	Chemicals	Tobacco	Print-ing	Furn-iture	Metal-lurgy	Paper	Hides and Leather	Cement	Total manuf.
1928	100	100	100	100	100	100	100	100	100	100	100	100	100	100
1929	80	105	104	116	88	112	104	114	86	102	132	97	109	98
1930	77	113	86	85	47	79	94	106	63	84	96	111	99	91
1931	96	105	75	87	47	78	97	70	71	74	124	108	190	92
1932	100	104	77	76	42	92	94	76	71	92	112	100	169	93
1933	112	119	81	80	52	90	98	94	74	133	176	122	257	104
1934	126	125	83	87	56	102	150	108	91	159	228	128	382	116
1935	150	131	96	111	65	120	112	121	97	176	304	147	416	130
1936	178	136	108	132	81	171	133	138	240	207	344	147	551	153
1937	192	129	110	132	88	173	158	162	277	230	412	153	649	160
1938	203	137	109	142	78	192	164	130	371	280	428	139	702	166
1939	236	141	127	124	81	186	132	141	306	407	448	231	793	182

SOURCES: For metallurgy, Villela and Suzigan (1973) p. 433; other series from Haddad (1974). Base year changed to 1928.

growth of textiles from 1928 to the end of the following decade was more than twice as fast as that of those three industries. This rapid increase in textiles would hardly have been possible but for the degree of unutilised capacity in the late 1920s, mentioned above, caused by increases in productive capacity in a period of stagnant production.[37] The vigorous process of diversification of industrial output that took place in the 1930s (see Fishlow, 1972, for details) was also influenced by investment initiatives taken in the 1920s and in earlier periods.[38]

A conclusion to be drawn from the above findings, therefore, is that the 1930s did not mean the sharp break with the past that some of the literature implies. Brazil's economic performance in that decade seems to have been closely related to previous developments, especially in what concerns the capacity of private agents to adjust promptly to the new set of relative prices.

On the other hand it should be clear that the emphasis placed by the ECLA school on the importance of the demand shock caused by the crisis is not challenged here; as pointed out before, recent treatments of the period have tended to confirm Furtado's classical analysis (1959) of this question. No doubt the process of capital accumulation as a whole was very much affected by the profits generated by the increase in production for the internal market in the period. The point is, rather, that the demand boom had the effect it had, in the 1930s, largely because the basis for supply expansion had been laid before, in many activities. The conditions that made possible such pre-1929 developments, especially in the industrial sector, are an important area of future research; but the evidence available so far – including that presented above – clearly indicates that the notion that the process of (export-led) industrial growth was nearing exhaustion before 1929 (an idea present in many ECLA writings) is simplistic at best. The expansion and transformation of productive structure in Brazilian industry seems to have been a more gradual process than is often supposed.

Pre-1929 developments may be also relevant to explaining the response of Brazilian policy-makers to the crisis. As Carlos Diaz Alejandro points out, those Latin American countries which displayed 'reactive' behaviour after the crisis, as regards economic policy, fared distinctly better in their performance during the 1930s.[39] From this point of view Brazil was typically a reactive country, having adopted, soon after the 1929 crisis, various relatively unorthodox measures, such as the abandonment of convertibility and exchange and import controls – not to speak of the coffee support programme, partly financed through monetary expansion. It can well be argued that those actions were made easier by the fact that measures of a similar nature had been adopted before (non-convertibility had been the rule rather than the exception; financing of governmental deficits by means of monetary expansion had been common; the tariff system had often been used to check selected imports, and so on). To that extent previous experiences may help to explain why Brazilian policy-makers reacted to the crisis the way they did (that is: to explain why they were 'reactive' and not 'passive', in Diaz Alejandro's terms). Also here, a sharp division between the periods before and after 1929 may be misleading.

NOTES

1. The basic source of information on industrial output for the period under consideration are the statistics on production subject to the consumption tax (see Brazil, Directoria da Receita Pública do Thesouro Nacional). These statistics were based on the tax stamps applied on the products as they were sold by their makers; they thus showed annual sales rather than annual production. From 1919 to 1923, however, the tax agents were instructed to collect also information on production. It so happened that, when the figures were later collected in a single volume (Brazil, Departamento Nacional de Estatística), the *production* data for 1919–23 were used, along with the *sales* data, for all remaining years. The resulting series are, therefore, a mixture of different things. This introduced an upward bias in the numbers for that five-year period; particularly noticeable is the extraordinary increase in the production of cotton textiles in 1923 (a 50% increase over the 1922 level), for which there is no correspondence in the sales data. The 1923 peak in the Villela – Suzigan and Haddad indices is derived from that spurious jump in the figures for textiles. (The Fishlow index, on the other hand, is correctly based, in the case of textiles, on the sales figures, thus not showing a rise in 1923.) All three indices, however, are in some degree distorted in the period 1919–23. For details see F. R. Versiani (1981).
2. On the early development of the textile industry, see F. R. Versiani (1980). The share of textiles in value added in industry, in the 1920s, was around 25%: cf. Villela and Suzigan (1973), Fishlow (1972), Haddad (1974).
3. Table 7.2 comprises practically all manufacturing sectors for which there is reliable statistical information in the period. Haddad's index is based on those ten sectors up to 1925; in 1926–30, paper, hides and leather, cement and tyres are also included.
4. The index in the first column of Table 7.3 is a simplified version of Haddad's overall manufacturing index: the basic data are the same, with a few exceptions (see previous note), but fixed weights are used, instead of Haddad's year-by-year weighting procedure (Haddad, 1974, pp. 4 ff.). In

comparison to Haddad's, Table 7.3's index tends to underestimate total manufacturing production by 3% to 5%, in the last years of the decade.

5. Compare the index of industrial equipment imports in Villela and Suzigan (1973, p.437). Note, on the other hand, that the additional indicators of industrial investment suggested by those authors (internal consumption of cement, and of rolled steel) also show a remarkable rise in the last years of the 1920s (Villela and Suzigan, ibid.).

6. See, on this, Villela and Suzigan (1973), Fritsch (1980), Peláez and Suzigan (1976), and Silber (1977).

7. For the relations between coffee prices and the exchange rate in the period before 1914, see F. R. Versiani (1980).

8. President Artur Bernardes took office in October 1922. For an interesting account of policy-making in the first part of his Administration see Fritsch (1980).

9. Exchange-rate data from *Comercio Exterior do Brasil* (various issues).

10. See UK, Department of Overseas Trade (1929, pp. 21–3).

11. Comprehensive information on tariff changes in the period can be found in Nunes and Silva (1929–32).

12. The gold quota was levied in accordance with the official *mil-réis*/gold parity.

13. On the contemporary debate about tariff policies see Luz (1961).

14. Tariff proceeds given in Villela and Suzigan (1973, pp. 418–19); import data from Brazil, Instituto Brasileiro de Geografia e Estatística (1941, p. 1359).

15. The cost-of-living index for Rio de Janeiro is one of the very few general price indices available for the period.

16. It is true that the rate of growth of demand suggested by the estimates in Table 7.5 is rather low; but see n. 27 below.

17. *Brazilian Business* (November 1925, p. 15).

18. Cf. UK Department of Overseas Trade (1927, p. 20).

19. Ibid. p. 7.

20. Ibid. p. 20.

21. *Brazilian Business* (July 1926, p. 10).

22. See F. R. Versiani (1972).

23. UK, Department of Overseas Trade (1925, p. 37; 1927, p. 45). The forced curtailment of production in São Paulo mills, in 1925, due to a severe power shortage, favoured an expansion of production in other States. See UK Department of Overseas Trade (1925, p. 25); *Brazilian Business* (September 1925, p. 22).

24. Stein (1959, chap. IX and X). On the increased importance of smaller mills in São Paulo see Mendonça de Barros and Graham (1981).

25. UK Department of Overseas Trade (1929, p. 14).

26. See data in Brazil, Departamento Nacional de Estatística (1933, p. 172).

27. It is possible, however, that available production data over-emphasise the bad performance of textiles, in the late 1920s. As we saw above, it is very likely that the share in domestic output of small mills, scattered around the country, increased in the period. A possible consequence of this fact is an underestimation of the output of the industry in official statistics. To recall, these statistics were a by-product of tax collection;

and the degree of tax evasion is expected to be larger in the case of small mills in the interior of the country than in the case of a large factory in São Paulo city.

28. For the case of the steel and cement industries see Baer (1969); Peláez (1972).
29. Dates of foundation of firms are given in Banas (1962a; 1962b; 1963a; 1963b).
30. See Dean, (1969, chap. vii); also Banas (1962a; 1962b; 1963a; 1963b).
31. *Brazilian Business* (February 1924, p. 24; July 1925, p. 7).
32. The quotation refers to the chemicals and drugs industry; *Brazilian Business* (September 1923, p. 23). See also 'The Opportunity of Paper', ibid. (p. 69).
33. Banas (1962a; 1962b; 1963a; 1963b); Department of Overseas Trade (1925, p. 25).
34. See, for instance, 'Estado e Sociedade no Brasil' and 'A Questão do Estado no Brasil', in F. H. Cardoso (1975). On policy-making and its relation to coffee interests in the 1920s see Fritsch (1980).
35. *Brazilian Business* (September 1923, p. 57).
36. US Department of Commerce (25 January, 1919, p. 388). See also the issues for 26 April, 9 May, 9 July and 30 August (1918).
37. In cotton textiles the average rate of output increase, from 1929 to 1937, was 11% a year; on the other hand, from 1925 to 1929 production had decreased by 18%, at the same time as the number of looms installed *increased* by more than 20%. (See data above, and Stein, p. 191.)
38. On industrial diversification in the pre-World War I period, see M. T. Versiani.
39. See Diaz Alejandro's contribution to this volume, Chapter 2.

REFERENCES

Werner Baer, *The Development of the Brazilian Steel Industry* (Nashville 1969).
W. Baer and Anibal V. Villela, 'Industrial growth and industrialization: Revisions in the Stages of Brazil's Economic Development', *Journal of Developing Areas*, 7 (1973) 217–34.
Geraldo Banas (1962a), *Anuário Banas: A Indústria de Material Electrônico, 1962* (São Paulo, 1962).
——— (1962b), *Anuário Banas: A Indústria Brasileira de Máquinas, 1962* (São Paulo, 1962).
——— (1963a), *Anuário Banas: Elétrica e Electrônica, 1963* (São Paulo, 1963).
——— (1963b), *Anúario Banas: Máquinas e Ferramentas, 1963* (São Paulo, 1963).
Brazil, Departamento Nacional de Estatística, *Estatística da Produção Industrial do Brasil (dos Produtos Sujeitos ao Imposto de Consumo Arrecadado pelo Governo Federal, 1915–1929* (Rio de Janeiro, 1933).

——— Directoria de Receita Pública do Thesouro Nacional, *Estatística Geral do Imposto de Consumo dos Estados Unidos do Brasil* (Rio de Janeiro, yearly).

——— Instituto Brasileiro de Geografia e Estatística, *Anuário Estatístico do Brasil, 1939/1940* (Rio de Janeiro, 1941).

Brazilian Business (Rio de Janeiro, monthly).

Eliana A. Cardoso, 'Celso Furtado Revisitado: a Década de 30' *Revista Brasileira de Economia*, 33 (3) (Julho/Setembro 1979) 373–98.

F. H. Cardoso, *Autoritarismo e Democratizacão* (Rio de Janeiro, 1975).

Comercio Exterior do Brasil, published yearly by the Directoria de Estatística Comercial (Ministério da Fazenda) and then by the Departamento Nacional de Estatística (Ministério do Trabalho, Indústria e Comércio).

W. Dean, *The Industrialisation of São Paulo 1880–1945* (Austin, 1969).

A. Fishlow, 'Origins and Consequences of Import Substitution in Brazil', in Luiz Eugenio di Marco (ed.), *International Economics and Development: Essays in Honor of Raúl Prebish* (New York, 1972).

A. G. Frank, *Capitalism and Underdevelopment in Latin America* (New York, 1969).

W. Fritsch (1924), *Pesquisa e Planejamento Econômica*, 10 (3) (December 1980) 713–74.

C. Furtado, *Formacão Econômica do Brasil* (Rio de Janeiro, 1959).

C. L. S. Haddad, *Growth of Brazilian Real Output, 1900–1947*, doctoral dissertation (Chicago, 1974).

N. V. Luz, *A Luta pela Industrialização do Brasil (1808 a 1930)* (São Paulo, 1961).

J. R. Mendonça de Barros and D. H. Graham, 'A Recuperacão Econômica e a Desconcentração do Mercado da Industria Textil Paulista durante a Grande Depressão: 1928–37', *Pesquisa e Planejamento Econômico*, 11 (1) (April 1981) 79–105.

J. F. Normano, *Brazil, a Study of Economic Types* (New York, 1968) (first published in 1935).

P. C. B. Nunes and J. R. Silva, *Tarifa das Alfandegas*, 4 vols (Rio de Janeiro, 1929–32).

C. M. Peláez, *História de Industrialização Brasileira* (Rio de Janeiro, 1972).

C. M. Peláez and W. Suzigan, *História Monetária do Brasil: Análise da Política, Comportamento e Instituções Monetárias* (Rio de Janeiro, 1976).

S. Silber, 'Análise da Política Econômica e do Comportamento da Economia Brasileira durante o Período 1929–1939, in F. R. Versiani and J. R. Mendonça de Barros (eds), *Formacão Econômica do Brasil, a Experiência da Industrialização* (São Paulo, 1977).

S. J. Stein, *The Brazilian Cotton Manufacture: Textile Enterprise in an Underdeveloped Area, 1850–1950* (Cambridge, Mass., 1959).

W. Suzigan, 'Industrialização e Política Econômica: uma Interpretacão em Perspectiva Histórica', *Pesquisa e Planejamento Econômico*, 5 (2) (December 1975) 433–74.

UK, Department of Overseas Trade, *Report on the Economic and Financial Conditions in Brazil*, dated September 1925, by Ernest Hamblock (London, 1925).

——— *Report on the Economic and Financial Conditions in Brazil*, dated October 1926, by Ernest Hamblock (London, 1927).

—— *Financial, Commercial and Economic Conditions in Brazil*, October 1928. Report by Stanley G. Irving (London, 1929).

US, Department of Commerce, Bureau of Foreign and Domestic Commerce, *Commerce Reports: Daily Consular and Trade Reports* (Washington, DC, daily).

F. R. Versiani, 'Industrialização e Emprego: O Problema da Reposição de Equipamentos', *Pesquisa e Planejamento Econômico*, 2 (1) (July 1972) 3–54.

—— 'Industrial Investment in an Export Economy: The Brazilian Experience before 1914', *Journal of Development Economics*, 7 (3) (September 1980) 307–29.

—— *Um Problema na Estatística da Produção Industrial na Decada de 1920*. Notas para Discussao no. 15 (Brasília, 1981).

M. T. R. O. Versiani, *Proteção Tarifária e o Crescimento Industrial Brasileiro dos Anos 1906–1912*. Textos de Discussao no. 78 (Brasília; 1981).

A. V. Villela and W. Suzigan, *Política do Governo e Crescimento da Economia Brasileira, 1899–1945* (Rio de Janeiro, 1973).

8 Argentina into the Depression: Problems of an Open Economy

ARTURO O'CONNELL

The Depression of the 1930s and the Second World War began a period of decline in international economic transactions and consequently the adoption of policies oriented towards economic autarchy. But once post-war reconstruction had taken place and international trade as well as capital movements were flourishing again, 'economic opening-up' reacquired its popularity.

Developing countries in particular have incessantly been advised to abandon the machinery and policy reflexes built up during that now distant era and to embrace the new credo. The 1930s – it sometimes seems to be intimated – were an aberration, a pathological era, with problems that will never be present again: consequently there would be no justification for pursuing policies geared to cope with such exceptional circumstances. On the contrary, the previous decade – that of the 1920s – is seen, at least in the case of Argentina and some of the other fairly advanced countries in South America, as the paradigm of a happy era of tight integration to the world economy and one where the State had not yet started intervening in the economy.

The argument of this paper will be that Argentina exemplifies well a different general view of the 1930s, namely that far from being such an exceptional period they are almost normal, even though depressingly low. In line with this we also want to challenge the view that sees the previous decade as unquestionably prosperous and harmonious. An open economy – that of Argentina – will be shown to be very

188

vulnerable to instability in the world economy which – admittedly in different degrees – was an element common to both decades and in fact present in the whole history of the world economy up to the 1980s. In addition, the fall in commodity prices which occurred during the Depression can in most cases be ascribed to long-run forces already active well before 1930.

The 1930s as one instance of the effects of instability and long-run trends in the world economy on a vulnerable open economy become, therefore, of much more than merely anecdotal interest.

An open economy, of course, is not only vulnerable to instability in the world economy, but also becomes part of a power system at a universal level, and one which may not always be that best suited for its further expansion or for the distribution of benefits from growth. Economic policy in the 1930s will be examined to show up to what point it was a response to these two issues, *instability* and *structural change*. Lack of autonomy in economic policy-making due to the openness of an economy like that of Argentina in the interwar period turns out under such an examination to be one of its main features.

This chapter takes the following form. In the first section we discuss the Argentine economy prior to the Depression and show how vulnerable it was to instability in the world economy and how this generated a rather typical business cycle. In the second section we turn to a description of the slump and later recovery in Argentina. The third section will be devoted to an examination of some of the policy responses to the Depression. In the fourth section some of the more lasting consequences of the Depression on the economic structure of the country are briefly reviewed, including the question of industrialisation.

THE ARGENTINE BUSINESS CYCLE

By the late 1920s a rather clear pattern of economic fluctuations had become well established and perceived in Argentina, to the point of having received a name: the 'Argentine business cycle'.[1]

Export and Capital Inflow Instability

As in other open export economies of that era the Argentine cycle originated in the instability of exports and capital inflows. Exports were almost exclusively made up of half a dozen rural sector products. Although apparently in a better position than a mono-export economy, Argentina – almost alone among present-day underdeveloped countries – was a temperate-zone producer in direct competition with the domestic production, and even the exports, of almost all the important economies of the world. Moreover, in the market of some of those products the country was far from a marginal supplier. In such a position it was decidedly vulnerable to the excess supply conditions building up in world agriculture, and further was not a price-taker in these markets.[2]

Both export prices and quantum showed marked variability. Export prices – in gold or foreign-exchange terms – linked Argentina to the world economy and the specific conditions in agricultural markets. These were anything but stable even before the 1930s. As to quantum, both harvest losses – due to drought every three to five years – and a cobweb-type cattle cycle generated sharp changes in output. Confronted with a steady trend in domestic absorption these fluctuations were borne by exportable surpluses.[3]

In addition to the above, monopoly positions in the export trade of the Republic had a significant influence on export prices and volumes. The 'Big Four' cereal houses handled 60 to 80% of grain exports, and the meat trade was organised around a 'pool' dominated by three American and two British firms allocating refrigerated cargo space from the River Plate to Great Britain. 'Transfer pricing' among the subsidiaries of these transnational firms, under-invoicing, price-wars and all the habitual practices in such circumstances worked to further destabilise export prices and volumes.[4]

In spite of some inverse relation between export prices and volumes – to be expected in a country which was not a price-taker – export values also showed a significant degree of instability. In the period 1917–29 it was higher than in any previous or later period in the life of Argentina and quite above anything experienced by LDCs in general after the Second World War.[5]

Had import prices oscillated in the same direction and degree as export prices their instability would have been unimportant in terms of import capacity and balance of payments, although far from a neutral phenomenon in its effects on income distribution within the country. But if anything the reverse was the case. Terms of trade for Argentina did experience wide swings before the 1930s and only recovered their pre-First World War level in the years 1946–50, although as we shall see later, these sharply improved in the midst of the Depression.[6]

Capital inflows also experienced significant oscillations in spite of the fact that they were almost entirely channelled into direct investment in public utilities and purchases of bonds issued either by the various levels of government or those same public utilities. The behaviour of these long-run capital movements was mainly determined by conditions in the capital markets of the 'centre' – London up to 1914 and New York after 1924 – which on the whole were unrelated to developments and needs in Argentina. When they were, their flow – as that of the quantitatively less important 'hot' money – was clearly destabilising, as they increased in times of boom and fell in slump.[7]

Transmission Mechanisms

Exports, in the period 1925–9, represented 24% of GDP and 67% of final demand for the 'Pampa' rural sector. Foreign capital, on the other hand, owned by the end of the 1920s 32% of all fixed capital, and gross current inflows represented more than 10% of gross fixed investment, mainly public works or infrastructure with significant multiplier and linkage effects. Instability of exports and capital inflows, therefore, was a powerful generator of instability in the whole economy through the workings of the income – expenditure system.[8]

External shocks were also transmitted through the fiscal and monetary systems which were intimately linked to external transactions. The country's monetary system had been christened one of 'sporadic gold standard'. Creation of high-powered money was regulated by gold and foreign-exchange flows. And unless the banks (there was no central bank till 1935 although the state-owned Banco de la Nación Argentina performed some of its functions) followed a deliberately compensatory cash reserve policy, lending and secondary money expansion was rigidly related to the ups and downs of the payments balance.[9]

The fiscal system of Argentina was also exceedingly dependent on balance-of-trade variations. Three-fourths of all government current revenue originated in customs and other import duties. Periods of boom in foreign trade induced fiscal laxity and expenditure commitments (usually compounded by an upsurge in public bond issues) which became rather inflexible in the later downturn.[10]

External Vulnerability and the Autonomy of Economic Policy

As with all debtor countries, Argentina faced a substantial annual fixed charge against its foreign-exchange proceeds. Even before the

First World War these charges had become larger than the trade balance. Consequently the country needed a fresh inflow of capital every single year to avoid serious balance-of-payments problems and the ensuing domestic disturbances.[11]

In addition to the above, imports – which also represented a significant fraction of GDP – showed a very high income elasticity. Moreover, import demand – it was surmised – revealed a rather perverse lagged response which meant that it would remain at a high level even after exports and the level of activity were falling, thus creating a severe external payments problem in the downward phase of the cycle. Imports, also, could not be easily reduced as they contributed in a decisive way to supply consumption, productive inputs and capital goods needs. Consequently imports as well as debt service represented a rather inflexible fixed charge against foreign-exchange proceeds, which as we have seen were highly unstable.[12]

The supply of foreign exchange, moreover, was basically in the hands of the few cereal houses and meat-packing firms. Consequently, to a substantial degree variations in foreign reserves – and under the 'sporadic' gold standard system, in money supply – were under monopoly control while there was no 'countervailing' state organisation intervening in the foreign-exchange market. Opportunities for exchange and rate of interest speculative movements were obvious, creating further instability.

Increased vulnerability – additional to that emerging from the above – followed from the triangular structure of Argentina's foreign trade, shipping and capital movements, which we have analysed in detail in another work and which is referred to in Abreu's chapter (chapter 6, above). First, the country was singularly dependent on sales to Great Britain, or at least this was true of one of its most important social groups, the cattle producers. Second, by running a surplus *vis-à-vis* Great Britain and a deficit *vis-à-vis* the USA, Argentina relied on either Great Britain being able and willing to finance an import surplus over and above its claims as a creditor – involving exchange of sterling into dollars – or the USA having the capacity for sustained net capital exports to Argentina.[13]

The Argentine economy, therefore, was not only vulnerable to overall developments in the world economy, but it was particularly vulnerable to the difficulties of the British economy and very specifically to its dollar deficit and the need to find outlets for the products of the old export industries.

As a consequence of the above, economic policy had very limited autonomy to enable it to cope with the Argentine business cycle. In a balance-of-payments situation like the one described and with demand for imports as income elastic as it was, attempts to reflate domestic demand via fiscal and/or monetary measures could easily lead to an external payments crisis. Anyway with such an elementary tax and monetary system some of the instruments required by such a policy were absent.

The essential character of most imports, on the other hand, made it extremely difficult to curtail this source of demand for foreign exchange during the downward phase of the cycle. As to the other 'drain' on foreign reserves, i.e. service of foreign capital, this represented a rather fixed amount unrelated to balance-of-payments difficulties. Further, default or retention of profits of foreign firms would have faced serious obstacles as the most important creditor of the country – Great Britain – was simultaneously its most important customer.[14]

The Business Cycle in the 1920s

The decade of the 1920s witnessed several oscillations in economic activity. There was first a decline from 1919 to 1921 originating in a sharp reduction in agricultural prices after the end of the First World War. Recovery followed from 1922 to 1924 with good harvests and the beginning of significant capital flows coming from the USA. A bad harvest in the 1924–5 season led to a new downturn accentuated by a renewed drop in agricultural prices during 1925 and 1926.

A new cycle started in 1926. Beginning in this year the Argentine peso – which had depreciated under inconvertibility – started to rise as both exports and capital inflows increased. At the beginning of 1927 the peso was touching parity. In this year export volumes and prices increased and there was a new upsurge in capital inflows, particularly in public borrowing. Gold entered the country and convertibility was resumed in August 1927, thus avoiding further peso appreciation. Banks accumulated sizeable foreign reserves.

Both currency and deposits increased but lending lagged behind as banks rebuilt their reserves and liquidated old credits hanging over from the previous downturn. Interest rates fell, both short- and long-run. Behind this behaviour of the banking sector one can detect the action of the Banco de la Nación Argentina which reduced its loans to other banks.[15]

THE DEPRESSION

The 1928 Capital Outflow

In 1928 exports increased less and imports increased more than in the previous year. In addition, there was a marked decline in public borrowing, leading – in spite of sizeable private investment – to a reduction in capital inflows. Gold imports were almost as high as in the previous year, but they were completely concentrated in the first half of 1928. In fact, during the second half, there was a net export of gold. A boom in Wall Street and a newly inaugurated tight-money policy by the Federal Reserve were draining away funds from Argentina. Even during the first few months of the year 1929 when exports were at a seasonal high gold exports continued. There was no public borrowing during 1929 and only a reduced level of private foreign investment.

Imports continued to increase throughout 1929, while there was a significant outflow of funds for speculative purposes. Moreover, due to a fall in prices, export values fell more than 10%. As a result gold imports of about 400 million pesos in the 1927–8 biennium were completely cancelled out by the late 1928 and 1929 outflow. In December 1929 the government took the decision to suspend convertibility.

In the meantime, credit was being expanded in spite of the decline in foreign reserves. Beginning in June 1928, heavy drawing on bank reserves permitted loans outstanding to increase 15% between September 1928 and December 1929. As a consequence, in that same period, reserve ratios fell from 24.7% to 12.3%. An active policy of lending to the government and to other banks by the Banco de la Nación Argentina was behind such an expansion. Spending and GDP increased, therefore, in 1929, in spite of the balance-of-payments crisis, but less aggregate figures were showing clear signs of a downturn in the second half of the year.

The Fall of Wheat and the Agricultural Depression

We have mentioned that one of the reasons behind the aggravation of the balance-of-payments situation in 1929 was a fall in the value of exports as a consequence of a sharp drop in world prices.[16] In the 1928/9 commercial year harvests in the main producing countries were much larger than in the previous years, and were added to already heavy stocks. Wheat prices experienced a marked decline beginning in mid-1928, which news of larger harvests in the Northern Hemisphere season by mid-1929 only accentuated. In Argentina wheat prices dropped almost 30% between May 1928 and May 1929. Again, well before the Wall Street crash, crisis had arrived in Argentina not only through the drying up of capital inflows, but also in the form of a sharp drop in export prices.[17]

In fact, from a long-run perspective, the 1928–9 fall in wheat prices was only part of a more fundamental crisis in world agriculture. World prices for many agricultural commodities had been falling since 1925. In the case of wheat, prices had been declining since the early 1880s.[18] Careful calculations produced by Mandelbaum on 'actual' and 'necessary' world wheat acreage showed that there was a gap between them that had increased from a level of 6.9% in the late nineteenth century to about 15% in the 1930s.[19] Reasons for the growing imbalance may be conventionally summarised as those affecting supply and those affecting demand.

On the demand side there were two different forces at work. The first one was the slow rate of growth of population, particularly in north-western Europe which was the main cereal importing area. The second was a reduction in per capita consumption of grains in favour of other food as incomes increased.

On the supply side the main factor was the recovery in European production levels, beginning in the year 1925, without a corresponding reduction in cultivation in the overseas exporting countries, the USA, Canada, Australia and Argentina, which had expanded their output in response to wartime needs.[20]

In such a situation protectionism became increasingly popular for agricultural goods. Mandelbaum has documented the extent of price divergence introduced by protectionism in France, Germany and Italy as compared with Great Britain, who in 1932 only adopted protection for wheat, and that in a mild form.[21]

Products other than wheat among Argentine exports fared somewhat better in the international market. Corn and linseed prices did experience an increase in the years just before the crisis although in the case of corn the peak for 1928 was well below the 1925 price. The case of beef, again, was somewhat different as the price collapse had taken place earlier in the decade. Prices even mildly recovered in 1927 after the 'Meat War' – a breaking up for two years of the *frigorífico* pool – as volumes were again firmly under control.[22]

In Argentina domestic prices for the whole rural sector clearly reflected the trend in world markets. The average for 1920–4 being

127.0 (1910/14 = 100.0), prices for such goods fell from 156.8 in 1925 to 128.6 and 131.0 in 1926 and 1927, experienced some recovery to 145.7 in 1928 and dropped again to 136.2 in 1929. Land prices followed the same trend. Land suitable for wheat cultivation in the province in Buenos Aires dropped from a price of 377 pesos per hectare in 1926 to 324 pesos in 1929, in spite of credit inflation. Land suitable for cattle fattening fell in those same years from 382 to 293 pesos per hectare.[23]

The drop in agricultural and related prices in Argentina in sympathy with world trends therefore preceded the year 1929, which is normally taken as marking the beginning of the Depression. Moreover Argentina was having to face not only instability in prices for its export products, but a more permanent decline in world markets for temperate food products.

Slump and Recovery

We have already seen that by late 1929, indeed beginning in the second half of 1928, there were clear indications of a downturn in economic activity initiated by the two classical forces of a fall in export prices and a reversion in capital inflows. To such a serious picture we must add harvest losses in the 1929–30 season. These factors led to a sharp fall in export volumes beginning in the last quarter of 1929.

From peak to trough – 1928 to 1932 – export prices for Argentina dropped 64%. As import prices fell 41% in the same period the external terms of trade declined 'only' 40%. This fall in the terms of trade was sharper than that of the beginning of the 1920s (23% in the 1919–22 period), but it made their level almost equal in both periods.[24]

Relative prices, however, do not show one important difference between the two situations: their lower absolute level. Export prices, which in the earlier crisis had just returned to their pre-war level, were now less than half that level. The severity of the agricultural depression was felt in enormously increased debt burdens on farmers.[25]

Export volumes, on the other hand, only varied with the weather. There were significant losses in 1930 – as we have seen – and again in 1933. In this the experience of Argentina does not seem to be different from that of other agrarian countries which typically maintained output in spite of the fall in prices.[26]

Price and quantity effects combined to produce a 67% drop in export values and a 45% fall in the purchasing power of exports in the same period, 1928–32.

As to the other traditional source of instability, foreign capital, non-compensatory inflows dried up almost completely in 1929–33,[27] while service on foreign capital declined much less than exports, with the result that by 1933 it was eating up 37.8% of their value.

Although there were some substantial gold exports – mainly during the first half of 1931 – and some accumulation of balances awaiting either a better exchange rate or authorisation to be sent abroad, imports had to fall precipitously to accomodate the simultaneous reduction in export values and foreign capital inflows in the presence of a rather inflexible amount of debt repayment. In the period 1928–32 import volumes fell 55%, more than the contraction of import capacity (53%).[28]

As we have already mentioned, output levels in the rural sector were maintained in spite of the fall in price levels. Thus activity in the whole economy was given a stability typical of agrarian countries. From peak to trough rural output fell around 6% while GDP fell 9.7%.[29] In fact, if five-year averages are taken, GDP actually increased 2% between the 1925–9 and the 1930–4 quinquennia, and Pampa (export-oriented) rural output by 3.7%.[30]

But if account is taken of the effect of changes in terms of trade and of service on foreign capital the resulting figure for national income shows a different picture. The terms of trade effect between those two quinquennia generated a fall in national income equivalent to almost 10% of GDP, and service on foreign capital increased its participation in this aggregate by 1%. As a result of both effects national income fell 9.4% between the pre-Depression quinquennium and the first of the Depression. In the case of Argentina, therefore, the fall in incomes during the Depression is not a consequence of a decline in productive activity, but of the external shock in terms of trade and the rigidity of debt service.[31]

Let us now make an attempt to trace the distribution of that fall in national income among the various sectors and groups. Domestic prices followed the same pattern as world markets. But peso depreciation – once the Caja de Conversión was closed at the end of 1929 – cushioned deflationary forces. In the period 1928–32, while export and import prices declined respectively more than 60% and 40%, wholesale prices in Argentina only fell 9%. The pound sterling and the US dollar were, respectively, 19% and 65% dearer by the end of the year.[32]

The overall wholesale price level, however, hides very important differences. The fall in non-rural prices had halted by July 1931 and by 1932 they were 3.4% above their 1928 level. Rural prices, on the contrary, fell 45.5% between 1928 and 1932 and a further 5.2% by November 1933. As a consequence of such disparate movements internal terms of trade between the rural and non-rural sectors fell 47.3% in that same period.[33]

At the same time interest rates tended to rise. From a level of 5.8% per annum in July 1928 they stood at 7.9% in December 1931 only to start a gradual decline to 7% by the end of 1932. Real interest rates for non-rural producers, therefore, were far from low although peso depreciation by inflating their prices lent a helping hand. But one can well imagine the plight of rural producers under the burden of debt. The difficulties of landowners – only 36% of 'pampean' land was owned by producers – were also great as the largest portion of land was rented in money terms and rents fell about 30 to 40% while mortgages paid the above-mentioned rates. Land prices, simultaneously, fell from 30 to 50% depending on the area. Urban land and buildings as well as rents were affected in a similar way.[34]

There is evidence (admittedly somewhat scattered) that monopoly export firms were rather successful in transferring the decline in terms of trade back to farmers and landowners. For instance, while profit rates for companies fell, on average, from 8.4% in 1928 to 1.8% in 1932, those of meat-packers went up from 6.7% to 8.3% in the same period. Grain-exporting firms like Bunge & Born or de Ridder were making profits in 1932 of around 10%. Banks, too, were rather successful in maintaing their profit levels.[35]

Using our figure for the fall in national income between the five years prior to the Depression and the first quinquennium of the Depression, it may be estimated that the rural sector bore the burden of adjustment almost alone *vis-à-vis* urban sectors in spite of the substantial peso depreciation. In fact the purchasing power of rural production fell more than 25% over the same period. The rural sector being almost one-third of GDP, this fall translates into more than 8% of national income, almost nine-tenths of our figure for the decline in national income. Only some guesses on the basis of information provided above may be made at this stage as to the distribution of that fall in rural incomes between workers, farmers, landowners and creditors.[36]

Urban incomes therefore probably maintined their aggregate value. No great changes in the distribution between wages and profits seem to have taken place. Evidence on nominal wages is scanty, but what is available shows, on the average for the first five years of the Depression, a fall similar to that of the cost of living, thus preserving real pre-Depression levels. Unfortunately, we have been unable to find systematic information on unemployment. If it did increase significantly, as is sometimes argued on the basis of somewhat impressionistic evidence, it would mean in the aggregate a redistribution of income towards profits in urban sectors.[37]

One important qualification to the above is population growth. Population grew almost 13% between 1925–9 and 1930–4. Consequently, per capita national income fell over the same period around 20%.[38]

We turn now to the recovery. In Argentina, as in other agrarian countries like those of the Danube basin, industrial growth stimulated by the fall of imports no doubt played some role in economic recovery. We shall see later, however, that at least in our case the overall rate of growth of industry during the 1930s was not particularly high. Rather, the main driving-force behind recovery was once more an external shock: an upsurge in export prices right in the middle of the Depression years.[39]

Export prices shot up by 43% in 1933–4 and again increased 21% in 1935–6 and 22% in 1936–7. By 1937 the terms of trade of Argentina were back to the 1928 level and, in fact, to the historically high 1913 level.[40]

The reason, despite the agricultural depression and the gloomy underlying situation in world markets for grains and meat, was a prolonged drought – beginning in 1933 and lasting an almost uninterrupted four harvest seasons – in the grain growing regions of the USA and Canada and extending to Australia also in 1934 and 1935. For three consecutive years the USA was a net importer of wheat and maize. Wheat prices in the 1936–7 grain year were on average 80% above their low 1933–4 value and about the same level as in 1928–9. The fall in production due to harvest losses allowed a temporary equilibrium to be established between supply and demand.[41]

Export volumes did not show any significant change, contrary to what seems to have happened in other Latin American economies. But as a consequence of the increase in prices export values increased by 128% between 1932 and 1937.[42]

Following hard on export prices the other external instability factor also reappeared. In the years 1934, 1935 and 1936 private capital, stimulated by the recovery, once more flowed into the country. It was now short-run in character and would abandon Argentina as soon as in 1937 the upswing came to an end.[43]

The positive change in the balance of payments allowed a much larger volume of imports and even some debt repatriation. In the period 1930–4 to 1935–9 import capacity increased 49%. Imports expanded by 74% between their 1932 low and their new peak in 1937.[44]

Stimulated by these external forces economic activity started to recover as of 1933. Between 1930–4 and 1935–9 GDP in constant prices increased 17.4%. In addition the terms of trade had now turned in favour of Argentina and with an increase in GDP the burden of service of foreign capital was reduced. As a consequence of these developments national income increased almost 28% between the two quinquennia. Income per capita increased over the same period by 17%.[45]

We may attempt to guess how that increase in income was distributed. Price increases in the world market for Argentine exports and imports worked through to domestic prices helped by some additional peso depreciation in 1933–4. From 1933 to 1937 the wholesale price index went up by more than 30%. As nominal interest rates fell beginning in June 1932, real interest rates came down from their previous high level. Furthermore, in the two 'inflationary' years of 1934 and 1937 real interest rates became markedly negative. In today's terminology debt started to be 'liquefied' in Argentina in 1934, to which a mortgage debt moratorium was added to help landowners.[46]

As prices increased substantially both for the rural and the non-rural sectors the weakening of the debt burden was significant in both cases. But relative prices underwent important changes. Non-rural prices only increased 22% from 1933 to 1937 while rural prices went up by 84% in the same period. In a reverse movement to that of the early phase of the Depression and in agreement with shifts in relative prices in the world market, internal terms of trade between the rural and non-rural sectors went up by more than 53%. Such violent ups and downs in the relative income positions of the different groups in the Argentine economy – and particularly of the rural sector *vis-à-vis* the urban sectors – were to become a permanent characteristic of contemporary life.

But although the direction of change of internal and external terms of trade is in agreement in both periods – the descending and the ascending phases – there is an important asymmetry when magnitudes are compared. Using averages for quinquennia, while external terms of trade fell 17% in 1930–4, compared with 1926–9, internal terms of trade fell even more, i.e. 35%. In the following period, while external terms of trade increased 19% from 1930–4 to 1935–9,

internal terms of trade went up only 15%. As a result of this difference the ratio between internal and external terms of trade came
down a further 3% between the two quinquennia. On average during
1935–9 it stood 34% below the level for 1926–9.[47]

Economic policy and social forces were clearly generating increasing discrimination against the rural sector. It may be estimated that
real incomes originating in the rural sector increased between 22 and
25%, a figure lower than that for national income, confirming that,
again, as during the descending phase of the cycle, income was being
transferred away from the rural sector.[48]

In addition, rents went up so that by 1937 it was estimated that rent
levels had risen to pre-Depression levels. Such information may be
confirmed by looking at land prices which in the wheat and maize
zones recovered almost all their earlier loss. Farmers, therefore, were
being squeezed between relative prices and increasing rent charges
favouring landlords, in their turn recipients of the benefits of the
mortgage moratoria.[49]

Urban rents also experienced some recovery and although house-
building did not recover pre-Depression levels there were comments
on the level of activity in new high-price flats in the affluent sections
of town.[50]

Urban incomes under the combined effect of the sharp increase in
national income and the mechanisms of income transfer away from
farmers should have gone up very significantly. Now, real wages if
anything tended to fall between 1930–4 and 1935–9. Consequently,
urban profits must have increased unless they were absorbed by the
expansion in employment, which was important – 14% in manufacturing. Figures for the distribution of national income, at current
prices, starting in 1935, do not show any definite trend in the share of
wages and salaries for the period 1935–9.[51]

The recovery did not last long. As news of a promising harvest in
North America arrived by the second quarter of 1937, prices for
grains in the world market started a fall. Concurrently capital began
to flow out of Argentina. In addition the 1937–8 harvest was hit by
drought. For the first time since 1930 the trade balance for 1938 was
negative. After a year in which important amounts of dollar debt had
been repatriated the government contracted a new loan in the USA.
Most estimates show a fall in GDP for 1938. The following year with
the beginning of the War everything changed again. Had we just experienced one more cycle in the economic life of Argentina? We shall
have an opportunity in the last section of this paper to point out some
permanent changes generated in the Depression decade. In the next

section we turn our attention to some elements of economic policy-
making during the early years of the decade.[52]

ECONOMIC POLICY DURING THE DEPRESSION

We have just seen that recovery – and later relapse – during the 1930s
in Argentina can be ascribed in the main to the well-known forces of
the foreign-induced business cycle. Given this, some of the drama
associated with the debate about economic policy during that decade
disappears. This, however, may help rational discussion.

Some Global Issues

Although they go beyond the limits of this paper we shall briefly review two global questions which have been – and still are – the object
of bitter controversy over economic policy-making in Argentina during these years.

On the one hand, there is no doubt that the degree of state intervention in the economic affairs of the country was radically expanded. The introduction of exchange control and the creation of
several marketing boards like the Junta Reguladora de Granos are
just two instances of such a process. It is true that quite a few of the
reforms enacted during those years had long been discussed in
Argentina. The need for more flexibility in the management of the
monetary system under external shocks had been widely acknowledged and quite comprehensive schemes for reform had been debated in Congress. A project for the introduction of an income tax,
also, had been submitted by President Yrigoyen during his first term
in office (1916–22). The fact remains that it was only under the impact of the Depression that those long-delayed reforms were introduced. In addition, with the passing of the emergency generated by
the Depression and the Second World War there was little if any
dismantling of the machinery put in place in the early 1930s.

Advocates of economic non-intervention have consequently put
the blame on the economic policy-makers of the 1930s for all the later
problems of the Argentine economy. In their opinion the country will
remain in its present unhealthy state unless an effort is made to go
back to a previous era of unblemished *laissez-faire*.

But, on the other hand, even if the other side of the spectrum in
public debate acknowledges the need for institutional reform, criti-

cism has not been spared from this quarter either. Among the ranks of those who would not oppose state intervention in general, the opinion is held by many that, far from being a neutral instrument employed to cope with the consequences of the Depression, there was a definite bias in favour of the interests of the 'establishment' and more specifically of British interests in Argentina. In their view economic reform during the 1930s, instead of transforming those aspects making the country vulnerable to instability and victim of an unfair system of foreign relations, if anything reinforced them. For instance, it is argued that commercial policy consecrated the orientation of the Argentine economy towards one market – that of Great Britain – as well as the whole chain of interests – railways, refined cattle-producers, meat-packers and shipping companies – involved in this trade. The wide and nationally sensitive powers conferred on the newly created central bank were hardly compatible – in the view of many critics – with the fact that representatives of foreign banks were seated on its board of directors.

More generally the wide powers acquired by the executive as a result of state interventionism were widely resented as a consequence of the fact that the governments of those years achieved office on the basis of electoral exclusions and fraud following the first military take-over in the history of contemporary Argentina, in September 1930. A balanced assessment of the era is further hampered by the acrimony created around financial scandals in connection with foreign concerns which some currents of opinion have traced back not so much to corruption as to leniency *vis-à-vis* some vested interest.

But in this chapter, rather than analysing such global issues, we turn our attention to a more modest examination of the utilisation of some of the orthodox and not-so-orthodox instruments of economic policy during the early part of the 1930s. One further question demands a clarification. It is not our task to discuss the originality or the technical competence with which economic policy was formulated and executed. The reader, by comparing the Argentine experience with that of the other Latin American countries covered in this volume and that of other agrarian countries both inside and outside the British Commonwealth, can perhaps draw his own conclusions.

Economic Policy during the Depression

We have already seen in some detail how limited was the autonomy of economic policy in Argentina confronted with the business cycle, of which the Depression was an unusually severe case. It became increasingly clear that exports could hardly be expanded and that capital markets, at least in the short run, had practically dried up. There seemed to be no way out other than introducing even further cuts in imports or in servicing of foreign capital.

But, simultaneously, the Depression was making it more difficult than ever to cope with the additional limitations imposed on the country by the presence of monopolies in its foreign transactions as well as by the triangular structure of Argentina's foreign payments. This was because, faced with their own problems, British interests and government had also adopted a strategy to deal with the external situation of Great Britain. This strategy implied, in the first place, making sure that profits on investments by British nationals (but not, or at least not with equal priority, service on foreign bonds floated in the London market) could be repatriated. And, in the second place, it implied ensuring that some of their industries in trouble would continue to find outlets not only in Empire markets.[53]

Therefore, limitations imposed on economic policy-making in Argentina cannot be forgotten. At the same time, however, everything cannot be explained in terms of mere external determination. It is also true that the previous period of active growth under an open economic environment had left intact, in spite of the Depression, the conviction that prosperity would be regained by the very same means. This could be particularly the case for those interests closer to the Concordancia government, the creature of the September 1930 military takeover. Insistence on maintaining service of the external debt even when confronted with outright suggestions of suspension by the British authorities – in the context of the Anglo–Argentine Agreement negotiations of 1933 – looks like a clear indication that such a set of ideas went beyond any external determination.[54]

The foreign-exchange bottleneck became the main preoccupation of economic policy-making in Argentina beginning with the Depression. Let us therefore start our survey of some major elements of economic policy by examining the exchange regime and policies.

The exchange regime progressed from inconvertibility (December 1929) to the introduction of exchange control in several stages, beginning in September 1931. In November 1933 an official and a free market were established and within the official market a margin was created between a purchasing rate and a selling rate. The free market was, at that time, for imports not covered by a prior permit and for capital outflows, and drew on receipts from non-traditional exports, capital imports, freight earnings, tourist expenses, etc. We shall see later how it was utilised for purposes of bilateral commercial policy. The free market was eliminated for merchandise transactions in August 1939.

Exchange-control authorities set priorities for the allocation of foreign exchange according to two sets of criteria. On the one hand, service of the public debt, essential imports and remittances by foreign-owned public utilities, in that order, were granted priority and capital flight was discouraged. Mandatory surrender of exchange proceeds by the big cereal firms was enforced, as it was established that they had been involved in large-scale speculative retention of export proceeds.[55] On the other hand, the exchange-control authorities, once a policy of preferential treatment for Argentina's customers was started, allocated exchange according to country of origin.

It has been argued that exchange control was the most effective way to cut down imports and consequently a fundamental tool to bring about industrialisation in Argentina during those years. Prima facie, however, by inducing an improvement in the supply/demand balance in the foreign-exchange market, exchange control was instrumental in maintaining the exchange rate at a level lower than the one that would have emerged from a free market and as such made imports more competitive with domestic production. In fact, it was later admitted that it was not very effective as an instrument of import restriction.[56]

As to the exchange rate, we should remember that it was an issue dividing exporters and the rural interest on the one hand, and creditors on the other, this meaning mainly British enterprise (with the inevitable sympathy of Ministers of Finance having to cope with the increased burden of servicing public debt with a depreciated peso). In addition as depreciation had traditionally been used as an inflationary policy partisans of controlling the balance of payments through deflation argued against depreciation. Thus in spite of the exporters' powerful interests several attempts at halting depreciation were seen, before and after the imposition of exchange control.

Careful calculation of real exchange rates shows that, in fact, there was real revaluation of the peso against the British pound in the period 1930–4, *vis-à-vis* 1926–9. This situation changed with the late 1933 devaluation leading to a real exchange rate in 1935–9 4% above that for 1926–9. The average for the whole Depression decade is slightly below the base period when the abundance of foreign exchange led to some degree of over-valuation. The situation *vis-à-vis* the US dollar is somewhat different with an increase of 11% and 17%

of the real exchange rate for non-rural goods for the first and the second Depression quinquennia, respectively.[57]

In no case do figures for the real exchange rate indicate real devaluations of the kind that the evidence in this volume on other Latin American countries seems to suggest. The low rate of real devaluation confirms the above view as to the impact of exchange control on exchange rates. One may add that it was precisely the kind of products imported from Great Britain for which there were in principle better prospects for production in Argentina.

The exchange margin within the official market was intended to provide fiscal revenue to pay for the increased peso burden of servicing the public debt after the simultaneous devaluation and finance the newly introduced minimum prices for wheat, linseed and maize.[58] These minimum prices were set at a level 20% above their previous level – the same as the increase in the rates for foreign currencies at the purchase 'window' – so that they could easily be paid by exporters. But it was thought that, confronted with the new, higher price, farmers would rush to sell thus driving down the price. In such a case it would have been the cereal houses alone that profited from the devaluation as in previous peso depreciations. The Junta Reguladora de Granos was set up to buy any grain offered at the minimum price and to sell it to exporters at the going price.[59]

In fact the Junta initially had to buy 86% of the wheat crop and sell part of it at a loss in the first months of its operations up to May 1934. Thereafter with the increase in world prices the Junta started making a profit on its sales so that by the end of the year Junta losses ended up being less than 10% of exchange margin profits. Consequently the exchange margin ended up as a tax on the rural producer; here and there a 'rebate' of such a tax would be granted in the form of an effective minimum price.

Further, the role of such a tax was, in combination with new higher tariffs, to introduce the spread we have seen developing between domestic relative prices and external terms of trade of agricultural products *vis-à-vis* the rest.[60]

Rural producers, therefore, were not granted the full benefits of the devaluation. But the most powerful group of creditors – the British railways – were instead granted in 1936 a rebate of about two-thirds of the difference between the rates, which meant that they benefited from a real revaluation of about 7%. In December 1936 the spread between the purchase and the selling rate was cut by half.[61]

It has already been mentioned that exchange control was also utilised for a policy of preferential treatment for those countries which were important customers for Argentine produce, foremost among them Great Britain. We shall first review the way in which the exchange regime was used towards such an end and later tackle the broader issues raised.

Under agreements signed beginning in May 1933 with Great Britain and other European countries, exchange was made available for payments to these countries up to the amount made available by their purchases of Argentine products (after a small deduction for service of that portion of the public debt issued in other countries, mainly the US issued debt). Such exchange was made available at the official selling rate. Payments to other countries either for imports or other reasons had to go through the 'free' market if insufficient exchange was available in the official market. In practice, such a scheme meant that imports from the USA – which as we have seen had become Argentina's first supplier after 1925 – were mainly channelled through the 'free' market while imports from Great Britain were only exceptionally not granted official exchange. The 'free' market, a device to prevent import excesses, was only applied to a few countries of which the USA was the most important. No wonder, therefore, that the US share of Argentine imports went down from 25% in 1925–9 to 15% in 1934–8. The UK share, at the same time, increased from 20 to 23%.

The system of preferences did not behave as well as desired. With the improvement in the balance of payments after mid-1934, the spread between the two rates came down from about 20% in January 1934 to less than 12% in April 1935. Differences in competitiveness were high enough for such a differential rate not to be enough for British exporters. Consequently, in May 1935, a 20% flat surcharge on the official selling rate was placed on all imports through the 'free' exchange market. The 'free' rate ceased to be relevant for merchandise trade in January 1938, when all at once the surcharge was reduced to 10% but the 'free' rate increased due to the new exchange tension developing after mid-1937.

In the field of what is usually considered commercial policy, i.e. tariff-making, there were significant increases both in tariff, valuations and in tariffs, the most important being the 10% flat additional tariff on all dutiable items introduced in October 1931.[62]

In the wider field of commercial policy the most significant development during the 1930s was of course the inauguration of a policy of bilateralism. The first and most important of the several agreements signed during the Depression decade was the Anglo–Argentine Treaty of May 1933 (better known as the Roca–Runciman agreement). We can only mention here some of its most relevant aspects for exchange and commercial policy. We have already noted the main provision of the May 1933 convention which became a model for the rest, i.e. that of allocation of exchange for import purchases up to the limit of a country's purchase of Argentine produce, a principle that conflicted directly with the triangular structure of Argentina's trade and payments. In addition the Supplementary Convention signed in September 1933 involved tariff adjustments for more than 300 items of special interest for British trade. (These concessions, however, were extended to all other countries under most-favoured-nation principles.)[63]

There should be no question about who took the initiative in bilateralism. It was Great Britain that began figuring in a series of treaties entailing bilateral advantages, some of them only of a trade character, others – as in the case of Argentina – involving exchange and payments clauses. We have already mentioned Tasca's opinion about the priority granted to the payments element. Another author said: 'Indeed the agreement [the Anglo-Argentine one] has been described merely as an instrument for debt collection . . . Britain is using her power as a large-scale purchaser of Argentine products to ensure payment of trade and capital debts due to her from Argentina.'[64]

In addition, therefore, to any convictions about external debt policies that the Argentine authorities themselves had, there were clear limits to any suggestion of default as was practised by most other Latin American countries not having Great Britain as their most important customer. And bilateralism was not a neutral policy for trade; 'in the 1930s Argentina in order to continue exporting has to buy consumer goods which it could well produce itself or dispense with, in order to acquire capital goods and other essential commodities in exchange . . . but . . . a country cannot of itself choose the most advantageous trade policy'.[65]

Fiscal and monetary policies were less adventurous although some significant technical innovations were introduced. After the experience of 1930 when the deficit was almost 40% of expenditure, fiscal policies became restrictive. Taxes were increased or new taxes were created and expenditure was cut, so that by 1933 equilibrium was close, in the midst of the worst of the Depression. Beginning in 1935, once the recovery based on the cereals export boom was well on its way, government expenditure started on an upward surge that took it from 12.8% to 15.9% of GDP four years later.[66]

The monetary field was where the greatest innovation was introduced with the creation of the Central Bank and the way bad banking debt was dealt with through a special institution devoted to the task. Monetary policy was also basically restrictive up to 1935. Not only did memories of wild inflations of the past loom large in the minds of policy makers of the time. As was the case with fiscal policies, the threat of inducing an import boom and the ensuing balance-of-payments crisis was very much in people's minds. In the initial years of the Depression, in spite of the basic restrictive stance, the crisis led to some emergency expansionary measures. Thus in April 1931 the old – and hitherto unused – rediscount law of 1914 was utilised to rediscount commercial paper at the Caja de Conversión. Next year a large proportion of the newly issued Empréstito Patriótico was also deposited in exchange for currency at the Caja de Conversión. With the creation of the central bank and its authority to engage in open-market operations a new innovation was brought into being. Confronted with an inflow of hot-money the central bank sold paper to absorb part of the expansion induced by these funds. Centralisation of the bank reserves in the central bank coupled with stringent liquidity requirements in loan policy helped prevent a renewed immobilisation of bank portfolios. The country was left, however, without a system of long-run credit for industrial investment, till 1944 when the Industrial Credit Bank was created.

SOME CONSEQUENCES OF THE DEPRESSION FOR THE ARGENTINE ECONOMY

The Depression, on the one hand, may be looked at as one more rather severe instance of the Argentine business cycle. But on the other hand, as we have argued in relation to the fate of Argentine exports, it did accelerate the bringing about of a new phase in the international division of labour and it entailed a period of reduced significance for international transactions.

Argentina, therefore, as an open economy, had not only to bear the full shock of the crisis but, in addition, had to undergo some basic changes to adapt to the new international order.

The first casualty, in this sense, of Depression was growth itself. As we have seen, growth was painfully slow during the Depression. In fact, in per capita terms, growth was negative, i.e. there was a fall of almost 7% in average income per head between the 1925–9 and the 1935–9 quinquennia.[67]

Second, as a consequence of the general retraction in trade and the bringing about of a new international division of labour in the agricultural sector, exports lost some significance. The ratio between exports and GDP fell from a level of 23.8% in the years 1925–9 to 19.1% by 1935–9. For the 'Pampean' rural sector external demand fell to 58% of the total from 67% – in those same two periods – and for the whole rural sector domestic demand now meant 57% of the total as compared with 49% before the Depression.[68]

Another way to look at the closing up of the Argentine economy is the reduction in import coefficients. Imports as a proportion of GDP fell from 25% to 15%. The fall was particularly strong in the direct import content of consumption, which fell almost 50% from a level of 13.3% to 6.8% in a ten-year span.[69]

Long-run private foreign capital almost ceased to be invested in Argentina if one looks at it in balance-of-payments terms. But based on other sources of finance foreign capital did play a significant role in the expansion of manufacturing output through branches of transnational companies and migrant European capital.[70]

In the third place, slow growth in output and incomes was associated with a low rate of investment. Fixed investment fell as a proportion of total domestic demand, from 33% in 1925–9 to 24% during the Depression decade.[71]

Under the impact both of the closing-up of the economy and the low rates of investment, the little growth that took place had characteristics which differed from the previous performance of the Argentine economy. First, while in the period 1925–9 to 1935–9 GDP increased by 19.8%, rural output only increased 16%. But more importantly 'Pampa' rural output grew just 10.8%, cereals and linseed only 2.1%. If the rural sector is subdivided – following Diaz Alejandro – into mainly traditional 'exportables' *vis-à-vis* 'new' activities the discrepancy is very evident. In that same time-span, while the first group of products grew 5%, the second grew 30%. Although some of the 'new' activities were involved in exporting they were mainly devoted to supplying domestic demand and their fast rate of growth was a consequence of import-substitution, as in the cases of rice, edible oils and cotton.[72]

Within exportables, there was also a significant shift from cereals and linseed towards cattle as this last activity grew almost 11%, a response to relative price movements.[73] Within the livestock sector there was a shift towards more refined cattle-fattening as the export quotas while almost maintaining chilled beef markets implied an important reduction in frozen beef.

A consequence of a shift away from agriculture towards extensively based cattle-fattening was the expulsion of labour. The contribution of this displaced labour to the industrial and building activities must have been important in filling the gap left by the fall in international migration.

Growth in manufacturing activities was higher than that of GDP – as in the period previous to 1930 – but it was not particularly fast for most branches. Comparing 1927–9 with 1941–3 GDP increased at an annual rate of 1.8% while manufacturing increased at a rate of 3.4% (1.9 times the rate of growth of GDP while this elasticity had been around 1.2 in the first thirty years of the century). As a consequence, its share in GDP increased from 18% in 1929 to 20.9% in 1939. Not only was manufacturing growth far from spectacular either in absolute or relative terms, but its share in new capital created over the period 1925–9 to 1940–4 was only 5.8%, less than its share of total existing capital during the first quinquennium.[74]

Manufacturing growth in addition was very uneven. For most branches it was either negative or negligible. Two fast-growing sectors increased their production on the basis of plants that had been installed on the basis of decisions taken before the Depression. These were petroleum refining (12.6% per year) and rubber products (39.0% per year). (The fastest-growing sector is in fact a statistical mirage; we refer to electrical machinery and appliances, which grew at a rate of more than 40% because it was almost non-existent before 1929.) As to the textile sector it is true that it did experience a rather fast rate of growth as was the universal experience of agrarian countries in those years (textile production grew at about 10% per year). But looking at figures for the share of imports in apparent consumption for this sector jointly with clothing one discovers that there was no import substitution at all: a result which is not surprising if one remembers the difficulties involved in granting more protection to an industry in which the British had a very important export interest. Import-substitution in the textile sector was to be more of a wartime phenomenon.[75]

Examination of capital – labour ratios as well as capital – output coefficients confirms that what growth there was in manufacturing was of a labour-intensive type. In fact, even if there was some new capacity, it is clear that to a great extent growth was based on an intensive use of already existing capacity.[76]

Manufacturing exports, despite the stimulus of a higher exchange rate, did not show any important increase till the Second World War.[77] The growth in manufactures that took place, therefore, left several important unsolved problems for the future. The main ones were run-down equipment and an accumulation of problems on the labour front, where as we have seen, real wages were declining during the decade.

CONCLUSIONS

We have seen that instability and marked cyclical behaviour were not new in the Argentine economy before 1930 and were intensified in their consequences by the vulnerability implied in the openness of the economy. We have also tried to show that the Depression in Argentina started in the second half of 1928, *before* the Wall Street crash, and as a consequence of the immediately preceding Wall Street boom.

The collapse in the prices of Argentine exports – mainly temperate-zone foodstuffs – also took place before October 1929 and can be ascribed to long-run forces in world markets which were indicating well before the Depression that the country had to find other avenues for growth.

To add to the elements of continuity between the two inter-War decades it has also been underlined that recovery and later decline during the 1930s followed very traditional lines, being mainly an outcome of a passing boom in Argentine exports as a consequence of intense droughts in North America. Once more, capital movements, in spite of the new machinery put into effect, played a fundamentally destabilising role.

Examination of economic policies pursued during the Depression has revealed their limited autonomy in an economy as open as Argentina and, more specifically, their extreme vulnerability to developments and demands in Great Britain. Of course the whole story was not mere repetition. The Argentine economy became much less open and industry increased its share of national income in a context of rural stagnation. New agencies were set up to deal with different aspects of the economic life of the country and they were utilised to try some new policies, although these typically had roots in previous experience. Both GDP and industry, however, grew at a very slow rate, significantly below the experience of other Latin American countries. That in spite of an easier balance-of-payments situation than that of most other Latin American countries Argentina had such a poor performance in the field of industrialization may not be wholly unrelated – we believe – to the caution which dominated economic policy-making and some of those more specific external restrictions we have already mentioned.

As instability has again become a feature of the world economy and Argentina – as well as other Latin American countries – is once more much more vulnerable to international trade and financial difficulties, an examination of the 1930s – and in fact of the whole inter-War period – looking for the underlying permanent aspects of economic life, can therefore be a useful field of study for us in the 1980s.

NOTES

1. See the *Revista Económica*, first published by the Banco de la Nación Argentina from 1928 to 1934, and thereafter by the newly created Banco Central de la República Argentina, for an early analysis of the Argentine business cycle. Throughout the life of this journal we can detect the inspiration and pen of Raúl Prebisch – head of the Economic Research Department of the Banco de la Nación in the late 1920s and General Manager of the Central Bank from its inception.

2. In the period 1925–9, 96% of Argentine exports were accounted for by agricultural and pastoral products. Cereals and linseed made up about 60% and livestock products about 40% of the total. The most important products were wheat (22% of the total), maize (19%), linseed (12%), beef (11%), wool (8%) and hides and skins (8%). Argentina was the second world exporter of wheat, with 20% of world exports; the first in maize (more than two-thirds of world exports), in linseed (80% of world exports) and in beef (61% of world exports). Europe and the USA were significant producers of almost all these products. See *Revista Económica* (n.s.) vol. 1, no. 2 (1937): 'Tendencias de la producción agropecuaria', and Taylor and Taylor (1943) for the volume and share of Argentine exports in world markets. For the composition of Argentine exports see Diaz Alejandro (1970) table 1.11, p. 18. The position of Argentina *vis-à-vis* the more advanced countries was closer to the predicament of present-day NIC's specialising in exports competitive with decaying labour-intensive industries in Europe and the USA than to that of the typical primary producer.

3. For an analysis of instability in the physical volume of exports see *Revista Económica*, vol. 3, no. 1 (January 1930) and also *RE* (n.s.) vol. 1, nos 2 and 3 (1937). See Dieguez (1972) for a systematic analysis of both price and quantum instability in terms of an instability index. This index was

estimated by Dieguez following MacBean as the percentage difference between annual figures and a five-year moving average. Export prices were normally less unstable than volumes. But in the period 1917–29 the instability index for prices was 12.5% while it was 12.2% for volumes.

4. See Nemirovsky (1933) pp. 142–3 for data on export concentration in the grain trade. For data and analysis on the 'frigorífico pool' see the official Anglo-Argentine Joint Committee of Enquiry (1938). The Sociedad Rural Argentina, back in 1928, had published 'El pool de los frigoríficos' written by Raúl Prebisch. It was shown that rather than smoothing out price fluctuations as they claimed to do the 'pool' transferred back any price decline while tending to retain price rises. Sizeable gaps existed between export prices declared to Argentine authorities and import prices in Great Britain. In one famous episode one of the meat-packing firms which had refused to provide cost data to an Argentine Congress Investigative Commission was caught red-handed smuggling cost sheets in corned beef tins. See Smith (1970). As to grain firms it was alleged that during a devaluation they forced down the international price so as to monopolise all the price advantage *vis-à-vis* the producer and the country. Their position was very much helped by lack of storage space, which forced Argentina to sell the whole crop immediately after the harvest.

5. The instability index for export values in the 1917–29 period was 16.8%. The same index estimated by MacBean for 35 countries in the 1948–58 period was only 9.06%. See Dieguez (1972) p. 34.

6. Terms of trade declined 24% from 1919 to 1922 then increased 37% up to 1925 to fall again 10% in 1926 and 1927, shoot up 35% and decline 7% in 1929. On the average terms of trade in the decade of the 1920s were 27% below their 1913 level; incidentally this was the same as the average for the 1930s. See Balboa (1972) for a yearly series of the terms of trade.

7. The classical instance of change in capital inflows totally unrelated to Argentine conditions is that described by A. G. Ford (1962). The Balkan Wars led to a halt in capital inflows and to a crisis in Argentina – aggravated thereafter by harvest failures – without any domestic justification. In the period 1926–8 long-run capital inflows represented 10% of the value of exports, being therefore a significant source of foreign exchange. Private investment contributed 41% and public borrowing 59% of the total. See *Revista Económica* (n.s.) vol. 1, no. 1 (1937) cuadro 6, for estimates of Argentina's balance of payments for 1926–36.

8. For export shares in GDP and the 'Pampa' rural sector see CEPAL (1959), cuadro 16, p. 18, and cuadro 20, p. 23. For foreign capital participation in total fixed capital see cuadro 27, p. 28, and cuadro 28, p. 29, for the figure on long-run gross capital inflow as well as cuadro XI, p. 114 for the figure on gross fixed capital formation, all for the period 1925–9. Figures in 1950 pesos have been converted into 1950 dollars using the purchasing parity rate of exchange for that year i.e. 6.30 pesos per US dollar. In net terms the contribution of foreign capital was, strictly speaking, clearly negative. The net annual outflow was, on the average, 249 million dollars of 1950 purchasing power, which represented 4.7% of GDP. Data from cuadro 28, p. 29 and cuadro 24, p. 26 in CEPAL (1959).

9. The expression 'sporadic gold standard' was coined by Alberto Hueyo, who was Minister of Finance from March 1932 to July 1933. See his

words in *Ministerio de Hacienda* (1932) p. 6. The country during the first three decades of the twentieth century was on gold till August 1914 and again from August 1927 to December 1929. Return to gold, both in 1899 and in 1927, was pushed by export sector interests confronted with an appreciating peso. Foreign investors, on the other hand, favoured a 'strong' peso for conversion of their peso earnings into foreign currencies. For Sir Otto Niemeyer's opinion adverse to the rigid credit system see *Revista Económica* (1934) vol. 7, nos 5–8, p. 132.

10. See *Revista Económica* (October, 1932) vol. 5, no. 9, cuadro 6, p. 178, for figures on tax revenues from various sources.

11. See V. L. Phelps (1938) appendix I, table 1, for figures on Argentina's balance of payments in gold pesos for the complete period 1914–35. Figures in current pesos, for the period 1926–36 are in *Revista Económica* (n.s.) vol. 1, no. 1 (1937) cuadro 6. (The Argentine gold peso as defined by law in 1891 had 1 451.61 milligrams of fine gold and was equal to a mint par of 47.58 pence, 5 French francs or 0.965 US dollars. The paper peso defined by the 1899 Conversion Law was equal to 0.44 gold pesos. See also Salera (1941) p. 21 for the pre-First World War period. The heavy indebtedness of Argentina had drawn the attention of Keynes (see Keynes (1919) p. 263). Service of foreign capital, in the period 1925–9, was taking up 31% of export proceeds and 8.5% of GDP; see CEPAL (1959) cuadro 28, p. 29, and cuadro 29, p. 30. For an analysis of the debt burden of agricultural countries, recipients in 1924–8 of 60% of all capital going into foreign securities, see Timoshenko (1933) chap. 3. In Argentina for the period 1924/5–1928/9 the net trade balance was 570 million gold pesos, against which remittances of private profit and interest of 563 million gold pesos – out of which 70% were sent to the British railway companies – and service of the public debt of 322 million gold pesos had to be settled, leaving a deficit of 315 million gold pesos. A net capital inflow of 675 million gold pesos not only made up for that deficit, but allowed a substantial accumulation of gold reserves; see V. L. Phelps (1938) for the source of these figures.

12. For the share of imports in GDP see CEPAL (1959) cuadro 24, p. 26. It was 24.8% in 1925–9, only slightly down from 26.1% in 1900–4. Imports in 1925–9 supplied 13.3% of consumption. In that same period intermediate-goods imports represented 8% of GDP and machinery and equipment 35.3% of domestic investment. See CEPAL (1959) cuadro 25, p. 27. The essential character of some imports for the level of domestic activity was shown during the First World War. Scarcity of imports in this period led to a sharp downturn of 20% in GDP from 1913 to 1917. Part of the fall, however, was due to reduced building activity as a consequence of financial difficulties. See Diaz Alejandro (1970) statistical appendix, table 19, for figures for GDP at factor cost. This depression was much more serious than that of the early 1930s.

13. See Fodor and O'Connell (1973). The position of Argentina was rather singular for primary producers at that time. Most other Latin American countries, for instance, had an export surplus with the USA and an import surplus with Great Britain and thus in this sense helped Britain's balance-of-payments problems.

14. For an examination of the limitations of countercyclical economic policy

in the Argentina of those years see Banco Central de la República Argentina, *Memoria Anual 1938*, capitulo II. Chilled beef exports, depending almost exclusively on the British market, were only 7.5% of total Argentine exports. Other export products could find outlets in the European continent although Great Britain normally represented an important customer. The British market, therefore, was more essential for cattle-producers than for Argentina as a whole.

15. The Banco de la Nación Argentina, a state-owned bank created after the 1890 crisis, had in 1926–8 45% of all deposits and 42% of all lending of the banking system. See *Revista Económica* (n.s.) vol. 1, no. 1 (1937) p. 39. For this description of the cycle of the late 1920s I have essentially relied on the analysis published in that and previous issues of the *Revista Económica*.

16. Export quantum fell 3.8% while export prices fell 9% relative to 1928; see Dieguez (1972).

17. See *Revista Económica* (English-language version), May 1929, pp. 74–80, for an early analysis of the crisis in the wheat market. Between May 1928 and May 1929 wheat prices fell from 11.81 to 8.44 pesos per quintal. For wheat, one quintal (100 kilogrammes) is equal to 3.68 bushels.

18. According to Timoshenko (1933) prices for fifteen important agricultural products – including wheat, wool and hides – were already falling by the mid-1920s. According to Mandelbaum (1953) wheat prices had been declining since the early 1880s. In Argentina, wheat prices fell from an average of 15.13 pesos per quintal – in the 1920/24 period – to 10.50 in 1927/28 and 9.68 in 1928/29.

19. Ibid. pp. 172–5.

20. For an analysis of these various factors see Mandelbaum (1953) and de Hevesy (1940). See also League of Nations (1931). The main variation in output during the War had taken place in North America as shipping difficulties had made it less attractive to expand production in Argentina and Australia.

21. See Mandelbaum (1953) fig. 11, p. 118. For an analysis of agricultural protectionism before 1930 see O'Connell (1983).

22. Corn prices were at 9.21 pesos per quintal in 1925, but at 8.53 pesos per quintal in 1928. See *Revista Económica*, vol. 3, no. 1 (1930) and also April – June (1934) in the English-language version 'The downward trend in agricultural and pastoral prices'. For the 'meat war' see Smith (1970).

23. For an index of rural sector prices see *Revista Económica* (English-language version) April – June 1934: 'The downward trend of agricultural and pastoral prices'. For land prices see *Sociedad Rural Argentina* (1979).

24. Figures for export and import prices as well as for terms of trade have been taken from Balboa (1972). In 1921–2 and in 1931–2 the average terms of trade were 60, 1913 = 100.

25. Export prices at their lowest level in 1922 had been 6% below pre-war prices. In 1932 they stood 54% below the 1913 level. See Balboa (1972).

26. For figures on export volumes see also Balboa (1972). On the experience of agricultural production during the Depression a good Argentine source is *Revista Económica* (n.s.) vol. 1, nos 2 and 3.

27. The exception was the issue by British railway companies of 245 and 68 million pesos in debentures, in 1930 and 1931 respectively. In 1930, also, short-run loans were extended by British and American banks, but they had to be repaid in 1931. See *Revista Económica* (n.s.) vol. 1, no. 1, for balance-of-payments figures. For the burden of debt service see Balboa (1972).
28. See Balboa (1972) and CEPAL (1959) vol. 1, cuadro XIV, p. 115, for figures on import capacity.
29. See Diaz Alejandro (1970) table 1.6 for structure of GDP at 1937 prices and statistical appendix, tables 33 and 19, respectively, for figures on rural output and GDP at factor cost year by year.
30. See CEPAL (1959) cuadro 11, col. E, p. 15, and cuadro 20, col. 1, p. 23.
31. Figures for terms of trade effect and debt service from CEPAL (1959).
32. Wholesale price indices from *Revista Económica*, various issues, and the same source for exchange rates. The wide disparity between the dollar and the pound is due to the pound's inconvertibility in September 1931. Prices, as measured by the overall wholesale price level, continued to decline till November 1933.
33. Ibid. for rural and non-rural prices.
34. The figures for interest rates were obtained from *Revista Económica*, several issues; those for ownership of land are taken from the Agricultural Census of 1937. For land prices see Sociedad Rural Argentina (1979) and for urban land and rents see *Revista Económica* (n.s.) 1937, vol. 1, no. 2, p. 73.
35. For figures on profit rates see *Revista Económica*, various issues. Rather high spreads between passive and active interest rates were maintained by banks so that their profit rates reveal an amazing stability, up to 1931: above 7%.
36. For figures on rural output see CEPAL (1959) cuadro 20, p. 23, and for relative wholesale prices *Revista Económica*, various issues.
37. For wage and cost-of-living figures see League of Nations (1941) tables 16 and 97.
38. See CEPAL (1959), chap. 11, p. 15, for population figures.
39. Even a party interested prima facie in claiming responsibility for the recovery for economic policy correctly asserted that the main reason behind recovery was the increase in world prices for Argentine export staples; see *Revista Económica* (series II), vol. 1, no. 1, 1937, p. 1.
40. See Balboa (1972) for figures on export and import prices in US dollars.
41. See *Revista Económica* (n.s.) vol. 1, nos 2 and 3, 1937, for an analysis of these years in the wheat and maize markets. The drought in North America and Australia allowed Argentina to expand output and exports beyond the quotas established under the recently signed International Wheat Agreement. The convention provided for a 15% acreage reduction in the USA and Canada, but for the maintenance of their export quantum by Argentina and Australia. Importing countries committed themselves not to further encourage their domestic production. See Mandelbaum (1953). There is a saying in the country that 'God is Argentinian'; it seems, indeed, to apply to this episode.
42. See Balboa (1972) for figures on export volumes and values.
43. See *Revista Económica* (n.s.) vol. 1, no. 1, 1937, for an analysis of these

movements.

44. See Balboa (1972) for figures on import quantum. In addition to debt repatriation, on the one hand, there was funding of blocked balances at the end of 1933 and the beginning of 1934, on the other, as compensatory movements. Figures for import capacity from CEPAL (1959) vol. 1, cuadro XIV, p. 115.

45. See CEPAL (1959) vol. 1, cuadro 11, pp. 15, 28, and p. 29, for figures on GDP, terms of trade effects, foreign remittances and population.

46. Figures both for wholesale prices and interest rates from *Revista Económica*, several issues. The mortgage moratorium law was passed in 1933. Interest rates fell from almost 8% per annum in June 1932 to slightly above 6.75% by mid-1933 and beginning in September 1933 fell to 5.0/5.5%. Prices, on the other hand, increased, both in 1934 and 1937, by 14 per cent.

47. Figures for wholesale prices and external terms of trade were taken from sources already mentioned. As the wholesale price index of the Banco de la Nación Argentina started in 1926, we have taken four instead of five years as our base.

48. Sources for the estimate are the same as in the 1930–4 period; see n. 36.

49. For information on rents and rural land prices see *Revista Económica* (new series) vol. 1, no. 2, 1937, and Sociedad Rural Argentina (1979).

50. See also *Revista Económica*, same issue.

51. Figures for nominal wages and cost of living from same source as in n. 37. Figures for national income distribution from Diaz Alejandro (1970) statistical appendix, table 3, p. 398; the same source, table 30, p. 428, for figures on employment by sector.

52. For figures on export volumes and prices as well as on terms of trade and balance of payments see Balboa (1972). Data on GDP from various tables in the statistical appendix of Diaz Alejandro (1970).

53. See Tasca's opinion in his 1939 book. Speaking of British policies, Tasca says: 'The flow of current trade has apparently been subordinated to debt collection' (Tasca, 1939, p. 94). But even if having lower priority it was also true – as stated by an Argentine authority – that 'we [Argentina] shall still have to import large quantities of other goods not only because we need them, but also because it is essential to continue to import in order to continue to export' (see Banco Central de la República Argentina *Memoria Anual*, 1942, pp. 90–1.

54. 'The period of outward growth . . . had profoundly influenced ideas' (CEPAL, 1949, p. 93). The section on Argentina of this report carries the undoubted authorship of Raúl Prebisch.

55. For this episode see Salera (1941) pp. 54, 59.

56. 'the foreign exchange permit in addition to being an instrument for the restriction of imports, also became a selective instrument and on the basis of experience, it can be asserted that the latter function became often more important than the former': see Banco Central de la República Argentina, *Memoria Anual* (1941) p. 12.

57. The average import rates for the sterling pound and the US dollar have been estimated on the basis of information about the exchange regime applicable in each case after November 1933. Figures for the UK and US

wholesale price index from League of Nations (1941). Differences in devaluations are mainly due to discriminatory treatment in rates of exchange.

58. The selling rate was determined by auction each market day; it started with a devaluation of about 26%. The average spread between purchasing and selling rates for 1934 was 13.87%. Late in 1935 the public auction system was discarded, and the selling rate was fixed at 17 pesos per pound.

59. The Junta was not supposed to engage in a valorisation scheme – such as that traditional in Brazil for coffee – by trying to withhold supplies from the market. Not only did the authorities think that such schemes were bound to be unsuccessful, but the traditional lack of storage space made such schemes unmanageable. For the operations of the Junta see *Revista Económica* (English-language-edition) vol. 7, no. 4 (October – December 1934).

60. It was widely accepted that import trade margins had decreased during the crisis, as could be gathered from examination of changes in foreign and domestic prices for imported products. Consequently, the spread between internal and external terms of trade could not have emerged from the import side. The 1933 devaluation would today be termed a 'compensated' devaluation.

61. See Salera (1941) pp. 135–6. The estimate of the real exchange rate is based on the overall wholesale index and not on the railway tariff levels as would have been desirable.

62. However, the situation was far from uniform for the different countries supplying Argentina. For Great Britain 54%, in 1932, of all imports, by value, were duty-free and consequently untouched by such a measure. The second-ranking country in this respect was Germany with 12% of its sales being duty free (Salera, 1941, pp. 79–80).

63. Argentina had only a conditional most-favoured-nation treaty signed with the USA; consequently it was in a technically impeccable position if it did not extend to the USA concessions made to the UK. But, in fact, tariff concessions were all extended. The 20% import surcharge was, of course, much more important. Argentina signed bilateral agreements of the exchange kind with Belgium (1934), the Netherlands (1934), Switzerland (1934), Germany (1934), Spain (1934), Italy (1937) and some other European countries. 55% of all imports into Argentina, by 1937, came from these countries. In addition to those agreements some unconditional most-favoured-nation treaties in the tariff field were concluded. See Salera (1941) pp. 87–8 and US Tariff Commission (1948).

64. See Tasca (1939) p. 94; Richardson (1936) p. 106. Preferential trade and payments agreements were signed in 1933 with Denmark and other Scandinavian countries as well as with Germany and several Central European countries in addition to Argentina, Brazil and Uruguay. As to the initiative of the bilateral system an Argentine authority may also be quoted: 'The system of bilateral trade was imposed by the force of circumstances rather than adopted by choice.' (CEPAL (1949) p. 193.)

65. Ibid. p. 104. The Anglo-Argentine agreement involved several other aspects. The first one was relevant for Argentine exports to Great Britain. Minimum quotas for beef – although at a level lower than the histor-

ical one – were obtained. A second aspect is that related to 'favourable treatment' of British capital in Argentina which allowed decisions like the special railway exchange rate. A third one related to the organisation of the meat trade. Blocked balances were also taken into account. Funding of those balances above some level was agreed upon as well as an exchange provision out of current export proceeds for the minor ones. Funding of sterling balances was made at 4% interest, five years of grace and fifteen years amortization at a rate of exchange of 43d. per peso (for the first £13 526 400) and 42d. per peso (for the additional tranche of £1 293 600). There was an additional issue on similar terms for Swiss Francs 100 316 545 and one of 2% Treasury bills to be amortised over fifteen years, at par at a rate of exchange of 1.135 pesos per dollar. British funding represented 58% of all funding and, as we have seen, it was Britain's practice to fund blocked balances. The funding of dollar balances did not involve any *quid pro quo* on the part of Argentina. In spite of both facts some authors insist on presenting the funding as an important concession obtained by Argentina that could justify by itself signing the Agreement. For data on the funding see *Revista Económica* (March – April 1934) p. 60.

66. See Diaz Alejandro (1970) table 13 in the statistical appendix and 2.16, p. 97.
67. Figures from CEPAL (1959) vol. 1, cuadro 11, pp. 15 and cuadro 28, p. 29.
68. Ibid. cuadro 16, pp. 18, and cuadro 20, p. 23.
69. Ibid. cuadro 25, p. 27.
70. See Diaz Alejandro (1970) table 99, statistical appendix, where it is shown that twenty-six plants were established during the 1930s by US-owned companies. See also D. M. Phelps (1936). German capital was very active during this decade in Argentina, mainly in the pharmaceutical and chemical industries, but also in metal industries.
71. See CEPAL (1959) vol. 1, cuadro X, p. 114.
72. See Diaz Alejandro (1970) tables 3.12, p. 164, and 111, p. 519.
73. Ibid. table 3.12, p. 164, and table 3.15, p. 172.
74. Ibid. table 2.3, p. 71, and table 2.4, p. 72, and CEPAL (1959) vol. 1, cuadro xv, p. 116. Road-building received the lion's share of new investments.
75. Ibid. table 4.6, p. 222, and table 4.14, p. 232.
76. See CEPAL (1959) for figures on capital-labour and capital-output coefficients.
77. See Diaz Alejandro (1970) table 4.28, p. 263. Manufacturing exports were 10.5 million dollars by 1937–9.

REFERENCES

M. Balboa, 'La evolucion del balançe de pagos de la República Argentina, 1913–1950', *Desarrollo Económico*, vol. 12, no. 45 (April – June 1972).
Banco Central de la República Argentina, *Memoria Anual* (Buenos Aires).
Comision Económica para América Latina (CEPAL), *Economic Survey of*

Latin America 1949 (Mexico, 1950).

Comision Económica para América Latina (CEPAL), *Analisis y proyecciones del desarrollo económico*, vol. v: *El desarrollo económico de la Argentina*: Part I: *Los problemas y perspectivas del crecimiento económico argentino* (Mexico, 1959).

C. F. Diaz Alejandro, *Essays on the Economic History of the Argentine Republic* (New Haven and London, 1970).

H. L. Dieguez, 'Crecimiento e inestabilidad del valor y el volumen físico de las exportaciones argentinas en el período 1864–1963', *Desarrollo Económico*, vol. 12, no. 46 (July – September 1972).

J. Fodor and A. O'Connell, 'La Argentina y la economia atlántica en la primera mitad del siglo 'XX', *Desarrollo Económico*, vol. 13, no. 49 (April – June 1973).

A. G. Ford, *The Gold Standard, 1880–1914, Britain and Argentina* (Oxford, 1962).

P. de Hevesy, *World Wheat Planning and Planning in General* (Oxford, 1940).

Joint Committee of Enquiry, *Report of the Joint Committee of Enquiry into the Anglo-Argentine Meat Trade* (London, 1938).

J. M. Keynes, *The Economic Consequences of the Peace* (London, 1919).

League of Nations, *La Crise Agricole* (Geneva, 1931).

—— *Statistical Yearbook 1940* (Geneva, 1941).

W. Mandelbaum, *The World Wheat Economy 1855–1939* (Cambridge, Mass., 1953).

L. Nemirovsky, *Estructura Económica y Orientación Política de la Agricultura Argentina* (Buenos Aires, 1933).

A. O'Connell, 'Free trade in One (primary-producing) Country: The Case of Argentina in the 1920s', Working Paper No. 114, Instituto Torcuato di Tella (Buenos Aires, 1984).

D. M. Phelps, *The Migration of Industry to South America* (New York, 1936).

V. L. Phelps, *The International Economic Position of Argentina* (Philadelphia, 1938).

República Argentina, Comisión Naciónal del Censo Agropecuario, *Censo Nacional Agropecuario año 1937* (Buenos Aires, 1939).

Revista Económica, Series I published by Banco de la Nación Argentina, Series II published by Banco Central de la República Argentina.

J. H. Richardson, *British Economic Foreign Policy* (London, 1936).

V. Salera, *Exchange Control and the Argentine Market* (New York, 1941).

P. Smith, *Politics and Beef in Argentina* (New York, 1970).

Sociedad Rural Argentina, 'Èl Precio de la Tierra' (Buenos Aires, 1979).

H. J. Tasca, *World Trading Systems: A Study of American and British Commercial Policies* (Paris, 1939).

H. C. Taylor and A. D. Taylor, *World Trade in Agricultural Products* (New York, 1943).

V. P. Timoshenko, *World Agriculture and the Depression*, vol. v, no. 5 (Ann Arbor, Michigan, 1933).

US Tariff Commission, *Economic Controls and Commercial Policy in the American Republics: Argentina* (Washington, DC, 1948).

9 The Great Depression and Industrialisation The Case of Mexico

ENRIQUE CÁRDENAS*

INTRODUCTION

Neither the effects of the Great Depression on the Mexican economy nor the latter's general performance during the 1930s have been clearly established in the literature. Perhaps one of the few agreements in the historiography of this period is that the structure of the economy suffered a fundamental change and that the basis was laid for postwar development.

In particular it is argued that the structural changes were carried out by a process of 'Reform and Reconstruction' (Reynolds, 1970). 'Reform' because a more active economic role of the government and its greater explicit commitment to the goal of redistributing income were recognised. 'Reform' also because a considerable redistribution of wealth took place through the oil industry's expropriation and the process of agrarian reform. The term 'Reconstruction' has been used to mean the efforts to restore the economic characteristics of pre-revolutionary times, from industry and railroads to confidence in paper money, and the undertaking of infrastructure pro-

* The basic ideas of this chapter were taken from parts of my doctoral dissertation. I am deeply indebted to Carlos Diaz Alejandro, Albert Fishlow, Leopoldo Solís and to the participants of the two conferences on the 'Effects of the Great Depression on Latin America'. Naturally, they are not responsible for any remaining errors that may have survived their comments. I am grateful to Rosemary Thorp for having invited me to participate in the conferences and to the Social Science Research Council for providing financial support to do so. My thanks also to Elia Solís, who typed the manuscript with proficiency and speed.

jects, ranging from roads and irrigation facilities to legal changes and developments banks. Similarly, it has been argued that during these years the basis for economic growth in the 1940s was established, meaning that a proper set of laws, financial institutions, agricultural infrastructure and property rights were preconditions for economic development.

With regard to the process of industrialisation it has been suggested that it started as a response to the Second World War when the unavailability of goods from the belligerent nations provided a great incentive for import-substitution. Although some substitution of imports is believed to have taken place in the 1930s, it has been considered to be unimportant and irrelevant (Villarreal, 1976). That is to say, unlike other Latin American countries such as Argentina, Colombia and Brazil where the Great Depression provided the impetus for import-substitution, this development had to wait until the Second World War to get underway in Mexico. Perhaps the single most important reason for this delay, it has been asserted, was the great uncertainty prevailing in the country at the time because of the government's intention of enforcing the 1917 Constitution, particularly in regard to the ownership of the nation's subsoil (Hansen, 1971, pp. 29–40). These conditions were later aggravated, so goes the argument, by Cárdenas's socialist policies and the government's emphasis on the agricultural sector.

The process of Mexican industrialisation during the 1930s is the main topic of this chapter. It will be argued that a fundamental change in the economy's structure took place: one in which the industrial sector began to acquire preponderance and a relatively independent dynamism, characteristics which were to mature in the following decades. That is to say, the years 1925–40 were indeed a period of restructuring and reconstruction in the midst of crisis. But such structural changes were not only related to institutions, public works, laws and the like. The economy itself was transformed and a process of change from outward to inward development and growth began to take shape. The Great Depression contributed to this transformation by facilitating the maturing of institutions and creating economic conditions which promoted domestic industrialisation. As a result, and partly because other sectors stagnated (agriculture, mining and to some extent oil), industry became the engine of growth during the 1930s.

The purpose of this chapter is to show how it was possible for the industrial sector to perform so well in this period, and to explore the particular role played by government policy and the Great Depression itself in this outcome. In particular the strength and transmission mechanism of the crisis will be considered as well as the process by which it promoted the maturing of an important institution, namely the Banco de México. The chapter has been structured chronologically. The following section considers the shock of the Great Depression, paying special attention to the transmission channels of the crisis and to the macroeconomic policies pursued. The third section deals with the recovery and the remaining years of the 1930s. Here the emphasis is placed on the distinction between policy measures and the exogenous forces which accelerated the recovery from the shock. In addition it is shown there how the financial authorities matured during the 1930s in terms of their capability to respond to foreign crises. In the concluding section we argue that the findings of the chapter show that Mexico's experience fits quite well with that of the other countries studied in this volume, and we discuss the implications of our analysis of industry for the usual interpretations of Mexican industrial development.

THE SHOCK OF THE GREAT DEPRESSION

Neither the Wall Street boom nor its corresponding crash a year later were the immediate causes of the Mexican Depression. Indeed, the impact of several depressive forces had been felt in the Mexican economy since about 1925 and were somewhat aggravated in 1927 by the US recession. The terms of trade had deteriorated 4% in the 1926–9 period, although the volume of demand for Mexican mineral exports had remained strong after the 1927 recession. The other major export – oil – had been decreasing steadily in importance since the early 1920s, so that the Great Depression simply accelerated its fall.

The forces making for Depression were exacerbated by the pro-cyclical, orthodox economic policies followed by the government. Like most other countries at the time, Mexico was officially on the gold standard and took economic measures accordingly. However, Mexico's peculiar monetary system gave her effectively a floating exchange-rate regime. Such a situation was unique in the Latin American context and deserves some explanation before we can deal with the role of economic policy during the Great Depression.

The point is that Mexico was *de facto* under a flexible exchange-rate regime because the monetary system was essentially composed by gold and silver coins, and because the only currency with full legal tender was the gold peso. However, since most transactions were carried out with silver currency, basically because of the long tradition of using silver, the relevant exchange rate was that of the silver peso *vis-à-vis* the dollar, and not with respect to the gold peso. Naturally, the relative value of the gold and silver currencies varied with the fluctuations in the international price of both metals and with their relative domestic supply and demand. Therefore, the silver peso would depreciate when the international price of gold increased relative to that of silver, or when pressures in the balance of payments occurred which made gold flow out and become scarce domestically, so that its price relative to that of silver would also rise. The government could counteract this process by reducing the coinage of silver money and increasing that of gold, thus leading to a decrease in the price of gold relative to silver and a consequent appreciation of the silver peso. Consequently, the fact that most domestic transactions were carried out in silver placed Mexico effectively under a flexible exchange-rate system.

Now, in spite of such an exchange-rate regime, the government tried to maintain both the official gold parity and a balanced budget from at least the second half of the 1920s through to the bottom of the Great Depression in early 1932. Consequently, every time the balance of payments was in an unfavourable position, gold would tend to flow out and therefore the money supply would diminish. As a result a tendency towards depreciation of the peso would take place, given the flexible exchange-rate system, which the authorities would try to prevent by halting the coinage of silver, thus decreasing the money supply even further. In addition the government would increase taxes when a lower level of income reduced the volume of fiscal revenues. Such an increase in taxation tended to reduce even more the level of aggregate demand.

As mentioned before, the increasing difficulties in the balance of payments from mid-1926 on were caused to a large extent by the slowing down of the US economy and the decreasing value of mineral and petroleum exports. The position was aggravated by the remittances made to the International Bankers Committee between 1926 and mid-1928 as debt payments under the Pani–Lamont agreement (Ortíz Mena, 1943, p. 283, and Simpson, 1932, pp. 6–7). As a result, the exchange rate depreciated and the federal government reacted by accelerating the coinage of gold and halting that of silver pesos in February 1927, and eventually interrupting the servicing of the foreign debt in the middle of 1928. This policy made the money supply fall 10% in 1927,[1] and caused the exchange rate to appreciate 10% between February 1927 and April 1928. Naturally this measure had a further depressing effect in addition to that caused by the fall in export demand, so that GDP in real terms fell 4.4% in 1927 and barely increased in 1928. In turn, the decline in income reduced the volume of imports in those years. Consequently, all these sources of tax revenues – exports, imports and income – fell and hence the amount of fiscal revenues. With a balanced budget policy, such a reduction implied an additional contractionary effect. However, it was not possible to reduce expenditures in the same proportion and deficits appeared in 1926 and 1927. Nevertheless, the fact that such deficits were essentially financed by accumulating arrears considerably reduced their potential expansionary impact.[2]

As a whole the period preceding the Wall Street crash witnessed a whole array of contractionary policies which continued after Luis Montes de Oca replaced Alberto J. Pani as Finance Minister in 1927. Indeed, expenditures were cut 15% between 1926 and 1929, essentially by reducing the government's payroll, and additional taxes were levied. The new taxes together with the economy's recovery allowed an increase in fiscal revenues, but only to finance a decreasing level of expenditure up to 1929.

Such a restrictive economic trend was substantially worsened by the Great Depression. Both the Mexican terms of trade and the volume of exports diminished drastically, basically because of the sudden decrease in foreign demand as income abroad fell, but partly due also to the increase in tariffs in the USA in 1930. GNP in that country fell at an average annual rate of 8.2% in real terms between the peak (1929) and the trough (1933) of the cycle. In turn the Mexican terms of trade deteriorated 21% while the volume of exports contracted 37% during 1929–32, which implied a fall of 50% in the purchasing power of exports (see Table 9.1).

The impact of the external shock on aggregate demand worked through various channels. First of all, the export sector itself was immediately affected by the reduction in prices and the absolute fall of demand. However, the fact that a considerable share of the sector was in foreign hands with a consequently low returned value from exports – 66% in 1926 – made the foreign shock milder in terms of its repercussions on the rest of the economy. Indeed, only 3% of the non-rural labour force worked in the oil and mining sector, which in turn represented approximately 65% of all exports (Cárdenas, 1982,

TABLE 9.1 *Macroeconomic variables during the shock*[a]

| | Percentage Change, 1929–32 | |
	Total	Yearly average
Exports (dollars)	−64.9	−23.0
Imports (dollars)	−67.8	−24.7
Terms of trade	−20.8	− 5.7
Capacity to import	−50.3	−16.0
Real total output	−17.6	− 4.7
Real industrial production	−31.3	− 9.0
Wholesale price index	−18.8	− 5.1
Nominal exchange rate[b]	47.0	10.1
Real exchange rate[b]	21.9	5.1
Central bank reserves (dollars)[c]	−53.4	−22.5
Money supply[d]	−60.2	−26.5

[a] All figures in nominal terms except when stated otherwise.
[b] Pesos per US dollar
[c] For the period 1929–31, the latter year being when reserves reached a minimum. Figures for 1929–32 are 23.6 and 5.4% respectively.
[d] For the period 1929–31, the money supply reaching a minimum in the latter year. Figures for 1929–32 are −45.6 and −14.1 respectively.

SOURCE: Cárdenas (1982) table 2.4.

pp. 22–30). The experience contrasts sharply with that observed in Brazil or Colombia where the main export product – coffee – is a labour-intensive activity, and therefore the shock was much more widely spread.

A second related channel through which the foreign shock was transmitted was that of the fiscal linkage. The fact that almost 50% of all taxes were related to the foreign sector made the level of fiscal revenues highly dependent on foreign economic fluctuations. Consequently it is not surprising to find that tax receipts dropped from 231 million pesos in 1929 to 155 in 1932, with 63% of the fall coming from the fall in taxes related to the foreign sector (Nacional Financiera S.A., 1978, p. 355). This decline in the flow of fiscal revenues took place in spite of government efforts to increase taxes. The new general tariff which came into effect in 1930, and even more the 1% extraordinary tax levied in 1931 on gross output of agricultural, industrial and commercial activities, should be seen as emergency measures to stop the declining trend in taxes. With regard to expenditures, these decreased substantially in 1931. Naturally these measures brought with them corresponding budget surpluses which were of a considerable magnitude and went beyond the government's plans to stabilise the net position of the Treasury. In fact the accumulated surpluses in the years 1929–31 were slightly smaller, in real terms, than the deficits accumulated in the four years bewteen 1937 and 1940 during President Cárdenas's expansionary Administration (Cárdenas, 1982, pp. 131 and 280).

The foreign and fiscal contractionary elements were coupled with a third transmission mechanism, namely, the monetary channel. As mentioned above, the balance of payments received a further shock with the Great Depression and the surplus in the trade account continued its downward trend. The level of international reserves began to decrease at the beginning of the second quarter of 1930[3] partly due to the worsening of the trade account, and partly because the government paid 10 million gold pesos to the foreign creditors in order to negotiate the resumption of servicing the public foreign debt. The exchange rate continued its depreciating trend and by the end of July 1931 the international reserves were practically exhausted, reaching a low point of US $6.1 million: the government had no choice but to reform the 1905 Monetary Law and demonetise gold.

The increasing discount of silver *vis-à-vis* gold during the previous few months had raised expectations of devaluation and the banking system suffered a run: more than 20 million pesos were withdrawn from the banks and exchanged into gold or foreign exchange the week before the enactment of the new Monetary Law (Simpson, 1932, p. 67). However, the authorities were reluctant to abandon what they considered the gold standard and, in addition to the providing of US $15 million to defend the exchange rate, the Treasury ordered the withdrawal of 10 million (silver) pesos from circulation and an increase in the reserve requirement (US Department of Commerce, 1932, p. 451; Banco de México 1931, p. 27).[4]

The deteriorating balance of payments coupled with these restrictive monetary measures, as well as the panic conditions prevailing during most of 1931, made the money supply fall sharply in that year. M_1 reached an all-time low value of 272 million pesos, more than a 60% decline in nominal terms and 54% at constant prices. The total resources of the banking system fell 21% in nominal terms and with them the volume of credit granted, though in a somewhat smaller proportion. As wholesale prices fell almost 20% in 1931, the drop in financial resources in real terms was 37% and real interest rates soared, thus further aggravating the economic depression.[5]

Summarising the argument so far, the Great Depression had its impact on the national economy essentially through three channels. First, it diminished demand and prices for the export sector. Second, it reduced the level of fiscal revenues, and thus expenditures, as a consequence of the decline of foreign trade. And finally, the restrictive monetary policy and the export of gold which both developed in response caused a decrease in the money supply. These contractionary elements, however, were somewhat counteracted by the depreciation of the exchange rate, and its effects on the relative price of imports and domestically produced import-competing products. As this relative price change took place, consumers tended to substitute imports for domestic goods and so domestic demand tended to increase. This price effect was to have a long-lasting impact on the industrial sector's performance during the 1930s.

Finally, an autonomous element which aggravated the effects of the 1929 Depression was the very bad crop of that year which resulted from adverse climatic conditions. The fact that the livelihood of a vast proportion of the population depended on agriculture and that much of this group constituted part of the market for industrial goods and services, made the 1929 crop failure contract even further the level aggregate demand in the early years of the Depression.

The resulting contraction of demand left installed capacity idle. At the beginning, the government prohibited the closing down of factories in order to prevent a higher level of unemployment but by the middle of 1931 that was no longer possible. Sales diminished, inventories accumulated, and finally the volume of output was also curtailed. Profits in industry tended to diminish partly because of idle capacity and partly because of the lag between sales and production. The continued forced production in the face of falling sales implied that the wage bill was probably reduced but not proportionately. That is, nominal wages were reduced but that did not prevent profits from declining. Moreover, wages were also pressured downwards by two additional factors. On the one hand, a total of over 310 000 Mexicans working in the USA were repatriated between 1920 and 1933,[6] which represented almost 6% of those employed in 1930 (Carreras de Velasco, 1974). On the other hand, the labour movement had gone astray with the withdrawal of government support in the late 1920s, a fact which hindered the process of collective bargaining and the defence of labour, wages and other prerogatives.

The failure of the financial authorities to manage the increasingly difficult economic situation made inevitable the resignation of the Minister Montes de Oca in late December 1931. Alberto J. Pani, who had already been the Treasury Minister under President Calles, became once more the head of the ministry in February 1931, and shortly after implemented several economic policies which significantly modified the trend of the economy.

RECOVERY AND PERFORMANCE DURING THE 1930s

Like various other Latin American nations the Mexican economy was able to recover relatively soon from the contractionary effects of the Great Depression. By 1932 the business cycle had reached its trough, probably before the end of the first half of the year, and it resumed a steady growth trend thereafter through the remainder of the decade. Two major factors on the demand side were responsible for the early recovery of the Mexican economy: an early increase in the value of exports and a series of expansionary monetary and fiscal policies. Let us consider these two elements in some detail.

The relatively early increase in the value of exports was made possible by the rise in prices of some exports and the exploitation of a new oil-field, elements which were strengthened by the rapid nominal and real devaluation of the peso since 1929. Indeed, the value of exports began to rise in 1933 only because the dollar price of all exports increased 8.5% in that year, while the volume only began to grow in 1934. In this latter year, as a result of a growing volume and price of exports, the export value experienced a substantial increase of 68% in dollar terms and 73% in peso value.

The rise was particularly strong in the mining and oil sectors which allowed these products to surpass their 1929 dollar value of sales abroad in 1934, thus contributing substantially to the early recovery of total exports. In fact, of the US $82 million increase in exports from 1932 to 1934, 77% came from gold, silver and petroleum products (Cárdenas, 1982, pp. 298, 319 and 322). Consequently, the somewhat privileged position of Mexico in owning silver and oil made it possible to accelerate the recovery by increasing demand and the capacity to import, thus allowing the purchase of foreign raw materials which, in the face of idle capacity, permitted the quick resumption of production. This evidence contrasts with that of other countries which had to rely on only one major export and where prices did not rise fast enough. Such is the case of Chile, for instance, which mainly exported copper which did not surpass its 1929 price until the 1940s. A less dramatic but similar case is that of coffee, the fundamental export of Brazil and Colombia. That is to say, while the sluggish recovery in the price of industrial metals significantly affected the behaviour of Mexican exports, such an effect was substantially counteracted by the rise of prices of other products. Using Diaz Alejandro's allegory, Mexico was quite lucky in the export 'commodity lottery'.

The second element which permitted a rapid recovery from the Great Depression, expansionary economic policy, is perhaps of greater interest since it implied a fundamental change of course. With regard to the exchange rate the new Minister, Pani, *de facto* abandoned the policy of stabilising, or rather defending, the exchange rate and in this sense the gold standard as well. The government implicitly made the decision to put the goal of full employment before the objective of external equilibrium by letting the peso float freely, at least in the first few months after the monetary reform of March 1932.[7] Such a decision was not taken exogenously, however, but was forced by the very low level of international reserves in the central bank. Naturally the peso continued to depreciate after the reform, experiencing wide fluctuations until the middle of 1933, when the exchange rate became fairly stable again. The export recovery had by then increased the supply of foreign exchange and the level of international reserves so that the monetary authorities decided to fix the peso parity in November 1933. The new value implied a depreciation of 35% with respect to February 1932, and 67% with respect to 1929. This parity would remain until March 1938, despite the abandonment of the gold standard by the USA in 1934.

With regard to monetary policy the 1932 measures undertaken by Minister Pani were essentially expansionary. As soon as he took office in March, he ordered the resumption of silver coinage and, more quietly, the use of Banco de México bills to pay government employees in order to increase the means of payment. From the time of the Monetary Reform until the end of 1933, the coinage of silver amounted to 89 million pesos, whereas the issue of bills in excess of rediscounts amounted to 53 million.[8] In addition the Banco de México reduced the discount rate and the reserve requirement a few weeks after the Reform. Naturally the general impact of these policies was very expansionary. According to the official figures the money supply increased 31% in 1932, and 15% in 1933. It is estimated that over 80% of the growth in the money supply was caused by the federal government via increases of high powered money. As was to be expected, the nominal interest rate diminished from 12% to

8% between 1931 to 1932, whereas in real terms the decrease was much larger (Banco de México, 1981, p. 117, and Banco de México, 1933, pp. 19–20).

On the fiscal side, which given the simple financial system was closely related to monetary policy, the declining trend in the level of public operations had continued through the bottom of the Depression with a balanced budget in 1932. Moreover, the surpluses obtained in the previous years were transformed into monetary (gold) reserves which partially evaporated with the deterioration in the balance of payments. By 1932 arrears had arisen again and 1933 showed an actual deficit. Both of these were indirectly covered with the seignorage gains which resulted from the extraordinary coinage of silver and the corresponding bill issue of those years.

It must be mentioned that these seignorage gains were considerable during 1932 and 1933, and actually implied fiscal deficits in both years of a relatively important magnitude. Although the official figures show an actual balanced budget in 1932, the fact that 33 million pesos were obtained as seignorage gains makes that the size of the relevant deficit, which amounted to 1.1% of GDP. The adjusted deficit for 1933 is 46 millions or 1.3% of GDP. This implies that about 17% of government expenditures was actually financed with seignorage gains in these two years. Moreover because relative changes and not levels are what matters, one can say that the change between 1931 and 1932 was very significant. From a surplus of 0.75% of GDP in the former year, the budget jumped to a deficit of 1.1% in 1932. The expansionary policy is then of almost two percentage points of GDP, which is by no means negligible. In fact these deficits were larger as a percentage of GDP than those run during the expansionary years of the Cárdenas Administration. Consequently it can be said that a quite significant expansionary fiscal policy was carried out at the very bottom of the Depression which accelerated the process of recovery, and complemented the expansionary monetary and exchange-rate policies discussed above.[9]

Finally, it is interesting to note that several indicators suggest that the response of the economic system to these expansionary measures was very rapid indeed. First, the wholesale price index began to rise in April 1932 and by December it had increased 18% with respect to the level of the previous March. Another indicator of quick response can be inferred from the difference between the expected and actual fiscal revenues of 1932. This difference, which was 13.3 million pesos in the first quarter, disappeared by August. Of the 16.2 million peso decrease in fiscal revenues during 1932, 95% correspond to the first quarter (Pani, 1941, p. 167).

But to emphasise the economic recovery is to divert attention from the important and deeper consequences of the Great Depression, namely the intense process of industrial development that took place in the 1930s and the more relevant role of the government in managing economic policy. It is in this decade that export-led growth gave way to growth based on the domestic market. Real industrial output increased at an average rate of 6.1% a year from the bottom of the Depression in 1932 to 1940, and it constituted the economy's engine of growth during the 1930s for the first time. Output per worker increased 37% during the decade and industry accounted for 38% of GDP growth while it had only on average a relative weight of 17% in GDP. It is in that sense that we call industry the 'engine of growth'.

Why was industry's performance so outstanding given the difficult economic circumstances? In general terms one can argue that increasing profits and a growing level of aggregate demand were the essential factors behind such a process. With regard to supply there was an 86% increase in the domestic terms of trade between 1929 and 1940, urban relative to rural prices, which invited a transfer of resources to the modern sector. In addition the agrarian reform programme, which was substantially accelerated during the 1930s, introduced an element of uncertainty that diminished expected profit rates in agriculture and thus investment in that sector. Consequently resources were reallocated to other areas where conditions were more favourable, such as industry. Similarly, the relative price of (industrial) import-competing commodities compared with non-traded goods and services also increased during the 1930s (38%) and resources tended to shift correspondingly.

Other elements which played a significant role in the increasing profits of industry were the availability of excess capacity in some key industries such as electric power and cement, and public investment outlays in various types of public works. In particular the construction of the road network was accelerated, merging most of the industrial and urban centres. This reduced transport costs and significantly enlarged the available market, thus increasing overall productivity. Some estimates show that the effect on productivity was substantial indeed, its growth contributing with approximately 27% of the industrial increase in output during the 1930s (Cárdenas, 1982, pp. 252–8 and 289). As a whole the increasing profitability of the modern sector was soon reflected in a strong process of capital accumulation, and given some public investment in agriculture too, the investment coefficient practically doubled during the 1930s.

On the demand side the 67% devaluation of the peso in 1929–33 was able to change relative prices of imports and import-competing products, fostering the substitution of domestic goods for those imported. In fact about 37% of industrial demand growth in the decade came from import-substitution, a process stronger in the consumer goods industries and less so in the intermediate good category. Moreover, the substitution of domestic for imported commodities seems to have been very rapid indeed, as is suggested by the high estimates made of elasticities of substitution in the early 1930s.

The contribution of import substitution to the growth of demand in the 1930s is high and comparable to that observed in Brazil, where industrialisation in that period was in considerable part induced by substituting imports (Cárdenas, 1982, pp. 166 and 181, and Fishlow, 1972). In fact foreign observers were aware of the magnitude and strength of that process: Joseph Pike, writing for the British Overseas Trade Department in 1936, said that the country was strongly heading towards self-sufficiency and that imports into Mexico would have to concentrate on raw materials and equipment rather than consumer goods. He listed many industries as being normally supplied by domestic production with the exception 'of a small demand in the largest cities, chiefly from foreign residents' (Department of Overseas Trade, 1936, pp. 9–17).

In addition to the process of import-substitution, expansionary government policies combined with a fixed exchange rate through most of the 1930s were instrumental in sustaining a high level of aggregate demand. As mentioned above, during 1932–3 monetary expansion financed about 17% of total public expenditures, a fact which helped the process of economic recovery. The following two years were basically characterised by an accommodating monetary policy and a fixed exchange rate. The growing foreign demand reflected the economic recovery abroad while the domestic economy approached a high level of employment. Domestic prices remained practically constant in those years while those abroad were increasing. With a fixed exchange rate the peso became somewhat undervalued and the *real* exchange rate depreciated 19% between 1933 and 1935. This price effect helped the diversification of exports and continued to strengthen the process of import-substitution.

From 1936 to 1940, especially in 1938, government expenditures were financed to a lesser degree (7% on average) by monetary expansion with corresponding budgetary deficits. This figure is not particularly high, but there was an important qualitative change: public expenditure shifted from administrative to social and economic projects. In addition to the supply-side effects these government outlays implied certain consequences for demand which affected the industrial sector. In particular the building of public works increased the demand for certain raw materials produced at home, especially those related to the cement and steel industries. Moreover, the construction of roads merged small communities with larger towns or cities. To the extent that previously isolated areas were effectively integrated, there was a growing demand for several products simply because the market became larger. In fact, this phenomenon had an international dimension as well as national. It has been claimed that international tourism was greatly enhanced during the post-depression years by the availability of roads connecting Texas and Mexico City (Banco de México, 1941). In addition to tourism's effect on the supply of foreign exchange, this activity demanded other industrial goods, especially the construction of hotels and other service-type facilities. In economic development terminology, road building had both forward and backward linkages which particularly affected the construction industry.

The previous discussion has shown that one important consequence of the Great Depression was the acceleration of the import-substitution process and domestic industrialisation by means of changing relative prices. This outcome was also influenced by an expansionary macroeconomic policy and the maintenance of a high level of aggregate demand through the remaining years of the 1930s. This fact is closely related to the second most important economic consequence of the Great Depression, namely, the wider role the government was able to play in macroeconomic policy management. In particular the authorities could implement monetary policy in a relatively autonomous fashion for the first time.

Indeed, it was only with the 1930s that the central bank could actually finance the budget deficit by printing money. One can argue that government economic policy between the mid-1920s and 1935 was essentially orthodox, in the sense that the authorities sought a balanced budget financed with fiscal resources, whereas in the second half of the decade a budget deficit was consciously and consistently obtained and financed through printing money. That is to say, the budget deficits observed in 1926–7 and 1932–3 were completely different in nature to those observed after 1936. The former deficits

TABLE 9.2   *Comparison of the Great Depression with the 1938 Recession*
(percentages)

	Great Depression[a]	1937–1938 recession[b]
Exports	−29.5	−25.2
Terms of trade	−15.8[c]	−23.5
Purchasing power of exports	−22.8	−22.2
International reserves	−31.7[c]	−56.3
Money supply	−18.4[d]	10.8
Output (GDP)	− 6.3	1.6
Industrial value added	−10.5	4.0

[a] 1929–32, average annual rate of change.
[b] 1937–8, rate of change.
[c] 1929–31, average annual rate of change. The reason is that these variables reached a minimum in 1931. The 1929–32 figures are −7.5% for the terms of trade and −8.6% for reserves.
[d] If the 1929–31 value had been computed instead, when M_1 reached a minimum, the result would have been larger in absolute terms: −25.4%.

SOURCE: Cárdenas (1982) table 3.3.

were forced by circumstances; in the specific case of 1932–3, the government apparently felt justified in paying its employees and other expenses with bills backed with silver earned through seignorage gains. By contrast, the deficits of the second half of the 1930s resulted from explicit policy measures. There was a determination to raise the level of aggregate demand even if financed with fresh-printed money. And by that time the central bank had finally acquired the *de facto* monopoly of paper money issue, a power acquired essentially as a consequence of the Great Depression.[10]

Such a change in policy proved to be extremely helpful during the 1937–8 recession. Indeed, it is possible to assert that the Mexican government was much more able to cope with an external shock in 1937 than just a few years earlier, managing to keep economic activity growing though at a lower rate. Although a comparison of the Great Depression with the 1937–8 recession poses some difficulties, since 1937–8 was not as bad an agricultural year as was 1929–30, it is worthwhile making a simple comparative exercise to see if such an assertion is valid or not. Table 9.2 shows the behaviour of several variables during the Great Depression and the 1937–8 recession. It is quite remarkable to see that whereas the external shock was at least as bad in 1938 as in the 1929–32 period, the effect on the level of output was considerably more favourable in 1938 than during the Great Depression. Indeed, exports and the terms of trade fell in such a way as to make the drop in the purchasing power of exports practically the same in both periods. Moreover the decrease in the level of international reserves was far more severe in 1938 than during the 1929 Depression. By contrast, GDP and industrial production had positive and much greater rates of growth in the latter recession than in the former.

Perhaps the single most important variable accounting for this difference was the money supply. During 1929–32 it fell 18.4% yearly on average (and 25.4% during 1929–31), whereas in 1938 it increased 10.8%. The government was instrumental in preventing the money supply from falling in 1938 by expanding domestic credit as much as possible. Therefore it is probably safe to assert that the monetary authorities played a fundamental role in counteracting the effects of the external shock. Which instruments did the government, and particularly the Banco de México, have in 1937 which they did not have in 1929, which helped to counteract the latter recession more quickly and effectively? Most important of all were the political will and the ability to expand aggregate demand directly through budget deficits. As opposed to the former period the public accepted the central bank's bills freely and institutional arrangements existed which made deficit financing possible. Furthermore, the exchange rate had become an instrument for stabilisation and no longer a goal of economic policy: the government was unwilling to sacrifice a rapid rate of development for the sake of a fixed exchange rate. That is to say, the Banco de México in particular and the government in general became much more capable of managing macroeconomic policy in the 1930s partly as a result of the Great Depression.

CONCLUSIONS

It has been argued in the previous pages that Mexico's experience, in terms of the shock, response, and consequences of the Great Depression, was not very different from that observed in other Latin American countries. Indeed, various other nations pursued expansionary macroeconomic policies in response to the crisis and experienced a strong process of import-substitution during the 1930s. Mexico was not an exception but rather confirms Diaz Alejandro's perception regarding the larger countries.[11] In particular one can say that the rapid process of industralisation in Mexico and in other Latin American countries was due, in the last analysis, to a responsive and strong economic policy, to the possibility of substitution for imports, and to a dynamic domestic (and foreign) industrial sector which was quick to react to new market opportunities. It is interesting to note in this regard that the process of import-substitution did not respond to an explicitly protective government policy. True the change in prices was caused by a devaluation of the exchange rate, which ultimately is a policy variable. But, at least in the case of Mexico, the government did not devalue the peso *in order to* promote import-substitution. This fact sharply contrasts with the postwar strategy of development, which relied so heavily on tariffs and other import restrictions to promote domestic industrialisation.

Finally, it is important to comment on some of the implications that this research has regarding the interpretation of the Mexican process of industrial development. First of all, it is no longer possible to argue that the Second World War was the turning-point in the country's modern industrialisation. The story that we have advanced in these pages has hopefully shown that such a turning-point should be traced back *at least* to 1929 or the Great Depression. We have shown elsewhere (Cárdenas, 1982, pp. 168–76) that a number of industries representing 35 or 40% of manufacturing output did not rely on imports to supply the domestic market as early as 1929, which suggests that a considerable development in some industries had taken place earlier; there seems to be evidence that such a process did appear in the 1920s, partly relying on excess installed capacity inherited from the pre-revolutionary years of the *Porfiriato*.

By looking at the 1920s and 1930s in this new fashion, and eventually at the revolutionary period too, it will be possible to have a long-term picture of the Mexican industrialisation process. It is very possible that such a process was far more continuous than is usually believed, so that the inter-War period was not a break with the long-term trend of development. In fact it could probably be argued that the period of revolutionary upheaval was quite short and mild with regard to its destructive effects. In this way it will then be possible to merge the *Porfiriato*'s industrial growth with that which occurred after the Revolution.

A second implication is related to postwar development. Mexican economic growth from the 1940s through part of the 1960s has been called the Mexican Miracle. This is because of the rapid growth of the economy in that period, and because it has not up to now been clear how that outstanding performance occurred or where it came from. The present story provides an explanation for the rapid growth during the 1940s, which was able to occur almost without any additional investment. Indeed, the strong capital accumulation that took place in the 1930s made the labour-intensive growth of the 1940s possible, and that makes the 'miracle' much less astonishing.

A final implication also related to the postwar period arises from the fact that the process of import-substitution had advanced substantially by 1940, especially in the non-durable consumer-good industries; that implies that there was not much more room for additional substitution of imports. Rather, there was room for a regression in such a process, so that most growth would have had to come from an expanding domestic market or from foreign demand, in contrast to what is usually believed. For the economy to have witnessed considerable import-substitution in the 1940s, as is currently believed to have happened, such a process would have had to have taken place in the consumer durable, raw materials or capital goods industries; the standard view does not argue this.

NOTES

1. The concept of money supply in this work is defined as M_1, namely, the sum of Banco de México bills and coins in circulation plus checking accounts. The official source is Banco de México and it does not specify whether the figures are in gold or silver pesos. My own impression is that the figures shown were revalued with respect to gold and consequently are expressed in silver pesos.
2. It is interesting to note that the increase in expenditures for 1927 was essentially due to the investment programmes on roads and irrigation and not for emergency purposes (Secretaria de Hacienda y Crédito Público, 1963, p. 84).
3. The fall in reserves came relatively late by Latin American standards, particularly for Brazil, where capital outflows and decreases in international reserves began to take place in response to the Wall Street boom which preceded the 1929 crash. Apparently the continued coinage of gold with the aim of stabilising the exchange rate led to a delay in the fall in international reserves in the Mexican case until mid-1930. Between January 1929 and July 1931, when the so-called gold standard was abandoned, the monetary authorities coined 48.3 million gold pesos (Secretaria de Hacienda y Crédito Público, 1932, p. 108).
4. The decision to continue the contraction of silver means of payment to prevent a further depreciation of the peso clearly indicates that there was no shift in exchange-rate policy, in spite of the gold demonetisation.

5. The level of aggregate output increased more than 3% however, because of an extraordinarily good agricultural year in 1931. Nevertheless industrial production fell 6% as a result of the monetary contraction and high interest rates, and in the face of substantial stockpiling. (See Cárdenas, 1982, pp. 284, 294, 302, and 306 for sources of figures.)

6. An additional implication of deportation was the fall in foreign-exchange remittances sent to Mexico, which reduced the supply of hard currency with the same contractionary effects that a decrease in exports implies.

7. In fact the monetary authorities tried to peg the exchange rate at the end of 1932, but had to abandon their attempt fairly quickly (Martínez Ostos, 1941, pp. 432–3, and Banco de México, 1934, pp. 21–2).

8. A most interesting question that arises at this point is why the public began to accept Banco de México notes after more than fifteen years of repudiation. I have argued elsewhere (Cárdenas, 1982, pp. 102–5) that a substantial excess demand for money emerged in 1931, caused by a fall in the money supply coupled with a relatively stable demand for money, to the point that barter transactions began to appear. Consequently the public was ready to accept a new means of payment as soon as it was available. Also, the Banco de México induced acceptance of its notes by paying government employees with paper money.

9. In comparative terms, however, one cannot really speak of a very vigorous contractionary or expansionary fiscal policy during the 1925–40 period. In terms of surpluses or deficits as a percentage of GDP it can be shown that the Roosevelt Administration did not intend to be as expansionary as it actually was (Brown, 1956, and Peppers, 1973).

10. See n. 8 above.

11. See his Chapter 2 in this volume.

REFERENCES

Banco de México, *Sexta asamblea general ordinaria de accionistas* (Mexico, 1931).

Banco de México, *Octava asamblea general ordinaria de accionistas* (Mexico, 1933).

Banco de México, *Novena asamblea general ordinaria de accionistas* (Mexico, 1934).

Banco de México, *El turismo norteamericano en México, 1934–1940* (Mexico, 1941).

Banco de México, *Estadísticas históricas, Moneda y Banca. Cuaderno 1925–1978* (Mexico, 1981).

C. Brown, 'Fiscal Policy in the Thirties: A Reappraisal', *American Economic Review*, 46 (1956).

E. Cárdenas, *Mexico's Industrialization During the Great Depression: Public Policy and Private Response* Ph.D. dissertation, Yale University (1982).

M. Carreras de Velasco, *Los mexicanos que devolvió la crisis, 1929–1932* (Mexico, 1974).

Department of Overseas Trade (Great Britain), *Report on the Economic and Financial Conditions of Mexico* (London, 1936).

A. Fishlow, 'Origins and Consequences of Import Substitution in Brazil', in L. E. Di Marco (ed.), *International Economics and Development. Essays in Honor of Raúl Prebisch* (New York, 1972).

R. Hansen, *The Politics of Mexican Development* (Baltimore, 1971).

R. Martínez Ostos, 'El Banco de México', in M. E. de Koch, *Banca Central* (Mexico, 1941).

Naciónal Financiera, *Statistics of the Mexican Economy* (Mexico, 1977).

R. Ortíz Mena, 'El sistema monetario mexicano', en *Sistemas monetarios latinoamericanos*, vol. 1 (Córdoba, Argentina, 1943).

A. J. Pani, *Tres monografías* (Mexico, 1941).

L. Peppers, 'Full Employment Surplus Analysis and Structual Change: The 1930s', *Explorations in Economic History*, 10 (1973).

C. Reynolds, *The Mexican Economy: Twentieth-Century Structure and Growth* (New Haven, 1970).

Secretaría de Hacienda y Crédito Público, *Memoria de la Casa de Moneda* (Mexico, 1932).

—— *La hacienda pública a través de los informes presidenciales*, vol. 2 (Mexico, 1963).

E. N. Simpson, *Recent Developments in Mexico in the Field of Money and Banking* (Mexico, 1932).

US Department of Commerce. Bureau of Foreign and Domestic Commerce, *Foreign Commerce Yearbook* (Washington, DC, 1932).

R. Villareal, *El desequilibrio externo en la industrialización de México, 1929–75* (Mexico City, 1976).

10 Restructuring through the Depression: The State and Capital Accumulation in Mexico, 1925–40*

E. V. K. FITZGERALD

MEXICO AND THE DEPRESSION

The shock-wave of the Depression, as it spread out from New York in 1929, dealt a severe blow to an economy still in the throes of reconstruction after the first major revolutionary upheaval on the American continent: between 1928 and 1932 the external terms of trade fell by 50%, the real value of exports by 75% and output by 21%. None the less, by 1935, production had recovered and despite an import capacity of about half its previous level, growth and accumulation began the long upward trend from which they have only recently departed. Although, as other chapters in this volume indicate, neither the degree of the shock nor the rapidity of the recovery were unique, the extent of Mexican 'openness' in trade, finance and ownership to the USA on the one hand, and the scale of the restructuring of the

* I am particularly indebted to Eugenio Rovzar for his collaboration on early stages of the drafting of his chapter; unfortunately he wasnot able to conclude the work, but much of the historical viewpoint was inspired by him. I am also extremely grateful to the Institute of Latin American Studies at Austin for the research facilities provided during the Fall Semester of 1981. This chapter forms part of a larger project on the State the capital accumulation in Mexico between 1925 and 1980.

economy under state direction on the other, do make Mexico an extreme, if not a special, case.

Relatively little economic history has been written about the 1925–40 period, even though it is the object of heated debate among political and social historians,[1] particularly because the continuity of the Mexican State implies a contemporary relevance for the events surrounding its foundation. However, it is interesting to note that the economic impact of the Depression is not cited in most studies as a major cause of socio-political change; other factors such as post-revolutionary state formation, agrarian reform, negotiation with foreign investors and organised labour movements are seen as dominant; the Depression enters, if at all, as an exacerbating element. The standard view of economic historians has been that although the impact was severe on the balance-of-payments and domestic activity it did not lead to import-substituting industrialisation along the lines of the 'ECLA paradigm'; rather the 1925–40 period was one of building up economic institutions such as the banks and the gaining of national control over national resources as a prelude to the industrialisation drive from 1940 onwards.[2] Some recent research has tended to confirm that view as far as manufacturing is concerned.[3] However, work on other areas of the economy has produced a different picture: one of increased state involvement in macroeconomic management as a direct result of the Depression[4] on the one hand; and of a deliberate restructuring of the export sector away from minerals towards agriculture on the other.[5] Although both of these are seen as the culmination of longer-term trends in the reconstruction of the economy after the Revolution, their relative contribution to the rapid recovery of the economy remains a contentious issue.[6]

The purpose of this chapter is to analyse some of the empirical evidence available on state intervention, production, trade, investment and income distribution during this period, in order to assess the impact of the US Depression on this process of economic restructuring between 1925 and 1940. First, we shall look at the changing structure of the economy during the period as a whole and the progress made by 1929; then we shall examine the impact of the Depression on that process; and finally we shall discuss the emergence of state management of the economy after 1930. The implication is that although 1929 was not in itself a turning-point in Mexican economic history, the Depression had an important part to play in the development of the Mexican model of accumulation – but a role that contrasts quite strikingly with its role in other Latin American economies (see the appendix to this chapter for an analysis of that role).

THE POST-REVOLUTIONARY ECONOMY

The immediate economic prelude to the Depression was not, as elsewhere in Latin America, the primary commodity cycle following the First World War, but rather a revolution; and the process of reconstructing a national capitalist economy is the central theme of the 1925–40 period. The economic impact of the Depression must be analysed, therefore, not in terms of its effect on growth or even on industrialisation, but rather upon that process of restructuring – involving changing patterns of production, trade, accumulation, income distribution, ownership and state intervention. Here, however, we can do no more than sketch in the relevant aspects of this process, for the 1925–35 period in particular.

The aftermath of the Revolution had left a certain 'vacuum' in the power structure, within which the State (sustained by its own bureaucracy and the Army – this latter to be replaced by organised labour by 1940) enjoyed a considerable degree of relative autonomy from a bourgeoisie weakened by agrarian upheaval. The 'Sonora group' which dominated this fledgling State, appears to have pursued a project based on agrarian modernisation, industrialisation and a certain degree of nationalism, although the form that these three were to take was to be determined by the pressure of subsequent events.[7] The major steps of the land reform, labour incorporation, nationalisation of mineral resources and consolidation of the large business groups, which were to define the nature of the development strategy after 1940, were only to come towards the end of our period. The early years, dominated by Calles rather than Cárdenas, were rather ones of reorganising the State itself and its relationships with foreign interests on the one hand and with the domestic private sector on the other.

The reorganisation of the State in the economic sphere between 1925 and 1930 involved a new fiscal system, which was mostly in place by 1928,[8] the expansion of public investment in infrastructure,[9] and the foundations of a new state banking system centred on the Banco de México as central bank;[10] as we shall see, it is these activities which develop most rapidly in the wake of the Depression. At the same time negotiations opened with foreign capital, mainly US interests. The claims commission on external debt and damages had started work in 1924, after the recognition of Obregón by the US government in 1923; but the Mexican government did not realistically seem able or willing to pay very much.[11] Increasing pressure was placed on both mining and oil companies, although with more progress in relation to the former.[12] In manufacturing, despite the first step towards local control of electric power, foreign investment was actively encouraged in technologically 'new' branches such as automobile assembly, as well as the use of foreign contractors in public works.[13] At this stage, therefore, the policy towards foreign investors was not unlike that followed further south some forty years later. Finally, as the third element in this restructuring of the control of the economy, a new relationship with the domestic private sector was established. A mutual understanding was achieved with the larger banks, a concentration of the smaller ones encouraged[14] and large-scale agricultural enterprise was promoted on the reassigned estates (the *ejidos* in 1930 accounted for only 13% of land) and underpinned by large irrigation works.[15] The development of the three large groupings of domestic entrepreneurs, who were later to form the core of private industry, relied on state tutelage and personal bureaucratic involvement.[16] The resulting pattern resembled by 1929 nothing less than the kind of 'triple alliance' later identified as a feature of post-war Latin American capitalism. As we shall see, it was destined to go through further strains, but the result was to temper rather than to weaken the system.

Despite the received view to the contrary[17] the years up to 1929 also saw considerable structural change, closely associated with the ownership changes just mentioned, which resulted in a certain internalisation of the economy. Traditionally mining had been the 'leading sector' in the Mexican economy, providing the foreign exchange needed for imported producer goods and luxury consumption, as well as considerable projects for foreign firms. However, the main branches, silver and oil, had already been struck by crisis before 1929: the world silver price collapsed in 1926 (falling from 80 cents to 62 in New York) bringing with it problems not only for the mining sector itself, but also the banks, heavily involved in the sector, and the value of the currency itself which was based on silver. Oil output also declined, from its peak of 143 million barrels to 64 in 1927 (international prices also weakened) partly due to local difficulties with the companies, but also to rapid depletion of fields and alternative sources in Venezuela, bringing fiscal receipts down with it.[18] The result, as Table 10.2 indicates (see end of chapter), was to start the decline in exports well before the effect of the Depression was felt through the deterioration of the terms of trade in 1930. Agriculture, in contrast, showed considerable signs of dynamism, at least in the northern capitalist sector, where communications, credit conditions (spurred on by the Banco Nacional de Crédito Argícola, founded in 1926) and irrigation were steadily improving; but in the centre and south, subsistence farming – which held the bulk of the rural population and had been the scene of agrarian unrest – seems actually to have been in decline; according to Meyer,[19] while agricultural output per head rose fivefold between 1907 and 1929 in the north, it had fallen by one-third in the south and centre. Maize production in particular, which had reached 7 million tons in 1910, was down to 3 million in 1924 and declined still further in our period (see Table 10.3). For workers in the extractive sectors and subsistence peasants, therefore, the crisis was already well-developed by 1929; foreign companies and domestic banks were also in serious difficulties. The only other sector to show promise, apart from commercial agriculture, was manufacturing. Here the general industrial production index (see Table 10.3) stood at 15 in 1920 but had steadily climbed to 24 by 1925 and 29 in 1930;[20] about 30% of the increase in material production between 1921 and 1929 was accounted for by industry (as opposed to 60% from agriculture and ranching);[21] most of the output was food-processing and textiles, based on an expanding urban market and the gradual reduction of imports. Thus, although estimated GDP was roughly stable between 1925 and 1929 (see Table 10.3), and so fell in per capita terms, this does not represent stagnation; rather it represents a shift in the dynamism of the economy from mining and subsistence agriculture towards commercial agriculture and industry – the start on modernisation.

Foreign trade was central to the economy, for the mineral exports (which made up 70% of exports in 1925, and still accounted for 60% in 1929, most of the rest being agricultural products) permitted the import of not only plant and equipment (50% of imports in 1929) and productive inputs (18%), but also a large amount of consumer goods (33%) because even 'early' import-substitution had not yet progressed very far, and indeed was not to do so before 1940.[22] The trade coefficient, none the less, was relatively low, standing in nominal terms at 11% in both 1923 and 1929. Trade had actually declined in the 1920s, exports falling from US $425 million in 1920 to 336 million in 1925 and 285 in 1929, for reasons we have outlined above; imports had fallen, similarly, from US $242 million in 1921 to 193 million in 1925 and 185 in 1929; thus in real terms the trade coefficient was probably diminishing. The implication is that while foreign trade was central to accumulation and the 'modern' sector it may have left a large part of the economy, and more particularly the population, untouched. Trade was also concentrated, naturally enough, on the USA: 80% of exports and 73% of imports in 1924, although these proportions had fallen to 61% and 69% in 1929 due to the collapse of minerals.

There are no firm estimates of the balance of payments for our period, but as the trade data in Table 10.2 indicate, even allowing for some unregistered imports across the Río Bravo, the commercial account was in considerable surplus in the 1920s, and indeed for the subsequent decade. The one available estimate (see Table 10.1) seems to be based on considerable detailed information, and indicates that the merchandise trade surplus was balanced by a massive outflow of profits, not only from mining and oil companies (although these accounted for the greater part), but also from public utilities, insurance companies, cotton and wool, gins and commercial enterprises as well as capital exports by Mexican residents. Indeed, Sherwell (1929) suggests that for 1921–7 the average outflow was 290 million pesos a year (as opposed to an average of 655 for exports) which 'represents in large part interest and profits on foreign capital invested in Mexico, possibly supplemented by a net withdrawal, or export, of capital by Mexico'.[23] It should be noted that in 1926 at least, the public debt service accounted for less than one-tenth of the total outflow. Therefore the pressure on the balance of payments as exports declined in the 1920s came not from imports, but the outflow of profits – mainly to the USA.

Despite this outflow of profits, the deteriorating trade position, and institutional reorganisation, capital accumulation did take place in the 1920s. The average ratio of gross fixed capital formation for 1925–30 (see Tables 10.5 and 10.6) to Gross Domestic Product (GDP) was some 5.3%: of this, about two-fifths was in transport and commerce (i.e. roads and motor-vehicles) and one-fifth in housing or urban infrastructure; but the balance appears to have been invested in agriculture and industry. The state share was also considerable (38%) reflecting large-scale programmes of public works in irrigation and roads – to the particular benefit of the northern capitalists.[24] Although the rate of investment was not high compared to the boom years of the 1950s and 1960s, it was not inconsiderable when compared to the average of 10% for the 1940s. When this rate of capital formation is taken in conjunction with the trade surplus (equivalent to 4.7% of GDP in 1925 and 4.5% in 1929) the implicit rate of gross savings (before profit outflows) would be of the order of 10% of GDP. It is not entirely clear how, in the last resort, this surplus was generated. The greater part was probably in the extractive sector, based on both natural resource rent and extremely low wages; but although this would account for the profit outflow (which Sherwell estimates was in reality 'non-returned value' from export receipts) it would presumably not have flowed into other sectors; moreover, the banks concentrated on the finance of trade in this period.[25] Public investment was mainly financed from the budget (going into roads and railways) and thus from taxes on imported and locally produced consumer goods – in other words, by urban consumers. Himes[26] suggests that in effect, a 'Lewis model' was also in operation, where real wages were held down by surplus labour from subsistence agriculture, providing sufficient profits to the 'new' modern sector for self-financing: certainly the early evidence on real wages and proletarianisation in both agriculture and industry would seem to support this view.[27]

In sum, then, the orthodox view of the decade leading up to 1929 in Mexico as one of economic and institutional stagnation, awaiting the reforms of the 1930s and growth in the 1940s, is not correct. It is in fact a period of considerable change: the basis of the modern State was laid; the crisis in the export sectors was well-advanced; commercial agriculture and manufacturing were emerging as new leading sectors; and pressure on both peasants' and workers' incomes was increasing. It is against this background that the impact of the Depression should be assessed.

THE IMPACT OF THE DEPRESSION ON THE MEXICAN ECONOMY

To trace the effect of the US Depression from 1929 onwards on the Mexcian economy is not entirely a straightforward task. In the paradigmatic Latin American economy the effect of falling world prices and demand for commodities is felt through foreign-exchange shortages and lower imports; this in turn forces substantial devaluation and eventually promotes import-substitution.[28] In Mexico, however, although exports did decline, the effect was felt as much through low prices transmitted into the economy as through a lack of foreign exchange; aggregate output recovered very quickly, but not as the result of a domestic demand stimulus; and import-substitution was not much advanced despite the lowered import coefficient. These somewhat peculiar phenomena derive, in fact, from the characteristics of the Mexican economy at the time: its extreme openness, and the process of structural change we have just discussed. The openness of the economy (then as now) went beyond the fact that trade and ownership of productive assets were concentrated on and in the USA: on the one hand, the open border meant that goods could move freely between the two countries, and thus that falling prices were transmitted directly from the US to the Mexican economy, depressing business through profit margins as well as through the volume of activity; on the other, the possibility of large liquid financial flows between the economies, without problems of convertibility throughout the period, gave little local control over the money supply. In other words, despite the dawn of 'structuralist' ideas elsewhere in the continent the most appropriate analytical model for Mexico, between 1925 and 1935 at least, may well be the 'monetary approach to the balance of payments'.[29] Under this perspective the effect of the Depression would be reduced price levels and lack of liquidity; not a shortage of foreign exchange as such. To this we must add two more features of the economy, which was only in the early stages of structural transformation: first the 'dual' nature of production, with a small 'enclave' mining sector providing foreign exchange for profits, and a large but impoverished peasant sector providing food for wages; and second, the uncertainty surrounding the major foreign enterprises as the Mexican government's attempt to gain national control strengthened.

The immediate impact of the Depression was felt in the mining sector, naturally enough. Although volumes had been declining for some years, and silver prices had already collapsed, these factors were now reinforced: the overall export price index fell by 32% between 1929 and 1932, and the dollar value fell from US $275 million to 97 million. Import prices appear to have declined by only 14% despite a far larger fall (32% in wholesale prices) in the USA; the effect was to reduce the purchasing power of Mexican exports by 50% in the space of three years. Thus the real 'value' of the extractive sector to the economy was reduced by more than the output figures indicate: none the less, the estimated volume of output in mining by 1932 was 55% of that in 1929; while that for oil was 83%.[30] However, in both branches, there was quite a rapid recovery, for two largely extraneous reasons: first, the value of silver exports rose as the result of the London Silver Agreement of 1933 and the US Silver Purchase Act of 1934, and lead recovered in sympathy; second, the discovery of a new oil-field in Poza Rica allowed output to expand from 33 million barrels in 1932 to 40 in 1935, while a growing domestic market from motorisation was able to absorb 40% of output in 1934 as opposed to 21% in 1928.[31] These improved results from the extractive sector, despite the uncertainty surrounding ownership, account for the rapid recovery of exports, which more than doubled in dollar value between 1932 and 1935, rising to US $208 million, while their purchasing power rose by 62%.[32] The terms of trade estimated with current weights, which had stood at 137 in 1925 (1929=100) and 79 in 1932, returned to 87 in 1935 (see Table 10.2, p. 274).

Imports also declined sharply, from US $178 million in 1929 to US $57 millions in 1932, a fall of some 63% in real terms. With no restrictions on imports, and the relatively modest intervening devaluation of the peso (from 2.26 in 1930 to 3.16 in 1932, a 'real' devaluation of only 29% when adjusted for wholesale prices in Mexico and the USA),[33] this decline cannot be attributed either to the price effect as such or to import restrictions; the answer must be sought on the demand side. Export receipts and national income recovered rapidly, and were fairly 'normal' by 1935; but imports remained at US $113 million in that year, and in fact in real terms remained at about half their 'pre-Depression' level for the rest of the decade. The unknown element is, of course, what was happening to the 'invisibles' account during this period. Debt payment was virtually suspended between 1929 and 1935,[34] but this, as we have seen, was not the greater part of the outflow. However, judging by the merchandise trade balance (the difference between exports f.o.b. and imports c.i.f. fell from US $97 million in 1929 to US $40 million in 1932) and the *improved* reserve position (see Table 10.2) the outflow of profits probably fell by about one-half – and presumably much of the burden was felt by the mining companies. However, once exports improved, although the merchandise trade balance (thus defined) rose again to US $95 million in 1935, the reserve position improved by a similar increment, which implies that profits were not flowing out again on so large a scale, although (as Table 10.1, p. 273, indicates) the outflow had regained its former strength by 1940. There is good reason to suggest, therefore, that the 'returned value' from exports did not decline as much as 'gross value', and thus much of the financial shock was absorbed by the foreign firms controlling the extractive enclaves. This was possibly a key contributory factor both to their relative lack of resistance to Mexican government policy, and to the relatively rapid recovery of the economy as a whole, given that it was restructuring away from mining in any case.

Meanwhile agriculture – the other pillar of the Mexican economy – was also going through a difficult period. Value added in the sector as a whole (Tables 10.3 and 10.4) was in fact fairly stable between 1929 and 1932, but while food output (mainly non-traded) rose, raw materials output declined by about 30%. The key product for peasant incomes and proletarian consumption levels was maize, and this (see again Table 10.3) was severely affected by not only the long-run downward trend, but also the drought of 1929–30, which reduced output from 2.17 million tonnes in 1928 to 1.50 million in 1929 and 1.38 million in 1930; the result was to cut apparent national consumption (even with increased imports) from 136 kilos per head to 83, a sudden fall in an essential component (along with beans, which had a similar fate) of not only small farmer incomes, but also the real wage. The recovery of this sector in 1932–5 was a natural one therefore, and helped lift the economy out of the Depression and apparently absorbed a great deal of unemployed 'modern sector' labour immigrants expelled from the USA. This crop cycle, therefore, was superimposed on the external shock. Commercial agriculture was severely affected by falling US prices transmitted across the border (especially sugar – for which a special government support scheme was instituted): both food-crops and raw materials prices fell by about one-quarter between 1928 and 1932, and were further hit by extensive flooding on the Pacific coast in 1932, although this sector exported less than one-third of its output, and was not greatly affected by declining US demand.[35] Between 1932 and 1935 total agricultural output rose by 13% and livestock by 26%; food output was stable, and raw materials rose by 42%, reflecting the recovery of the commercial sector, but the continued stagnation of subsistence agriculture as prices recovered and weather conditions improved.[36]

The industrial sector was exposed to the Depression mainly through the effects on other sectors. There is no record of shortages of imported inputs being a problem, so the main effects were through price and demand, and possibly domestic raw materials supply. The output index (see Table 10.3) does not record an immediate decline, but rather one in 1932; from peak (1930) to trough (1933) there was a fall of 20%, but this was easily recovered by 1936; value added moved similarly (see Table 10.4) but rather more violently, with a decline of

31%, but very rapid recovery thereafter. This cycle seems to have been distributed over the whole of the sector; cement output fell from 227 thousand tons in 1930 to 138 in 1933, but recovered to 252 in 1935; beer production fell from 72 million litres in 1930 to 42 in 1932 and rose to 83 in 1935; cotton textile production fell from 37 thousand tons in 1930 (as opposed to 36 in 1925) to 32 thousand in 1932 and rose to 42 thousand in 1934; electricity generation actually rose from 1.46 million kWh in 1930 to 1.53 in 1933 and 2.06 in 1935, despite the decline in demand from their best client, the mines.[37] The impact of the Depression was, therefore, only temporary and the upward trend continued through the rest of the decade. Although the textile sector appears to have been affected by lack of raw materials supply to some extent, resulting from the decline in cotton output (due to low 'imported' prices) the main effect on manufacturing was doubtless through demand, both from wage-consumption in the export sectors[38] and the temporary decline in investment. Once demand recovered there was more than adequate capacity to meet it. The question is, how did demand fall? Clearly, as GDP declined by 21% between 1928 and 1932, but recovered the 1928 level by 1935 (as the combined result of the sectoral cycles we have discussed) there was bound to be a sharp fluctuation, but the composition also varied. In the first place, with respect to consumption, the volume of wage expenditure from mining and commercial agriculture fell not so much from real wage cuts as from unemployment; but as important seems to have been the lower prices transmitted into the economy from the USA, which apparently were squeezing commercial margins and forcing merchants to run down stocks in order to meet their financial obligations with the banks.[39] As exports and agriculture recovered, consumer demand expanded as well, but the abandonment of the fixed parity and the issue of paper money on a substantial scale (see the fourth section below) allowed prices to rise again: the Mexico City wholesale price index, having fallen by one-fifth between 1929 and 1933, was up to its former level by 1936. Commerce revived, probably generating a restocking effect to add to the expansion of consumer demand as such; in other words, we have the effect of an inventory cycle superimposed on the production cycle.

Fixed capital formation did not decline until 1931, doubtless because of the lag in investment decisions, but in 1933 it was down to half its 1930 level; however, by 1935, both public and private investment had recovered to above this former level; the revival of public investment was the result of deliberate government policy, but that of private investment is remarkable[40] under the circumstances. In industry, moreover, there was no accelerated process of import-substitution; the tariff measures imposed (see the fourth section below) were mainly for fiscal purposes, and relatively mild, while the composition of imports did not alter substantially; but the relatively rapid recovery of the export sector and, more significantly, the lack of any real restriction on imports during the period, meant that there was comparatively little stimulus to import-substitution other than real devaluation. The most reliable study of this process concludes that the effect was somewhat different: 'the Depression meant in the case of Mexico, rather than an effective stimulus to industrialisation and import substitution, putting in evidence the contradictions and limitations of an enclave economy'.[41] Despite the sustained growth of industry for the rest of the decade, Villarreal's indicator of import-substitution for manufacturing only declines from 0.567 in 1929 to 0.486 in 1939.[42] The investment in both manufacturing and commercial agriculture appears to have been in modernisation and in existing branches, rather than to compete with imports. None the less, a whole series of branches connected to transport (cement, car assembly) and agriculture (inputs, processing) were to expand as the economy was restructured, while consumer goods branches absorbed most of domestic demand. The ratio of imports to GDP at current prices in 1935 stood at 14.3%, as opposed to 12.5% in 1930, and only fell to 13.3% in 1940. The 'step' reduction in dollar value corresponds to a change in the composition of consumption and investment from imported to home goods: this might have been due to the shift in wages and salaries from mining towards commercial agriculture and industry involving different expenditure patterns, while the shift of investment towards infrastructure and urbanisation clearly favoured home investment goods (construction).

The effect of the Depression on income distribution is not entirely clear, although it is of considerable relevance, not only for demand composition, but also for subsequent political developments. Average GDP per capita[43] had already fallen from 2 447 pesos (at 1960 prices) in 1925 to 2 251 in 1929; by 1932 it had fallen another 12% to 1763; but from then on rose steadily, albeit checked by population growth, to 2 137 in 1935, although it had not yet reached the 1925 level by 1940. The effect on employment and wages is hard to gauge in the absence of aggregate statistics. In agriculture the peasant sector suffered from the basic grains cycle as we have seen; it also appears to have absorbed unemployed labour from the export sectors and immigrants expelled from the USA.[44] Recorded unemployment rates are unreliable and mainly urban, but those tripled between 1930 and 1932, returning to the former level by 1934.[45] In the textile sector there was an 11% decline in employment between 1929 and 1932, but this was mainly due to modernisation; real wages were reduced severely,[46] however, and this presumably applied to the rest of manufacturing. The bureaucracy took a nominal wage reduction, but as wage-goods prices were declining too, real salaries do not seem to have suffered.[47] In commercial agriculture, where there are some data, there was the most drastic effect, as real wages declined by 46% between 1928 and 1930.[48] From 1934 onwards there do exist earnings data, but although employment presumably recovered with output as a whole (although not in mining) real wages were fairly stable in the second half of the 1930s.[49] As a whole a very rough judgement would be as follows: peasants (about half the labour force at this time) experienced falling real incomes, which stayed down afterwards, but due to the structural features of their sector; rural wage labour (about one-quarter of the labour force) suffered a sharp real wage decline, and little recovery; urban wage labour experienced a lesser decline, but no recovery either. This would tend, therefore, to support the argument that as far as the new 'leading sectors' were concerned, profits recovered even more rapidly from the Depression than value added.

In sum we have the picture of a sharp but short cycle between 1930 and 1935, related to the transmission of prices rather than foreign-exchange shortages, and aggravated by an inventory cycle, but with the main causal factors being other than aggregate demand movements – the special circumstances of mining and the environmental impact on agriculture. We have also suggested that wages fell and stayed down as a result of the shock. However, the experience of the attempt at management of the economy did lead to changes which were to have a considerable impact in subsequent years, and it is to this that we must now return.

THE EMERGENCE OF ECONOMIC MANAGEMENT

Although the impact of the Depression on production and accumulation may well have been less severe than elsewhere in Latin America, the consequences for the financial system were possibly greater; the cycle, despite its brevity, so demonstrated the shortcomings of both the banking and fiscal structures themselves and the instruments of macroeconomic management that the basis for a new system (which survived more or less intact for almost half a century) was laid between 1932 and 1936. The effect was not only to permit a stabilising monetary policy, but also to strengthen the position of the State in the accumulation process.[50]

The major economic issue of the 1930s was not the reorganisation of the fiscal and monetary systems, of course, but rather the dispute over foreign ownership of basic economic sectors.[51] In 1928 Calles had been forced to make concessions to foreign oil companies in order to stimulate exploration, but nationalist pressure increased and Petromex was founded as a mixed enterprise in 1933; the conflict came to a head under Cárdenas, leading to nationalisation in 1938. Mining was in decline anyway, but government controls were tightened and foreign companies steadily withdrew from the sector. In 1933 the Comisión Federal de Electricidad was established to control foreign power companies, tariffs were held down and expansion began to be planned by the government, so investor interest declined and a steady nationalisation process started, to be completed in the late 1950s. Finally, the rapid advance of land reform in the second half of the 1930s involved not only the creation of *ejidos*, but also the expropriation of a considerable number of foreign-owned plantations. However, it appears that those nationalisations were not really the result of the Depression as such, so are not our concern here except in so far as they strengthened the position of the State in relation to the private sector; although it could be argued[52] that the effect of the Depression on the USA itself (concern with domestic problems, changing attitudes towards large companies and the policies of the New Deal) was such as to reduce US opposition to such moves.

Despite the measures to strengthen the fiscal system before 1929, and the concessions to mineral enterprises which had virtually removed export duties as a source of government income, the effect of the Depression on external trade was rapidly reflected in tax receipts through the fall in import tariff income. Federal budget income fell by about one-third between 1929 and 1932, although the simultaneous price decline maintained its real value, and the decline in output actually raised fiscal pressure (income as a proportion of GDP) from 6.5% in 1929 to 7.0% in 1932. In that year, while the economy was still depressed, the government undertook new programmes which raised expenditure for 1933 slightly (see Table 10.5) and from then on expenditure rose quite rapidly. However, until 1936 it was not technically possible to run budget deficits – and even in the late 1930s when it was possible they only averaged half of 1% of GDP – and thus there was no real macroeconomic effect of the budget, stabilising or otherwise, during that period. Import tariffs had been used before 1929 to stimulate domestic production, particularly of textiles; but the 1930 Tariff Code raised both levels and coverage in order to maintain fiscal income and protect to some extent the balance of payments, in which it seems to have been relatively effective.[53] The new tariffs do not, however, appear to have been designed as, nor to have acted effectively as, a means of stimulating industry as such, because as with the 1935 Customs Law, protection was relatively low and covered existing as well as new industries – it was only with the 1936 'Law of Industrial Saturation', which closed entry to branches with excess capacity, that the codes actually began to promote industry. Indeed, as the tariffs were specific duties, the *ad valorem* rate fell off as prices recovered, declining from 29% on average for 1930–4 to 22% in 1935–9.[54]

Any effect of public expenditure, therefore, would have been more from changes in composition than from any addition to aggregate demand. On current account the shift identified by Wilkie away from administration (particularly defence) towards economic and social expenditure is not really discernible in this period; so the main impact must have been through the expenditure of bureaucratic salaries, although as these apparently accounted for as much as one-quarter of the population of the capital[55] the effect on commerce and industry may have been considerable. Public investment, however, did have an effect on economic recovery: in real terms it stagnated rather than fell between 1929 and 1933, and rose thereafter (see Table 10.5), reflecting the lagged public works and rail programme of the Calles Administration. In 1960 prices it rose from an average of 1.06 billion pesos in 1925–30 to 1.22 in 1931–5 and 1.86 in 1936–40; as a share of total investment it moved from 39% to 47% to 42% in the three sub-periods; and as a proportion of GDP from 2.0% to 2.6% and 3.2%. Although the composition of investment was overwhelmingly in transport (90%) in 1929–34, it was shifting from rail to road, and in the 1935–40 period, irrigation works were to rise from 10% to 20% of the total.[56] In turn the effect of expanding public expenditure must have been such as to stimulate the rest of the economy (particularly manufacturing, construction and commerce), even though it was not counter cyclical or aggregate-demand-increasing as such.

External public credits had been in the past, and would be in the future, a source of deficit finance. Attempts had been made to settle the outstanding debt with the USA (which in fact accounted for only 21% of the total, as opposed to 33% with France and 22% with the UK) during the 1920s precisely in order to regain access to the New York capital market. In 1929 Finance Minister Montes de Oca had nearly concluded the matter, but the events on Wall Street intervened; in 1931 two more years' respite on payments was achieved and with the support of the private banking sector (Banamex) the debt was restructured; but by 1935 little or no progress on renegotiation was made, and it had become clear that Mexico was neither able nor willing to pay; only in 1940 was an understanding reached with the USA.[57] Thus, on balance, the effect of external debt on the fiscal and macroeconomic balance was neutral.

In sum, although public expenditure was a key feature in the restructuring of the economy, neither expenditure nor taxation were flexible or strong enough instruments to be used in demand management.

The Mexican banking system had suffered considerably during the Revolution (not least from unrequited loans to the government), but the larger Porfirian bankers had managed to survive, so that although the ratio of bank assets to GDP had fallen from one-third to one-fifth between 1910 and 1925 and was not to return to pre-revolutionary levels until 1940,[58] there was still a high degree of concentration (three private banks having three-quarters of credit in 1928) and considerable foreign ownership.[59] Attempts had been made to bring the banking system under control with the founding of the Banco de México in 1925, but with little success as the private banks opposed the move towards reserve requirements and paper money very strongly[60] despite the close association between the Banco de México and the US Federal Reserve; the only step forward was the foundation of the Asociación de Banqueros Méxicanos under state patronage in 1928. However, the massive outflow of (silver) money from Mexico in the wake of the Depression suddenly reduced the money supply (which was halved between 1930 and 1932 – see Table 10.5) and threw the banks into a severe crisis.[61] The government, although it maintained an extremely orthodox monetary policy until 1932, did begin to make moves to achieve two aims: the restoration of confidence in the banks and to channel remaining resources towards productive investment.[62] On the first objective the 1932 organic law for the Banco de México cut its operations with the general public and reduced reserve requirements (equivalent to a government levy) on the banks, making it more acceptable to the banks while the obligatory affiliation effectively 'Mexicanised' shareholdings in the financial sector and the lack of silver coinage finally made paper money generally acceptable – notes rising from 11% of the total money supply in 1932 to 18% in 1934 and 35% in 1935.[63] Despite this understanding between State and bankers, it did not prove possible to channel their funds away from commerce towards production:[64] in 1926 the Banco Nacional de Credito Agricola had been set up to support large commercial farmers; in 1933 the Naciónal Financiera (for industry), Banco Naciónal de Obras Públicas (public works), Banco Ejidal (land-reform enterprises), Banco Naciónal de Comercio Exterior (foreign trade), the Banco Naciónal Azucarero and the Banco Algodonero Refaccionario were all established. Although their volume of operations was not large until after 1940, they formed the basis of a new system of state finance which, in combination with the Banco de México, could provide finance for public sector investment and exert some leverage on private accumulation.[65]

Thus, while the emergence of state banks must mainly be attributed to the long-run structural changes we have identified, the freedom of action they acquired, the achievement of a domestic currency supply and the establishment of a satisfactory relationship between the Banco de México and private banks can be attributed to the Depression, even if these objectives had been official ones from at least 1925. It should be noted, however, that the 'open frontier' for finance had not been closed thereby, and thus large flows of funds (outflows in particular, as in 1938) across the exchanges could not be controlled by the authorities.

It is generally accepted that the post-Depression years mark the birth of macroeconomic management in Mexico, in the sense of the use of monetary policy to affect economic level through the level of aggregate demand.[66] Further, in the absence of a sufficiently flexible fiscal or budgetary system, and open exchanges, this system remained in place for nearly half a century.[67] In this chapter we will not deal with the operation of monetary policy in detail, because it is lucidly discussed elsewhere in this volume;[68] here we shall only discuss its relationship to the restructuring of the economy.

Monetary policy in the immediate aftermath of 1929 was, under Montes de Oca as Minister of Finance, extremely orthodox in sticking to what were in effect 'gold-standard' rules, holding the peso parity by bringing the money supply down with the balance-of-payments deficit between 1929 and 1932.[69] The effect, as we have seen, was to touch off severe difficulties in the commercial sector by reinforcing the 'imported' decline in prices as banks withdrew revolving credits from merchants and forced inventories on to the market; political pressure for reflation, particularly from the commercial sector, grew during 1931, the object apparently being the restoration of profit margins as much as sales volume[70] – a 'classical' rather than a 'Keynesian' approach to the problem. The reappointment of Calles's Finance Minister, Pani (he had already held office in the 1920s and reorganised government finance), marked a significant change in policy; he not only engineered the hegemony of the Banco de México, but also started an active monetary policy, initially based on silver coinage but later on paper emissions. The money supply increased rapidly between 1932 and 1936 and the peso was allowed to devalue, balancing the increased demand for money as the economy expanded, although it was not until the latter year that the central bank could serve as a form of deficit finance for the government. Thus, although the new policy was probably a reaction to events at this stage, when the next external shock was generated in the form of the downturn of the US economy in 1937, followed by the massive outflow of capital in 1938 connected to the expropriations, monetary policy was consciously used to maintain economic activity, albeit with inflationary consequences and further parity decline.[71] The expansive monetary policy also permitted the State to finance much of its increased investment, permitted by the 1936 monetary laws, without recourse to further taxation. It is difficult to argue, however, that the State had acquired macroeconomic control, for the level of activity depended on the structure of production and external trade rather than aggregate demand, while the overall money supply was still sensitive to short-term capital flows across the exchanges in response to essentially political factors.

In sum the major impact of the Depression was on the financial system, the consequent restructuring of which resulted in increased state control of the economy even though this did not really extend to 'economic management' in the Keynesian sense. During the 1930s governments attempted to extend this control by introducing some sort of 'planning', for which there was in fact provision in the 1917 Constitution. In 1928 Calles had already introduced a Ley Naciónal de Planificación, but to little effect; this was followed by a Consejo Naciónal de Economía in 1933; finally Cárdenas formulated a Plan Sexenal in 1934; but in no case were the instruments available or even proposed.[72] None the less it can be argued that the Depression, by underlining the vulnerability of the economy to external fluctuations, directly stimulated (even if it did not originate) attempts at state control of the economy.[73]

CONCLUDING REMARKS

The main conclusions of this chapter should be fairly clear by now, and may be summarised as follows. First, the impact of the US Depression on external prices and trade was felt mostly on the foreign-owned minerals sector and the invisible account (profit outflows) of the balance of payments, ameliorating the shock to agriculture and industry. Second, the post-revolutionary shift towards commercial agriculture and manufacturing as engines of growth was accelerated by the Depression, even though import-substitution was not a characteristic of this period, nor the foreign-exchange shortage a constraint on production. Third, the main brunt of the shock was borne by banking and commerce, which recovered rapidly as real output expanded. Fourth, the effect on income distribution probably was to stabilise salaries, reduce real wages and severely depress peasant incomes, leading to a higher profit share. Fifth, the major consequence of the Depression was to provide the conditions for the strengthening of state control over capital accumulation and a lasting accommodation with the national private sector. Although this result reflects the overall Latin American experience, as revealed in this volume, of the Depression strengthening existing trends in the restructuring of national economies, the Mexican experience was very different from the ECLA paradigm of forced import-substituting industrialisation under foreign-exchange constraint; a difference which arose from the openness of the Mexican economy and the post-revolutionary nature of the Mexican State.

Our discussion of the impact of the Depression has been confined to the 'political economy', in which we have suggested that there was substantial continuity, at least of strategic logic. However, there was clearly a considerable political and even social change between the regimes of Calles and Cárdenas; and it has been suggested that the impact of the Depression, particularly on employment and living standards, was such as to exacerbate class conflict, reactivating popular movements after two decades of demobilisation, and providing a new mass base for the State.[74] This is beyond the scope of our discussion here, but it is consistent with the economic analysis we have presented, although we have suggested that the relationship with domestic capital during the late 1930s was one of accommodation rather than conflict, allowing the rate of private accumulation to rise, and perhaps making the developments after 1940 more understandable.

To draw close parallels with the present condition of the Mexican economy would be unwise, but the renewed reliance on mineral exports, the exposure of the financial system to the balance of payments, the transmission of recession from the USA and the structural constraints on agriculture are all familiar themes, despite the enormous progress in industrialisation during the intervening half-century. Moreover, possibly due to the essential continuity of the regime during that period, the political debate again centres around the themes of the 1930s – state intervention, financial orthodoxy, industrialisation, foreign ownership and income distribution[75] – and explicitly refers to the different interpretations of the Depression we have noted. One significant difference is that the case for an active State is now argued by the opposition rather than the regime.[76]

In sum the effect of the Depression on Mexico was to push forward the restructuring of the economy that was already under way. But after all, as Schumpeter pointed out, this is the historical role of the trade cycle.

NOTES

1. Cordova (1974), Hansen (1971) and Cline (1963) are typical of alternative views.
2. Solis (1970) and Reynolds (1970); these are still the standard sources on post-revolutionary economic history.
3. Villarreal (1976) and Kate (1980), for example.
4. Cavazos-Lerma (1976) is a good example of the Banco de México's own view of the period with, naturally enough, monetary policy playing a key part in the cycle.
5. Meyer (1978) and Krause (1977), which are part of the important new multi-part history of the Mexico Revolution conducted by the Colegio de México under the original direction of Daniel Cosio-Villegas. See also Rovzar (1975, 1978), who contributed much of the economic data to Krause (1977).
6. See the 'concluding remarks' to this chapter.
7. Glade and Anderson (1963), Rovzar (1975), Krause (1977) and Leal (1972). All trace this new relationship between reformist State and modernising capitalists from different points of view.

8. Iturriaga (1976) is the only detailed study of Calles's fiscal reforms; Wilkie (1970) places them in the context of expenditure patterns; FitzGerald (1978) analyses them in relation to resource mobilisation.
9. Reynolds (1970) pp. 156–7.
10. Moore (1963) provides a good survey of institutional changes.
11. Sherwell (1929) was sent south to provide an independent report for the bankers on the eve of the Depression; Cline (1963) places the debt in the context of wider geopolitical considerations.
12. Krause (1977) pp. 253–68.
13. Wionczek (1967) part I, Krause (1977) pp. 289–94, on electricity and manufacturing respectively.
14. Hamilton (1978, 1982), Cordero (1979) provide new evidence on the relationship between the Porfirian bankers and the new regime.
15. Hewitt (1978) and Stevenhagen (1968) both stress the emergence of capitalist agriculture during this period.
16. Mosk (1950) traces the origins of his 'new group' of industrialists to this period, as does Fragoso (1979), albeit from a somewhat different viewpoint.
17. Reynolds (1970), Solis (1970) chap. 3.
18. Meyer (1978) chap. I.
19. Meyer (1972) is the best survey of the oil conflict.
20. Nafinsa (1977) p. 156.
21. Calculated from Solis (1970) p. 90.
22. Villarreal (1976) chap. 1.
23. Sherwell (1929) p. 18.
24. Redfern (1980) stresses the importance of irrigation policy in the subsequent agricultural boom.
25. Moore (1963).
26. Himes (1965) alone appears to have tackled the problem of the 'sources of accumulation' during this period, but takes a very 'dualistic' view.
27. Stevenhagen (1968) suggests that as much as half the rural workforce was landless labour in 1930, before the Cárdenas land reform, but this is probably rather too high, as it does not account for seasonal labour properly. There are no urban wage indices before 1934 (for 1934 onwards see Nafinsa (1977)), but de la Peña (1934) gives evidence for the textile industry; the anonymous 'R.F.F.' gives figures for rural wages.
28. See the Introduction to this volume, and the appendix to this chapter.
29. Jo Love has kindly informed me that much of the early work on what is now known as the 'monetary approach to the balance of payments' was in fact worked out at the Banco de México in the 1940s.
30. Solis (1970) p. 91; also Table 10.4, p.000.
31. Meyer (1972) pp. 51–6.
32. See Table 10.2; we are using here the Paasche-weighted index worked out by the Banco de México, and reported in Cárdenas (1982). The index given in ECLA (1951) does not seem to be very reliable, especially as it shows dollar import prices rising sharply between 1932 and 1935.
33. Villarreal (1976) p. 34.
34. Bazant (1968); we shall return to this point later.
35. Meyer (1978) pp. 26 et seq.
36. Nafinsa (1977) p. 106.

37. Ibid. pp. 73, 185, 203, 214.
38. De la Peña (1934).
39. S.E.N. (1948) and HMSO (1933) both report this as being the main *specific* impact beyond the effect on exports and tax receipts.
40. This rapid recovery of accumulation is, in fact, paralleled elsewhere in Latin America; see the appendix to this chapter.
41. Villarreal (1976) p. 36.
42. Ibid. p. 44; the ratio is that of imports to imports plus value added in local production. Most progress was made in consumer goods, but even here the decline was from 0.353 to 0.222.
43. Nafinsa (1977) p. 19.
44. Meyer (1978) p. 83, on the basis of US Consular Reports.
45. Meyer, loc. cit. cites the Dirección General de Estadística as recording open unemployment as 1.7% in 1930, 6% at its peak in 1932, and back down to 1% in 1934. This is obviously too low (as Meyer points out), but taken as representative of 'modern sector' employment (perhaps one-quarter of the total workforce) this would be quite plausible..
46. De la Peña (1934).
47. Meyer (1978) p. 87.
48. R.F.F. (1935).
49. Nafinsa (1977) p. 414.
50. See Moore (1963) and Cordero (1979) for contrasting views.
51. On oil see Meyer (1972); on mining, Meyer (1978) section i.4; on electricity, Wionczek (1967); and on agriculture, Stevenhagen (1968). A general, albeit sympathetic, view from the other side of the border is Gordon (1941).
52. Cline (1963) correlated the changing US attitude with the changing presidential administrations in *both* countries.
53. Kate (1980); see also FitzGerald (1978).
54. Villarreal (1976) p. 29; he also calculates a 'real' exchange rate (on the basis of the nominal parity adjusted for the relative rates of wholesale price inflation in Mexico and the USA), the index for which (1930=100) roughly represents real devaluation; the index stood at 114 in 1931, and 129 in 1932, rising rapidly to 161 in 1935, which would represent a considerable relative price effect in favour of home goods, except that the index *fell* to 137 in 1937.
55. Wilkie (1970) chap. 4, 'The Rise of the Active State', Banamex (1978) p. 134.
56. See the notes to Table 10.6, p. 000.
57. Bazant (1968).
58. Goldsmith (1966).
59. S.H.C.P. (1930).
60. Mosk (1950).
61. Meyer (1978) pp. 67–73.
62. Moore (1963), Bennet (1965).
63. Fernandez-Hurtado (1976) p. 142; this ratio has been more or less maintained to this day.
64. Bennet (1965) and Moore (1963) both remark on this problem, which is still a key aspect of Mexican banking, according to FitzGerald (1981).
65. Bennet and Sharp (1979).

66. Cavazos-Lerma (1976).
67. FitzGerald (1979) makes this point in analysing the ineffectiveness of monetary policy in the 1960s and 1970s.
68. The piece by Cárdenas elsewhere in this volume provides an excellent analysis. On Pani himself see Rovzar (1978).
69. Cavazos-Lerma (1976).
70. S.E.N. (1948), HMSO (1933).
71. Cavazos-Lerma (1976), Cárdenas (1982).
72. Proel (1973), Solis (1975) pp. 11–26, 106–20; in fact a Ministry of Planning was not established until 1976.
73. Velasco (1981).
74. Cordova (1972), (1974).
75. Tello and Cordera (1981) set out the 'nationalist' and 'liberal' models.
76. M.A.P. (1981).

REFERENCES

Banamex, *Examen de la Situación Económica de Mexico, 1925–76* (Mexico City, 1978).
J. Bazant, *Historia de la deuda exterior de Mexico, 1823–1946* (Mexico City, 1968).
D. Bennet and K. Sharp, 'El estado como banquero y empresario: el caracter de última instancia de la intervención económica del estado mexicano, 1917–70', *Foro International*, xx, no. 1 (1979).
R. L. Bennet, *The Financial Sector and Economic Development: The Mexican Case* (Baltimore, 1965).
E. Cárdenas, 'Mexico's Industrialization during the Great Depression; Public Policy and Private Response' (doctoral dissertation) (Yale University, 1982).
M. Cavazos-Lerma, *Cincuenta años de política monetaria*, in Fernandez-Hurtado (1976).
H. F. Cline, *The United States and Mexico* (Cambridge, Mass., 1963).
R. Cordera (ed.), *Desarrollo y crisis de la economía Mexicana: ensayos de interpretación história* (Mexico City, 1981).
M. E. Cordero, 'Estructura monetaria y financiera de México, 1932–40', *Revista Mexicana de Sociología*, xvi. 3 (1979).
A. Cordova, *La formación del poder político en Mexico* (Mexico City, 1972).
——— *La política de masas del cardenismo* (Mexico City, 1974).
M. de la Peña, 'Los salarios en la industria textil', *El Trimestre Económico*, i (1934).
Economic Commission for Latin America, *Economic Survey of Latin America, 1949* (New York, 1951).
E. Fernandez-Hurtado (ed.), *Cincuenta años de banca central* (Mexico City, 1976).
E. V. K. FitzGerald, 'Patterns of Public Sector Income and Expenditure in Mexico', *ILAS Technical Papers Series* (Austin, 1978).
——— 'Stabilisation Policy in Mexico: The Fiscal Deficit and Macroeconomic Equilibrium 1960–77', in R. Thorp and L. Whitehead, *Inflation and Stabilisation in Latin America* (London, 1979).

—— 'El deficit presupuestal y el financiamiento de la inversión: una nota sobre la acumulación de capital en Mexico', in Cordera (1981).

J. M. Fragoso, *El poder de la gran burguesía* (Mexico City, 1979).

W. P. Glade and C. W. Anderson, *The Political Economy of Mexico* (Madison, Wisconsin, 1963).

R. W. Goldsmith, *The Financial Development of Mexico* (Paris, 1966).

W. Gordon, *The Expropriation of Foreign-owned Property in Mexico* (Washington, DC, 1941).

N. Hamilton, 'Mexico: The Limits of State Autonomy', doctoral dissertation, Wisconsin University (1978).

—— 'The State and the National Bourgeoisie in Postrevolutionary Mexico: 1920–40', *Latin American Perspectives*, 9. 4 (1982).

R. D. Hansen, *The Politics of Mexican Development* (Baltimore, 1971).

HMSO, *Economic Conditions of Mexico* (London, 1933).

C. Hewitt de Alcantara, *La Modernización de la agricultura Mexicana, 1940–70* (Mexico City, 1978).

J. R. Himes, 'La formación de Capital en Mexico', *El Trimestre Económico*, xxxii, no. 125 (1965).

J. Iturriaga, *La resolución hacendaria: la hacienda pública con el Presidente Calles* (Mexico City, 1976).

A. Kate, *Protection and Economic Development in Mexico*, (Farnborough, Hants, 1980).

E. Krause, *Historia de la revolución Mexicana: período 1924–28*, vol. 10 (Mexico City, 1977).

J. F. Leal, *La burguesía y el estado mexicano* (Mexico City, 1972).

L. Meyer, *Mexico y los Estados Unidos en el conflicto petrolero, 1917–42*, 2nd edn (Mexico City, 1972).

—— *Historia de la revolución Mexicana, período 1928–34*, vol. 13 (Mexico City, 1978).

O. E. Moore, *Evolución de las instituciones financieras en Mexico* (Mexico City, 1963).

S. A. Mosk, *Industrial Revolution in Mexico* (Berkeley, California, 1950).

MAP, *Tesis y Programa* (Mexico City, 1981).

Nafinsa, *La economía mexicana en cifras* (Mexico City, 1977).

A. L. Olmedo, 'La balanza mexicana de pagos', *El Trimestre Económico*, viii (1942).

J. Proel, 'Los intentos de planificación económica en Mexico', *Comercio Exterior*, vol. 23, no. 1 (1973).

D. Redfern, 'Mexican Irrigation Policy', paper delivered at the 1980 Conference of the Development Studies Association, Swansea (1980).

C. W. Reynolds, *The Mexican Economy: Twentieth Century Structure and Growth* (New Haven, 1970).

'R.F.F.', 'El Salario mínimo en el sector agrícola', *El Trimestre Económico*, iii (1935).

E. F. Rovzar, 'La economía Mexicana en vísperas de la crisis internacional de 1929', tesis profesional, Mexico City, Universidad de Anahuac (1975).

—— 'Alberto J. Pani: un capitalista revolucionario', *Investigación Económica*, xxvii (1978).

SEN, *Trimestre de Barómetros Nacionales* (Mexico City, 1948).

—— *Revista de economía*, vol. i, (Mexico City, 1933).

SHCP, *Boletín de la Comisión Nacional Bancaria*, no. 18 (1930).

G. B. Sherwell, *Mexico's Capacity to Pay: A General Analysis of the Present Economic Position of Mexico* (Washington, DC, 1929).

L. Solis, *La realidad económica Mexicana: retrovisión y perspectivas* (Mexico City, 1970).

——— *Planes y desarrollo económico y social en Mexico*, (Mexico, 1975).

R. Stevenhagen (ed.), *Neolatifundismo y explotación de Emiliano Zapata a Anderson Clayton* (Mexico City, 1968).

C. Tello and R. Cordera, *Mexico: la disputa por la nación* (Mexico City, 1981).

R. Torres-Caytan, *Un siglo de devaluaciones del peso mexicano* (Mexico City, 1980).

C. Velasco, 'El desarrollo industrial de Mexico en la década 1930–40: las bases del proceso de industrialización', in Cordera (1981).

R. Villarreal, *El desequilibrio externo en la industrialización de Mexico, 1929–75* (Mexico City, 1976).

J. W. Wilkie, *The Mexican Revolution: Federal Expenditure and Social Change since 1910* (Berkeley, Calif. 1970).

M. S. Wionczek, *El nacionalismo Mexicano y la inversión extranjera* (Mexico City, 1967).

APPENDIX

A Note on Income Distribution, Accumulation and Recovery in the Depression: An Alternative View

(EDITOR'S NOTE: as explained in the Introduction to this volume, this short piece results from a particularly stimulating intervention in the Workshop debate, which the author was requested to write up. As its length and tentative nature do not merit a separate chapter it has been placed as a somewhat disconnected 'appendix' to FitzGerald's chapter on Mexico.)

1. THE ECLA MODEL

The original model constructed by the Economic Commission for Latin America to explain economic underdevelopment in the region was based on a secular accumulation theory which held that the productivity gains from technical progress in industry are not reflected in lower industrial prices, but rather are retained at the Centre by monopoly pricing, while at the Periphery productivity gains in the primary sector are few and wages are held down by surplus labour, any advances being dissipated by competition between exporters.[1] The shift in the terms of trade is also, in the ECLA model, the main transmission mechanism of depression (i.e. downswing of the trade cycle) from Centre to Periphery. Wage inflexibility in the Centre and flexibility at the Periphery imply that unemployment in depression will be much worse at the Centre than on the Periphery; while profitability in the (primary) export sector of the Periphery is much more affected than the (manufacturing) export sector of the Centre; but by implication 'classical' adjustment would be much more rapid on the Periphery than at the Centre. The 1930s were seen by ECLA as a particularly acute example of a more general cyclical characteristic of the capitalist world economy which permits adjustment of income distribution and renewed accumulation. The post-First World War boom was regarded as naturally followed by the decline in the terms of trade and import capacity of nearly one-half between 1928–9 to 1931–2; while the reduction in export volume was seen mainly as the result of the decline in import propensity at the Centre as part of its own adjustment.[2] Hence, the functional income distribution and the pattern of capital accumulation play a central part in ECLA *theory*, true to its roots in classical political economy.[3]

However, as the introductory chapter has argued, the main emphasis of ECLA's *historical* analysis of the 1930s, once the decline in import capacity has been noted, is not so much on unequal exchange as on state-led aggregate demand shifts and response to exogenous relative prices,[4] in what might be termed a 'Keynesian view' (if not a 'neo-classical synthesis' thereof); an approach shared by most of the case studies in this volume. The question that raises is whether such a focus does not underplay the importance of the balance of investment and consumption on the one hand, and the factor income distribution on the other; both of these being affected by the supply of various categories of commodities. Moreover, a demand-side analysis does not fully explain the stability of the domestic financial system. Despite the strong elements of continuity in the growth and industrialisation of the Latin American economies after the initial shock, it will be our argument that the adjustment does require more explanation than a mere price and demand shift as a stimulus for capital restructuring from imports towards home production, particularly since the response was so rapid and the new pattern was retained after the shock passed. The theoretical model requires further development to accommodate the observed behaviour of wages, profits and accumulation.

2. INCOME DISTRIBUTION AND ACCUMULATION

Data on functional income distribution and investment patterns in Latin America during our period are hard to come by. What evidence there is indicates, however, that although money wages fell in most countries, the effect probably being transmitted from the export sectors towards urban areas, real wages (particularly in manufacturing) did not fall, because the internal terms of trade moved against food production. Certainly this is true of Mexico, Argentina, Chile, Peru and Colombia.[5] In other words, the internal effect of the world price shift was also against the primary sector, despite which it proved possible to preserve the real wage fund (i.e. the total supply of wage-goods) intact, and thus prevent popular living standards from falling. Thus the largely non-capitalist or small-business food sector acted as a 'cushion' in the adjustment process, allowing real wages to be maintained.[6] In cases such as Argentina where food was an export, the effect on local prices was much the same, but at the expense of land rents – again, not of money profits or real wages. Governments naturally attempted to stimulate domestic food production as the simplest way to save foreign exchange if the country was also a food importer (e.g. Peru), thus favouring real wages too.

At the same time there seems to have been a considerable acceleration in the proletarianisation of the Latin American workforce. In manufacturing, ECLA records a rapid substitution of factory employment for artisan activity, which fell from three-quarters of the total in 1925 to only one-half in 1940 for Latin America as a whole, while absolute factory employment increased as a proportion of the urban active population from 9% in 1925 to 10% in 1930 and 12% in 1935; it reached 13% in 1940 but the *peak* attained in 1945, was only 15%. Yet at the same time there was a severe slide in industrial employment as a share of total non-agricultural employment between 1925 and 1933 in Chile, Colombia, Peru and Venezuela, a slight decline in Argentina and Brazil and a rise only in Mexico.[7] These trends, in the face of the industrialisation and urbanisation (discussed elsewhere in this volume) would be consistent with a process of concentration of the industrial workforce (probably accompanied by ownership concentration as well – for which there is direct evidence for Mexico and Chile) accompanied by extensive internal migration in response to the unemployment in hinterland export sectors and the impact of deteriorating internal terms of trade on peasant incomes.

Despite the external financial shock, the collapse of export rents and default on foreign debt, Latin American banks did not collapse, unlike their metropolitan cousins; on the contrary, they seemed able to respond to new industrial finance requirements and replace foreign loans, thereby completely restructuring both their assets and their liabilities. In part this was due to state support, made institutionally possible by the earlier foundation of central banks or strengthening of currency boards in response to the violent fluctuations in reserves after the First World War, but full support operations ('lender of last resort') did not become common until the mid-1930s (Prebisch's own Banco Central de Argentina leading the way, closely followed by the Banco de México), when the full shock had passed and recuperation was well under way. The intersectoral concentration of ownership (then, as now, banks operated as central 'treasurers' to groups of export, industrial, commercial, real estate and agricultural firms) undoubtedly prevented both the panic withdrawal of funds and bankrupties causing a chain-reaction through the economy. None the less the increase in the supply of money must have been met by a concomitant demand for currency and deposits; the increase in *transactions* demand for money could only come later as real incomes recovered.

Most significantly of all, the rate of accumulation of fixed assets began to recover very rapidly indeed after 1929; in Brazil, for instance, capital formation fell from an average 200 million cruzeiros (at 1937 prices) in 1928–9 to 50 in 1930–1, but climbed steadily to reach the previous 'boom' level by 1937; in Chile, capital formation fell from an average 2 000 million pesos (at 1940 prices) in 1925–30 to 250 in 1932–3, but was back up to 1 000 in 1936–8; in Mexico, capital formation fell to half of the 1925–9 level by 1932, but by 1934 it was back to normal levels again.[8] Throughout Latin America fixed investment seems to have recovered in five years at most; if some allowance is made for the fact that much of the pre-1929 imports of 'transport equipment' were really private automobiles, the real recovery was probably even quicker; indeed the revival of investor confidence (taking into account the lag between investment decisions and actual formation) seems to have even preceded the 'new economic policies' of the mid-1930s. The explicit priority given by all governments in foreign-exchange allocation to imports of equipment (freely available from the USA, unlike the war periods) also helped, of course. The composition had changed, too, towards construction and probably also greater investment in working capital (wage-bills) rather than fixed assets, and towards lines with low imported input content. The expansion of manufactured wagegoods branches (e.g. textiles), construction goods (e.g. cement) and simple industrial inputs (e.g. chemicals) all reflect this change due as much to the changing patterns of income distribution and accumulation as to the demand pattern of lack of imported finished commodities.

3. AN ALTERNATIVE VIEW

An approach to economic analysis where accumulation is linked directly to income distribution and real-goods supply (in our case, imports on the one hand and wage-goods on the other) would be useful in explaining these phenomena, which do not easily fit into the orthodox (Keynesian, neo-classical or ECLA-historical) interpretation of the rapid recovery of output in Latin America after 1929. ECLA theory might potentially provide an answer, but it was not sufficiently developed, as we have seen. An analysis of the peripheral economy in a similar tradition is provided, however, by Kalecki.[9] There are three sectors: primary exports, which provide (transmuted by exogenous terms of trade) foreign exchange to import producer goods and superior consumer goods, organised by capitalist (often foreign) firms; small-scale production of food by small farmers and peasants (who also supply seasonal labour to exporters); and an incipient urban secondary sector. There are thus three types of commodities: producer goods, necessary consumption goods (wage-goods) and non-necessary consumption goods (for capitalist consumption). Wage-goods are consumed by workers, and their supply (fundamentally by small producers, particularly peasants and artisans) can be treated as exogenous (i.e. 'structurally' determined by land tenure and so on); the real value of the wage-fund is thus determinate, and for a given level of employment (in exports, industry, construction and so on), so is the average real wage. Profits are spent on investment or capitalist consumption; their real value depends upon the supply of producer goods and non-necessaries, and in the peripheral economy in the early stages of industrialisation, upon the capacity to import. The balance between those two uses of foreign exchange depends in turn, upon the rate of accumulation, which varies with capitalists' expectations of profitability in the various branches of the economy.

The application of this model to the case of recovery from the Depression would imply that despite the fall in import capacity, in profits and rents in the primary export sector, and in money wages (transmitted from the export hinterland to the urban secondary sector), the real wage-fund would be maintained. The maintenance of real wages from the workers' point of view (i.e. nominal wages deflated by wage-goods prices) would mean, none the less, lower wage-costs for capitalists: that is, nominal wages deflated by manufacturing prices would *fall* (looked at another way, less manufactures need be exchanged with farmers for wage-goods) and thus increase urban profits. The increase in urban profits would be confronted with a reduction in the (imported) supply of producer goods and non-necessary consumer goods. In the first instance savings would rise in a monetary form; then capitalists would shift towards investment involving 'cheap' labour and domestic inputs, and thus move import composition towards capital goods. On the savings side the general movements in the balance of payments in our period, by virtue of the collapse in import capacity (although the non-payment of debt and the reduction of remittances by foreign enterprise should be set against this[10]), would imply that 'external savings' fell heavily; so that as investment rates rose again, they must have done so on the basis of domestic savings – that is, increased profits. The first 'stop' for such savings would logically have been the banking system, as the secondary sector profits (if they had been in the primary sector, they would have been exported) were deposited in the banks. This must have helped them 'weather the shock', unlike at the Centre, where the general public withdrew its cash balances to maintain consumption at a time of massive unemployment, thus bringing the financial system towards collapse. Further, those deposits then allowed the 'unplanned' budget deficits of Latin American governments to be met without the destabilising consequences which, in a small open economy (as modern monetarists and traditional suppoerters of 'sound finance' observe) would not have the desired 'Keynesian' effect.

The remarkable recovery of public and private accumulation, in line with (but hardly preceded by) the recovery of production, took a new form, using more labour and less imported inputs – textiles and construction being key sectors. This brought about an accelerated proletarianisation that was not to be repeated, which in turn supported the market for *manufactured* wage-goods; the expansion of non-necessary consumer goods production came at a later stage.

4. CONCLUDING REMARKS

In sum the effect of the external shock on the Latin American economy of the 1930s can be seen to have been, in considerable part, a function of its incomplete nature (an incipient industry and traditional agriculture) which protected wage-goods supply and provided a 'buffer' in the form of imported ecessary consumption goods; this provided a basis for renewed accumulation which was as important as relative price changes or aggregate demand stimulation, if not more so.

The contrast with the experience during the First World War is instructive: food prices rose, and despite severe problems with exports (still dominated by the UK market) the USA was willing and able to supply consumer goods, so that 'increases in production and profits during the War were not accompanied by significant new investment or a diversification of Latin America's industrial structure.[11] Continued import-substitution and industrial expansion, on the one hand, and commercialisation of agriculture on the other, after the Second World War, meant that wage-goods and industrial employment were heavily dependent on imports, while local industries supplied non-necessaries and investment goods had become more technologically sophisticated. Thus the two 'buffers' of peasant food-supply and imported non-necessaries were no longer available, so reduced import capacity would have a quite different effect upon income distribution. In consequence, real-wage repression became a central element of stabilisation in the Periphery as in the Centre.[12]

The 1930s retain, therefore, much of their historical specificity, as ECLA itself was the first to recognise.

NOTES

1. ECLA (1951). As Rodríguez (1980) points out, this 'classical' formulation of the terms-of-trade problem was soon replaced by the better-known 'elasticities' formulation (the so-called 'Prebisch – Singer' theory) which has less insight. See FitzGerald and Floto (forthcoming) for a further elaboration of this and other elements of ECLA thought in relation to economic development theory.
2. As ECLA (1951) puts it (p. 57): 'the cycle has been the mode of growth of the capitalist economy'. See also op.cit. pp. 57–61 for a detailed description of the ECLA cycle theory.
3. See Love (1981) and Braun (1973).
4. See ECLA (1951, 1965) as canonical sources, and Sunkel and Paz (1970) and Furtado (1970) for economic histories by leading members of the *cepalino* school.
5. See Diaz Alejandro (1970) on the Argentine case, and other chapters in this volume for other countries.
6. Gordon (1965) pp. 373–4. This, interestingly, is written from the 'institutionalist' viewpoint, itself very much a part of Depression economics in the USA.
7. ECLA (1965).
8. ECLA (1951) various country chapters.
9. Kalecki (1976); but see FitzGerald (1983) for an attempt to elucidate and develop Kalecki's characteristically enigmatic essay on 'Financing Economic Development'.
10. See Chapter 2 by Diaz Alejandro, above.
11. Miller (1981).
12. PREALC (1982).

REFERENCES

O. Braun, *Imperialismo y comercio internacional* (Beunos Aires, 1978).

C. Diaz Alejandro, *Essays on the Economic History of the Argentine Republic* (New Haven, 1970).

ECLA, *Economic Survey of Latin America, 1949* (New York, 1951).

―――― *The Process of Industrial Development in Latin America* (New York, 1965).

E. V. K. FitzGerald, 'Kalecki on the Financing of Development: An Elucidation and an Extension', *Working Papers*, Series no. 8 (The Hague, 1983).

―――― and E. Floto, *ECLA and Economic Theory on the Periphery* (London, forthcoming).

C. Furtado, *The Economic Development of Latin America* (Cambridge, 1970).

W. Gordon, *The Political Economy of Latin America* (New York, 1965).

M. Kalecki, *Essays on Developing Economies* (Hassocks, 1976).

J. Love, 'Raúl Prebisch and the Origins of the Doctrine of Unequal Exchange', *Latin American Research Review*, at proof (1981).

R. Miller, 'Latin American Manufacturing and the First World War: An Exploratory Essay', *World Development*, vol. 5. 8 (1981).

PREALC, *External Adjustment, Employment and Wages in Latin America and the Caribbean* (Santiago de Chile, 1982).

O. Rodriguez, *La teoría del subdesarollo de la CEPAL* (Mexico City, 1980).

O. Sunkel and P. Paz, *La teoría del desarollo y del subdesarollo de America Latina* (Mexico City, 1970).

TABLE 10.1   *Balance of payments, 1926 and 1940*
(million pesos)

	1926		1940	
1. Merchandise trade:				
Exports	677		778	
Imports	−381		−669	
Adjustments	−13		−39	
		282		71
2. Gold coins and ingots		15		182
3. Interest and dividends:				
Public debt service	−27		−10	
Profits of foreign companies	−221		−316	
Dividents to foreigners	−69		−74	
		−317		−400
4. Other current transactions:				
Income	36		79	
Expenditure	−34		−42	
		2		37
Current Account		−17		−110
5. Capital movements:				
Oil industry	12		−15	
Other branches	4		125	
		16		110
6. Errors and omissions		1		−
Capital Account		17		110

SOURCES: Olmedo (1942); his 1926 figures were taken from Sherwell (1929); 1940 was estimated by the Banco de México.

TABLE 10.2 Foreign trade, 1925–40

	1925	1926	1927	1928	1929	1930	1931	1932
Exports, fob (mn US $)	336	334	299	285	275	203	151	97
Imports, cif (mm US $)	193	184	163	172	178	155	82	57
Trade balance (mn US $)	143	150	136	113	97	48	69	40
Reserves (mn US $)	27.4	17.7	16.2	19.8	25.0	13.6	9.7	31.2
Export prices (1929 = 100)	147	118	102	99	100	93	68	68
Import prices (1929 = 100)	107	99	95	104	100	106	94	86
Terms of trade (1929 = 100)	137	119	107	95	100	88	72	79

	1933	1934	1935	1936	1937	1938	1939	1940
Exports, fob (mn US $)	104	179	208	215	248	185	176	178
Imports, cif (mn US $)	70	93	113	129	171	109	121	124
Trade balance (mn US $)	34	86	95	86	77	76	55	54
Reserves (mn US $)	36.8	52.9	93.2	89.0	55.4	43.2	41.4	63.4
Export prices (1929 = 100)	83	110	94	72	88	57	64	69
Import prices (1929 = 100)	93	101	108	115	114	130	121	123
Terms of trade (1929 = 100)	90	110	87	63	77	44	53	56

SOURCES: Nafinsa (1977) for trade flows and reserves; Cárdenas (1982) for price indices, based on Paasche-weighted indices prepared by the Banco de México.

TABLE 10.3 *Output, 1925–40*

	1925	1926	1927	1928	1929	1930	1931	1932
GDP (bn 1960 pesos)	37.4	39.6	37.9	38.1	36.7	34.4	35.5	30.2
Index (1925 = 100)	100.0	105.9	101.3	101.9	98.1	92.0	94.9	80.7
GDP deflator (1960 = 100)	13.2	13.0	12.4	12.4	12.5	12.8	11.2	10.0
Wholesale price (1954 = 100)	20.9	20.4	19.9	19.2	19.2	19.2	16.7	15.6
Manufacturing output (1950 = 100)	23.9	27.1	24.6	25.7	27.3	28.7	34.2	24.8
Food output (1950 = 100)	53.8	58.4	58.5	58.5	45.8	43.8	57.9	50.7
Agricultural raw materials (1950 = 100)	33.0	42.8	33.1	39.4	35.9	30.0	30.5	25.3
Maize (mn tons)	2.0	2.1	2.1	2.2	1.5	1.4	2.1	2.0
Textiles ('000 tons[a])	44.0	45.0	43.8	4.19	42.8	44.7	38.7	40.2

	1933	1934	1935	1936	1937	1938	1939	1940
GDP (bn 1960 pesos)	33.6	35.9	38.5	41.7	43.0	43.7	46.1	46.7
Index (1925 = 100)	89.8	96.0	102.9	111.5	115.0	116.8	123.3	124.9
GDP deflator (1960 = 100)	10.6	10.9	11.1	12.1	14.9	15.7	15.9	16.6
Wholesale prices (1954 = 100)	16.7	17.6	17.6	18.7	22.2	23.6	23.6	23.9
Manufacturing output (1950 = 100)	22.9	34.2	33.3	38.3	40.1	41.3	43.8	46.1
Food output (1950 = 100)	52.5	47.7	49.4	53.5	50.8	53.4	59.9	56.5
Agricultural raw materials (1950 = 100)	33.7	32.9	35.8	43.1	39.1	35.8	37.6	38.1
Maize (mn tons)	1.9	1.7	1.7	1.6	1.6	1.7	2.0	1.6
Textiles ('000 tons[a])	45.6	59.6	58.1	61.5	63.5	63.3	64.3	63.9

[a] Fibres consumed in manufacture, about 80% cotton.
SOURCE: Nafinsa (1977).

TABLE 10.4 *Gross domestic product, 1925–40*
(billion pesos at 1950 prices)

	Agri-culture	Livestock etc.[a]	Mining	Oil	Manu-facturing	Cons-truction	Electric energy	Trans-port	Govern-ment	Commerce	Other	Total GDP
1925	2.42	1.59	1.09	1.27	2.09	0.26	0.09	0.59	0.31	3.07	2.06	14.82
1926	2.81	1.83	1.26	1.11	2.33	0.27	0.11	0.58	0.41	3.63	2.28	16.62
1927	2.61	1.71	1.44	0.75	2.36	0.25	0.12	0.61	0.40	3.32	2.18	15.74
1928	2.76	1.82	1.51	0.62	2.29	0.30	0.12	0.63	0.39	2.46	2.22	16.12
1929	2.50	1.64	1.61	0.56	2.43	0.29	0.12	0.80	0.37	3.55	2.24	16.12
1930	2.28	1.49	1.46	0.53	2.42	0.30	0.12	0.79	0.37	3.59	2.17	15.54
1931	2.65	1.72	1.27	0.45	2.30	0.27	0.13	0.75	0.34	3.94	2.22	16.02
1932	2.57	1.73	0.88	0.46	1.68	0.22	0.13	0.68	0.34	2.98	1.87	13.55
1933	2.94	1.75	0.92	0.51	2.24	0.32	0.13	0.59	0.38	3.82	2.18	15.76
1934	2.69	2.15	1.10	0.61	2.43	0.41	0.15	0.81	0.41	3.60	2.30	16.65
1935	2.90	2.10	1.14	0.62	2.82	0.35	0.17	0.76	0.45	4.18	2.49	17.98
1936	3.20	2.19	1.19	0.58	3.20	0.49	0.19	0.83	0.57	4.35	2.70	19.49
1937	3.22	2.23	1.36	0.67	3.28	0.57	0.21	0.92	0.57	4.67	2.84	20.55
1938	3.32	2.25	1.37	0.65	3.47	0.60	0.21	0.91	0.58	4.73	2.89	20.92
1939	3.24	2.23	1.26	0.60	4.00	0.41	0.21	0.83	0.88	5.84	3.13	22.62
1940	2.90	2.27	1.24	0.57	4.26	0.50	0.21	0.87	0.89	5.92	3.25	22.89

[a] Includes fishing and forestry.

SOURCE: Solis (1970) p. 91; note that this has different price base from other tables.

TABLE 10.5   *Accumulation, 1925–40*

	1925	1926	1927	1928	1929	1930	1931	1932
GFCF (bn 1960 pesos):								
public	0.88	1.13	1.13	1.04	1.08	1.10	1.14	1.00
private	1.38	1.43	1.44	1.91	1.66	2.21	1.35	0.92
total	2.26	2.56	2.57	2.95	2.74	3.31	2.49	1.92
Total GFCF as % of GDP	4.3	4.5	4.7	5.9	5.5	7.1	5.0	4.6
GDP (bn current pesos)	4.94	5.15	4.70	4.73	4.58	4.40	3.98	3.02
Money supply (bn current pesos)	0.46	0.53	0.49	0.63	0.66	0.68	0.32	0.30
Velocity of circulation	10.7	9.7	9.6	7.5	6.9	6.5	12.4	10.1
Federal receipts (in pesos)	322	309	295	300	322	289	256	212
Federal expenditures (in pesos)	298	325	310	288	276	279	226	212
Average/GDP (%)	6.3	6.2	6.4	6.2	6.5	6.5	6.1	7.0

	1933	1934	1935	1936	1937	1938	1939	1940
GFCF (bn 1960 pesos):								
public	1.15	1.18	1.63	1.83	1.71	1.65	1.91	2.18
private	1.41	2.20	2.07	1.99	2.68	2.51	2.44	3.15
total	2.56	3.38	3.70	3.82	4.39	4.16	4.35	5.33
Total GFCF as % of GDP	5.3	7.2	7.2	6.9	7.6	7.3	7.2	9.1
GDP (bn current pesos)	3.56	3.91	4.28	5.04	6.41	6.86	7.34	7.77
Money supply (bn current pesos)	0.38	0.54	0.51	0.57	0.69	0.67	0.88	1.06
Velocity of circulation	9.4	7.2	8.4	8.8	9.3	10.2	8.3	7.3
Federal receipts (in pesos)	223	295	313	385	451	438	566	577
Federal expenditures (in pesos)	245	265	301	406	479	504	571	610
Average/GDP (%)	6.6	7.2	7.2	7.8	7.3	6.9	7.7	7.6

SOURCE: Nafinsa (1977) for all data except Gross Fixed Capital Formation (GFCF), for which the source is as for Table 10.6.

TABLE 10.6 Gross fixed capital formation at current prices
(billion pesos, annual averages)

	1925–30			1931–5			1936–40		
	Public	Private	Total	Public	Private	Total	Public	Private	Total
1. Agriculture etc.	0.02	0.03	0.05	0.02	0.03	0.05	0.04	0.05	0.09
2. Industry etc.	–	0.05	0.05	–	0.05	0.05	0.02	0.11	0.13
3. Production (1 + 2)	0.02	0.08	0.10	0.02	0.08	0.10	0.06	0.16	0.22
4. Habitat[a]	0.01	0.04	0.05	0.01	0.02	0.03	0.02	0.07	0.09
5. Other[b]	0.07	0.03	0.10	0.07	0.02	0.09	0.14	0.07	0.21
6. Services (4 + 5)	0.08	0.07	0.15	0.08	0.04	0.12	0.16	0.14	0.30
7. Total (3 + 6)	0.10	0.15	0.25	0.10	0.12	0.22	0.22	0.30	0.52

[a] Housing and urbanisation.
[b] Transport, commerce and services.

SOURCES: Unpublished SNI estimates (Sistema Naciónal de Información, *Estadísticas de Inversión, 1925–40* (Mexico City, 1979) carried out under the author's supervision. Overall investment based on imported capital goods (by sector), a revised construction index (based on cement consumption) and livestock, from *Anuario Estadística 1941* (Dirección General de Estadística, Mexico City, 1943). Public investment from Secretaria de la Presidencia *Inversión Federal 1925–63* (Mexico City, 1963); private sector by difference.

11 Central America in the Inter-War Period

VICTOR BULMER-THOMAS

INTRODUCTION

This chapter[1] will concentrate on economic developments in Central America until the 1960s, the impact of the Depression must have been period (1920–40) has been seriously neglected in Central American scholarship, so that the region's performance has not been taken adequately into account in works purporting to offer an overview of the Latin American experience (e.g. Furtado, 1970).

In place of studies based on primary sources, a 'received wisdom' has been built up derived from *a priori* reasoning. Thus, it has been argued, since industrialisation did not begin seriously in Central America until the 1960s, the impact of the Depression must have been particularly severe. This in turn has justified the most sweeping generalisations regarding economic performance.[3]

The main reason for the neglect of this period in Central American economic studies has been the lack of appropriate statistics. Before writing this chapter, therefore, it was necessary to construct estimates of national income for each republic from available primary sources (details are given in the Appendix). These estimates are in real terms and have been built up sector by sector, so that the performance of the main branches of the economy can be assessed.

After allowing for all the well-known problems associated with national income estimates, the results show a very different picture from the prevailing one; despite the severity of the impact of the Depression, which was felt above all in the form of falling commodity prices, regional Gross Domestic Product (GDP) recovered fairly quickly in real terms and the second half of the 1930s was marked by steady growth in several republics. How this was possible, despite the

279

weakness of industry, will be discussed below, but first the main features of the Central American economy in the 1920s must be outlined.

CENTRAL AMERICA IN THE 1920S

The liberal reforms which swept Central America in the 1870s created the framework for the economic structure which exists in large part to this day. Communal ownership of land was abolished, banks were started, railroads laid down and ports improved; an export economy, based first on coffee and later on bananas as well, was established to the interests of which the State was completely subservient.

The First World War interrupted the consolidation of the liberal reforms, but did not lead to any change in direction. The ruling class waited patiently for an end to the War, which had disrupted its European markets (particularly for coffee), and then proceeded to re-establish even more firmly the dominance of the two traditional exports – bananas and coffee. This was helped in the early 1920s by a series of currency reforms which led to the adoption of fixed exchange rates under the gold standard (see Young, 1925). These rates were rigidly adhered to and even today two of the republics (Honduras and Guatemala) preserve the parities established during this period.

The model of export-led growth based on traditional exports[4] reached its highest expression in the 1920s. By 1926, for example, earnings from coffee and bananas accounted for over 90% of exports by value in Costa Rica, Guatemala and El Salvador, while in Honduras and Nicaragua (where exports of precious metals continued to be important), traditional exports represented over 70% of export earnings.

The growth of exports in real terms was achieved through increases in acreage rather than yields. This brought with it a number of implications of great importance; first, the increase in area devoted to coffee began to encroach on land used for domestic crops (particularly in El Salvador); second, the increased use of labour by the export sector also reduced the workforce available for supplying the home market, so that for both these reasons imports of foodstuffs rose;[5] third, the expansion of the volume of banana exports through increases in acreage depended crucially on direct foreign investment, so that the influence of the multinational fruit companies rose sharply in the 1920s.

The region's financial system was largely built around the export sector in the 1920s. Exports paid for imports and taxes on external trade accounted for the bulk of public revenues;[6] the budget of each republic was usually balanced and total public debt (both internal and external) was very modest;[7] movements in the money supply were therefore determined above all by surpluses and deficits in the balance of payments and the credit extended to the export sector was usually supplied from abroad. The commercial banking system played only a minor role in stimulating productive economic activity.

The export-led model was therefore very simple. Increases (decreases) in sales of traditional exports brought rises (falls) in factor incomes in the export sector, with profits being the most volatile element in income; with a high marginal propensity to import out of profits, imports responded quickly to changes in exports and external equilibrium became almost automatic. Public revenues also rose (fell) with increases (decreases) in external trade and public expenditure moved in line with revenue; thus, both private and public consumption moved pro-cyclically and adverse developments in the export sector set in motion a train of events, which restored external equilibrium at a lower level of output, incomes and employment.

The failure to operate any sort of countercyclical demand management policy can be explained in several ways; first, governments were very weak and controlled directly only a small part of total expenditure; second, the ideology of *laissez-faire* was embraced wholeheartedly by the political leadership and, third, the belief that adverse developments in the export sector would only be temporary was widespread. Thus, the response to the 1921 world recession, which savagely reduced the value of export earnings from Central America, was one of non-intervention and, indeed, export prices and earnings did recover very quickly.

The consolidation of the traditional model of export-led growth in the 1920s was achieved in an atmosphere of comparative political stability, with the exception of Nicaragua, which continued to be occupied by US marines (see Black, 1981); in Guatemala, the liberals José Maria Orellana (1921–6) and Lázaro Chacón (1926–30) gave the republic a chance to recover from the suffocating dictatorship of Estrada Cabrera, while in El Salvador the Meléndez family governed in the interest of the coffee aristocracy until 1927. In Honduras, after the civil war of 1923, a unique decade of political stability was achieved under alternating presidents and in Costa Rica two conservatives (Ricardo Jiménez and Cleto González) succeeded each other in power from 1924 to 1936 and thus became the only country not to institute a long dictatorship in the wake of the Depression.

Some efforts at export diversification were made in the 1920s,[8] but in general the leadership in each country felt content to consolidate the achievements of the past half-century based on traditional exports (coffee and bananas). Throughout the isthmus, the political elite concurred in the belief that the market was too small to justify industrialisation[9] and that demand for the region's traditional exports could be expected to grow without limit; the main problems were seen as smoothing the obstacles to expansion on the supply side. In Guatemala, for example, the leadership remained preoccupied with the problem of ensuring an adequate labour supply,[10] while in Honduras the emphasis was on improving transportation and encouraging foreign investment. In El Salvador, however, the main constraint on export expansion was becoming a shortage of suitable land.[11]

Only a few voices were raised against the dominance of the traditional model in the 1920s, but with the benefit of hindsight its diminishing utility becomes apparent. On the supply side the expansion of coffee was increasing dependence on imported foodstuffs and reducing the region's ability to secure an automatic adjustment to external equilibrium (since food imports cannot be cut so easily). In the case of bananas, expansion involved mortgaging vast tracts of land in perpetuity to banana companies,[12] while the accompanying social infrastructure served the needs of the banana sector only.[13]

On the demand side the low-income elasticity for both coffee and bananas was bound to affect the region's rate of growth sooner or later. In three republics the rate of growth of real GDP fell in the second half of the 1920s (see Table 11.1) while the rise in Nicaragua and Honduras is accounted for by the opening up of new lands for the production of bananas, which replaced exports from elsewhere in the Caribbean.

The main criticism, however, of the traditional model concerns the distortions it introduced into the allocation of resources. The region's investment effort was geared almost exclusively to the needs of the traditional export sector, so that alternative activities were squeezed out. Non-traditional suffered from a shortage of land where infrastructure was available and an absence of infrastructure where land was available; manufacturing developments, where permitted by market size, were choked off by a shortage of credit and the region's mineral potential went largely unexploited.

TABLE 11.1 *Central America: quinquennial rates of growth of GDP and GDP per head (in brackets), 1920–49* (rates expressed as geometric annual averages)

Period	Costa Rica	Guatemala	Honduras	Nicaragua	El Salvador	Central America (unweighted arithmetic average)
1920–24	3.0 (1.0)	5.4 (1.5)	0.5 (−1.7)	1.9 (−0.3)	4.3 (2.5)	3.0 (0.6)
1924–29	0.2 (−2.1)	3.8 (0.8)	8.3 (5.9)	6.4 (4.0)	2.6 (0.9)	4.3 (1.9)
1929–34	0.1 (−2.1)	−0.6 (−3.2)	−2.4 (−4.5)	−5.2 (−7.4)	−0.7 (−2.1)	−1.8 (−3.9)
1934–39	8.0 (5.5)	12.5 (10.3)	0.2 (−2.6)	2.4 (0.3)	3.3 (2.0)	5.3 (3.1)
1939–44	−2.8 (−5.2)	−4.9 (−7.0)	2.3 (0.3)	4.6 (2.4)	3.5 (2.2)	0.5 (−1.5)
1944–49	10.9 (7.8)	6.6 (3.9)	5.3 (2.9)	6.9 (4.1)	6.8 (5.4)	7.3 (4.8)

SOURCE: derived by the author from national accounts estimates. See Appendix (p. 305).

THE ONSET OF THE DEPRESSION

For most of the 1920s the value of exports and imports rose steadily in Central America (see Figure 11.1). This was due principally to the persistent and sharp rise in coffee prices from 1921 to 1925[14] and the less marked tendency for upward revision of the administered export price for bananas.[15] The advent of the Depression, however, was signalled by a collapse of export values.

The turning-point in the cycle (see Figure 11.1) did not coincide with the year (1929), often thought of as marking the arrival of the Depression in developed countries. On the contrary the value of exports peaked as early as 1927 in Guatemala and 1926 in Nicaragua. In Costa Rica and El Salvador the down-turn commenced in 1928, while in Honduras it was delayed until after 1930.[16]

The difference in timing can be most easily explained by reference to the prices of traditional exports. Much Central American coffee in the 1920s was being sold in forward markets,[17] which appear to have anticipated the Depression; thus, Guatemalan coffee prices reached their peak in the period 1925–7 and fell steadily thereafter until 1934.

Banana prices, by contrast, held up much better and did not decline until the period 1931–2. There were two reasons for this: first, the export price – being an administered price – reflected auction prices in consumer countries only after a considerable lag; second, retail banana prices did not fall anything like as far or as fast as retail coffee prices in the Depression.

A third factor affecting the timing of the decline in export values was the volume of banana exports;[18] in Costa Rica, for example, production of bananas went into decline as a result of disease as early as 1926 and fell in each of the following ten years; in Honduras, the export of bananas rose sharply in the late 1920s and continued to rise until 1931 when a dramatic decline (also caused by disease) set in.

The initial decline in export values was not considered very serious in Central America. The cyclical nature of export earnings was accepted and reserves built up in good years were used to support imports in bad years; thus in all the republics except Honduras[19] a visible trade deficit was at first tolerated (see Figure 11.1). By 1930, however, the severity of the Depression had become apparent and imports by value fell even more rapidly than the value of exports; thus all Central American countries ran surpluses on visible trade in the worst years of the Depression.

The sharp decline in the value of imports during the Depression (to

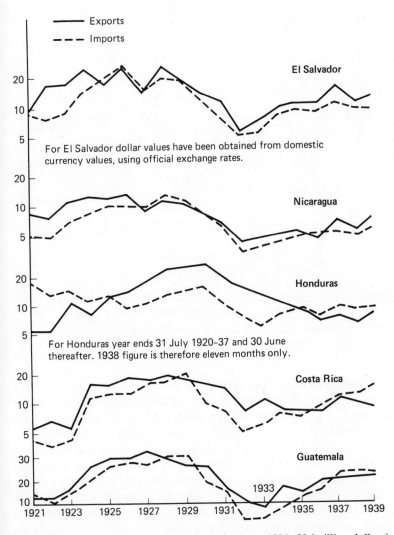

FIGURE 11.1 *Central America: imports and exports 1921–39* (million dollars)

Note: exports valued f.o.b. exclusive of export duties. Imports valued c.i.f. (El Salvador, Costa Rica), f.o.b. (Nicaragua, Honduras) and f.a.s. (Guatemala)

SOURCES: 1920–9 League of Nations, *International Trade Statistics*. 1930–9 UN, *Yearbook of International Trade Statistics*.

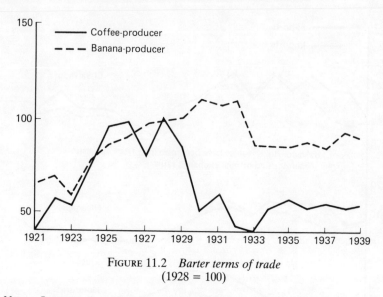

FIGURE 11.2 *Barter terms of trade*
(1928 = 100)

Note: Import prices have been derived from data on real and money values of imports for Honduras (see Banco Central de Honduras, 1956).

Coffee prices are unit values for El Salvador and banana prices are unit values for Costa Rica.

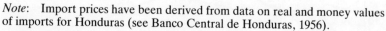

about one-quarter of peak levels) was not all due to volume changes. Import prices in dollar terms did fall, although the evidence is rather indirect.[20] The barter terms of trade, however, initially rose or fell depending on whether a republic specialised in bananas or coffee (see Figure 11.2).[21] Thus in the case of Honduras (where the bulk of exports was accounted for by bananas) the terms of trade index rose steadily until 1930 and did not fall below the 1928 level until 1933.

Coffee-producers were not so fortunate. The steep fall in coffee prices brought a sharp decline in the barter terms of trade after 1928 which was only reversed in 1934 (see Figure 11.2). El Salvador, for example, whose export earnings came almost entirely from coffee, was the worst affected, although the other coffee-producing countries also experienced a deterioration in the barter terms of trade.

The decline in the value of external trade reduced government income from trade taxes, the most important component of public revenue. The latter peaked in the period 1928–9 and fell sharply in the following three years (see Table 11.2). Public expenditure reductions followed with a short lag, although the fall was generally of a smaller

TABLE 11.2 *Central America: summary of budget accounts*
(receipts in millions of units of domestic currency. Expenditure in brackets)

Year	Costa Rica	Year	El Salvador	Nicaragua	Honduras	Guatemala
1928	33.3 (26.9)	1928/9	27.0 (27.2)	n.a.	13.7 (13.1)	15.4 (16.4)
1929	35.4 (36.2)	1929/30	24.6 (25.8)	5.9 (3.8)	14.3 (15.0)	13.4 (14.3)
1930	27.5 (32.5)	1930/1	20.5 (n.a.)	5.4 (4.9)	11.8 (13.9)	10.7 (13.2)
1931	24.8 (27.6)	1931/2	14.4 (17.9)	4.7 (4.8)	10.9 (10.1)	9.2 (9.9)
1932	23.1 (25.0)	1932/3	17.4 (16.6)	3.8 (4.2)	9.0 (12.3)	8.3 (8.3)
1933	23.9 (24.2)	1933/4	14.6 (15.6)	4.2 (4.7)	10.1 (12.7)	8.6 (8.2)
1934	26.4 (25.9)	1934/5	19.4 (16.1)	5.0 (4.9)	10.8 (12.5)	9.6 (8.8)
1935	27.2 (30.8)	1935/6	17.7 (19.9)	5.3 (5.5)	10.0 (14.1)	10.5 (10.0)
1936	34.5 (32.5)	1936/7	19.9 (19.4)	7.5 (6.9)	11.7 (11.7)	11.6 (10.4)

SOURCES: League of Nations, *Public Finance, 1928–37*.

amount than in the case of revenue and budget deficits were therefore common in the first half of the 1930s.[22]

SHORT-RUN RESPONSE TO DEPRESSION

The steep fall in the value of external trade, beginning in the late 1920s, did not at first cause undue problems. The region had experienced such declines before, most notably in 1921, and the long-run repercussions had been minimal; each republic had the resources and the means to run a trade and/or budget deficit for a year or so; the former was made possible by healthy exchange reserves, while the latter depended on a pliable banking system.

During the period 1930–1 it had become clear that the recession was much deeper and might last longer than previous downturns in the trade cycle. The collapse in the value of external trade, which had fallen to half of its peak levels by 1931, was putting intolerable strain on public revenues and salary bills in the public sector were in many cases simply 'deferred' (see, for example, Grieb, 1979, p. 55).

A political crisis was therefore inevitable and the first casualty was Guatemala. A period of constitutional confusion in the latter half of 1930 (see Grieb, 1979) was resolved when Jorge Ubico was elected president as the sole candidate in 1931. In El Salvador the victor in the presidential elections of 1931, Arturo Araujo, was overthrown and his constitutional successor General Maximiliano Hernández Martínez ruled like Ubico through a policy of *continuismo* until 1944 (see White, 1973).

In Nicaragua and Honduras the transfer of power did not occur until 1933, but the Depression contributed to the discontent against the Moncada regime and the presence of US marines in Nicaragua; the Sandinista revolt ended when the liberal Juan Bautista Sacasa took office in 1933, but this was to prove merely a temporary interlude and Anastasio Somoza succeeded to the presidency in 1936 (see Black, 1981). In Honduras the better export performance may have contributed to the survival of the Mejía Colindres regime until 1933, when Tiburco Carías – the successful conservative candidate in the 1932 elections – took power and ruled through *continuismo* until 1948 (see Stokes, 1950).

In Costa Rica the electoral system survived the crisis and power changed hands peacefully in 1932, 1936 and 1940 (see Bell, 1971). None the less, political developments in the depths of the recession were of some importance; the Communist Party was formed by Manuel Mora Valverde and was powerful enough to lead a successful strike against the United Fruit Company in 1934.

The most serious problem faced by each government in the immediate wake of the Depression was the maintenance of external equilibrium. International reserves could not be expected to finance imports at their previous levels and foreign capital flows (both public and private) virtually dried up.[23] The decline in imports was initially achieved through a non-price rationing of available foreign exchange by commercial banks and was in most cases highly successful (with the value of imports falling more steeply than exports).

The key to the success in reducing imports was provided by their structure; the import bill was dominated by consumer goods, whose purchase could be indefinitely postponed without affecting the profitability of the export sector or the rate of growth of GDP. None the less, that imports fell *more* steeply suggests that foreign exchange was required for repatriated profits and/or capital outflows;[24] little evidence is available for this, although the need for foreign exchange to meet fixed interest charges on the public external debt was rising in proportionate and, in some cases, absolute terms.[25]

With the collapse of the gold standard in 1931, the Administration in each republic faced a new crisis – the management of the exchange rate. The initial response was to peg to the US dollar in the case of Guatemala, Honduras and Nicaragua, although Costa Rica and El Salvador allowed their rates to float. The Costa Rican colón, which throughout the second half of the 1920s, had been quoted at 4 to the US dollar, fell gradually to 6 colones to the dollar by 1936,[26] while in El Salvador a depreciation of 33% between 1932 and 1933 was followed by a mild appreciation until the rate was pegged in 1935 at its current level.

It is fair to say, therefore, that Central America followed a passive exchange-rate policy, since the rates even in Costa Rica and El Salvador did not change very dramatically. They preferred to avoid active use of an instrument which proved very useful in promoting recovery elsewhere in Latin America.[27] Despite this it is difficult to question the wisdom of the policy; exchange-rate depreciation alone was not capable of promoting a programme of import-substituting industrialisation (ISI) and the government of each republic preferred other methods to stimulate the external sector (see next section).[28]

The fall in the value of exports, imports and public revenue increased in proportionate terms the burden of the service on the exter-

TABLE 11.3 *Central America: total public debt (internal debt in brackets)*
(in millions of units of domestic currency)

Year	Costa Rica[a]	El Salvador[a]	Nicaragua[b]	Honduras[c]	Guatemala[a]
1928	83.6 (15.0)	45.8 (4.7)	23.5 (20.2)	28.4 (17.2)	17.6 (2.9)
1929	87.8 (17.9)	42.7 (3.7)	23.2 (20.1)	29.4 (18.6)	15.6 (2.1)
1930	94.1 (25.8)	43.6 (7.6)	22.5 (19.7)	27.0 (16.6)	20.0 (4.6)
1931	101.8 (27.4)	46.6 (11.8)	21.9 (19.3)	25.5 (17.0)	20.9 (6.4)
1932	108.4 (30.9)	49.0 (12.3)	21.6 (19.2)	25.6 (16.2)	21.3 (7.1)
1933	114.5 (30.6)	46.9 (9.8)	17.9 (15.5)	28.0 (19.1)	22.2 (7.6)
1934	115.5 (31.8)	45.3 (8.6)	10.0 (7.7)	28.7 (21.1)	22.1 (7.6)
1935	119.7 (36.7)	45.7 (6.2)	8.2 (5.9)	27.8 (20.8)	22.2 (7.2)
1936	141.9 (37.7)	42.1 (6.2)	9.0 (6.7)	28.3 (21.8)	20.2 (6.0)

[a] 31 December.
[b] 1928–32, 31 March. 1932–6, 28 February.
[c] 31 July.

SOURCES: League of Nations, *Public Finance 1928–37*.

nal debt[29] and forced several republics into default and renegotiation. Costa Rica, Guatemala and El Salvador defaulted in the year 1932/3, while Honduras defaulted on its *domestic* debt only. Nicaragua had to postpone the repayment of certain foreign loans starting in 1932, although interest payments on the external debt were met promptly. By 1937, however, the foreign debt had been successfully renegotiated in each case.

The extreme difficulty of obtaining additional capital from abroad[30] forced several governments to increase their internal public indebtedness to meet the budget deficits during the early years of the Depression. In Costa Rica, Guatemala and El Salvador there was a sharp rise in the public debt (see Table 11.3), although the fiscal rectitude of Nicaragua and Honduras (until 1931) made such an increase unnecessary. In Honduras, however, the floating debt rose sharply, when the government failed to pay civil servants on time and this became increasingly serious between 1931 and 1934.

With such abrupt falls in the value of exports, imports, public revenue and expenditure, combined with the rise in indebtedness, it is easy to see why the impact of the Depression on Central America has been assumed to have been very severe (see p. 279). When the monetary veil is stripped from the figures, however, the position does not look so bad. The volume of agricultural exports in general held up well (see Table 11.4) and the decline in real GDP from its peak in the late 1920s was surprisingly mild for all countries except Nicaragua (see Figure 11.3).

All elsewhere in much of Latin America, therefore, the impact of the Depression was felt more through price than quantity changes. Employment, real incomes and real consumption certainly fell,[31] but the declines were less steep and less rapid than those experienced, for example, by Nicaragua in the period 1977–9 and El Salvador in the period 1979–81. Why the impact in real terms was so mild and why Central America was able to grow rapidly in the second half of the 1930s is something to which we must now turn.

RECOVERY FROM THE DEPRESSION – EXPORT PROMOTION

Although export volumes held up well in the early years of the Depression they did fall below their previous peak levels (see Table 11.4, p. 295)[32] and the deterioration of the barter terms of trade (see Figure 11.2) meant that even the maintenance of previous export levels would still reduce the capacity to import. The road to recovery was therefore likely to depend on more than just the promotion of traditional exports.

This, as we shall see, was the case. Policy, however, concentrated heavily on the traditional export sector for a number of reasons; first, it was felt that world commodity prices for traditional exports would improve and the level of activity in the export sector should therefore be maintained; second, influencing the level of exports through variations in policy instruments was a familiar role for Central American Administrations and, third, the political elite throughout the Depression and despite its severity remained wedded to the traditional export-led model.

There was a sharp contrast, however, between the positions of coffee and banana exports. Coffee production and sales, being largely in national hands,[33] could be influenced with the policy instruments available, but banana exports were quite different; first, they were almost entirely controlled[34] by the United Fruit Company and the Standard Fruit and Steamship Company, and these two giants of the fruit trade determined production in individual Central American republics on a global basis; second, banana production was very susceptible to diseases for which at that time (see Karnes, 1978) no known antidote existed.[35]

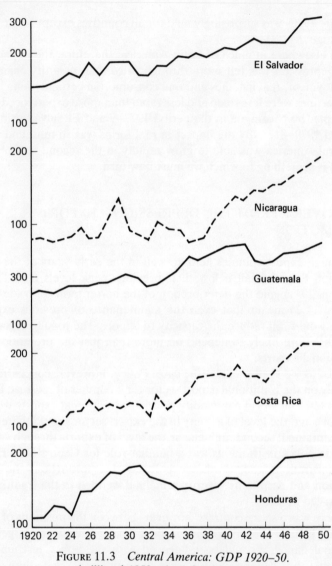

FIGURE 11.3 *Central America: GDP 1920–50.*
(million $ 1950 prices. Semi-log scale.)

SOURCE: derived by the author from national accounts estimates. See
Appendix.

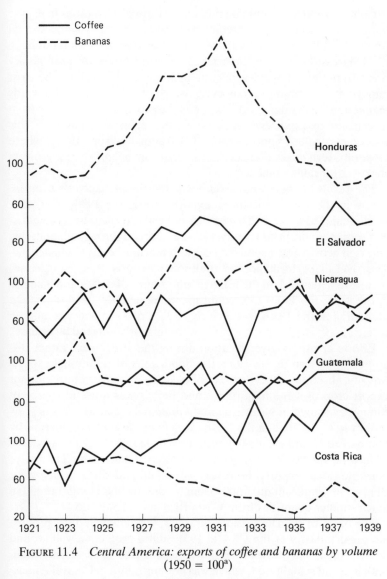

FIGURE 11.4   *Central America: exports of coffee and bananas by volume*
$(1950 = 100^a)$

[a] Except banana exports from Nicaragua, when 1928 = 100.

SOURCE: Appendix.

Coffee production could be influenced through variations in export duties, the availability of credit, exchange rate changes and special funds.[36] All these instruments were used by one or other republic in the Depression and the impact of low world prices on profitability was also mitigated by the reduction in labour costs. Perhaps the most important contribution, however, which the State made towards maintenance of coffee production was the protection of growers from foreclosure by exporters and bankers when debts were not paid. This was of particular importance in El Salvador (Wilson, 1970), where General Hernández Martínez intervened on behalf of the growers shortly after taking office.[37]

The result of these endeavours was the maintenance or even increase in the volume of coffee exports during the 1930s over peak levels achieved in the 1920s (see Figure 11.4). At the same time banana production dropped steeply as disease spread through plantations, although activity was maintained close to previous levels in Guatemala. The overall performance of traditional exports (see Table 11.4) therefore depended on the relative importance of coffee and bananas in the total; this helps to account for the poor GDP performance of Honduras in the 1930s (see Figure 11.3), since she had virtually no coffee exports and banana exports were seriously affected by disease.

Efforts at export diversification during the 1930s were rather disappointing. Even in the 1920s the dominance of traditional exports was not absolute; in several republics sugar had grown into a minor export crop of some importance and timber was a useful source of foreign exchange in Nicaragua and Guatemala. Cacao exports grew rapidly in Costa Rica in the 1920s, largely because of experiments by United Fruit on idle banana lands, and chicle remained a vital source of income for the Petén region in northern Guatemala. The major non-traditional exports, however, were gold and silver, which were shipped in significant quantities from Nicaragua and Honduras and in much smaller quantities from Costa Rica and El Salvador.

The onset of the Depression, however, virtually killed the promising sugar industry as the USA in 1931 built a protective wall around its own sugar activities. Much the same was true of the cattle trade, both live and slaughtered, which was not important in Central America in the 1920s (except for Nicaragua, which exported to Costa Rica), but which was effectively prevented from establishing itself in the 1930s by world-wide protectionist policies.

There were some successful attempts at diversification, however; cotton from Nicaragua, now the mainstay of that country's economy,

TABLE 11.4   *Central America: real value of agricultural exports*
(1950 = 100)

Year	Costa Rica	Guatemala	Honduras[a]	Nicaragua	El Salvador
1940	52.5	89.8	107.7	67.1	81.6
1939	61.8	103.8	93.4	86.7	80.5
1938	72.3	100.5	82.3	81.0	77.6
1937	78.2	95.4	79.3	92.3	97.5
1936	61.2	86.1	99.3	68.4	71.3
1935	59.3	66.9	102.4	94.4	72.2
1934	52.6	71.5	139.4	77.2	71.9
1933	73.6	61.7	154.6	83.1	81.1
1932	58.7	70.2	186.2	63.6	57.2
1931	70.1	67.3	223.9	85.6	78.8
1930	76.5	81.7	197.7	101.6	84.6
1929	71.0	75.5	184.9	106.7	67.5
1928	76.4	72.8	186.6	111.0	76.6
1927	74.0	78.9	152.1	83.1	52.2
1926	82.7	73.2	123.9	93.8	73.0
1925	75.9	75.3	113.8	96.3	46.3
1924	77.1	84.6	86.8	102.9	70.4
1923	62.4	76.0	86.8	99.9	60.6
1922	72.4	69.8	99.2	70.4	62.1
1921	67.6	68.2	86.1	73.2	40.8
1920	73.9	63.8	70.0	65.6	54.2

[a] Year ends 31 July.

SOURCE: derived by the author as explained in the Appendix.

appears on the export list in the 1930s and by 1937 had reached 7.5%
by value of total exports. Timber exports also steadily increased in
importance from Nicaragua after a collapse in 1931–2. In Costa Rica
the cacao experiment grew in importance as more and more idle
banana lands on the Atlantic coast were turned over to cacao production by the United Fruit Company and tobacco began to appear for
the first time among the export statistics in Honduras.

The major scope for diversification, however, for the region was
into mining activities and both Honduras and Nicaragua intensified
their production and export of precious metals.[38] In Nicaragua the
output of the gold mines grew fairly steadily so that by 1938 production at 1522 kg. was twice the level achieved in 1928; the 1938 figure,
however, was more than doubled the following year and by 1940 was
seven times greater than in 1928. Gold exports also grew steadily in
Honduras in the 1930s, although silver exports were fairly static, but
El Salvador emerged from the Depression as an important producer

of gold for the first time with production rising fivefold between 1933 and 1934.

The pattern of exports by area of destination was changed only slightly by these efforts at diversification, the main changes being accounted for by the change in the relative importance of coffee and bananas. In Costa Rica, for example, the decline in importance of bananas reduced the USA to a less important market for exports than the UK by the mid-1920s, although this was reversed again after 1933. In Guatemala Germany competed with the USA as the principal market for exports with the former more important in 1933, while in Honduras and Nicaragua the USA remained the principal market throughout the two decades 1920 and 1940. The German market, however, accounted for over 25% of El Salvador's exports from 1925 to 1934 and during this period was more important than the USA as a market for El Salvador's exports.

RECOVERY FROM THE DEPRESSION – IMPORT-SUBSTITUTION

The decline in the barter terms of trade combined with a (slight) fall in the volume of traditional exports brought about a deterioration in the income terms of trade for Central America and a reduction in the capacity to import. With the tightness of the international reserve position, and the drying up of capital flows from abroad, the capacity to import proved to be a fairly accurate determinant of real imports and Central America was faced with a choice between forgoing consumption of goods previously imported or producing them herself.

This was a similar choice to that faced elsewhere in Latin America, but there were differences. The level of industrial (and particularly manufacturing) output was extremely low in the 1920s[39] and the spare capacity to increase production without importing additional equipment simply did not exist; on the other hand, half a century's reliance on the traditional export-led model had left the region heavily dependent on imported foodstuffs.

Import-substitution therefore occurred in two quite separate activities in Central America and import-substituting agriculture (ISA) turned out to be more important than import-substituting industrialisation (ISI). The performance of domestic use agriculture and industry in each republic between 1921 and 1939 is summarised in Figure 11.5 and a number of patterns can be discerned. First, in the

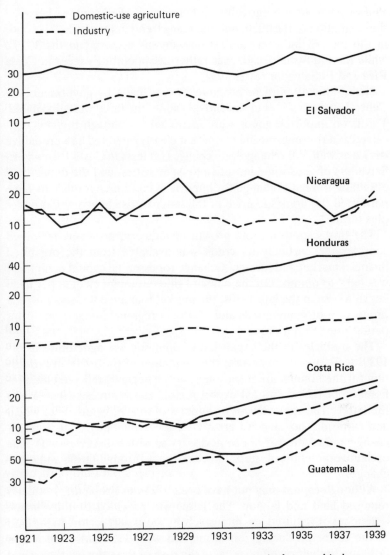

FIGURE 11.5 *Central America: domestic-use agriculture and industry, contributions to GDP; million US dollars* (1950 prices)

SOURCE: Derived by the author; see the Appendix.

case of domestic use agriculture, there is a marked contrast between the stagnation of the 1920s and the rising trend in the 1930s;[40] second, in the case of industry modest growth was achieved in the 1920s, while the following decade was rather disappointing except in Costa Rica and El Salvador (after 1932).

No serious attempt to promote ISI was made by governments in Central America,[41] but incentives none the less were available. Tariffs on imported goods were increased;[42] although this was conceived as a revenue-raising measure it clearly operated as a protective device as well.[43] Exchange-rate changes (at least in Costa Rica and El Salvador) offered some incentive to ISI activities, and the difficulty of obtaining foreign exchange for imports of consumer goods may have permitted the domestic price of the latter to rise above world prices plus tariffs.[44]

The obstacles to a rapid growth of industry, however, remained considerable; virtually no credit was available from the organised financial market and foreign exchange for essential capital equipment was hard to obtain. On the demand side, although income per head began to rise in the late 1930s, the market remained too small for the production of many goods and efforts at regional integration in this period came to nothing.

The obstacles to the expansion of domestic use agriculture in the 1930s were much less severe; the stagnation of the 1920s in production for the home market (in some cases a decline) reflected the profitability of the traditional export sector, as resources switched into the latter. The replacement of imports of maize, beans, rice, wheat and cattle did not depend greatly on the availability of foreign exchange and credit was not so necessary as with ISI. At the same time each government took steps to promote ISA through tariffs and other changes.

Although capital may not have been a serious problem, ISA clearly required land and labour. The latter was provided by those made redundant or required less intensively by the export sector. In the case of the coffee-producing zones, migrant workers could often return full-time to their own farms or, in the case of the colonos, they could rent a bigger plot on the unoccupied part of the estate; in the banana zones, however, the labour force in general had no access to land of its own and the presence of a large, depressed banana zone was a serious impediment to economic recovery.

Other factors were also at work in promoting ISA. In Guatemala, for example, which experienced a particularly sharp rise in domestic-use agriculture in the 1930s, production for the home market was affected in two quite separate ways; first, the labour laws were changed in 1934 and the legalised system of debt peonage was replaced by an anti-vagrancy law. The latter was intended to ensure a regular supply of labour to the export sector, but it also had the effect of increasing the labour-time supplied by a given workforce (see Jones, 1940, p. 164); with the weakness of the traditional export sector, much of the increase in labour-time supplied must have gone into domestic-use agriculture.[45]

The second influence in Guatemala (felt to a lesser extent throughout the region) was the massive road-building programme initiated by Ubico in the 1930s, which brought an almost fivefold increase in the road network in a decade (see Grieb, 1979, p. 137). As the programme relied essentially on forced labour, it gave Ubico a highly unsavoury reputation in liberal circles, particularly when coupled with his wholehearted admiration for European fascism; the new roads, however, did open up parts of the country which had previously been isolated and gave remote villages the opportunity to market a surplus where none had existed before.

THE PUBLIC SECTOR

In the early years of the Depression there was no element of final expenditure which operated countercyclically. Real consumption and investment followed traditional exports downwards and this was true also of government expenditure on current and capital account. Public expenditure peaked in real terms (see Table 11.5) between 1929 and 1930 and fell steadily until 1934.[46]

The pro-cyclical nature of government expenditure is not hard to explain. The ideology of *laissez-faire* during the hey-day of the traditional export-led model had kept government participation in the economy to very modest levels. In 1924, for example, the contribution of general government to GDP[47] was between 2% and 4%, except in Nicaragua where it did not even reach 1%.

By 1929, as a result of a boom in public revenue induced by the trade cycle, the range had risen to between 4% and 7% in Costa Rica, Guatemala and El Salvador, although in Honduras and Nicaragua there was no increase.[48] These levels of expenditure, however, did not provide much scope for increased government intervention during the Depression.

TABLE 11.5 *Central America: government expenditure (current and capital account) in real terms*[a]
(1950 prices)

Year	Costa Rica	Guatemala	Honduras	Nicaragua	El Salvador
1940	66 384	11 268	14 478	35 292	36 605
1939	61 578	10 521	14 825	21 982	36 244
1938	60 585	10 489	16 534	16 171	36 993
1937	53 547	10 521	14 825	15 319	34 847
1936	50 375	10 209	13 798	8 449	33 115
1935	46 046	9 919	13 001	7 173	29 232
1934	40 455	8 855	14 362	7 498	28 293
1933	38 381	8 821	14 594	7 058	27 651
1932	38 500	11 661	14 029	6 930	29 211
1931	41 124	14 653	15 043	7 227	34 394
1930	46 215	16 458	15 043	6 186	36 235
1929	50 100	18 235	14 246	8 928	33 892
1928	38 198	16 295	13 913	8 300	31 971
1927	32 364	13 228	12 089	6 831	29 043
1926	32 454	12 610	12 205	6 379	27 397
1925	36 840	9 685	14 710	6 719	26 800
1924	29 714	8 725	n.a.	6 053	24 949
1923	27 672	7 139	n.a.	5 752	20 683
1922	26 313	6 274	n.a.	4 043	20 140
1921	n.a	6 977	n.a.	4 247	20 880
1920	n.a	3 533	n.a.	6 755	24 665

[a] For method of estimation and sources, see Appendix.
[b] Excluding expenditure on capital account.

A further constraint was provided by the difficulty of financing public-sector deficits. As explained above (see p. 228), each republic ran a budget deficit in the worst years of the Depression, which was mainly funded through increases in the domestic debt; the non-floating domestic debt consisted, above all, of loans contracted with banks, while the floating domestic debt was essentially a euphemism for unpaid salary bills. There were, therefore, political obstacles to the expansion of the latter and financial obstacles to the expansion of the former.

Despite these obstacles the domestic debt did rise sharply in several republics (see Table 11.3, p. 290); the Nicaraguan government, for example, contracted loans from the National Bank in 1932, 1933 and 1934 to cover budget deficits, while the Guatemalan government obtained a US $3 million loan in 1931 from the local subsidiary of a foreign bank; the sharp rise in the non-floating debt in Costa Rica (from 1.2 million colones in 1931 to 10.0 million colones in 1934) was due almost entirely to borrowing from the banking system.[49]

These efforts to fund budget deficits did not, however, amount to much, and the contribution of general government to GDP actually declined between 1929 and 1934 in Costa Rica, Guatemala and El Salvador, although it remained virtually the same in Nicaragua (1%) and Honduras (2%). The position, moreover, was not very different in 1939, and we may conclude that the *direct* impact of government expenditure on economic recovery was minimal.

Despite this it is worth singling out a few examples of direct government intervention, for there were areas where expenditure actually increased. In El Salvador a special fund for Social Improvement was set up (with incomings earmarked from the duty on coffee exports), to be used for the acquisition of land and houses by the peasantry. In Honduras 'law and order' expenditure rose between 1929 and 1931 and in Costa Rica money expenditure on public works and agriculture nearly trebled in 1929 (although they fell back sharply thereafter).

In no sense can these interventions be described as Keynesian, and government expenditure was essentially pro-cyclical. The *indirect* influence of government intervention, however, was considerable, and examples are provided by the road-building programme in Guatemala, the rescue of producers of traditional exports from foreclosure and the impact of exchange control and/or tariff changes on import-substitution.

RECOVERY FROM THE DEPRESSION – DEMAND-SIDE CHANGES

The short-run response to falling world commodity prices was insufficient to prevent a downturn in real economic activity, but in most of Central America the bottom of the Depression had been reached by 1932 (see Figure 11.3).[50] The drop in the level of activity was surprisingly modest, although the impact on real living-standards is much more severe when population growth and the terms of trade effect are taken into account.

After 1932, however, there follows nearly a decade of steady growth in Guatemala, El Salvador and Costa Rica (in Nicaragua and Honduras recovery does not begin until the period 1936–8). During the five-year period 1934–9 only Honduras failed to achieve an increase in real product per person and in several republics the rise in living-standards was impressive (see Table 11.1, p. 283). By 1935 Costa Rica, Guatemala and El Salvador had all surpassed or reached the pre-Depression peak in GDP.

In previous sections we have considered what factors contributed to the recovery of the economy and how these were made manifest through changes in the output of different sectors. This, however, is the economics of the supply-side and it should be possible to relate a consistent story on the demand-side.

In two cases – export agriculture and mining – the consistency is automatic; demand-side changes in the main refer only to foreign demand and this is also the source used to determine the change in supply (see Appendix, below, p. 305). Similarly, the supply- and demand-side of public administration are not independent.

With agriculture for domestic use, however, and industry (other othan mining) the two sides are independent and it is important to consider whether demand for these sectors could have changed at a rate consistent with the estimated change on the supply-side.

One approach to this question might be to use some variant of the Chenery 'sources of growth' equation (see, for example, Robinson and Kubo, 1979). This enables us to decompose the change in output of any sector into the change due to variations in (a) home demand, (b) foreign demand, (c) import coefficients and (d) technological coefficients. Neither (b) or (d) is of much relevance in the 1930s for the two sectors in question, so we are left with (a) and (c).

We have already argued that import-substitution in agriculture and industry was important in initiating economic recovery. It is doubtful, however, if it could account for the dramatic increases recorded by some republics in these two sectors (see Figure 11.5, p. 297). It follows that changes in home demand must also have been important.

The change in demand, however, for any sector depends on the change in real income, the income and price elasticity of demand, and income distribution. Ignoring import-substitution this means that a sector can only grow faster or slower than GDP if the elasticities and/or income distribution changes permit it.

In Central America, after 1932, the growth of domestic-use agriculture and manufacturing was faster than GDP in several countries.[51] This can be explained satisfactorily in the case of manufacturing by income elasticities greater than unity together with import-substitution effects; in the case of domestic-use agriculture, however, it is at first somewhat puzzling.

The key to the puzzle is provided not by income elasticities (which are unlikely to have exceeded unity) nor by price elasticities nor by import-substitution (although this certainly played a part). The answer, on the contrary, must be found in income distribution changes.

As we have seen, the arrival of the Depression in Central America was heralded by a sharp fall in world commodity prices. This put a squeeze on the profit share of national income, to which capitalists and landowners responded by trying to drive down money-wage costs. The scanty evidence at our disposal suggests that these efforts were only partially successful[52] and that the worst years of the Depression were marked by a shift away from profits in the export sector.

In the period of recovery after 1932, world commodity prices continued at low levels while coffee and banana workers, for example, achieved modest increases in money wages.[53] In the urban economy it is not unreasonable to argue that a similar shift in income distribution was taking place, since the profitability of the most important sector (commerce) would have been highly dependent on the level of imports and labour-intensive activities (e.g. construction) were growing significantly.[54] Thus, we may surmise that in the urban economy and export agriculture, labour incomes rose faster than non-labour incomes in the 1930s.

If the shift in the functional distribution of income did occur, it helps to explain how domestic-use agriculture grew faster than real GDP. The marginal propensity to consume foodstuffs must have been higher for labour than non-labour incomes. At the same time a shift towards greater equality in the distribution of income during the 1930s is not inconsistent with what one might expect in primary-producing countries where the non-labour share of national income is heavily dependent on world commodity prices.

CONCLUSIONS

The most obvious conclusion from this study of Central America is that the impact of the Depression was less severe than had previously been thought. The received wisdom on this question can now be seen to have arisen from a confusion of price and quantity changes; while the former fell sharply in the worst years of the Depression, the decline in volumes was much more modest and in this respect the performance of Central America mirrors that of other Latin American countries described in this book.

Real GDP, however, did fall in every case from the peak level achieved in the late 1920s and real consumption per person fell further for two reasons; first, population growth in the period was quite rapid (above 2% per annum in all countries except El Salvador) and the terms-of-trade effect was negative.[55] The hardships associated with the Depression were greatest in the banana zones; although banana exports held up well in the first years of the Depression, the eventual collapse from disease led to unemployment among banana workers, who usually had no lands of their own to which they could return.[56]

Many factors contributed to the recovery from the Depression; one of the most important was the willingness of the government to intervene in the coffee sector to maintain or even increase the volume of exports despite low world prices. This intervention did not come easily to governments accustomed to minimising the role of the State in economic affairs, although the rise of *caudillos* in four of the five republics may have helped. Other factors contributing to recovery were import-substitution in domestic use agriculture and industry and income-distribution changes; export diversification, however, played only a minor part.

One important consideration in the timing and speed of the recovery was the composition of traditional exports. Republics with a large, foreign-owned banana enclave were at a severe disadvantage. They could not influence the level of banana exports with the instruments at their disposal, while a reduction in activity led to unemployment of both the land and the labour force[57] rather than to resource reallocation. This hampered efforts at import-substitution in agriculture and export diversification.

Despite the speed of recovery from the Depression the 1930s is not a decade to which Central America can turn back with pride. It was in many ways a decade of missed opportunities; there was no fundamental break with the traditional export-led model and only a few serious attempts at export diversification were made. Although new export crops were introduced in the 1950s (cotton) and 1960s (sugar, meat), the region remains to this day over-dependent on the export of coffee and bananas and the grip of the fruit companies is still considerable.

There were, nevertheless, some changes made in the 1930s which had favourable long-term implications. First, recognition of the need for some degree of state intervention in the economy is indispensable in a primary-producing region such as Central America and the first real steps in this direction were taken after the onset of the Depression.

Second, the traditional export-led model had led to the sad neglect of financial institutions. Credit for the export sector came from foreign merchants in the case of coffee, and the fruit companies in the case of bananas and loans for new productive activities from domestic financial sources were virtually unavailable. This began to change in the 1930s with the emergence of new banks,[58] and the strengthening of old ones and financial institutions started to play a much more active part in determining the allocation of resources.

It is tempting to conclude by looking for parallels between the present economic decline in Central America and the Depression initiated fifty years before. Both downturns have been marked by falling commodity prices (particularly for coffee) and changes in political regimes. In both periods an earlier export boom had led to increased dependence on imported foodstuffs, local production of which could take the edge off the impact of the recession. There, however, the parallels cease; much of the present economic crisis in Central America is the result of internal disturbances – fiscal and monetary (Costa Rica), as well as political (Nicaragua, El Salvador, Guatemala) – and by no means all export commodity price movements have been unfavourable in the last few years. The complexity of the economy has increased considerably and political and social developments since the 1930s mean that no government, however authoritarian, can now afford to ignore internal equilibrium.

APPENDIX

Sources and Methods for Estimation of Gross Domestic Product (GDP)

The estimates of sectoral output and GDP presented in this chapter are in the main unofficial; they have not been previously published and much of the interpretation in this chapter depends on their accuracy. The sources and methods used to prepare the estimates therefore deserve some comment.

Official estimates of national accounts for some of the inter-War period have been prepared; in the case of Guatemala, for example (see Banco Central de Guatemala, 1955), an expenditure-based estimate starting in 1923 has been presented, but it works with current prices and was therefore not very helpful for my purposes. Guatemala also has a quasi-official net output estimate (see Adler *et al.*, 1952) for the period 1936/7 to 1947/8 in real terms, which proved useful for the last years of the inter-War period.

Honduras, however, has an official estimate of GDP (see Banco Central de Honduras, 1956) in real and money terms from both the expenditure and net output sides, which starts in 1925. When my own work began I did not know of the existence of this series and was relieved to find a high correlation between my own and the official estimates.[59] I therefore decided to use the latter, modified to allow for the difference in base year (see below).

The method used was to estimate net output sector by sector,[60] 'grossing-up' to GDP to allow for those sectors for which no estimate was possible. The estimated sectors represent for each republic 70–80% of GDP in 1950 (the first year for which official estimates for all countries in Central America are available), so that grossing-up covered about one-quarter of GDP.[61]

The base year chosen was 1950 and its choice was dictated by several factors. It is the first year for which official GDP figures covering the whole of Central America are available; the figures, estimated from the net output side at market prices, are roughly comparable and are presented in the original sources in considerable detail.

The official estimates for 1950 are in the currency of the country in question. These were converted to US dollars (Central American pesos) at the offcial exchange rate; this is unlikely to have introduced serious distortions, as the difference between the official domestic currency – US dollar rate differs from the purchasing-power parity rate by a similar margin in each republic (see Kravis *et al.*, 1978) and because, within Central America, official exchange rates were not under pressure in 1950 (with the possible exception of Costa Rica). The numéraire in the national accounts estimates for the inter-War period is therefore 1950 dollars.

The sectors for which an estimate proved possible were (a) export agriculture, (b) domestic-use agriculture, (c) mining, (d) manufacturing, (e) commerce and (f) general government. The estimates suggest that agriculture's contribution to GDP in the 1920s averaged some 50% in Costa Rica, Nicaragua and El Salvador, falling to 35% in Guatemala and rising to 65% in Honduras. Industry's share, on the other hand, averaged less than 10% in Costa Rica, Honduras and El Salvador, while the higher figure (15%) for Nicaragua and Guatemala is explained by mineral exports and market size respectively.

For each of these sectors, and for products within each sector, a production series was constructed in index number form (1950 = 100) and applied to the equivalent net output figure in the 1950 national accounts. This gave sectoral net output in each previous year back to 1920, although the method is forced to assume that the share of value added in each sector's gross output did not change over the period.

Export agriculture was defined for each republic as covering those products for which foreign demand was the dominant source. This meant that production could be estimated from external trade figures in volume terms. Domestic-use agriculture[62] was defined as non-export agriculture and the estimate for each republic was based on a list of the major ten or so products for which official production figures exist. The principal source used for these figures was the Institute of Agriculture's *International Yearbook of Agricultural Statistics*.

Mining output was estimated in the main from external trade figures, but manufacturing was first broken down into (a) food-processing, (b) drink, (c) tobacco and (d) other industry. Food-processing was then estimated from the production series used for agriculture, while drink and tobacco – being in several cases government monopolies – were estimated from government figures on output, sales, taxes, etc. Other industry was estimated, using as index the volume of imports under Class III of the Brussels nomenclature; the latter is defined as 'materials, raw or partly manufactured' and it was assumed that these were destined for use as complementary imports in industry.

The net output of commerce was prepared from an index formed by adding up all those commodities thought to be subject to distribution margins, i.e. domestic-use agriculture, industry and imports all in real terms. The general government estimate was formed by adjusting public expenditure figures for price changes; the implicit price deflator was obtained from the official GDP series for Honduras, which gives the contribution of general government to GDP in real and money terms.

In Table 11.6 the national accounts for each republic are presented in summary form for 1929. One may note that the ranking of sectors in terms of GDP per head has changed in the intervening fifty years with Honduras becoming the poorest, although Costa Rica had already established its position as the country with the highest average living-standards. In terms of economic structure, Central America in 1929 resembled some of the poorer African countries today and a very dramatic shift in sectoral shares has been recorded since then.

NOTES

1. I have been helped considerably in the writing of this chapter by the comments of Carlos Diaz Alejandro and Laurence Whitehead, although the latter in particular may not agree with all its contents. I am also very grateful to Rosemary Thorp for suggesting the idea in the first place.
2. The phrase 'Great Depression' in fact is something of a misnomer, as we shall see, because other periods in Central American history have been equally (if not more) traumatic in terms of their economic consequences. The phrase is maintained here, however, because of its long-established tradition.
3. Anderson (1971) p. 12, for example, claims that national income in El Salvador fell by 50% in the Depression.
4. Throughout this chapter the phrase 'traditional exports' refers to coffee and bananas; in El Salvador, however, there were no banana exports,

TABLE 11.6 *Central America: national accounts, 1929*
(1950 prices)

	Costa Rica	Guatemala	Honduras	Nicaragua	El Salvador
Export agriculture (% of GDP)	38.1	14.9	52.5	30.9	26.8
Domestic-use agriculture (% of GDP)	9.2	17.4	19.3	24.6	19.5
Mining (% of GDP)	0.1	0.1	1.1	1.2	0.1
Manufacturing (% of GDP)	9.5	14.4	4.7	9.7	11.2
Commerce (% of GDP)	13.1	25.5	8.9	9.7	19.6
General government (% of GDP)	4.7	6.7	2.1	0.9	4.5
GDP (million dollars)	110.9	314.4	161.4	118.0	180.7
GDP per head (dollars)	225	177	184	185	128

SOURCE: see text.

while in Honduras coffee exports were negligible during the inter-War period. In the other republics both products were of great importance.

5. By 1929 imports of food and drink (excluding live animals) represented nearly 20% of the import bill in each republic.

6. Trade taxes accounted for some 65% of government revenue in the 1920s.

7. Public debt per person in nominal terms varied from US $42 for Costa Rica to US $9 in Guatemala. The external public debt was less than US $15 per person in each republic except Costa Rica.

8. Attempts were made to establish cotton as an export crop in El Salvador, but the experiment failed through disease.

9. By the end of the 1920s the population of Central America was 5.2 million, of which 1.8 million lived in Guatemala and 1.4 million in El Salvador. Natural and artificial barriers to trade between the republics meant that intra-regional commerce was negligible and within each country much of the rural population was not in a position to purchase industrial goods. The effective market for industrial output was therefore limited to the main urban centres in each republic.

10. The problem of labour supply is a recurring theme in Guatemalan colonial and post-colonial history (see Jones, 1940).

11. The alienation of communal lands in El Salvador continued long after the initiation of liberal reforms in the 1870s and was one factor accounting for the peasant uprising of 1932, brutally suppressed by General Maximiliano Hernández Martínez (see Anderson, 1971).

12. In Costa Rica, for example, the United Fruit Company controlled 274 000 hectares on the Atlantic coast at the start of the Depression, although the area cultivated never rose above 20 000 hectares. By the end of the 1930s the Company had added another 118 000 hectares to its holdings on the Pacific (see Seligson, 1980, chap. 3).

13. The best example is provided by Honduras, where the transport system could be used for little else but the movement of bananas. It did not even connect the capital with the coast.

14. Coffee prices peaked in 1925 in all republics except Costa Rica, where the peak is reached in 1927/8. Costa Rican coffee data in this period, however, are quoted c.i.f. and this might account for the difference.

15. Throughout the inter-War period the export price of bananas reflected nothing more than the fruit companies' needs for local currency expenditure. Thus the companies did not have to surrender foreign exchange from export sales before purchasing imported equipment, repatriating profits, etc. (see May *et al.*, 1952, pp. 231–2). Since local currency costs were dominated by labour expenses, the export price tended to vary in line with the wage rate. For an excellent description of this and other aspects of the banana industry see Kepner and Soothill (1935) and Kepner (1936).

16. This is fiscal year 1930, i.e. 1 August 1929 to 31 July 1930.

17. This was not true of Nicaraguan coffee, which (being of inferior quality) was sold in spot markets. Nicaragua, however, is the exception which proves the rule, because its coffee prices only fell sharply after 1929.

18. The volume of coffee exports, by contrast, held up well in the Depression. See Figure 11.4, p. 293.

19. Honduras had no need to run a deficit in the first years of the Depression, because the value of exports did not peak until 1930.

20. The only source for import prices in Central America in the inter-War period is unit values constructed from trade data. In Honduras, however, official estimates of real imports (see Banco Central de Honduras, 1956) have been obtained from *weighted* unit values, using as weights the five classes in the Brussels trade nomenclature and the implicit price deflator obtained by comparing the real and money values of Honduran imports is therefore the best guide to import prices in Central America. For that reason, I have used Honduran import prices in constructing the barter terms of trade indices in Figure 11.2.

21. The terms of trade indices in Figure 11.2 are theoretical. They represent the case of a republic which obtains all its export revenue from either coffee or bananas. In practice the indices reflect closely the reality in Central America, because Honduras obtained 75% of export earnings from bananas while in 1928 Costa Rica, Guatemala, Nicaragua and El Salvador obtained 62%, 82%, 58% and 93% of export earnings from coffee respectively.

22. In no sense, however, can these budget deficits be regarded as Keynesian in spirit. Internal equilibrium (full employment) was not a policy objective in this period.

23. The book value of foreign direct investment, for example, which had built up rapidly during the 1920s to reach $288 million by the end of 1929, fell thereafter and was estimated at $197 million in the period 1935–9 (see Rosenthal, 1973, pp. 74–6).

24. Other than the profits of the international fruit companies – see n. 15.

25. In Costa Rica, for example, the service on the public debt (most of which was external) as a proportion of government expenditure rose from 17% in 1928 to 28% in 1932. This also represented a rise in absolute terms.

26. The Costa Rican colón was pegged in 1937 at ₡5.6 to the US dollar.

27. In the case of Nicaragua and Honduras the adoption of a passive exchange-rate policy was undoubtedly influenced by their semi-colonial status. In Guatemala, however, the same policy may have been adopted in reaction to the chaotic monetary conditions prevailing in the early 1920s before the 1925 currency reform.

28. Central America experienced in the inter-War period some of the structural rigidities of countries which run the risk of price increases and output falls following a devaluation (this is known in the literature as a 'contractionary devaluation' – see Krugman and Taylor, 1978). A contractionary devaluation also involves a worsening of income distribution and this would almost certainly have occurred in Central America if greater use had been made of exchange-rate depreciation.

29. Exchange-rate depreciation added further to this burden, although the devaluation of the British pound sterling against the US dollar reduced the domestic currency cost of servicing the British-held debt. Sterling obligations formed a part of the public external debt for most of the republics.

30. An example is provided by the Swedish Match loan to Guatemala in 1930, which was only obtained after the republic had agreed to humiliating and onerous terms (see Grieb, 1979, p. 179).

31. Although the fall in real product was not as severe as one might have expected, real consumption per person must have fallen further because of population growth and the adverse terms-of-trade effect. Serious labour unrest, however, was not common in the Depression, the most important exceptions being the peasant revolt in El Salvador in 1932 and the banana strike in Costa Rica in 1934. The civil war in Nicaragua broke out before the onset of the Depression and had much broader origins.

32. Table 11.4 (p. 295) refers to the real value of *agricultural* exports, but this is a very close approximation to the real value of total exports in Central America in the inter-War period.

33. Both the production and export of coffee in Guatemala, however, involved a high level of participation by foreigners, although the foreigners concerned (mainly German) did reside in the country (see Fergusson, 1940).

34. The United Fruit Company bought out Sam Zemurray's Cuyamel Company in 1929, leaving only Standard Fruit as a serious rival (see Wilson, 1947). It should be pointed out that, although these two companies totally dominated the export of bananas, they did not exercise the same control over production, part of which remained in the hands of independent growers (see Kepner, 1936).

35. In the inter-War period, the preferred method of dealing with disease was to abandon affected plantations and start new ones. This is the main reason why the companies owned far more land than they cultivated.

36. El Salvador, for example, set up a special fund administered by the Mortgage Bank to aid coffee-growers.

37. This interpretation is disputed by Anderson (1971), who argues that forced sales of coffee estates in the Depression brought about a sharp rise in the concentration of ownership. It seems certain, however, that without the intervention of the state concentration would have risen still further.

38. In both countries the mines were foreign-owned and the rate of production was outside the scope of government influence.

39. The proportion of GDP accounted for by manufacturing in each republic at the end of the 1920s is given in the Appendix (Table 11.6).

40. There is no rising trend in Nicaragua, where – on the contrary – there is a sharp fall in agricultural production for domestic use from 1933 to 1937. This could have been in reaction to the earlier civil war, although the latter would in any case have made the estimate of production somewhat unreliable.

41. With the possible exception of Costa Rica (see Soley Güell, 1949, vol. II, pp. 329–32).

42. In Nicaragua, for example, the ratio of the value of tariffs collected to the value of imports rose from 34% in 1928 to 50% in 1933. It should also be remembered that some duties were specific, not *ad valorem*, and in a period of declining export prices the *ad valorem* equivalent of such taxes would have been rising.

43. The incentive to producers is measured by the *effective* not *nominal* rate of protection, but even in this period of their history Central American Administrations taxed consumer good imports more heavily than intermediate and capital goods. It is quite possible, therefore, that the effective rate of protection also rose in the 1930s.

44. The most important industrial developments in Central America after 1929 were the establishment of a textile industry in Nicaragua and El Salvador, using in the main locally grown cotton, the establishment of cement production in Nicaragua and the expansion of the shoe industry throughout the isthmus.

45. Agricultural workers cultivating 'with their personal work' three man-zanas of corn in a hot zone, four manzanas in a cold zone, or four man-zanas of wheat, potatoes, vegetables or other products in any zone were exempted from the provisions of the anti-vagrancy law. If Wagley's (1941) study of Chimaltenango is representative, a significant minority of the rural population would have had access to farms of this size and the incentive to increase production of domestic crops would have risen accordingly. This incentive was reinforced in 1937, when rural workers cultivating at least $1^5/_{16}$ manzanas of land on their own account were required to work for others a minimum of 100 days per year rather than the 150 days applied to landless labourers.

46. In Honduras, public expenditure did not rise in real terms until 1936.

47. Based on my own estimates of the national accounts in this period – see the Appendix, p. 305.

48. Taxes on the export of bananas were negligible in the 1920s (unlike the case of coffee taxes); that is one reason why the growth of Honduran public expenditure was so restrained in the second half of the 1920s. In Nicaragua, by contrast, government expenditure was very closely con-trolled by US officials.

49. Despite the rise in the internal public debt in Central America, monetary contraction rather than expansion was the rule. This occurred, because of the downward pressure on the money supply exerted by the fall in international reserves. Throughout the inter-War period, changes in the stock of net foreign assets held by the banking system (money of external origin) is a much better guide to changes in the money supply than changes in net domestic assets (money of internal origin).

50. In Honduras the turning-point was not reached until 1937, while in Nicaragua 1932 represented only a *local* minimum – the global minimum was not reached until 1936.

51. Between 1932 and 1940 domestic-use agriculture grew faster than GDP in Costa Rica, Guatemala and El Salvador. In Honduras the same sector expanded while GDP was shrinking between 1932 and 1936, although it grew more slowly than GDP between 1936 and 1940. Manufacturing grew faster than GDP between 1932 and 1940 in Costa Rica, Honduras and El Salvador.

52. We must again distinguish between those republics for which coffee was the dominant export crop and those for which it was bananas. In the latter the fall in the export price reflected the fall in labour costs in the banana zones (see n. 15), so that, *ceteris paribus*, such republics would not have experienced a shift in income distribution.

53. In Guatemala the rise in money wages in the mid-1930s was consider-able, as employers reacted to the change in the labour laws by competing for workers (see Jones, 1940, p. 165). Guatemala is also the country which experienced the sharpest rise in domestic-use agriculture.

54. The shift in the distribution of income within the urban economy runs against what was happening in the larger Latin American republics in the 1930s. In the latter case, however, the shift towards profits is associated with the sharp rise in industrial output – a phenomenon which, as we have seen, did not occur in Central America.
55. Although it was probably positive in Honduras until 1932 (see Figure 11.2).
56. It is in fact the thesis of one author (Seligson, 1980) that in Costa Rica at least many workers only took jobs in the banana zones because they had lost access to land in the coffee-producing highlands. It is also well-documented that in Honduras many banana labourers were landless migrants from El Salvador.
57. In Costa Rica banana lands ravaged by disease were eventually leased to former employees by the United Fruit Company for growing cacao. This did not, however, become important until nearly a decade after disease started spreading. In Costa Rica there were also legal impediments to the migration of the banana workers (mainly black) to the rest of the country (see Seligson, 1980, chap. 3).
58. The Banco Central de Reserva, for example, was established in El Salvador in 1934.
59. In only one of the years in question (1925–40) do the two series not move in the same direction and in that year (1929) the official series falls by 0.5% while mine rises by 0.3%.
60. An expenditure-based series was rejected on the grounds that it would prove impossible to estimate private consumption in real terms. The factor shares approach was ruled out by the absence of suitable data on labour income.
61. Grossing-up was done by a simple 'blow-up' method. More sophisticated techniques seemed wholly inappropriate.
62. The estimate of net output in domestic-use agriculture was the most difficult. Production figures were sometimes incomplete or inconsistent and had to be supplemented by other data (e.g. on stocks or trade flows) in order to obtain a more reliable picture. Production figures refer (at least in theory) to total output, so that the subsistence sector is included.

REFERENCES

J. H. Adler, E. R. Schlesinger and E. C. Olson, *Public Finance and Economic Development in Guatemala* (Stanford, 1952).

T. Anderson, *Matanza – El Salvador's Communist Revolt of 1932* (Lincoln, 1971).

J. P. Bell, *Crisis in Costa Rica – The Revolution of 1948* (Austin, 1971).

G. Black, *Triumph of the People – the Sandinista Revolution in Nicaragua* (London, 1981).

E. Fergusson, *Guatemala* (New York, 1940).

C. Furtado, *Economic Development of Latin America* (Cambridge, 1970).

K. Grieb, *Guatemalan Caudillo – the Regime of Jorge Ubico* (Columbus, Ohio, 1979).

Banco Central, Guatemala, *Memoria* (Guatemala, 1955).

Banco Central, Honduras, *Cuentas Nacionales, 1925–55* (Tegucigalpa, 1956).

C. L. Jones, *Guatemala Past and Present* (Minneapolis, 1940).

T. L. Karnes, *Tropical Enterprise: The Standard Fruit and Steamship Co.* Baton Rouge, (Louisiana, 1978).

C. D. Kepner, *Social Aspects of the Banana Industry* (New York, 1936).

——— and J. H. Soothill, *The Banana Empire: A Case Study in Economic Imperialism* (New York, 1935).

W. H. Koebel, *Central America* (New York, n.d.).

I. B. Kravis, A. Heston and R. Summers, 'Real GDP *per capita* for more than one hundred countries', *Economic Journal* (June 1978).

P. Krugman and L. Taylor, 'Contractionary Effects of Devaluation', *Journal of International Economics* (November 1978).

League of Nations, *Public Finance, 1928–35* (Geneva, 1937).

S. May and others, *Costa Rica: A Study in Economic Development* (New York, 1952).

D. G. Munro, *The Five Republics of Central America* (New York, 1918).

F. D. Parker, *The Central American Republics* (Oxford, 1964).

S. Robinson and Y. Kubo, 'Sources of Industrial Growth and Structural Changes: A Comparative Analysis of Eight Countries', paper presented to Seventh International Conference on Input–Output Techniques (Innsbruck,1979).

G. Rosenthal, 'The Role of Private Foreign Investment in the Development of the Central American Common Market', mimeo (Guatemala, 1973).

M. Seligson, *Peasants of Costa Rica and the Development of Agrarian Capitalism* (Madison, 1980).

T. Soley Güell, *Historia Económica y Hacendaria de Costa Rica* (San José, 1949).

W. S. Stokes, *Honduras–An Area Study in Government* (Madion, Wisconsin, 1950).

C. Wagley, 'Economics of a Guatemalan Village', *Memoirs of the American Anthropological Association*, no. 58 (1941).

A. White, *El Salvador* (London, 1973).

E. A. Wilson, 'The Crisis of National Integration in El Salvador 1919–35', unpublished Ph.D. thesis, Stanford University (1970).

C. M. Wilson, *Empire in Green and Gold: The Story of the American Banana Trade* (New York, 1947).

J. P. Young, *Central American Currency and Finance* (Princeton, N.J., 1925).

12 The 1929 World Depression in Latin America – from the Outside

CHARLES P. KINDLEBERGER

I was an impostor at a meeting of Latin American experts. I know little of the area, read neither Portuguese nor Spanish and, apart from a few yards into Mexico at various points in Texas and California, have not even been to the area except to Panama and Cuban territorial waters in 1929 and 1930, rather before the events under discussion, and when I had no knowledge of or interest in economic history. I came to Manchester to learn. But my hope was to stimulate thought by reading the papers, listening to the discussion, commenting on them from the vantage-point of what I may know, and comparing one account with another. Herewith the result.

The chapter begins with a general comment on Latin America's contribution to the start and continuation of the Depression. I then turn to the chapters and discuss their content, first in relation to uniformity and diversity, especially in regard to commodities and policy response. The following sections take up the chapters' views on the role of prices; foreign borrowing and its halting; foreign direct investment; the capacity to transform the economy, and finally dependence versus self-reliance. For complete coverage of the chapters, one should address the question of the political consequences of the Depression, but my ignorance at this level is so abysmal that I leave it to others.

LATIN AMERICA'S CONTRIBUTION TO THE START AND CONTINUATION OF THE DEPRESSION

The usual positions on the start of the 1929 World Depression are that it started exclusively in the USA, as Friedman and Schwartz (1963) assert, or that it was the consequence of European mistakes, as President Hoover of the USA insisted (1953, vol. III). As between these two positions it seems to be sensible to give the answer of R. C. O. Matthews (1954) on the issue of whether the 1936–7 Depression was caused by Britain or the USA: so intricate is the chain of causation linking the two areas that the question cannot be answered. Few have found causes of the 1929 Depression outside the USA and Europe, apart from A. J. H. Latham, who ascribes a portion of its origin to Asian overproduction of rice (added, to be sure, to world surpluses of wheat (1981)).

I come to the role of commodity prices later, but at this stage consider the difference between the price collapses of 1921 on the one hand, and of 1929 on the other. The year 1921 was traumatic for producers of many commodities, but recovery proceeded relatively quickly thereafter (except in Britain, burdened by heavy debt structures piled on the 1920 boom). In 1929 prices fell sharply, but failed to recover – in fact continuing to decline worldwide. The difference between the two periods has been ascribed to a change in the downward flexibility of wages – union contracts after 1921 no longer providing for two-way adjustment to the cost of living (Temin, 1971, p. 67) and to the earlier absence of bank failures. The essential difference seems to me to lie in the difference in world commodity production and stocks. In 1921 correction of the boomlet left production barely recovering in Europe and stocks low worldwide. In 1929, on the other hand, the sellers' market of the early 1920s had turned into a buyers' market. Prices of agricultural products and minerals had been slipping since 1925 as European production after the War was added to expanded wartime supplies outside Europe. Cobwebs in some products, especially sugar and coffee, led to excessive responses to postwar price increases, and production in minerals – petroleum, copper, lead, zinc and in Asia tin – had expanded dangerously. Attempts to hold up prices in coffee and linseed accumulated stocks over the market. Latin America contributed to much of this oversupply which accounted for the failure of prices and production to recover quickly after the sharp drop in commodity prices communicated from the stock market to commodity markets.

Second, Latin America was hit hard – especially Argentina, Brazil, Colombia – by the abrupt halt in foreign lending in June 1928 when the New York stock market started its meteoric rise and interest rates tightened on the call money market. On this score a number of Latin American countries date the start of the Depression from the second half of 1928. Argentina lost $111 million in gold in 1929. In addition, its exchange rate started to slip from 97 cents to the US dollar in the first half of 1928 to 95 cents at the end of 1928, a rate held through November 1929 when exchange depreciation went further.

Third, Latin America (and Australia – New Zealand) contributed to the World Depression by early depreciation of their exchange rates in the face of falling commodity prices, exhausted reserves and inability to borrow. Few other choices existed, but in a world poised on the edge of deflation, depreciation leaves domestic prices unchanged and the corresponding appreciation reduces them abroad. The area cannot be blamed for looking after its own interests at a cost to the rest of the world, since it had no responsibility for world economic stability. It may be observed further, that in a world of shortages, poised on the edge of inflation, depreciation raises domestic prices and appreciation abroad leaves them unchanged there. The ratchet works for world inflation under the conditions of the 1970s, for structural deflation under those of the 1930s.

UNIFORMITY AND DIVERSITY

The standard paradigm for the 1929 Depression in Latin America referred to by many of the papers is that prior to 1929 Latin America was a dependent area, tightly attached to the world economy and led by changes in spending and lending in Europe and the United States. With the world Depression, export-led growth and fluctuations gave way to import-substitution in the form of manufacturing industry because of adverse balances of payments, and to more active stabilisation policies, requiring in some instances the development of appropriate institutions. Most papers at the conference found this generalised description oversimplified, failing in one or more respects to fit the particular country under consideration. The break was less sharp, or went back to 1920–1 or to the First World War. Import-substitution as a process had long been under way, as had the construction of central banks, the imposition of tariffs, exchange depreciation and the like. O'Connell insists that Argentine troubles began much earlier than 1928 or 1929, and Palma traced industrialisation in Chile back to the collapse of nitrates exports in 1919 following the development of synthetic nitrates during the War. Cuba's troubles went back to 1925, whereas those of Honduras did not start until 1932. In the case of Brazil, industrialisation of the 1930s rested on excess capacity in textiles built in the 1920s, and the positive policy seen by Furtado in coffee valorisation financed by central bank credit was an extension of policies on coffee prices that originated as early as 1900.

While separate scholars quite properly emphasise the distinctive features of the national experience they study, divergences from the paradigm take off in different directions so that the generalisation holds up as an average description. The question remains perhaps whether the central tendency is sufficiently peaked to warrant its use as a description of the experience of the area as a whole.

Commodities. The various chapters explicitly and implicitly insist that one export commodity differs from another. Bulmer-Thomas points to the wide differences in Central America between coffee and bananas, the former produced on the whole by small producers, the latter foreign-owned, marketed by foreigners, subject to disease. Thorp and Londoño ring the changes on the differences between Colombian coffee, benefiting from Brazil's attempt at sustaining prices and the American preference for soft coffee, but requiring social overhead capital to bring it cheaply to market, and Peruvian metals, foreign-owned, needing little public construction. Fitzgerald observes similar differences within Mexico between metals and agricultural exports, and O'Connell notes the different demand and supply conditions in wheat and beef, although both are marketed by a handful of oligopolistic sellers. Implicit in these distinctions is the need for a staple theory relevant to depression and recovery comparable to that developed by Harold Innis for Canadian commodities with respect to growth. In a paper given in another symposium at the same Congress John Fogarty explored the relevance of Innis's staple theory for Argentina, Australia and Canada, and found it limited. The econometric work of Michael Twomey (not published in this volume) found that Latin American exports were generally in highly inelastic supply (at least for price decreases). My reading of the chapters, however, emphasises diversity, and Diaz Alejandro's expression, 'the commodity lottery', emphasises that cyclical outcomes depended to a considerable extent on the nature of the commodity – its ownership, production function, linkages, demand conditions and marketing – that a country happened to produce for export.

Policy responses. Diaz Alejandro divided the countries of Latin America into two categories, the 'reactive' and the 'passive'. He insisted that this is not the same distinction as between the large and the small. Among medium-size countries, for example, Chile and Uruguay were active and Cuba, without a central bank until 1935 and with the US dollar circulating side-by-side with the peso, was passive. Argentina was far less active than Brazil and Colombia was passive until late in 1931, maintaining its exchange rate and debt service through 1932, but then becoming very active.

An interesting generalisation emerged during the discussion to the effect that policy in a number of countries was held within highly orthodox lines by the memory of disasters consequent on financial unorthodoxy of the past. Argentina's financial woes of 1890–3, the Colombian inflation from the Thousand Days' War of the same epoch, Mexico's experience with wildcat issuance of banknotes after the 1914 revolution and continuing through to the early 1920s and Central American inflationary experience in the 1920–1 commodity bubble all inhibited policy for a time, until the need to take some kind of governmental action became overwhelming. The examples echo a series of extra-Latin American episodes – John Law's Mississippi bubble and the *assignats* in France, the revaluation of the pound sterling in 1925 followed by a decade of high unemployment and German hyper-inflation of 1923 – where 'collective memories' appear to have inhibited the adoption of rational policies for periods as long as fifty years or even (in the case of John Law) more than a century (Kindleberger, 1982).

Some considerable difference of opinion surfaced over the question whether active policies required the antecedent construction of appropriate institutions, or whether such institutions could be hastily built when the need became acute (as the Coase theorem (1937) implies). There was plenty of antecedent experience with tariffs and exchange depreciation, and foreign-exchange controls were put into action with some alacrity once the need was clear. In Central America, however, fiscal policy implied monetary policy, since there was no money or capital market on which domestic debt could be issued, whereas the Andean countries had benefited from the visit by Edwin Kemmerer in the 1920s, setting up central banks to operate the gold standard, even though in the case of Peru, the gold standard was adopted in a single day (information communicated by Paul Drake) so that the roots of the institution could be said not to penetrate deeply.

There was something of a temptation to say that the Monetarism of the 1920s was followed by Keynesianism in the 1930s, but in discussion the symposium decided that this was overstating it. Neither the gold standard of the 1920s nor the combination of government deficits, combined with tariffs, depreciation and in most cases foreign-exchange control represented coherent and thought-out conscious policies so much as spontaneous reactions to the exigencies of foreign financial advisers capable of blessing foreign loans in the case of the gold standard, and to declines in exports and consequently government revenues in the later period. In fact government deficits in a number of Central American countries represented primarily unpaid civil-servant salaries.

Considerable discussion turned on whether conscious policy choices were made in the general interest or on behalf of a particular dominant elite. Where the dominant economic interest was foreign, as in Cuba, policy might be undertaken deliberately on behalf of small native planters. Surprise was implied in Versiani's statement that the interests of the coffee elite were not always consistently pursued, and in some important instances were opposed. Debate took place over whether the Roca–Runciman treaty between Argentina and Britain in 1933 strongly favoured the cattle interests, as O'Connell and Abreu thought, or could be interpreted as providing the country as a whole with important financial gains, permitting raising wheat prices and conversion of the internal debt to a lower rate of interest and the government to balance its budget, as Alhadeff insisted. In Central America, passivity seems to have favoured the working classes, as wages were depressed less than profits, but there was dispute as to whether the end of peonage and the passage of a vagrancy law in Guatemala were beneficial in enabling the proletariat to plant food crops in land rented beneath the coffee trees, or constituted a device to force it to work on behalf of landowners to the latter's benefit.

The useful suggestion was made that import-substitution and deficit financing were induced prior to about 1932 in most countries and undertaken more actively as chosen policy thereafter. This would make the dividing-line between orthodox and Keynesian policies not 1929 but later, at a time when governments found themselves forced to do something – perhaps anything. But there was considerable variation from country to country.

PRICES AND THE TERMS OF TRADE

A number of the papers emphasise that Latin America suffered but little in real terms, as measured by Gross Domestic product (GDP), and recovered 1929 levels of output early in the subsequent decade. Suffering, however, should be measured by gross national income, not GDP, taking into account the relative fall in export and import prices. On this score Chile and Cuba were the worst-hit countries of Latin America, and Chile the worst-hit in the world. There were some buffers, notably the decline in profits which made the fall in the terms of trade on returned value (foreign sales less profits, or more positively, primarily wages and taxes) considerably less than that in exports and imports as a whole. Other buffers were default, and blocking of profits. The fact that GDP was sustained may help relieve unemployment, but if the terms of trade turn sharply adverse, does little to maintain consumption and investment.

A number of points on the fall of export prices are worth noting. Most of us are so bemused by Keynesian analysis that we tend to think of a decline in prices as affecting national income through its impact on the value of exports. This is by no means the only connection. Where a country consumes a substantial portion of the goods it exports the price decline on the retained amount may have significant macroeconomic consequences. Modern monetary theorists tend to dismiss changes in prices within a country as unimportant, suggesting that the loss of a producer whose price has fallen is made up for by the gain of a consumer or purchaser who gets it more cheaply. To think otherwise, in their view, is 'money illusion', i.e. to confuse nominal quantities with real quantities. I am unable to accept this view as it applies to 1929. As FitzGerald rightly says, depression can be transmitted through prices without impinging on the balance of payments. There are lags between the losses of the producer and the recognition of gains by the domestic consumer. In addition the producers' bank may fail, and the consumer is unlikely to start new banks. The dynamic consequences of price changes are ignored at the analyst's peril, and Ragnar Nurkse, for example, made a serious mistake when he said that the fact of an export surplus in the balance of payments of the USA in 1932 meant that it was wrong for the USA to devalue because the balance of payments was expansionary (1947). In reality the deflation communicated through falling world prices was driving down imports faster than exports were being reduced, and the impact of the outside world on the USA was highly deflationary. The point, while worth noting, is not extensively relevant to Latin America, which for the most part exports 'colonial products', defining that category as goods not extensively consumed in the exporting country or produced in the importing country.

It is worth mentioning in this connection that Latin American banks on the whole did not fail in the 1929 Depression. The reason, brought out in the discussion rather than treated in the chapters, was that many were state and provincial banks with governmental support. In Argentina, for example, the state bank had 30% of the system's loans and 40% of deposits. The contrast with the 1970s and 1980s is striking, since in the latter period there have been banking crises in Argentina, Chile, Colombia and Mexico, and the end of such crises is not in sight.

It has already been noted that currency depreciation in depression by Latin American countries with heavy stocks of commodities tended to push world prices down further. O'Connell observes that devaluation in Argentina failed to raise domestic prices. It follows that it lowered them abroad. This was especially true in wheat where lack of storage space in Argentina (and Australia) made export supply unresponsive to price. Canada and the USA tried through their Wheat Pool and Farm Board to hold the price up, but failed as early as May 1929. The unremitting availability of Argentine and Australian wheat hurt, especially after France imposed quantitative restrictions in 1930 as it struggled to raise the price paid to its farmers.

One further item on prices, in part to correct a mistake I made in *The World in Depression, 1929–1939* (1973). In that work I emphasised how the liquidity crisis in the New York stock market had been communicated to the commodity markets through a squeeze on New York banks. Typically in those days, commodities were shipped to New York to be sold on consignment, rather than bought in the producing region and imported for the owner's account. A financial seizure caused by withdrawal of call-money from the stock market spread to commodities when the New York banks stopped other lending in order to be ready to replace out-of-town banks and 'others' withdrawing call funds. Merchandise shipped to New York for sale on consignment could not find buyers for lack of credit, and prices fell drastically between September and December 1929. Commodities financed in the interior of the USA such as wheat, corn, sugar did not fall to the same degree as rubber (26%), hides (18%), zinc (17%). I originally included in this list coffee, which fell from 22½ cents to 15 cents, or by one-third, but I learn from Ocampo's neat discussion of coffee prices that this was due in part, perhaps large part, to the collapse in October 1929 of Brazilian efforts to stabilise prices, as well as to lack of credit on the part of New York commision merchants.

FOREIGN BORROWING AND ITS HALTING

Like 'commodity lottery', the expression 'Dance of the Millions' is new to me. I find it in the Thorp and Londoño chapter and in Pollitt's oral presentation on Cuba, and it is graphic. Thorp and Londoño are particularly eloquent on the speculation, corruption, greed and waste that accompanied the frenzied borrowing, largely from the USA and after 1925. These seem to be endemic in booms, called 'manias' on occasion (Kindleberger, 1978). The question is how to think today about this borrowing.

Diaz Alejandro blames the lenders for pushing loans on the borrowers, and is disposed to explain away Latin American default on the ground that everybody defaulted: the British on War debts, the Germans on short-term balances under the Standstill Agreements, the USA in repudiating the gold clause in its bonds. There are other ways to view it. Borrowing helped stimulate the boom and default cushioned the Depression for Latin America. An important difference from the borrowing of the 1920s and that of half a century later is that the earlier debts were mostly owed to private individuals whose losses had little effect in spreading depression, apart from a wealth effect that may have reduced consumption. Default on the debts of the 1970s contracted to banks if it takes place would have a much greater spread effect by threatening the stability of individual banks, and possibly of the financial system as a whole if two or more large defaults occurred close to one another and impaired the capital of several important banks. Unlike the 1920s the public good of world monetary stability is involved in the contract along with what might be regarded as a private national interest.

Whatever the merits of US bankers in pushing foreign lending from 1925 to 1928, they were surely at fault in cutting it off abruptly in June of the latter year. Deflation is imposed by the Centre on the

Periphery whenever the former suddenly stops lending, as in 1825, 1857, 1866, 1873, 1890 and 1907. First halting lending and then cutting way down on imports is a recipe for disaster. It is worth noting that in the 1890s world bankers, who can do nothing about the decline in developed-country imports from the developing world, are acutely conscious of the need to avoid a sudden cut-off in lending that would precipitate serious deflation at the Periphery, certain to reflect back on the developed world and on their institutions.

The national interest of separate countries contemplating default then and now involves one argument scarcely mentioned in the chapters: the need or desire of the borrowing country to maintain access to the international capital market. History suggests that there has been typically a thirty-year lag between default and a country's being welcomed back into good standing as a borrower. Latin American defaults in the nineteenth-century took place in 1825, 1857, 1890. A lending boom under way in the period from 1910 to 1913 would probably have become excessive and ended in repudiation of debt had not the First World War supervened. This stretched the new borrowing to the second half of the 1920s and default to the 1930s. The Mexican Revolution of 1914 involved an earlier default which was about to be repaired in the Pani – Lamont agreement until its operation was rendered impossible by the Depression.

An interesting point to me is the connection running between devaluation and default, stressed by Thorp and Londoño. Colombia hung on to the gold standard and paying its debts on the nail as long as it could. Devaluation, says Ocampo, was then undertaken in the interest of the coffee elite, but brought about a drastic increase in the local-currency cost of servicing foreign debt leading thus to default.

FOREIGN DIRECT INVESTMENT

Direct investment is mentioned at many points in the various chapters, but I find it hard to draw much in the way of generalisations. Foreign owners of mines suffered major losses in profits in Peru, Mexico and Chile. In addition such positive profits as remained in Chile were practically blocked. In Mexico prospects were so discouraging that a process of withdrawal was begun. The banana-exporting countries had little control over the price, quantity, or growth of exports which were entirely in the hands of the big fruit companies, and in Cuba the large American growers with extensive plantations, plus the American and Canadian banks which lent to them, left the Cuban government with little control over events in its jurisdiction. The British government bargained strongly on behalf of its nationals owning the Argentine railroads in the Roca–Runciman agreement, taking advantage of Argentina's dependence on the British market and responding to Dominion demands put forward at Ottawa in 1932. Argentine utilities increasingly were owned by US investors rather than British, the financial switch occurring also in borrowing through bonds and compounding over the long run the problem of selling to Britain and buying from the USA, when sterling was not convertible.

The role of foreign direct investment in import-substitution was little stressed. The 1920s saw the beginnings of foreign investment in automobiles, tyres, cement, electrical appliances, some of it protected by new tariffs which the foreign entrepreneurs 'jumped', to use Diaz Alejandro's phrase. Presumably local entrepreneurship was too little developed for tariffs combined with restrictions on foreign direct investment, such as are widespread today, to have produced locally led industry. Versiani observed the development into factories, of some repair shops required in the First World War by shortages of manufactured parts, but they seem not to have been many. There was also some infusion of entrepreneurship from European immigration. I judge that at this early stage of industrialisation, however, direct investment from abroad in industry was welcomed as a contributor to industrialisation, and that most governments were willing to provide it with tariffs and other inducements. O'Connell emphasised in discussion that the 1930 road-building programme of Argentina ran not from farms to railheads to assist the agriculturalists, but parallel to trunk line rails, presumably to stimulate the birth of the automobile age.

CAPACITY TO TRANSFORM

In his contribution to the Triffin *Festschrift*, Diaz Alejandro calls Latin American capacity to transform resources into new sectors impressive (1982, p. 179). Leading sectors were textiles, building materials, especialy cement, oil-refining, tyres, toiletries and food-processing. The role of foreign enterprise has already been noted, along with the expansion of cotton-growing in Brazil and Nicaragua under the umbrella of US efforts to raise prices. Much of the transformation was in import-substituting agriculture, and some of that was at the expense of other Latin American countries. O'Connell cites a shift from cattle-breeding to cattle-fattening with its induced demand for feed-grains, but also observes the transformation of Argentine agriculture from its traditional beef, wheat, maize and linseed to new products such as sunflower seeds, cotton, and peanuts for the domestic market. There was intense competition within the region in export products – coffee, bananas and petroleum – and a movement to substitute domestic production for such imports as sugar.

This transformation occurred largely in the reactive countries. Others such as Peru, Cuba and Central America waited for recovery of the world market. Diaz Alejandro hypothesised that active policies of import-substitution in world Depression produced a less satisfactory outcome than would the absence of the Depression and continued reliance on export-led growth. It is not clear whether this judgement assumes that import-substitution would have continued as a natural process, resulting from the spillover of demand from export staples into market-oriented products, giving rise to the growth of local industry, or not.

A significant point was made by Bulmer-Thomas about Central America: that export-led growth led to the neglect of financial institutions. Coffee exports were financed by foreign merchants, bananas by the fruit companies, and little savings were available for other productive activities. Perhaps this was so in Central America in this period. It may be observed, however, that export-led growth of Sweden in feed-grains, timber and iron in the 1850s and 1860s, originally financed by foreign merchants, did not inhibit the rapid development of strong financial institutions capable of intermediating between foreign capital and local borrowers, and in fact doubtless accelerated it. Bulmer-Thomas's point may have more to do with Central America than with export-led growth in general.

DEPENDENCE V. SELF-RELIANCE

Diaz Alejandro's chapter ends with the statement that the time has come for Latin America to achieve self-reliance. The Cocoyoc declaration of 1976 made a similar demand. I have not seen the paper by Johan Galtung entitled 'Self-reliance: An Overriding Strategy for Transition' (1982) but the experience of Latin America in the Depression raises a number of issues related to self-reliance by developing countries in a large world.

In the first place there is a strong contrast between the experience of Argentina on the one hand and Brazil on the other. Both were potentially dependent on triangular trade, selling to one trading partner and buying from another, but, as Abreu shows, Argentina suffered from the fact that its trade partner, Britain, was prepared to take advantage of its position, whereas Brazil, selling mainly to the USA, found the latter unwilling to exploit its bilateral advantage. The USA, unlike Great Britain, did not use its import market to collect debts owed to its investors, force trade into bilateral channels or object when Brazil slipped into advantageous bilateral trading relations with Germany, displacing the USA from the German cotton market. Abreu may even approve of the emerging hegemonic USA in the 1930s as he notes the absence of a hegemonic country in the world economy today.

While Brazil benefited from the indifference of the USA to exploitation of its position, that indifference came close to being harmful for Mexico, whose interests in silver were, to say the least, totally ignored. Cárdenas describes how, when Mexico ran out of gold, it got a benefit from coining silver, then low in price, through gaining substantial seignorage. This failed to last, as the US Treasury, under pressure from western silver senators, started bidding up the price of silver. The seignorage was lost, but Mexican silver mines got a better price. With great good luck, and possibly some management, the Bank of Mexico found its peso notes gradually gain acceptance in place of coins. Thus Mexico gained a high price for its silver as bullion, and 100% seignorage on currency issues, instead of the earlier 60%. Had it had to depend solely on silver for money creation, however, it might have found itself drained of its money supply, as proved to be the fate of China.

Second, it is not clear in this context whether self-reliance means reliance on self by country, region, continent, hemisphere or by developing countries on some world basis. Thorp and Londoño note how Colombia prospered under Brazilian efforts to raise the price of coffee; Colombia's gain was at Brazil's expense. The same was true of a certain amount of agricultural import-substitution, especially in sugar.

Price-raising activities, moreover, have to extend beyond Latin American boundaries, as was then evident in copper, tin, petroleum, lead, silver and zinc, and is now true of coffee as well, in that Latin

American producers of basic commodities share the world market with other countries outside the hemisphere.

Since the Second World War attempts at integration involving groups such as the Central American republics, the Andean countries and Latin America as a whole have fallen short of widely held hopes for self-reliance by regional blocs.

It may be argued, as some of the participants do for separate countries, that machinery is needed before policy can be formulated and implemented – machinery going beyond trade policy for the region perhaps into monetary and fiscal policy, public works, even commodity-price stabilisation. Efforts in these directions in Europe and in the wider Atlantic community, including that honorary Atlantic power, Japan, do not offer strong hope. Self-reliance, it would seem, must take hold at the national level, and may thus contain substantial elements of beggar-thy-good-neighbour about it. If the USA were not losing in power and concern, it might well be that dependence of the separate members of the Periphery on the American public role of stabiliser would be preferable. It is widely agreed among political scientists that the best form of government is benevolent despotism, so long as one can rest completely assured that the despot remains benevolent. That hope, alas, seems generally vain.

Perhaps a better long-run guide to policy would be to strengthen the responses of economic elements to the market on trend, and to reserve strong government policy – on an international basis to the greatest extent possible – to the (it is hoped) rare lapses from trend into crisis in commodity markets (either dearth or glut), in capital flows or in finance.

REFERENCES

H. R. Coase, 'The Nature of the Firm', *Economics*, n.s., vol. 4 (1937) 386–405.

C. D. Diaz Alejandro, 'Some Historical Vicissitudes of Open Economies in Latin America', in R. N. Cooper *et al.* (eds), *The International Monetary System under Flexible Exchange Rates* (Cambridge, Mass., 1982).

M. Friedman and A. J. Schwartz, *A Monetary History of the United States, 1867–1960* (Princeton, N. J., 1963).

J. Galtung, 'Self-reliance: An Overriding Strategy for Transition', in R. Falk *et al.* (eds), *Toward a Just World Order* (New York, 1982).

H. Hoover, *The Memoirs of Herbert Hoover*, vol. III, *The Great Depression, 1929–1941* (New York, 1952).

C. P. Kindleberger, *The World in Depression, 1929–1939* (Berkeley, Calif., 1973).

—— *Manias, Panics and Crashes: A History of Financial Crises* (New York, 1978).

—— 'Collective Memory vs. Rational Expectation: Some Historical Puzzles in Economic Behavior', in *National Ekonomisk Tidsskrift* (1982) 860–71.

R. C. O. Matthews, *A Study of Trade-Cycle History: Economic Fluctuations in Great Britain, 1832–1842* (Cambridge, 1954).

R. Nurkse, 'Equilibrium in Foreign Exchange', in American Economic Association, *Readings in the Theory of International Trade* (Philadelphia, 1947) 1–25.

P. Temin, 'Three Problems in Economic History', *Journal of Economic History*, xxxi, no. 1 (1971) 58–75.

M. Twomey, 'Aggregate Supply and Demand during the Great Depression', mimeo, University of Michigan (1981).

Statistical Appendix

TABLE 1   *Latin America: external trade indices*
(1929 = 100)

	Export quantum	Terms of trade	Capacity to import
1925	78	104	81
1926	81	98	80
1927	91	104	95
1928	94	106	101
1929	100	100	100
1930	83	82	69
1931	90	67	61
1932	75	72	55
1933	78	74	58
1934	79	93	73
1935	86	87	75
1936	83	96	80
1937	92	103	95
1938	83	86	73
1939	89	84	76
1940	79	80	64

SOURCE: UN ECLA (1950).

TABLE 2 *Exports, mil. US dollars*

	Argentina	Brazil	Costa Rica	Chile	Colombia	Guatemala	Honduras	Mexico	Nicaragua	Peru	El Salvador
1925	793	491	16.4	229	83	29.6	12.0	336	12.4	94	17
1926	730	461	19.0	201	110	29.0	13.5	334	13.0	99	25
1927	972	431	18.1	206	106	33.9	17.6	299	9.0	107	14
1928	1017	475	19.6	236	131	28.2	23.1	285	11.7	111	24
1929	907	456	18.2	279	123	24.9	24.6	275	10.9	117	18
1930	513	311	16.3	162	109	23.6	25.1	203	8.3	83	14
1931	428	239	14.3	100	95	15.2	18.6	151	6.6	55	11
1932	331	181	8.5	35	67	10.7	14.8	97	4.5	38	6
1933	359	222	10.7	52	59	9.3	12.3	104	4.9	48	7
1934	418	287	8.7	97	94	14.8	10.5	179	5.2	70	9
1935	449	269	8.3	97	80	12.5	8.6	208	5.7	74	11
1936	483	320	8.8	116	90	16.9	7.0	215	4.6	84	10
1937	757	440	11.5	186	87	17.9	7.5	248	7.0	92	16
1938	438	280	10.1	131	82	18.2	6.6	185	5.9	78	11
1939	481	330	9.1	128	78	18.8	9.1	176	8.3	72	13

SOURCES: Those used in country chapters, supplemented by Wilkie (1974).

333

TABLE 3 *Imports, mil. US dollars*

	Argentina	Brazil	Costa Rica	Chile	Colombia	Guatemala	Honduras	Mexico	Nicaragua	Peru	El Salvador
1925	801	412	14	149	86	25	13	193	10	73	19
1926	758	391	14	157	109	29	10	184	10	73	26
1927	825	388	16	131	123	26	11	163	10	72	15
1928	807	442	18	146	145	31	13	172	13	70	19
1929	820	417	20	197	122	30	15	178	12	76	18
1930	617	251	11	170	61	16	16	155	8	51	12
1931	345	132	9	86	40	13	10	82	6	29	7
1932	215	108	5	26	29	7	8	57	3	16	5
1933	287	170	6	27	40	8	6	70	4	20	6
1934	327	208	9	50	54	10	8	93	5	39	8
1935	340	225	8	63	60	12	10	113	5	43	9
1936	328	247	9	71	69	14	8	129	6	50	8
1937	482	460	12	89	95	21	10	171	6	59	10
1938	443	280	13	103	84	21	9	114	5	59	9
1939	325	290	17	85	103	19	10	128	6	48	9

SOURCE: Wilkie (1974).

TABLE 4 *Real GDP 1925–40*
(*indices 1929 = 100*)

	Argentina	Brazil	Costa Rica	Chile	Colombia	Mexico	Guatemala	Honduras	Nicaragua	El Salvador
1925	80	76	99	70	75	92	81	81	81	82
1926	84	80	109	62	82	103	82	82	70	97
1927	90	89	99	66	90	98	88	90	71	85
1928	96	99	104	92	97	100	90	101	89	100
1929	100	100	100	100	100	100	100	100	100	100
1930	96	98	105	86	99	96	104	106	81	103
1931	89	95	104	68	98	99	97	109	76	92
1932	86	99	95	67	104	84	85	97	68	82
1933	90	108	113	78	110	98	86	91	86	94
1934	97	118	100	89	117	103	97	89	78	97
1935	102	121	108	91	120	112	112	85	79	106
1936	103	136	116	95	126	121	154	86	63	104
1937	111	142	135	103	128	128	151	82	68	114
1938	113	148	143	104	136	130	156	87	70	106
1939	117	152	147	101	145	140	175	89	88	114
1940	114	150	141	107	148	142	200	96	96	123

NOTE: Argentina, 1970 prices; Brazil, 1939 prices (Haddad's estimates have been used in preference to Fishlow and Villela/Suzigan); Central America: see the appendix to the chapter by Bulmer-Thomas in this volume; Chile, 1940 prices; Colombia, 1950 prices; Mexico, 1950 prices; Peru has been omitted because the only estimate available is considered too unreliable to use.

SOURCES: These are discussed in more detail in the country chapters. The sources are: Argentina: Wilkie (1978); Brazil: Haddad (1974); Chile: Palma (1979); Colombia: UN ECLA *Anexo* (1957); Mexico: Solis (1970); Central America: see Bulmer-Thomas, appendix to Ch. 11 in this volume.

TABLE 5 *The value of industrial production*
(indices 1929 = 100)

	Argentina	Brazil	Costa Rica	Chile	Colombia	Guatemala	Honduras	Mexico	Nicaragua	El Salvador
1925	82	84	98	101	84	89	77	86	113	80
1926	80	86	116	92	93	95	81	96	98	90
1927	85	96	98	89	93	95	85	97	95	86
1928	95	102	111	93	95	95	90	95	94	93
1929	100	100	100	100	100	100	100	100	100	100
1930	99	93	109	95	97	110	101	100	88	85
1931	88	94	115	77	95	115	94	95	87	73
1932	83	96	110	77	109	82	92	69	71	66
1933	94	107	134	87	128	86	94	92	84	80
1934	106	119	128	98	136	106	92	100	83	84
1935	109	133	134	111	151	122	105	116	85	87
1936	116	156	147	117	164	158	114	132	77	90
1937	123	164	171	123	193	140	116	135	85	100
1938	130	170	201	128	197	119	122	141	103	91
1939	135	186	225	130	242	105	124	165	155	97

SOURCES: Argentina: Diaz Alejandro (1970); Brazil: Haddad (1974); Central America: Bulmer-Thomas, appendix to chapter in this volume and unpublished work; Chile: Muñoz (1968); Colombia: CEPAL *Anexo* (1957); Mexico: Solis (1970).

TABLE 6   *Wholesale prices*
(indices 1929 = 100)

	Argentina	Brazil	Chile	Colombia	Mexico	Peru
1925	n.a.	116	n.a.	107	109	109
1926	104	95	n.a.	107	107	109
1927	102	93	n.a.	100	104	109
1928	102	104	100	100	100	103
1929	100	100	100	100	100	100
1930	96	88	87	79	102	96
1931	92	78	79	69	90	94
1932	93	79	119	53	83	91
1933	89	78	179	55	87	97
1934	102	83	178	77	90	101
1935	101	87	178	80	91	102
1936	103	88	197	85	96	103
1937	118	96	236	88	114	110
1938	109	99	224	n.a.	119	110
1939	112	101	218	n.a.	122	116

SOURCES: Argentina, *Revista Económica*; Brazil, Malan *et al.* (1977); Chile *Estadística Chilena*; Colombia, *Revista del Banco de la Republica*; Mexico, Wilkie (1978) p. 520; Peru, *Extracto Estadístico*.

TABLE 7   *Urban/rural terms of trade[a]*
(indices 1929 = 100)

	Argentina	Brazil	Chile	Peru	Mexico
1925	n.a.	91	n.a.	98	n.a.
1926	108	113	n.a.	94	n.a.
1927	107	108	n.a.	90	n.a.
1928	94	105	102	97	n.a.
1929	100	100	100	100	100
1930	119	95	108	100	108
1931	161	128	125	101	148
1932	179	125	125	106	168
1933	178	127	141	107	170
1934	163	128	138	106	155
1935	156	124	126	109	162
1936	129	136	114	107	160
1937	118	122	107	107	150
1938	131	128	109	104	155
1939	149	141	118	110	164

[a] Argentina: wholesale prices, non-rural and rural.
Brazil and Mexico: implicit price deflators; Chile and Peru: ratio of *general* wholesale price index and wholesale agricultural prices. These data, it should be noted, are *not* accurate measures of the terms of trade.

SOURCES: Argentina, *Revista Económica*; Brazil, Haddad (1974); Chile, *Estadística Chilena*; Peru, *Extracto Estadístico*; Mexico, Mosk (1950).

REFERENCES

C. F. Diaz Alejandro, *Essays on the Economic History of the Argentine Republic* (New Haven and London, 1970).

Estadística Chilena (Santiago).

Extracto Estadística (Lima).

C. Haddad, 'Growth of Brazilian Real Output, 1900–1947', doctoral dissertation (University of Chicago, 1974).

P. S. Malan *et al.*, *Política Económica Externa e Industrialização no Brasil 1939/52* (Rio de Janeiro, 1977).

S. Mosk, *Industrial Revolution in Mexico* (Berkeley, 1950).

O. Muñoz, *Creimiento Industrial de Chile* (Santiago, 1963).

J. G. Palma, 'Growth and Structure of Chilean Manufacturing Industry from 1830 to 1935', D. Phil. thesis (Oxford University, 1979).

Revista del Banco de la República (Bogotá).

Revista Económica (Buenos Aires).

L. Solis, *La Realidad Económica Mexicana* (Mexico, 1970).

UN, Economic Commission for Latin America, *Anexo Estadístico* to *El Desarrollo Económico de Colombia* (Mexico, 1957).

——, *Economic Survey for Latin America 1949* (New York, 1950).

J. Wilkie, *Statistics and National Policy*, Supplement 3 (1974) to UCLA, *Statistical Abstract of Latin America* (Los Angeles).

——, *La Revolución Mexicana; Gasto Federal y Cambio Social* (Mexico, 1978).

Index

Index